W9-AKE-634

PALM BEACH COUNTY
LIBRARY SYSTEM
3650 Summit Boulevard
West Palm Beach, FL 33406-4198

GOLD DIGGERS

GOLD DIGGERS

STRIKING IT RICH *in the* KLONDIKE

———————————✦———————————

CHARLOTTE GRAY

COUNTERPOINT
BERKELEY

Copyright © 2010 by Charlotte Gray. All rights reserved under International and
Pan-American Copyright Conventions.

Library of Congress Cataloging-in-Publication Data

Gray, Charlotte, 1948–
Gold diggers : striking it rich in the Klondike / by Charlotte Gray.
p. cm.
ISBN 978-1-58243-611-1
1. Klondike River Valley (Yukon)—History—19th century. 2. Gold mines and mining—
Yukon—Klondike River Valley—History—19th century. 3. Frontier and pioneer life—Yukon—
Klondike River Valley. 4. Klondike River Valley (Yukon)—Gold discoveries. 5. Klondike River
Valley (Yukon)—Biography. 6. Dawson (Yukon)—History—19th century. I. Title.

F1095.K5G68 2010
971.9'1—dc22
2010017805

COUNTERPOINT
1919 Fifth Street
Berkeley, CA 94710

www.counterpointpress.com
Distributed by Publishers Group West

10 9 8 7 6 5 4 3 2 1

For friends in Dawson, then and now

CONTENTS

PREFACE

IN 2008, THREE FRIENDS and I rafted down a section of the wide, silty Yukon River in the endless sunlight of four long June days. The scenery was breathtaking—no visible human habitations, distant snow-capped mountains under a vast sky, a black bear at the water's edge, and two moose standing motionless in a swamp. Massive log pile-ups littered the riverbanks like timeless sculptures. I heard the croak of ravens, the hiss of river sediment against the rubber raft, the howling wolves. I watched a branch bob along in the water, then realized it was a fifty-foot spruce tree, wrenched from the bank by a current strong enough to carve out new channels and treacherous gravel bars. My fingers went numb when I dipped them into the icy water.

I faced none of the risks and few of the discomforts confronted by those who had made the same journey in the 1890s, during the Klondike Gold Rush. We had life jackets, a Global Positioning System, down sleeping bags, Therm-a-Rests, bug repellent, a four-burner gas cooker, and all the other gear designed for extreme adventurers today. Even though I felt a lifetime away from my family south of the sixtieth parallel, I could return home within a few hours by plane.

Nevertheless, I felt the menace—the sense that we were trespassers on the immense silence. In four days of travel, we saw only three other boats, two of them with Hān men at the tiller. If, with all the protective paraphernalia that we had stowed, I felt overwhelmed by the savage beauty of the surroundings, how much more intense must it have been for those intrepid adventurers at the peak of the Gold Rush? If one of them drowned, it would take months for the news to reach his family back home. If he was alone when he toppled into the water, his name would be forgotten and his fate unknown.

Yet 110 years ago, stampeders streamed north in their tens of thousands in one of the great quests of the nineteenth century. Primarily from the United States but also from Canada, Britain, Australia, Sweden, France, Japan, Italy, and dozens of other countries, they undertook a brutal journey toward the Arctic. They were gamblers and dreamers: the Gold Rush was the chance to reinvent themselves—to escape the claustrophobia of cramped lives, and to share the adrenaline rush of mother lode fantasies and frontier adventure. In an earlier era, similar urges had impelled Europeans to set sail across uncharted oceans. In a later era, the same appetite for speculation persuaded investors to embrace the promise of dot-com stocks.

Different motives impelled me north. My river trip was the culmination of a three-month sojourn in the Yukon. I had hankered to spend time in the immense and almost impenetrable North American wilderness that stretches from the sixtieth parallel to the North Pole, and which freezes into an icy solitude for more than half the year. Moreover, I have three sons, who love to pit themselves against white water, steep mountains, and jagged rock faces. They revel in perilous adventures that fill me with terror of the unknown. They return from such trips exhilarated by their own stamina and courage, humbled by the power of raw nature, and at peace with themselves. I sought a glimpse of their elation.

Most of all, I wanted to see the Yukon with my own eyes. By now I had read dozens of books by survivors of the collective get-rich-quick madness of the 1890s. When I caught sight of the Moosehide Slide, above the confluence of the Klondike and Yukon rivers, I knew the surge of relief and excitement recorded by so many of the men and women who stampeded into the Far North toward the Klondike gold fields. Like me, most of those people had no idea what the terrain was like, no backwoods skills, and only the haziest notion of how to pan for gold.

I was particularly curious about a handful of obsessive, reckless individuals within that torrent of humanity that flowed north. I had heard their voices in memoirs, handwritten letters, or stories. Now I wanted to see and feel for myself what they had seen and felt, to help me understand why they faced such hazards. Why did they hurl themselves so far beyond the horizon's rim?

This is the true story, taken from their own words, of six people whose paths crossed during the Gold Rush drama. Had they not made that journey, they would never have met. Woven together, their accounts show how a community develops and how history is built from the ground up. Individual stories have a psychological depth too often missing from the grand narratives of the past, where crowds are faceless and personal motives irrelevant. My six Klondikers were the selfless Jesuit Father William Judge; Belinda Mulrooney, the feisty and ruthless entrepreneur; Jack London, a tough youngster desperate to make his mark on the world; the imperious and imperial Flora Shaw, special correspondent for the *Times* of London; Superintendent Sam Steele of the Mounties, the barrel-chested lion of the North; and the engaging prospector Bill Haskell. Each of them sought and found riches—although not always the yellow metal itself. Bill Haskell was the first of the six to make that arduous journey. If it weren't for men like Bill, with his incredible tenacity and hunger for adventure, the Klondike Gold Rush might never have happened.

PART 4: COLOR AND CHAOS

CHAPTER 1
Arctic Secrets, June 1896

THE WIDE RIVER SWEPT the little boat along in its silty current. All the two men had to do was steer clear of hazards—shifting gravel bars, uprooted trees, ice cakes. A thick branch jutting out from the bank could easily catch and swamp their homemade craft. But Bill Haskell couldn't resist glancing up from time to time.

"Mile after mile of wildest grandeur glided by like a continuous panorama," he recalled later. It was early June now, and the days were long. Light lingered in the northern sky until after midnight. Sheer cliffs glowed yellow in the midday sunshine or deep purple in the evening shadow. Hillsides were covered in dark spruce forests or slender white birches. Snow still capped the distant mountains.

But Bill and his partner, Joe Meeker, hadn't seen a human habitation for days, and they were intimidated by the landscape's vastness. The beauty was suffused with menace. The hiss of the river's sediment scraping along the side of the boat, and the harsh croaks of ravens, emphasized the eerie silence rather than broke it. Occasionally, a great bull moose would appear at the water's edge and stare at them. When they pulled their craft onto the bank, they found fresh bear scat and the bleached bones of animals torn to pieces by wolves. At night, wolf howls prickled the hair on the back of Bill's neck. When a sudden shower fell, the raindrops were hard, cold pellets of moisture, a stinging reminder that summer here was brief.

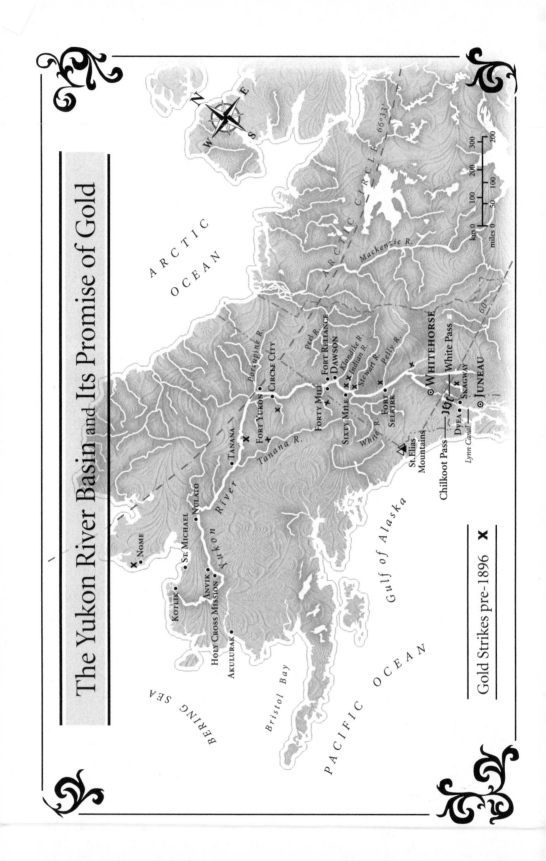

The Yukon River Basin and Its Promise of Gold

Gold Strikes pre-1896 ✕

The two men exchanged hardly a word as their clumsy boat swirled erratically in the channel. Bill, a husky, blond farmboy from Vermont, let out the occasional exclamation at the sight of a golden eagle wheeling overhead or a brilliant patch of purple fireweed. Joe, a wiry Irishman from South Carolina, was not much of a talker at the best of times; he stared ahead, gripping an oar. The two Americans were tired, and too sick of each other's company for much conversation. It had taken them three months to get here—a journey that had included avalanches, blizzards, an almost vertical climb, fierce rapids and treacherous whirlpools, and faces so swollen by insect bites that they could barely open their eyes. Now they were far, far from any civilization they would recognize. There were no cities, farms, railroads, or telegraph lines for hundreds of miles. They had almost reached the Arctic Circle.

Bill and Joe were traveling along the Yukon River, the waterway that meanders for 2,000 miles through conifers, tundra, and ice in the Far North. From the Yukon's headwaters, only 50 miles from the Pacific coast, the river flows toward the North Pole until it is about 120 miles from the Arctic Ocean, then curves southwest to flow for another 1,200 miles through impenetrable forests and black swamps. The mosquitoes are terrible, the landscape sometimes dramatic and at other points dreary and monotonous. Finally, after slicing an immense arc through the middle of Alaska, the river trickles through the many fingers of a wide, shallow delta before reaching the salt water of the Bering Sea in the topmost corner of North America's west coast. Covered in a layer of ice several feet thick for seven or eight months of the year, the powerful Yukon waterway is today still only half explored.

Why were Bill Haskell and Joe Meeker floating through this wilderness, their knuckles taut with fear? What hunger drove them to travel so far, and face such dangers?

Gold had enticed the two men north. In the 1890s, gold was as important as oil is today: it made the world turn. Gold was crucial for governments because every country's currency depended on its gold holdings, and money and credit for economic expansion rested on increasing gold supplies. And like oil today, in the second half of the nineteenth century supplies of gold seemed to be dwindling, putting a squeeze on the world's economies. Banks were failing, breadlines lengthening.

Gold was also the basis for individual fortunes, because a prospector who struck a mother lode would never have to work again in his life. An ounce of pure gold dust (enough to fill a teaspoon) was and is worth a lot of money—nearly twenty dollars in 1896 and more than $1,000 today. Miners like Bill and Joe had been drifting into the Yukon basin for nearly twenty years, drawn by rumors of gold dust in the river's gravel bars and nuggets in its tributaries. They arrived with their shovels, gold pans, and picks, eager to make their fortunes. There were other lures, too—the chance to conquer unknown territories, live on the frontier, escape the rules and regulations of more ordered societies. Wild-eyed and leather-skinned, muscular and pugnacious, they clung to their dreams like warriors on a crusade. By 1896, there were perhaps a thousand such adventurers in the Northwest, alongside the uncounted indigenous people, including the Tutchone, Tlingit, Inuit, Hän, and Tagish, who had made this inhospitable region their home for generations.

Gold bound Bill and Joe together. If their partnership was successful in striking gold, it would let them vault out of poverty, hunger, hopelessness and into a gleaming future. Joe clung to this vision with tight-lipped fury, refusing to speculate how he would use his wealth until he actually felt the heavy yellow dust trickle through his fingers. Easygoing Bill loved to fantasize how he would spend his precious nuggets—on a rich man's toys like one of the new horseless carriages, or on travel to distant cities like Paris that otherwise he could never hope to see. But how long would it take to find the stuff?

Each morning on the long journey, Joe would unfold a rough map of the Yukon River to gauge their progress. Narrowing his eyes, he looked for landmarks in the vast landscape. Bill, impatient to get started, would pile their meager possessions into the boat and slap the mosquitoes away from his puffy, sunburned face. They had already ticked off Windy Lake, Marsh Lake, the terrifying White Horse Rapids, Lake Laberge, the mouths of the Pelly, White, and Stewart rivers, and Fort Selkirk, an abandoned Hudson's Bay Company trading post. "We stopped upon the banks but little, for the mosquitoes make camp life an excruciating experience," Bill recorded. A couple of weeks after they had launched their clumsy craft, they saw a big white scar, left by a rock slide, on a hillside ahead of them. From their map, the men learned that this was nicknamed the Moosehide Slide because it looked like the hide of a moose stretched out to dry. Below the slide, a river gushed clear as gin into the soupy brown Yukon. The river was known as Tr'ondëk, or "Thron'diuk" as Bill spelled it. On each bank of the Tr'ondëk lay a narrow apron of flat ground, squeezed between the two rivers and a steep hillside. There was a small Indian settlement on the Tr'ondëk's left bank, but otherwise the mudflats were covered in alder shoots cropped to waist height by moose during the winter. Bill's trigger finger itched as he surveyed this prime hunting ground.

The Tr'ondëk was one of the favorite fishing rivers of the Hän people. Its name meant "hammer stones" because for generations Hän had hammered stakes across the mouth of the river, then slung fish traps between them to catch salmon as they swam upstream to their spawning grounds. Their leader, Chief Isaac, came with his family each spring to camp on the stream's south bank and harvest the salmon run. From the river, Bill saw a huddle of people by huts built in the characteristic Hän style—low-slung birch constructions, roofed with canvas anchored by more birch saplings. A tall, dark man stared at them as their boat floated past. Was this the Hän chief who was well known to prospectors muscling into his territory? Chief Isaac had learned English from the newcomers, and had even allowed an American missionary to convert him to Christianity.

If Bill and Joe had steered their boat to the riverbank and stopped to speak to the Hān families, they could have saved themselves so much trouble. But they were impatient, and had no time for people they had been raised to disparage. So what if these strangers had for generation after generation fished and hunted all over this hostile landscape, learned the migration patterns of caribou and medicinal properties of vegetation, and knew how to survive the cruel winters? So what if they were canny traders who had dominated the commerce in fox, bear, and lynx furs with the Hudson's Bay Company for years? Even Bill's hunger for human companionship wouldn't persuade him to mix with the Hān. When one of the fishermen shouted at them in his own tongue, Bill hooted with derisive laughter because the Hān language sounded to his untrained ear as though the speaker was "doing his best to strangle himself with it." He and Joe allowed the river to sweep them past the settlement.

So Bill Haskell never discovered that the people who lived here knew this river was special—that soft yellow stones glittered in the Tr'ondëk gravel. He never heard how Hān children competed to find the largest of these magic pebbles. Gold had no value for the Indians, and Bill saw no value in talking to people who understood this magnificent and mysterious land.

Besides, Bill and Joe were in a hurry: the Yukon's dangers and loneliness had unnerved them. Bill was hungry for the company of men like himself—the tough, grizzled, backslapping prospectors in the mining camps downriver, who shared his lust for gold and contempt for anyone who didn't speak English properly. Joe wanted to take stock of their dwindling provisions and cash. Bill would reflect a couple of years later that "but for the fact that we were now anxious to arrive at the center of the gold diggings we might have stopped a day to see what we could bag in this moose pasture." So the two men floated past the Tr'ondëk—which the world would come to know as the Klondike—"in blissful ignorance of what lay under the tundra of its creeks."

CHAPTER 2
Bill Haskell's Dreams of Gold, 1889–1896

BILL HASKELL RECORDED his Klondike adventure in a memoir entitled *Two Years in the Klondike and Alaskan Gold-Fields,* published only two years after he first saw the Yukon River. He began his tale in an unassuming tone: "This is the plain story of one who began life in a little township of Vermont about thirty-two years ago, and who, several times during the past two years, has been dangerously near losing it in a search for gold along the glacier-bound coasts of Alaska, in the frozen regions of the Yukon, and in the rich gulches of the Klondike."

But it was not a plain story. Bill was caught up in two extraordinary phenomena that reverberated throughout nineteenth-century America. The first was the surge of settlers who moved westward across the continent, pushing the American frontier all the way to the Pacific. The second was the obsession with gold, as a route out of cramped lives and into a fantasy of untold wealth. Bill's subtitle was *A Thrilling Narrative* . . . and it *was* thrilling. He was born on a hardscrabble New England farm and grew up entirely ignorant of either geography or geology. Although his parents, at considerable financial sacrifice to themselves, sent him off to a good school, he showed little promise. All he knew was that he wanted something from life beyond unremitting toil on rocky fields. Yet there was more to Bill than adolescent frustration: he had imagination, and an unquenchable appetite for books about quests and exploration. His account of his months in the

North has the drama and color of the bestsellers he most likely read—
W. L. Stevenson, for example, on the South Seas, or Bret Harte's short
stories about the California Gold Rush.

But first young William Haskell had to get himself out of eastern
seaboard inertia. In 1889, when he was twenty-two, Bill had found
himself behind the counter in a big Boston dry goods store, his fists
constantly clenched with sheer boredom. "What business had I, built
on Vermont lines, broad, muscular and tough—dallying behind a
dry-goods counter! Stuck up in a corner like a house plant when I
sighed for the free open air, the winds and the storm." For a century,
restless Americans had migrated westward. Horace Greeley, founding
editor of the *New York Tribune,* had popularized the slogan "Go west,
young man!" in 1865 and, as Bill was the first to admit, "To a spirit
like mine the possibilities of the great West naturally appealed." So with
thirty dollars in his pocket, he caught a transcontinental train.

Gold fever bit when Bill reached the Rockies. Sitting in a Colorado
Springs bar one day, the young New Englander heard a tale about three
Frenchmen who knew nothing about prospecting. They had staked a
claim on a stream bed and, according to Bill's drinking companion, "in
a few days one o' them durn'd Frenchmen picked up a nugget wuth over
six thousand." Soon everybody at the table was trading such anecdotes.
Bill listened avidly to the story of "two fellers trampin' up the coast"
who had been looking for wood for their campfire and stumbled on a
lump of gold. "That lump was sold afterwards in Los Angeles for two
thousand seven hundred and fifty dollars!"

Over the next few days, Bill heard plenty of such tales. One of his
new friends was a veteran of the 1849 California Gold Rush, the first
international mass stampede to a gold field in history. The old man
grew misty eyed as he recalled how news of the strike in a creek bed
in northern California had flashed along the newly invented telegraph
and he had found himself one of 300,000 gold seekers, or "argonauts,"
who streamed into the Sacramento valley. Others reeled off litanies of

later gold rushes, when they had been part of an army of prospectors that struggled north up the Cordillera and into Canadian territory. In 1871, the rich Cariboo District of British Columbia was explored; in 1874, gold fields were discovered in the Cassiar Mountains. Old-timers loved rehashing their tales of strikes in front of this fresh-faced young-ster, with his patched pants and hands as big as hams. Inevitably, as the bottles continued to circulate, Bill's buddies would start speculating about men who had kept going—into the basin of the Yukon River, up the creeks of distant rivers like the Lewes and the Stewart, named after long-dead Hudson's Bay Company explorers. Some had returned with wild stories. Many others were never heard of again because they had perished on remote mountain passes, in raging torrents, or during the hideous cold of northern winters.

Bill Haskell listened to the veterans talk of the seductive glitter of gold, as their stiff, calloused fingers curled around shot glasses of cheap whiskey. He realized that it was not just gold that kept them prospect-ing. Most were like him—rootless men who had hated the idea of working for paltry wages in ill-lit offices, factories, or stores. Joining the rush west was a bid for freedom: a gesture of reckless self-preservation for loners desperate to escape the grinding conformity of the modern world. There was little in their lives besides the quest for gold. After a mid-century burst of prosperity and expansion, the early 1890s were years of profound cultural and economic instability in North America. Alongside technological miracles like the transcontinental railroad and the telephone were unemployment and grinding poverty. Money was in short supply, banks failed with dismal regularity, families were thrown out of their homes, and four million men drifted around the conti-nent looking for work. Bill had seen the bleak headlines that filled every newspaper.

As the miners traded anecdotes among themselves, Bill's eyes wid-ened. "The effect of such conversation upon a tenderfoot with but a little silver in his pocket may be imagined." Cheerful and enthusiastic, he was eager to find a quest on which to focus his energies. He did not kid himself that success was a sure thing. Despite the talk of "fabulous fortunes and sudden wealth," none of his companions had ever struck gold themselves. There was never a mention of the thousands of prospectors who came up empty handed every time. Nevertheless, he decided to learn everything he could about gold mining, from both books and practical experience. "The next day I started with a party of a dozen others on my first rush to the goldfields."

Experienced prospectors in the party stared thoughtfully at the mountain ranges, carefully examined loose rocks, and trickled gravel through their fingers. Bill watched, then peppered them with questions until they gruffly told him to shove off. A few had torn charts and dog-eared volumes of geology in their packs, which he would borrow. It was hard work, squinting at small print by the light of a campfire, but he slowly acquired some basic knowledge. He learned that there are two ways to mine gold: lode mining (sometimes known as hard rock mining) and placer mining. Bill's companions were not interested in lode mining, since that required teams of men using expensive, heavy equipment to extract and crush the hard rock containing a vein, or lode, of gold. Bill's crowd consisted of placer miners, whose tools were rock picks and gold pans. (A pan was a tin basin about a foot across at the bottom, with flared sides.) They were looking for alluvial gold, released from the rock in which it had been deposited by the action of wind or water. Placer gold, lying near the surface of the earth like burst sacks of spilled treasure, just needed someone to come along and gather it up. A lone man, Bill heard, could end up with a pan full of gold entirely by his own efforts. A single man could beat the odds and become a millionaire.

As Bill learned by tedious experience, a man had to know where to look. The theory was simple enough: placer gold fields occur in mountain belts, where gold-bearing rocks have been forced upward in the ancient convulsions of the earth's surface. Placer gold might be found along the dried-up paths of ancient waterways, or in the gravel at the edge of flowing rivers. However, there was no fixed rule about where the gold lay or why, and no reliable geological charts to help a prospector. Ancient stream beds zigzagged under running streams like a serpent wrapped around a stick. Sometimes an experienced miner could tell from instinct and experience which creek or gravel bar looked hopeful; sometimes a complete rookie might wander around and by sheer luck blunder on placer gold.

In Colorado mountain valleys, Bill watched prospectors squat in chill streams, sink a pan of gravel under a stream's surface, and swish it around in water. Gold is heavy—nineteen times heavier than water and a lot heavier than every other mineral in a miner's pan. Each miner prayed that a few "colors," or gold flakes, would separate from lighter rocks such as silica, schist, and granite. The flakes would sink to the bottom of the pan; the lighter rocks would be swished out into the stream.

Panning for gold was backbreaking work and took practice. A skilled veteran could shake out more gold in a day with expert swirls than a greenhorn could collect in a week. But Bill was young, fit, and eager to learn. After about his fortieth try, he acquired the rhythm that encouraged the gold to gravitate to the pan's bottom and the sand to spill out over the lip. He spent the next couple of years wandering over mountains, along creeks and streams, and through gulches with his pan—"an inseparable companion," as he called it. He learned to recognize mica, galena, chalcopyrite, and gold. He taught himself to distinguish granite, sandstone, limestone, slate, serpentine, and schist, as well as talc, dolerite, dolomite, and porphyry.

From time to time, he found enough color to keep him going to the next stage: sinking a shaft through the overlay of muck, gravel, and sand toward the bedrock because the richest pans were usually closest to the bedrock. What constituted a rich pan? The rule of thumb was that with one ounce of gold worth twenty dollars, a single pan that yielded ten cents' worth of gold showed promise. Twenty such pans, which might take a day or two to accumulate, would yield gold to the value of two dollars. It wasn't much, but it would have taken Bill three days to earn that amount behind the counter of the Boston dry goods store.

"It was on the whole an agreeable life," Bill later wrote. But it was frustrating: his yields were enough to feed him but not enough to make him a rich man. Yet he had caught Prospectors' Disease. He convinced himself that his next strike might be "the big pan-out" that would make his fortune: "Every pan of dirt is a gamble. Dame Nature is dealing the cards. Will the player make a big stake, or will he lose?"

Bill might have spent the final years of the century, and the rest of his youth, shaking pans in the Rockies were it not for an encounter in the fall of 1895. Joe Meeker, a couple of years older than Bill, was a small, dark-haired, wiry man who shared Bill's rural background, impatience with clerking jobs, and sense of adventure. Gold was more than a dream to Joe: he was obsessed with the search for it. He had already ventured to the Far North and explored the lower reaches of the Yukon River. He described the river's quiet beauty in summer, its ice-bound magnificence in winter, and the rumors of glittering sandbars in its tributaries. Bill could see that the North's wild splendor and promise of hidden wealth held a strange fascination for Joe.

One night, the two men sat convivially by a campfire in the Colorado mining camp, watching the flames. Coffee was brewing in a battered enamel coffee pot; the smells of sweat and wood smoke mingled in the cooling air; overhead, stars sparkled in the clear, dark sky. Then Joe turned his face from the flames, stared intently at the broad-shouldered New Englander, and blurted out a bold suggestion. "The only place to hunt for gold now is in the upper Yukon. I believe that's the place for us, and if we put our money together it will be enough to buy a good outfit and pay our way." Joe explained to Bill that he had seen with his own eyes that the Yukon basin was similar to river valleys in California, Colorado, or British Columbia—rugged terrain, igneous rock formations, swift-flowing streams. But the odds of finding gold in the North, he argued, were better than in southern latitudes. Because the ground was frozen for eight months out of twelve, the gold had been locked into the permafrost for thousands of years instead of being dispersed over a large area by running water. It was *waiting* for them, Joe insisted, his dark eyes fierce with conviction. Yes, reaching the frozen gold in the Yukon was one hell of a challenge. But think about it, he urged his companion. The Yukon region's placer deposits could be thicker, richer, and purer than any of the deposits found farther south. "Color" there wouldn't be just flakes or dust—it could be whole nuggets.

Bill hesitated. He knew nothing about the North. He was barely aware that the United States had purchased the immense terrain of Alaska from Russia in 1867. He had no idea that the headwaters of the Yukon were in Canadian, rather than American, territory. But Joe's intensity gathered force. "There's gold there," he insisted, "and I know it." His own knowledge of the vast land was hazy, but who cared? The previous winter he had heard that gold had been found on the creeks flowing into the upper Yukon and that there was a string of small mining camps along the river—Rampart City, Circle City, Eagle, Forty Mile, Fort Reliance, Sixty Mile, and Fort Selkirk. He knew that living conditions were unbelievably harsh but that the Alaska Commercial Company already had trading stations in these camps. Settlements originally established by fur traders were now supplying provisions to prospectors. Joe's year in Alaska had convinced him, as he told Bill, that the Yukon basin would be the next eldorado.

Between them, the two men could muster about $1,500. This was a substantial sum for a couple of unskilled laborers, but it was hardly enough to cover the cost of travel, food supplies, and equipment if they headed north. It seemed madness to leave behind the congeniality of the Colorado mining camps and head off into the unknown.

But as Bill stared into the fire, a vision of gold glinting in the arctic mud exploded in his imagination. He recalled other stories of the North—the flickering mystery of the northern lights, the splendor of snow-capped mountain ranges, the fluid magnificence of the caribou herds, and the savage claws of grizzly bears. Bill was a gold miner, but he was also a resourceful young man eager to see the world and marvel at its wonders. Colorado was crawling with old-timers; the Yukon was tomorrow's country—the final frontier. What's more, he trusted Joe. The southerner might be surly at times, but he was experienced and straight. What the hell! Bill leaned back, then turned to Joe with a grin. "I'll go," he announced cheerfully.

Reaching the North now consumed all Joe and Bill's money and energy. They spent the winter of 1895–1896 in San Francisco, assembling what Joe decreed they needed for their expedition. "As our purchases were delivered, I began to get a dim realization of what Joe was preparing for," Bill later wrote. The total outfit included not only food for a year (everything from 800 pounds of flour to 50 pounds of dried apricots, plus bacon, beans, rice, sugar, rolled oats, coffee, tea, tobacco, candles, soap, and salt) but also hardware (30 pounds of nails, two pairs of snow goggles, shovels, knives, tin plates, cooking pots), clothes (extra heavy underwear, leather-heeled wool socks, blanket-lined coats, double-breasted flannel overshirts), tents, sleeping bags, fishing lines, a medicine case, two compasses, a Yukon stove, two gold pans, and a gold scale. Bill lost count of the number of implements Joe purchased (whipsaw, crosscut saw, ripsaw, ax, long-handled shovel, spade, pick, brace and bits, chisels, hatchet, as well as 3 pounds of oakum, 5 pounds of pitch, 150 pounds of rope). He winced at the weight of it all—over one and a half tons—and gave his partner an inquiring look. "You will think it weighs five times that before you get it on the Yukon," Joe remarked, "but it's a mighty good outfit, and I hope we shall get it there all right." Bill repressed his misgivings, but Joe's next comment didn't reassure him. "It'll be the roughest roughing it you ever saw. But you've got grit, and that's more than half."

On March 15, 1896, the two men sailed out of San Francisco and headed up the coast. They were bound for the little port of Dyea. An uneasy mix of excitement and apprehension filled Bill: he had never been on an ocean before, or traveled so far north. A forested coastline shrouded in fog slipped by as the vessel made its way through the cold, gray waters. Twelve days after they had waved California goodbye, the boat nosed into the Lynn Canal, a narrow inlet walled by steep, black cliffs with jagged peaks. At the head of the inlet was Dyea's dismal beach, onto which their possessions were abruptly dumped. Bill and Joe worked against the clock, hauling their outfit out of reach of the incoming tide. Big snowflakes started to fall, and Bill found himself pitching their tent in a foot of snow. Thanks to Joe, they were better prepared than others they had met on the steamer: "There was a noticeable change in the faces of those who were less inured to hardship." Among them were several women, clutching valises and staring helplessly at their desolate surroundings.

From the mouth of the tent, the two men looked up at the St. Elias mountain range, which they would have to cross. The wall of mountains towered above them, sheer and intimidating. Bill searched in vain on the steep, rocky, ice-covered slopes for the sign of a pass. Occasionally, the fogs and snowstorms parted and allowed him to glimpse a trail leading almost vertically up to a slight cleft among the peaks. This was the notorious Chilkoot Trail, the first and by far the toughest section of the best-known route to the gold fields. Joe saw the dismay on his partner's face, so quickly put Bill to work. It was impossible to haul all their supplies up the mountain in one load each, so at Dyea the two men methodically divided their supplies into eight sledloads. Then they set out, each hauling a fully loaded, clumsy wooden sled. Each would have to make the teeth-gritting, face-freezing return journey four times as they ferried their goods forward. If Bill found the trail incredibly hard going, others less brawny than he found it appalling. "Those who have not tried it can hardly imagine what it is to tramp twenty-five [sic] miles, half the way pulling four

As Bill and Joe discovered, a man had to be ingenious to pitch a tent on the steep slopes of the trail.

hundred pounds, in an intermittent snow storm, over a road which, while smooth for Alaska, would be deemed almost impassable in New England."

Compared to accounts of the journey to the gold fields written by subsequent stampeders, Bill did not dwell on its horrors in his memoirs. He had never been one to panic in the face of adversity. In fact, he enjoyed pitting his muscles against the hostile terrain as an occasional watery sun broke through black clouds and north winds screamed round his ears. He took the same kind of pleasure in the physical challenge as a young man or woman today takes in a solo round-the-world voyage or a rigorous climbing trip. He was still young enough to believe he was immortal; he didn't see disaster or death lurking in every precipitous rock face or icy whiteout. There is a note of pride in his memoir as he looks back at the ordeal: "There was a novelty in the experience which was exhilarating, so that it did not fatigue us as much as it might otherwise have done."

The first day was relatively easy: ten miles of gently rising bog and sand through a thinly wooded valley. Then the real climb began as the trail became an obstacle course of boulders, with few resting places. After a couple of miles of this, the trail leveled out again as it wound through a forest in which immense fir trees blocked the view of the sky. Soon the treeline was behind the two men, and mountain sheep and goats appeared occasionally in the distance. Bill kept his eyes on the ground as he gasped for air.

The men made four trips each to Sheep Camp, beyond which lay nothing but naked rock and vertiginous cliffs. Bill's muscles already ached with the effort of hauling the cumbersome sled, but he knew the worst was still ahead. Sleds were useless on the final four miles. First came an incline of about eighteen degrees to a landmark known as Stone House because the huge boulders appeared to be in roughly symmetrical formation. Next came a steeper, twenty-five-degree climb to The Scales, where Tlingit porters would weigh bags to assess the cost of packing them up the final stretch. The last part of the ascent was a precipitous rise with an incline of almost forty-five degrees. This stretch has remained forever in the world's memory, thanks to photos taken in 1897 by Seattle photographer Eric Hegg. The Hegg photos show a continuous thin, dark line of climbers, loaded with packs and bales, dark greatcoats stark against the snow-covered mountainside, stumbling up the ice like figures out of Dante's *Inferno*. In 1896, there were never more than a handful of people on the trail, so Bill and Joe could go at their own pace. Nevertheless, those two well-muscled young men had to make the grueling climb from Sheep Camp to the summit a total of twenty leg-cramping, lung-bursting times each.

At Sheep Camp, the two men had repacked all their provisions into smaller bundles they could carry up on their backs, then waited for two long weeks while a snowstorm imprisoned them in their tent. How did they pass the time, as they huddled together in their canvas shelter, listening to the wind? "It was a very dreary camp during those two

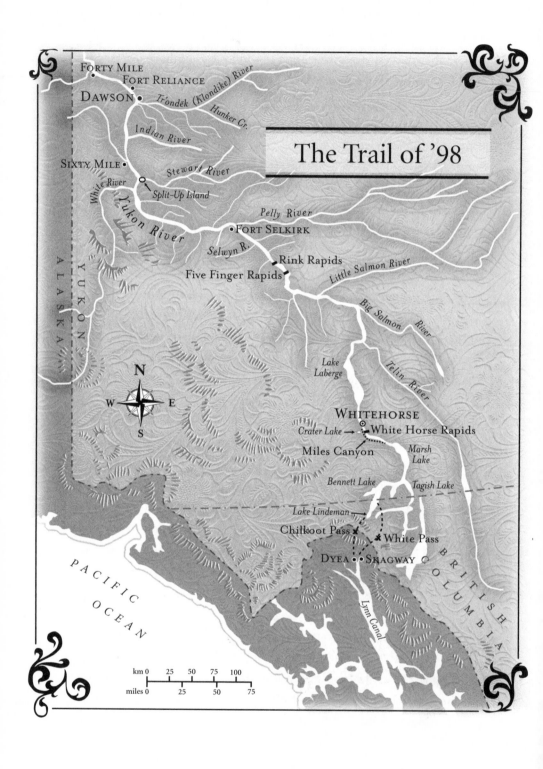

The Trail of '98

FORTY MILE

FORT RELIANCE

DAWSON

Tr'ondëk (Klondike) River

Hunker Cr.

Indian River

SIXTY MILE

White River

Stewart River

Split-Up Island

Yukon River

Pelly River

FORT SELKIRK

Selwyn R.

Rink Rapids

Five Finger Rapids

Little Salmon River

Big Salmon River

Telin River

Lake Laberge

WHITEHORSE

Crater Lake → White Horse Rapids

Miles Canyon

Marsh Lake

ALASKA

YUKON

Bennett Lake

Tagish Lake

Lake Lindeman

Chilkoot Pass

White Pass

DYEA • SKAGWAY

BRITISH COLUMBIA

PACIFIC OCEAN

Lynn Canal

km 0   25   50   75   100

miles 0   25   50   75

weeks," Bill recalled. Difficult as it was to climb the mountains, dread of the coming ordeal was worse. "There is nothing so hard as to keep still in these regions, especially when the mercury is far below zero." Finally, once the blizzard abated, they set off. Often they found themselves clinging perilously to loose rocks as they pushed upward on hands and knees. The wind howled, and the rumble of avalanches was often disturbingly close. Bill did not dare look behind him. Both men suffered searing sunburns as they sweated up the rocky terrain. "My face became so swollen," recalled Bill, "that I could hardly see out of my eyes." For protection, they blackened their faces with burnt cork or charcoal. "We were gruesome objects with our black faces and goggles."

Finally, Bill Haskell collapsed on the bleak, windswept summit of the Chilkoot Pass, 3,500 feet above sea level, with his last bundle. He was suffused with a sense of victory after such superhuman efforts. The seventeen-mile journey from Dyea to the top of the pass had taken twenty-three days. His back ached and his legs were weak with effort, but if he could hack that trail, he could take on *anything*. The landscape ahead was dazzling in its sparsely populated magnificence. "What a picture! It seems not of this world: it is so strange, so unique. Snow peaks and their shining glaciers!" He flung an arm round Joe's shoulders and told him that the tramp was nothing but "a rather long and at times agreeable method of premeditated suicide." His flippancy hid the sense of awe at the harshness of the climb they had made and the journey ahead. He decided that anybody who actually made it into the Yukon basin was going to be a pretty good fellow.

On the other side of the Chilkoot Pass was a steep, 500-foot drop to the frozen lakes below. The contrast between the partners was evident as they started downhill. Joe carefully checked their outfit and prepared to take the sled down in a controlled slide. Bill perched himself astride a bundle of their supplies, kicked off, and skidded down the slope at terrific speed, whooping as he went.

Bill Haskell took the rigors of the journey cheerfully in stride, but another side of his character emerged in his encounters with Tlingit porters. The Tlingit were an aggressive, proud, coastal people who had guarded the routes across the St. Elias Mountains for hundreds of years and prevented Russians from moving inland in the early nineteenth century. In 1880, Washington had sent a U.S. Navy warship under the command of Captain Lester A. Beardslee into the region because the American government considered Tlingit actions a threat to national interests. Beardslee had escorted a group of miners up the Lynn Canal and warned that he would turn his guns on Tlingit chiefs unless they opened the passes to American prospectors. In exchange, he agreed that the Tlingit would be engaged as local packers and that no trading would take place. The agreement enabled miners to cross the mountains to the headwaters of the Yukon, then fan out in search of gold.

It was not an altogether happy bargain. Over the previous decade, traders and prospectors had encroached on Tlingit territories, despoiled their coastal villages and fishing grounds, and disrupted their communities by taking Tlingit wives. The newcomers were a source of wealth, since they needed packers. As porters, the Tlingit displayed extraordinary strength: while southerners struggled with eighty-pound loads, the men and women who had grown up in these mountains shouldered packs weighing more than a hundred pounds. Moreover, they understood the coastal range's weather systems, and refused to break trail when they knew a blizzard was on its way or an avalanche threatened. But the incoming miners were deaf to Tlingit wisdom because they were steeped in the assumptions of racial superiority that prevailed among non-native North Americans back then. Bill was typical in his ignorant dismissal of the porters. "These people may be interesting to ethnologists," he declared, "and they may seem promising material for devout missionaries, but for the man who is in a hurry to get to the gold regions they are more often a hindrance than a help."

Once over the St. Elias range, Bill and Joe had to traverse four lakes. Crater Lake and Lake Lindeman, on the far side of the Chilkoot Pass, were both still frozen, so the two men pressed north on foot, pulling heavily laden sleds. They discovered that the way to keep the wooden runners sliding easily over ice was to freeze water on them before starting. An icy wind blew down Lake Lindeman's six-mile length, so Bill rigged up a canvas sail and off they sped, with Bill shouting, "This is sport!" More hard work lay ahead—a portage to Bennett Lake, then a thirty-four-mile tramp across the lake's frozen surface until they reached the far shore, then across Caribou Crossing to Tagish Lake. By now it was May 1, and the big melt had begun. "I guess the worst is over for a time," announced Joe, who decreed they would spend the next couple of weeks building a boat to take them the rest of the journey.

Several other parties had decided to do the same thing, so there was a jolly community camped by the lakeside. "We did not lack for company." At first, Bill tried to help Joe work on their vessel, but Joe lost patience with Bill's clumsy carpentry and happy chatter. He preferred working by himself. For the next ten days, Bill teamed up with some of the other prospectors to hunt for ptarmigan and rabbit. He tramped across spongy muskeg and over icy streams, chasing birds that were still in their winter white plumage and rabbits stringy from lack of food. "We would have lived like epicures," he liked to joke, "if I [had] made fewer disastrous experiments in cooking." Soon, the hairy stems of purple pasqueflowers were poking through the snow, and mountainsides were covered in forget-me-nots, Dutchman's breeches, alpine geraniums, and harebells. The temperature rose and the days grew longer. The honking of geese heading north filled the air, and water gurgled under the moss and fell in lacy cascades from bare peaks. Joe hammered away at a sturdy, sharp-nosed, blunt-sterned little vessel, paying little heed to Bill's exuberant tales of encounters with moose and bears. Soon it was time to move on.

The churning waters of White Horse Rapids claimed dozens of lives during the Klondike Gold Rush.

There was still a long way to go. The men's destination was Circle City, Alaska, 600 miles farther north, just below the point where the surging Yukon River crossed the Arctic Circle. Circle City, in the spring of 1896, was the center of the gold diggings. The men floated down the upper reaches of the Yukon River in their *Tar Stater*. (In a flash of patriotism, Joe had named their boat after his home state of North Carolina, a major producer of tar.) The first of many obstacles was Miles Canyon, where the river squeezed between looming granite cliffs and water poured through the rapids with a roar that could be heard for miles. Next came the notorious White Horse Rapids, where the white foam on towering waves curled like a horse's mane. The *Tar Stater* was nearly swamped at several points here, and the partners then lost a large part of their supplies farther downriver, in Squaw Rapids. Even Bill's nerve faltered as they were swept along in the heaving torrent. "Joe, we're goners sure," he screamed at his partner as the waters suddenly dropped nine feet, and the men shot through standing waves and dense spray. Somehow, they survived—unlike many others. Once through, the partners hugged each other silently, in feverish relief. Then, with the resilience of youth, Bill forgot his terror. "Standing on the bank in safety, the eye is charmed by the waters that leap and foam around the highly-colored rocks. You may watch it for hours and turn away with regret."

The river was in spring flood and Joe and Bill made rapid progress across the thirty-one-mile length of Lake Laberge, then past the mouths of numerous salmon rivers, through the surging Five Finger Rapids and the churning Rink Rapids. Where the Pelly River joined the Yukon River, they saw the tumbledown traces of Fort Selkirk, an old Hudson's Bay Company post. By now the river was racing: it took them only a day to travel over a hundred miles to the mouth of the Stewart River, where they saw a dilapidated trading post on an island, and farther on, at Sixtymile River, a lumber mill. A few miles beyond that, they noticed on the right the big rock slide and the river they had learned was called the Tr'ondëk. Ignoring the Hän fishing village at the mouth of the Tr'ondëk, they paddled on toward Forty Mile, a trading post on the Canadian side of the Alaska–Yukon border that served trappers, prospectors, and the native communities. It had acquired its name because it was forty miles north of Fort Reliance, an abandoned trading post about six miles downriver from the mouth of the Tr'ondëk River.

For weeks, the only human habitations that Joe and Bill had seen were a scattering of wooden huts and grubby tents. Bill expected Forty Mile to be little better than Fort Selkirk—a handful of ramshackle wooden buildings with a few greasy-hatted prospectors smoking their pipes on the bench outside the store. So when the *Tar Stater* rounded a bend in the river and the trading post came into view, he was astonished. There had been a settlement here since coarse gold had been panned on the Fortymile River in 1886, and by now it boasted nearly a hundred log buildings, including a sawmill, a couple of bakeries, and several blacksmiths' forges, restaurants, billiard halls, saloons, dance halls, and even a large, false-fronted barn of a building that declared itself to be the

Opera House. Bill's heart leaped. *This,* in his view, was "the vortex of white civilization on the Yukon."

Forty Mile gave Bill his first taste of mining culture in the North. Some of its aspects were familiar—Colorado mining camps had boasted muddy streets lined with false-fronted saloons and bars, resounding with the squeal of fiddles and plonking notes of honky-tonk pianos. But most of Forty Mile's residents had left the Outside, as lands to the south were known, months if not years ago, and they were much, much rougher. In the Opera House, Bill watched haggard women in grubby satin gowns perform their tired routines. The bristle-chinned miners, who had spent months in isolated mining camps near Forty Mile, loved them—and paid dearly for female company. "It is one of the peculiarities of mining regions," mused Bill, "that much of the gold goes to those who do not dig it."

Behind the Opera House, Bill was even more surprised to discover a small wooden chapel. At its door stood a tall, stooped, older man with little wire-framed glasses, a clean-shaven face, and a wooden cross hanging round his neck outside his thick "parky" jacket. This curious character in sealskin boots and a fur-trimmed hood was far too frail to be a prospector. A fellow miner told Bill that this was Father Judge, a Jesuit priest who had been in the North for years. The priest rarely smiled, yet he radiated a gentle benevolence that was a startling contrast to the grim resolve on the faces of most Arctic veterans. Bill, who had inherited his parents' Presbyterian distrust of Papists, gave a polite nod to Father Judge, then quickly walked on.

It was now late June, and the creeks around Forty Mile overflowed with miners. Joe had heard rumors of new strikes near Circle City in Alaska, 170 miles farther north. Prospectors were converging on the remote trading station downstream like crows round carrion. Joe wanted to join the rush. So the two men quickly replaced the provisions they had lost in the rapids, pushed off from Forty Mile's muddy wharf, and paddled the *Tar Stater* back into the Yukon's fast-flowing current.

Circle City was an even bigger surprise than Forty Mile. The largest log city in the world, in 1896 its residents claimed that it was the Paris of the North. Its twenty-eight saloons and eight dance halls made Forty Mile look like a village. When Bill and Joe approached the Circle City wharf, they were greeted by "a cosmopolitan crowd of men and women from everywhere in North America, a sprinkling of dirty Indians, and a crowd of howling dogs." Under the midnight sun, men hung around telling stories, playing cards, or drifting into the saloons to watch one of the burlesque shows. In the most remote region of North America was a thriving community of over a thousand people including, to Bill's astonishment, "respectable families . . . People talked glibly of the coming metropolis of the Yukon."

Two years later, Bill would recall Circle City with nostalgia. "No one could have imagined a livelier place of its size. Neither could anyone in the busy place anticipate that within a year it would be as dead as a door post—almost a silent city."

CHAPTER 3
Mob Justice and Wild Dogs, June–September 1896

DURING HIS FIRST SUMMER in the North, Bill Haskell quickly learned that life there was different—very different from the humdrum predictability of his existence up to now. This was a region through which were scattered uncounted aboriginal people, about a thousand ornery prospectors scrabbling for gold and, as yet, no police forces, courts, or lawyers.

Bill's first taste of this came when he observed a "miners' meeting," the informal institution through which justice was dispensed. For years, prospectors in Alaskan mining camps had organized these get-togethers when squabbles erupted. Such meetings, in this remote corner of North America, were captured in phrases the miners loved, such as "rough justice" and "brotherhood of the North." Everybody could attend, hear each side of the story, and then vote on the outcome. But a miners' meeting was accorded fearsome powers: it could hang a man, give him a divorce, imprison, banish, or lash him.

Bill had blundered into a miners' meeting in Forty Mile. In his book, he vividly describes the ill-lit saloon in which it took place, and the brutal way the men spoke to each other. Most of the participants were swilling back rotgut whiskey that tasted like carbolic acid, and the air was thick with tobacco smoke and male sweat. The case involved a French Canadian known as French Joe. En route from his claim on a remote creek to the trading station, Joe had agreed to a neighbor's request to deliver some gold dust to a man called Dick Robinson. But when French Joe arrived in Forty Mile and presented Robinson with two ounces of gold dust, Robinson had objected that he was owed three ounces. French Joe indignantly replied, "I don't know for dat. He gif me two hounce—der she was. Dat's all I know." (With his novelist's ear, Bill delighted in catching the accents and slang his fellow prospectors used when he recorded events like this.) Robinson demanded a miners' meeting, knowing that his burly fellow Americans would easily outnumber everybody else. Sure enough, the majority decided that French Joe probably stole the third ounce, and should therefore make it up himself, pay the costs of the meeting, and buy a round of drinks for everybody present.

Was French Joe lying? Had he stolen an ounce of gold? Bill Haskell had an innate sense of fairness and an instinctive revulsion for mob rule. The Forty Mile residents had already hanged at least two Indians, on suspicion that they had committed a murder. As the dejected and impoverished French Canadian miner left the saloon, Bill hurried to catch up with him and hear his side of the story again. It seemed to him that French Joe was a pretty straight fellow who had just tried to do a friend a favor. Their chat confirmed Bill's suspicions and left a sour taste in his mouth. Miners' meetings, he decided, were too easily manipulated by men who depended "less on their hands and muscles than their wits."

Bill's next lesson in northern living came a few days later, when he and Joe moored the *Tar Stater* close to the wharf at Circle City. He had already noted the packs of short-haired, ravenous dogs that roamed through northern mining camps, barking and howling: he wondered why nobody shot them. Now he learned how cunning they were. After a long night in the saloons picking up gossip about the creeks, Joe and he made their way back to their vessel. "While we were away the dogs had swum out to our boat, chewed off the rope by which it was held, and dragged it ashore. There they tore open every sack of provisions we had . . . They had even chewed up some of the flour sacks and the dishrag, the flavor of which was undoubtedly agreeable to them." The two men groaned as they surveyed the ransacked remnants of their supplies and calculated their losses.

Yukon old-timers had no sympathy for the mess the dogs had made of Joe's and Bill's outfit. It was the newcomers' fault for not being smarter. They should have done what everybody else did—put their provisions in a cache and suspended it out of reach of the snapping jaws of the dogs. *Everyone* knew that a sled dog, which would generally be fed dried fish only once a day, would steal anything edible it could reach: its own leather harness, a piece of bacon out of a boiling pot of beans, a man's hat. Sled dogs' thievery was never held against them. Two good dogs could haul up to 600 pounds on a trail and run twenty-five miles in six hours. They might howl all night and steal food, but they could save your life. They were so precious that many owners provided their faithful animals with buckskin moccasins to prevent their paws from being ripped raw by ice. "Everyone who gets along well in Alaska," Bill noted grimly, "must have a proper understanding of dogs."

Joe Meeker did not want to waste a moment hanging around Circle City's saloons. Birch Creek and its tributaries, some distance from town, were full of possibilities; Joe told Bill "that the creeks will continue to pay well for five years." But Bill was intrigued by this booming settlement and decided to stick around and earn some money, building log cabins. Privately, he thought a few weeks away from Joe would be a relief: his partner was a fine fellow, but he was so goddamn serious. And Circle City was fun, with its lively mix of Norwegians, Swiss, French and English Canadians, Germans, Irish, Scots, French, Russians, and Americans. Despite their different backgrounds, these men shared particular characteristics—restlessness, independence, a trust in luck, and an incurable credulity. Hope and privation glued them together, and although Bill recognized they were a tough crowd, he felt at home among them.

A log cabin was a palace for a man who had lived in a tent for months, struggling to stay fairly clean despite the mud and dirt.

So the partners separated. Joe packed up his tent, gun, and provisions and headed out of town. Bill started work for the sawmill owner and learned how to construct a log dwelling that would keep the cold out in the winter and the mosquitoes out in the summer. Soon he was stripping and notching logs, laying beams to make walls to the height of six feet, hammering wooden pegs into roof logs to support a gable four feet high, constructing a roof of split poles, and finally, covering the poles with a thick layer of earth for insulation. A cabin like this required forty-eight logs plus several sacks of moss for chinking. Properly finished, Bill liked to boast, "such a dwelling is a palace on the Yukon." In late August, Bill Haskell decided to see how his partner was doing and take him some provisions. He had to walk close to a hundred miles, asking miners along the way if they knew where Joe Meeker had claimed, before he found the remote creek on which Joe had pitched his tent. Along the way, he passed gurgling creeks with names like Birch, Deadwood Gulch, Miller, Eagle, Greenhorn, Preacher, and (thanks to the bones found near it) Mastodon Creek. It was hard going: the ground was either squelchy with mud or dusty with rocky boulders. The scenery was some of the least interesting of the whole river course: swampy, flat, and featureless. Bill struggled through muskeg, swatting away the whining clouds of mosquitoes that settled on his mouth, up his nose, in his hair. Relentlessly upbeat, he bragged, "I made fair time over the rough trail."

Along the way, Bill realized that these Arctic regions had spawned a new kind of placer mining. Up here, creeks and rivers were solid ice at least half the year, and under the surface of the ground soil there was a layer of permafrost, or permanently frozen soil. The paydirt, where you might find gold, was buried deep below frozen layers of moss, decayed vegetation, clay, sand, and other muck. How could a prospector even begin to pan for gold when the ground was, in Bill's words, "a solid, compact, adamantine mass"?

The first prospectors to reach the Yukon valley had tried to break up the ground with pickaxes, and then with dynamite. Their efforts didn't budge the frozen earth. Then they tried lighting fires to thaw the ground, shoveling off the ashes and any melted gravel when the fire was spent, then waiting for the sun to melt the next layer. But this was still irritatingly slow, and even during the brief arctic summer, the sun's warmth rarely penetrated much below the earth's surface. Undeterred, the miners continued to experiment. By the time Bill strode through the diggings surrounding Circle City, they had developed open fires into a year-round process. They would pile logs where they wanted to sink shafts, light bonfires, and allow them to burn all night. The following day, prospectors could shovel out the ashes and almost a foot of thawed muck. Over each shaft, a windlass was erected with which to pull buckets of muck and gravel to the surface. Eventually, a prospector's shaft might reach a layer of loose stones that he hoped was paydirt. He would pan a couple of shovel-loads, looking for nuggets or gold

In Yukon mines, shafts did not have to be cribbed with beams and pillars because the frozen muck was hard as granite.

dust. If there was nothing but gravel, he would have to start all over again on some other spot. But if there was gold, he would start digging, or "drifting," horizontally underground, in the direction in which he hoped the pay streak went. Most men worked in pairs, with one partner below ground and one above.

If the miner was lucky, as winter progressed, two large piles would slowly grow next to his shaft. One would be useless muck. The other would be the paydirt that contained gold. It was unbelievably hard, dangerous work, involving far more digging than panning. Men fell down shafts, breaking limbs, or wrecked their backs lifting heavy loads. Men working at the top of shafts, hauling up buckets of muck, were exposed to wind, snow, and cold, and risked snow blindness and frostbite. Below the surface, if a tunnel collapsed when a miner was "drifting," he would be buried alive. There was the constant risk of asphyxiation by smoke or methane gas in the tunnels. And during the long winters, the miners suffered all the ailments triggered by bitter cold and malnutrition—bronchitis, pneumonia, stomach flu, scurvy, diarrhea, toothache, fever, and pleurisy.

Throughout the winter, a thick pall of smoke hung in the frigid air. When miners weren't burrowing underground or hauling up buckets, they were cutting trees for firewood. Once spring came and streams began to flow, miners would start washing out the piles of paydirt dumped to the sides of their shafts. Like hawks, they would watch for nuggets or dust, desperately hoping that the payoff would make them rich. It was an uncertain future if no gold emerged.

At Birch Creek, Bill stopped to watch some of the miners washing their paydirt. Some used rockers: wooden boxes with two filters at the bottom. The first filter, made of sheet metal, had quarter-inch holes in it; this filter separated out all but the nuggets, gold dust, and tiniest pieces of gravel. The second filter was a heavy wool blanket, which caught the gold but let the water drain. "Having put some paydirt in, with one hand the miner rocks the cradle," explained Bill, "and with the other he pours in water . . . At intervals the blanket is taken out and washed" so the gold could be collected. This technique, Bill realized, was the cheapest method of harvesting the gold, but it was also the slowest and most labor intensive.

There was a second, faster method. Miners who could afford to buy milled lumber would build sluice boxes—a series of wooden boxes that slotted into each other like the joints of a telescope. Strips of wood known as riffle bars were placed across the bottom of the boxes, and then the sluice boxes were positioned so that the streams that came rushing down the hillsides, fed by melting snow, flowed through them. This could happen only from late June to mid-September on the Yukon, but Bill saw plenty of action as he hiked along. Miners were dumping shovel-loads of gravel into the sluice boxes, so that the water would carry away the muck while any particles of gold would sink and collect between the riffle bars.

Once built, sluice boxes required less labor than panning or rocking, but tending them was still backbreaking work.

Once there was a pile-up of material behind the riffle bars, the miners would stop the flow of water for the "clean-up." A couple of old guys had struck lucky: they bragged that they were cleaning up $1,000 of gold dust every day. They made it all sound so easy—but Bill looked at their lined faces, bloodshot eyes, and bent backs, and he knew that it wasn't. They had only ten weeks to collect this valuable harvest, after nine harsh winter months of burning, digging, shoveling, hauling, and dumping. For years before that, these two miners had just scraped a living from one poorly producing claim after another. Now they were going to take their newfound wealth to the saloons and gaming tables of Circle City and get themselves a good time. And chances were, mused Bill, that they would be poor men again before the onset of the next winter.

Bill delivered the provisions to Joe, who had cleared the brush off his claim and was now hell-bent on digging throughout the winter. By the spring of 1897, Joe told Bill, he, too, would have a pile of paydirt speckled with gold dust. But Bill had a hard time getting excited about the prospect. All that Joe could talk about was digging, drifting, and dirt. Bill's spirit faltered as he noticed how Joe's shoulders were already slumped with fatigue and the lines in his face were etched with dust. He looked at Joe's campsite a few yards from the creek—the cramped little tent, cache of dried food hanging in a tree, litter of empty tin cans, ash-filled firepit. From where he stood, he could see only one other tent; otherwise, he thought, there was no one between him and the North Pole. In the clear, late summer air, the surrounding hills glowed green and gold with spruce and birch. All too soon, frosts would leach the color out of the scenery.

The partners couldn't do much until the land froze again—if they started digging any earlier, the holes would just fill with water. And much as he lusted after gold, Bill still yearned to see more of this vast, mysterious terrain, which dwarfed the scattered trading posts and Indian villages. He wasn't ready to settle down just yet. Instead, he decided to work as a deckhand on one of the handful of shallow-bottomed steam paddle-wheelers that spent each summer on the Yukon River. In the spring, the vessels started their voyage at the desolate little port of St. Michael, just north of the mouth of the Yukon River on the Bering Sea, with its stink of rotting fish and its rusty Russian cannon. The steamers carried booze, provisions, traders, and rookie miners upstream to the mining camps, and then turned round and delivered exhausted prospectors and any gold they had accumulated to the coast. The season was so short that most boats completed only two or three round trips each year.

Bill Haskell made the 2,000-mile round trip from Circle City to St. Michael and back again, and decided to stay on the paddle-steamer as it continued upstream to Forty Mile. He arrived there in mid-September, and was taken aback. Instead of dozens of boats jostling for space to tie up at the riverbank, as there had been when he visited ten weeks earlier, there were only a couple of old wooden rafts. Nobody rushed out to greet the new arrivals. No smoke rose out of the log saloon chimneys, no music spilled out of the dance hall doors. The almost abandoned settlement looked particularly depressing under a gray sky and intermittent drizzle. There was already a chill in the air, and nighttime frosts had turned the handful of vegetable gardens into clusters of drooping, blackened plants. Most of the cabins were not just deserted: they were missing doors and walls as though they had been hastily torn apart. The settlement he had called the "vortex of white civilization on the Yukon" had become a ghost town.

Bill and the steamer captain scanned the scene and noticed one saloon where an oil lamp in the grimy window and a wisp of chimney smoke hinted at life inside. They disembarked from the steamer, walked over to it, pulled open the door, and stared at the handful of surly, red-cheeked drinkers inside the smoky room. This was not the cream of the prospecting crop. Many had homemade crutches lying on the floor next to them, others were bleary eyed, and all displayed the grim exhaustion of miners who had lost faith in Lady Luck. Harry Ash, the proprietor, greeted them laconically. "What happened?" asked Bill. Harry was soon launched on a story that centered on an intense Canadian loner called Robert Henderson and an amiable Californian called George Carmack.

Although Bill had never met Robert Henderson, he had often heard stories about the tall, lean figure with a hawk nose and burning eyes. The son of a Nova Scotian lighthouse keeper, Henderson had drifted into Alaska in 1894, after years of unsuccessful gold digging in both the southern and northern hemispheres. He spent the next two years combing the Yukon River and its tributaries for nuggets. While Bill Haskell was getting to know Alaska's Circle City in the summer of 1896, Henderson had been exploring a series of tributaries that flowed into the Yukon closer to its source. Henderson's prospecting activities were financed, or "grubstaked," as it was known in northern lingo, by another well-known figure in the North: a trader called Joseph Ladue. Bill Haskell immediately recognized Joe Ladue's name when he heard it, and remembered his reputation for being "full of grit, industry, honesty and determination." Ladue was a canny entrepreneur who ran the lumber mill at Sixtymile River, where he sold the staples of a miners' life—sluice box lumber, picks and pans, and provisions. His fortune would be made if anybody found gold near his sawmill, so he was eager to see the river's upper reaches opened up. Grubstaking Henderson could pay off for him.

With Ladue's help, Henderson had spent months beating paths through the swamps, tangled moose pastures, rank grasses, and rock falls of the region around Indian River. He had stumbled across streams, waded through creeks, poled himself along rivers, and scrambled up and down gulches. He had endured in drafty cabins for two winters, and covered himself in bear grease against the blackfly for two springs. Indian River yielded nothing much; a tributary named Dominion Creek was equally disappointing. Looming over the area was a big hill, known as King Solomon's Dome. One day, Henderson climbed it and just beyond the peak found an uncharted creek flowing in the opposite direction. He walked a little way along it, then bent down and collected a panful of water, swirled it, and saw color. This looked like such a good prospect that Henderson named the creek "Gold Bottom" because, he said later, "I had a daydream that when I got my shaft down to bedrock it might be like the streets of the New Jerusalem." Within a few weeks, he had taken out $750 worth of gold—a small fortune.

Sitting in the Forty Mile bar, Bill Haskell gasped at these figures, and leaned forward to hear what came next. By late July, Harry Ash continued, Henderson's provisions were running short. So he set off to restock in Forty Mile. Once he reached the Yukon River, Henderson had drifted along in the rapid current, rounded a bend and seen the

It was tough to spend a winter digging out paydirt, and even tougher if no color showed at the bottom of the pan.

Hān fishing camp on the mudflat where the Tr'ondëk emptied into the river. Henderson called into the camp and found an old comrade from Californian mining days: George Washington Carmack. Carmack was what American prospectors called a "squawman." He had taken up with a woman from the Tagish people, and spent more time with her family than with his fellow Americans. At the mouth of the Tr'ondëk, Carmack was fishing for salmon with his wife, Shaaw Tláa, known as Kate to Carmack; Kate's brother, Keish, whom Carmack liked to call Skookum Jim; and Keish's nephew, Káa Goox, nicknamed Tagish Charlie. They had hung their catch to dry over a smoldering fire, and the smell of dried fish, destined to be dog food, hit Henderson as he pulled up to shore.

The version of the Tr'ondëk strike story that Bill heard in the Forty Mile bar was the one that quickly became a Klondike legend. "It is one of the articles of the miner's code that he shall proclaim all discoveries

made by him as soon as possible," Bill wrote later in his memoir. Col-
laboration between miners was often the only way they could survive,
and it might also guarantee you company on a creek. So Henderson told
Carmack that he thought Gold Bottom Creek had potential. Then, with
a dismissive comment to Carmack's Tagish companions, he carried on
downriver to Forty Mile. Carmack and his party decided to test out
Henderson's tip because the fishing was slow. They struggled up one
of the creeks that flowed into the Tr'ondëk, then branched off across
a ridge that, they assumed, divided the creek from Henderson's Gold
Bottom. There was no trail. The group forced its way across fallen trees
and through impenetrable underbrush and thickets of wild raspberry
bushes. "It was a rough, agonizing journey," according to Bill's account,
"but Carmack and his Indians were hardened to such conditions." They
didn't mind the mosquitoes or the steep climbs; they were used to having to wade up to their thighs in rushing, ice-cold water. But Carmack
was not impressed by Gold Bottom, and decided to return to fishing.

On the way home, Carmack's party passed a stream known as Rabbit
Creek. As Bill heard the story, Carmack pulled out his pan and got to
work on the exposed bedrock. Carmack hoped for perhaps ten cents'
worth of gold. The first panful yielded an incredible four dollars' worth,
or close to a quarter of an ounce. The find was not just miraculously
rich. It was also amazingly easy to reach: a thick layer of raw gold lay
between flaky slabs of schist rock, like cheese in a sandwich. "In a few
moments," Bill was told, Carmack had "panned out twelve dollars and
seventy-five cents worth of gold," including a couple of fine nuggets.
Carmack had carefully tipped the nuggets and gold dust into an empty
cartridge shell and whittled a piece of wood down to fit as a cork. Then
he staked his claim according to the mining rules that every prospector had committed to memory. He hammered stakes into a rectangle
of land 500 feet by 500 feet, then attached to one of the stakes a notice
stating his name, the number of the claim, and the date of the notice:
August 10, 1896. Carmack's claim, as the first on the creek, became the

"Discovery Claim." As the discoverer, he was entitled to another claim for himself, so he staked "No. 1 below" in his own name and "No. 2 below" for Charlie. The first claim upstream, "No. 1 above," he gave to Jim. To ensure that they all secured their claims, they now had to get to the nearest mining recorder's office—in this case, a new police post at Forty Mile—as fast as possible and pay $2.50 for each one.

Sitting in the dingy, half-deserted bar at Forty Mile only two months later, Bill Haskell heard how Carmack and his pals had burst into the trading post and gleefully displayed the contents of his cartridge shell. At first, they met a wall of skepticism: Carmack did not have a great reputation as a prospector, and many of the Americans distrusted a man who had "gone native," as they called it. But the nuggets were real enough: a couple of the men described to Bill the size and weight of them. Moreover, old-timers could look at a nugget and know from its shape, color, and purity which creek it came from. Carmack's gold came from no source they recognized. The audience stopped jeering and agreed that he had to have found them somewhere.

Was this really how the great Yukon Gold Rush started? Was George Carmack the first person to find gold on a tributary of the Klondike River? Different stories have emerged in the years since Bill Haskell sat in that Forty Mile bar and heard the account that was rapidly enshrined in Yukon folklore. Most versions propose that George Carmack was asleep when the gold was found. One aboriginal account suggests that Carmack's Tagish relatives killed a moose in the area and saw gold glinting in a stream near the carcass. Then there is the version spread by Patsy Henderson, younger brother of Káa Goox, who years after the event told an interviewer that Skookum Jim had gone to the creek to get a drink of water, seen gold there, and called out, "George! Come down here. Bring down gold-pan and shovel." Yet another version suggests that Carmack's wife, Shaaw Tláa, probably made the discovery while she was rinsing dishes in the creek. The common theme to these stories is that Carmack was too lazy a fellow to have panned himself, but he took the credit because, as he told his brother-in-law, nobody would believe a Tagish man. Shaaw Tláa, doubly disadvantaged by being both Tagish and a woman, was quickly written out of the tale. Carmack's party had then failed to send a message to Henderson about the find because, the story went, the surly Nova Scotian had treated the Tagish people rudely.

All that Bill Haskell knew was that word of George's fistful of gold had spread through the crowded little settlement like a forest fire a few days after the strike. Gold fever took off. Men piled into the motley flotilla of boats tied up at the riverbank and started furiously poling, paddling, or rowing upstream. "Men who had been drunk for weeks and weeks," Bill heard, "were tumbled into the boats and taken up without any knowledge that they were travelers. One man, it was related, was so drunk that he did not realize that he had left Forty Mile until he was two-thirds of the way [to the creek]. Yet this same man is settled on one of the best claims." Vessels that were falling apart were patched with the lumber wrenched from cabins. Three days later, there wasn't a boat left in Forty Mile.

Bill Haskell listened to the story and scratched his beard. His first instinct was to resist the siren call of a stampede. He knew that it didn't take much to send a bunch of prospectors chasing off into the unknown, particularly when winter loomed and they were feeling the "bluest of the blue" because they had toiled for months without making a single strike. Besides, Joe was sweating away on their claim near Circle City, and Bill was starting to feel guilty about abandoning his partner. But a couple of days after he had arrived in Forty Mile, one of the guys who had rushed upstream in the first wave of miners returned. "It's a big thing," he announced gleefully, as he swigged a double. "Everybody is finding big pans." Another prospector reappeared, equally optimistic. The surface yields were so good, he said, that "if it went down it would be the biggest thing on earth." The miners had already renamed the Tr'ondëk River "the Klondike" because they couldn't pronounce its

Hān name properly, and Rabbit Creek "Bonanza" because they were convinced it would make their fortunes.

The enthusiasm was not universal: a couple of Yukon veterans came back in disgust, convinced it was a hullabaloo about nothing. "The valley was too wide, the willows did not lean the right way, [or] the waters did not taste right." But skeptics were soon drowned out as yet more miners poured into Forty Mile to pick up supplies for the winter before hot-footing it back to this glittering tributary of the Tr'ondëk. The hairs on the back of Bill's neck prickled. Maybe this was more than the usual pack hysteria. He felt himself being pulled into the frenzy. Could he afford to miss the big pan-out? "I determined that I would put out and see for myself." His decision meant that he was among the first to join the Yukon Gold Rush—the last great gold rush in history.

Chapter 4
"Five dollars to the pan!"
October 1896–April 1897

ONCE HE HAD MADE UP HIS MIND, Bill acted fast. With the money he had earned as a deckhand, he bought a small boat and some provisions, recruited three destitute miners eager to reach the new gold strike, and set off upstream toward the Klondike. But getting there took all their strength. Bill's boat was loaded to the gunwales, and the Yukon's current was too swift to permit paddling except for brief stretches. Most of the time, two men tramped through mud and thick bushes along the bank, hauling the boat against the current while the other two kept the vessel in midstream. Even bright-eyed Bill found the laborious voyage upstream in a constant drizzling autumn rain demoralizing: "We ate hurriedly, slept little, and hour after hour dragged the tow line over rough places on the shore, the boat all the time pulling a dead weight against us." Their feet and hands grew steadily more blistered as they slipped and sprawled along the rocks on the bank. Bill missed Joe: his new companions lacked Joe's muscles, stamina, and indefatigable determination. What's more, he now found himself the expedition leader—a position he had always ceded to Joe before. He had to deal with the constant grumbling of his new partners, even as he wondered if he was crazy to be joining the stampede. But he kept going because coming in the other direction were boats full of miners eager to register claims at

Forty Mile. "Hurry up, boys!" they yelled at Bill and his companions. "It's a great thing! Five dollars to the pan!"

After three days, the four men rounded a bend in the river and saw the mouth of the Klondike. Bill, who had been clambering over the rocks at the water's edge with the tow rope over his shoulder, straightened up and stared in amazement. In mid-May, when he and Joe had passed this spot, there had been only the Hän huts in the settlement on the bank of the Klondike where it joined the Yukon. Now it looked as though a circus of about fifty dirty white tents had come to town— except that there was no town, just a scrubby mudflat squeezed between the river and a steep hill. Bill and his crew were too tired and footsore to set off for the creeks that evening, so they pitched a couple of cramped little pup tents and dragged the boat up onto the beach. "We had a bite, a little hot coffee, and then a pipe, then sat and listened to the stories of those who had been in." They also stashed most of their provisions in a cache, out of reach of dogs, so they would not be too encumbered on the trail.

By now a cold, damp night had fallen, cloud hid the stars, and Bill was acutely aware of the whisper of the Yukon's current, the growling of dogs, and the occasional distant howl of wolves. It was a strange and lonely cluster of men around the campfires—the sole source of light in this murky landscape. In theory, they were all competing with each other for the most lucrative claims. In practice, they huddled together, thousands of miles from a half-decent town, dependent on each other in an emergency, wondering if they were all just grasping at fantasy. There were grunts of recognition from those who knew each other from Circle City or Forty Mile. When a stranger appeared, those already close to the fires shuffled aside to make room for the newcomer. The smell of sour breath and sweaty, damp clothing mingled with wood smoke and coffee. Some men never uttered a word. Others couldn't shut up.

Bill pulled his thick wool jacket tighter around him, tugged on a pair of knitted mittens, and glowered into the flames. As he listened to men who were returning to Forty Mile to register claims, he began to lose his nerve. There was plenty of talk of big strikes, "but we were shown little gold." Most of the prospectors had simply staked out claims on the creek with no idea if there was any color in them. Others planned to sell the claims they had staked before winter closed in. Bill could tell from their remarks that they were hustlers after a quick buck and didn't know a rocker from a sluice box. He began to wish that he had returned to Circle City and rejoined Joe, rather than allowing himself to be swept along in a burst of mass hysteria.

Suddenly there was a wild whoop, followed by a volley of yells and the sound of rocks tumbling down the hill. The men round the campfire rose, startled. Was this an Indian attack, Bill wondered? An avalanche?

It was a bunch of men returning from Bonanza. Bill shouted at the guy in front, "How is it?" A ripple of excitement ran through the crowd when the reply came: "Ten dollars to the pan, right in the bank of the creek." Someone threw more wood on the fire and began frying bacon as the newcomers were peppered with questions about what was happening in the hills behind them. Bill's spirits rose as he heard that three men had panned out seventy-five dollars' worth of gold in four hours, including a single nugget worth twelve dollars. A couple of men had even got two lengths of sluice boxes going already, and they had taken out $4,000. It was all still just talk: nobody in the shabby little campsite produced any nuggets or dust. But as Bill observed, "It was enough to set the miners wild!"

Within a few minutes, men started slipping quietly away from the fire, strapping on their packs, and starting up the path to the creek. They clung to the bushes as they attempted the steep incline in the dark. "They could not wait a moment after hearing the stories of those wonderful pans." But Bill watched the way that the miners who had come running down the trail now fell on the bacon and hot coffee as though half starved. The hike into gold country was obviously brutal, and Bill had little faith in

Essential tent furnishings included a bottle of whiskey, warm fur bedding, and a pair of scales for weighing gold.

his companions' stamina. He decided they should wait until dawn. He crawled inside his tent, wrapped himself in a blanket, and fell asleep. Yet all night, he periodically woke to hear the rattle of gravel as more boats arrived and were hauled onto shore. Their passengers would disembark, cook a quick meal, then scramble up the steep track.

The trail to Bonanza Creek began more easily than Bill expected. Granted, he and his three companions had to wade through a swamp and couldn't find any decent water to drink, but the low bushes along the path glowed scarlet with cranberries that helped slake their thirsts. Every so often, they would meet miners coming the other way. Some told of rich prospects along the creek; others declared the whole thing a fraud. But Bill was back in the grip of gold fever and eager to dismiss pessimists, who always looked "weary and fagged out . . . I knew they had had no breakfast."

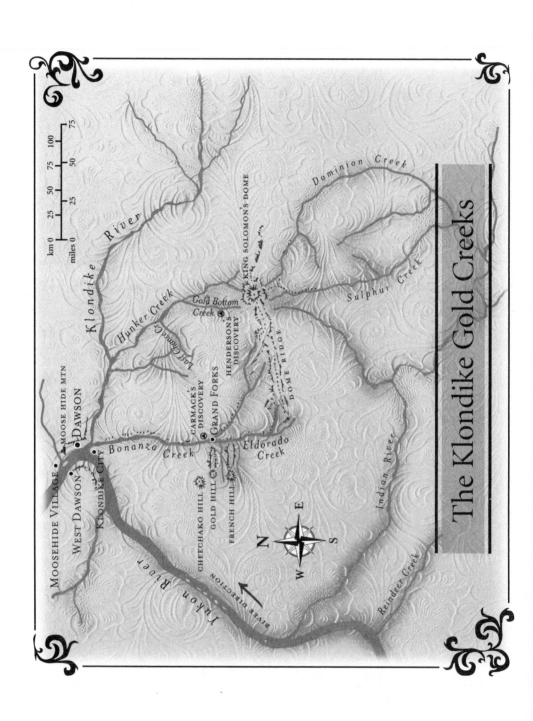

The Klondike Gold Creeks

The four men finally reached the summit of the first hill, and drank deep from a spring of fresh water. Bill looked around. After the previous night's drizzle, the sky had cleared, and in the crisp autumn air the landscape of low green hills, dark granite, trees tinged scarlet, and high sandy cliffs spread itself below him like a magnificent tapestry. He could trace the silvery thread of water for fifty miles, and he could see the snow-clad peaks of distant mountains. Every ravine in the far distance held a glittering little glacier, which converged on the main glacier like branches on a tree trunk. The whole glorious picture reminded Bill of "an outline drawing in chalk of a leafless tree."

Bill could have rested there for hours, admiring a spectacular landscape that few non-natives would ever see. "Never mind the mountains," barked his companions, so they all trudged on, first along the ridge, then down a perilously steep incline. A steady, soaking rain started to fall, making the trail soft, slippery, and easy to lose. It wasn't even a well-trodden path, thought Bill grimly: the hills around Circle City had been easier to hike across. The party stumbled and slid onward, past several creeks that nobody had yet panned and into a shallow swamp covered with what the miners called "niggerheads"—grassy clumps that looked like secure footings but were the cause of more twisted ankles and falls than any other feature of the Klondike landscape. By the time the men arrived at the first claim stake on Bonanza Creek, which was numbered 64 Below Discovery, they were tired, damp, and dirty. Bill's early euphoria had evaporated. As he stared at the creek's muddy banks and a few quartz pebbles, his spirits sank further.

There were ten and a half claims in a mile, which meant they were still a long way from Carmack's original find—"Six more miles on paper," Bill calculated, "several more times that on foot." Would they ever get to Discovery Claim? Did Bonanza really offer, in the words of an Irishman they met on the trail, "all the goold in the worruld"? Or was the man just another blowhard caught up in stampede frenzy?

On and on the four men trudged, clambering over rocks and fallen trees, wondering if they would ever reach clear ground. When they were still two miles short of Carmack's claim, one stopped in his tracks, let his heavy pack slide to the ground, and declared this was it: he could go no farther. It was almost dark, and Bill's shoulders ached. He organized a campfire and a pot of tea, then sat gloomily on the ground, wondering what the hell he was doing in this lousy moose pasture. No one said a word. Early next morning, he woke chilled through, with a white frost clinging to his blanket. Hot tea and a mouthful of bread helped a little, but it was a wretched party that struggled up the trail to Carmack's Discovery Claim.

Gold can work miracles. The sight of it glinting in Carmack's sluice boxes gave new energy to each of them. Carmack himself slapped them all on their backs, then proudly pulled three nuggets out of his pocket. With a big grin, Bill shouldered his pack and soldiered on, past the mouth of another creek—a "pup"—that emptied into Bonanza, past eager miners swishing gravel and water in their gold pans, past half-built log cabins being readied for the winter. Finally, eighteen hours after they had left Carmack, Bill and his boys came to the last of the claim stakes above the Discovery Claim. They staked out a 500-foot square each, tacked up notices of claims, then wearily looked around. They had no idea if their claims were any good. Since their mission had been to stake, not pan, they hadn't brought their pans with them, and they had no energy left to scrabble around on the stream bed. "It's all chance," Bill thought to himself, as he squatted by the creek, staring into the water. "Gold might be there and it might not. It certainly looks little like it." At least, however, they had secured their claims on the creek where there might be "all the goold in the worruld."

The return journey back to the mouth of the Klondike was much easier, now that the pressure was off. They met plenty of men coming up as they went down. "How is it?" the newcomers asked anxiously. Forgetting the doubts they had felt only hours earlier, Bill's gang replied in unison: "It's a big thing!" Once in sight of the makeshift camp at the

The sight of other men collecting nuggets and gold dust in their sluice boxes on Bonanza Creek gave new energy to Bill and his party.

river's mouth, "we, in our turn, yelled like Comanches and jumped and tumbled down the hills with the rattling rocks." So what if there was no gold on their claims? At least they were in the game: they now each owned the one claim an individual was legally allowed on a creek and its tributaries. Eager newcomers crowded round Bill and his companions, desperate for an update on the creeks because "we were in the delightful position of having staked our claims."

Once Bill had recovered from his race to stake, he hiked back into the hills to check whether any of Bonanza's tributaries held out more promise than the claims already secured. "It makes a great difference in carrying a pack on a trail whether a person is in a hurry or not," reflected Bill, as he strapped on a pack three times heavier than he had carried before. This time, the pace was more leisurely and, as frost crept into the ground, the trail firmer. None of the other pups looked worth trading his Bonanza claim for. Soon the deciduous trees shed their last leaves, there were no more cranberries to pick, and snowflakes started to drift across the path. Bill decided to retrace his footsteps to the mouth of the Klondike.

As Bill Haskell crested the last peak before the descent to the Yukon, an extraordinary sight met his eyes. On the far shore of the Klondike River, across the water from the cramped area where they had camped a few days earlier, was an even larger spread of dirty tents, and even the beginnings of several log buildings. The dreary mudflat covered in alder and stunted willows, opposite the former Hān fishing camp, had been transformed, in Bill's words, into "a new metropolis."

In later years, Bill enjoyed explaining how "a clever man could see that this flat was about the only place available for a city in that rugged region, and there was a clever man who saw it." The clever man was Joseph Ladue, the trader upriver who had grubstaked Robert Henderson. News of the rich find on Bonanza had ripped up and down the Yukon River in August, and when it reached Ladue at Sixty Mile, he moved fast. Grasping the need for a trading post near the gold fields, he had rushed downriver to the confluence of the Klondike and the Yukon. There, he carefully assessed the mudflat and recognized that although the gold-bearing creeks all flowed into the river from the south, only the river's northern bank could accommodate both a decent-sized community and a good steamboat landing. He then quickly continued downriver past Fort Reliance to Forty Mile and filed an application at the Canadian police post there to register plans for a townsite of 160 acres. Rowing and poling his way laboriously upriver for a hundred miles took a couple of weeks. But once back at Sixty Mile, he built a raft out of all his dressed lumber, loaded his sawmill onto it, and floated it downriver to the mouth of the Klondike.

By the time Bill Haskell returned from his second hike into the gold fields, Joe Ladue had set himself up on the Klondike's northern bank. He had purchased some gold claims for himself, got his sawmill working day and night, and built a warehouse plus a small cabin that also served as a saloon. He was only just ahead of the crowd. By late October about 600 claims had been staked on Bonanza Creek and its pup, named Eldorado. There were now over a thousand men in the Klondike valley, all clamoring for wood to build shanties and cabins. They had to cross the river to get to Joe Ladue's townsite and sawmill, but there were plenty of canoes and boats available in which to pole through the shallow waters. And once the river froze over, they could walk.

Ladue's townsite buzzed with anticipation. The site was strategically positioned to be the supply center for what the trader insisted would be the richest gold field in the world. The Yukon River was navigable by steamboats; the Klondike River was not. So the settlement at the junction of the two rivers was poised to become a booming business and transportation center. Ladue announced that his townsite was like San Francisco in 1849, before the California Gold Rush, and he started selling building lots for five to twenty dollars each.

And yet, as Bill recognized, there was still an aura of make-believe about the Klondike gold strike. Half the hard-bitten prospectors who had pulled their boats up on the mudflat and set off to Bonanza were acting out of force of habit. This was just one more roll of the dice for them. They had staked in previous stampedes, and they would stake again. Once the ritual was performed, many of them were happy to take refuge in the crowded little cabin that was Ladue's home and office, light their pipes, and try to sell their claims to the next eager arrival. Bill Haskell could see that, sick and discouraged by years of poor diggings, they thought the Klondike "a last chance, merely, and a mighty poor-looking one at that. They had nothing better to do and so rushed in." They didn't believe any of that "all the goold in the worruld" rubbish: their goal was to find suckers who would buy their claims off them. Bill himself watched how "claims which were afterwards worth thousands could have been picked up by the dozen in September or October for a hundred or two dollars."

Nevertheless, Bill himself was young enough to cling to the dream. He was swept along by the unbridled enthusiasm of those convinced that this was a gold field to beat all others and would make their fortunes. In Joe Ladue's cabin, Bill was one of the optimists, insisting that in all his days in Colorado, he'd never seen a better prospect. It was thrilling to be on the ground floor of a real stampede—one of the guys in the bar who could tell the greenhorns that the trail was hell but the payoff worth it. He bought Ladue's vision of a city that would outshine all the other mining towns in the North. Bill sent word to Joe Meeker in Circle City, advising him to come upstream and join him on the Klondike.

Once the sun set these days, the temperature dropped like a stone, and in early November a thin layer of snow covered the ground. The Yukon froze, and Bill Haskell was faced with a choice. Should he hang around Joe Ladue's townsite and earn some cash working in the sawmill? Even George Carmack himself, the Bonanza discoverer, was compelled to cut logs for Ladue in order to afford the provisions he needed for a winter on the creek. Or should Bill, who still had a bit of cash left, get straight back to his claim and prepare the cabin and the ground for a long, cold season of digging?

At first, Bill thought he would stick around on the mudflat until his partner arrived. He was fascinated by the way that the community grew from day to day: every evening there were new faces in the saloons, every few weeks there was a new saloon. Lines of canvas tents, most less than six by six, crept up along Second, then Third Avenue. The streets might be dirt tracks, but a city was emerging from the bush—just as two years earlier first Forty Mile and then Circle City had emerged on the banks of the Yukon.

The Yukon River was frozen solid by early November, cutting all links with the world south of the St. Elias mountain range. But the Klondike was a magnet for the hundreds of prospectors who had been in the great Northwest for years and who now made their way to Ladue's townsite, then headed for the hills. Both Bonanza and Eldorado were already staked, but weather-beaten veterans refused to work on somebody else's claim—even for wages of fifteen dollars a day that beat anything they could earn Outside. They wanted to stake their own claims on the dozens of nearby creeks that might, just might, prove even richer.

Prospectors were not the only people who swarmed to the Klondike. Bartenders, merchants, cardsharps, pimps, and hookers arrived from the bars, brothels, and stores of Forty Mile, Circle City, and other trading posts. Ladue's townsite now had over a thousand residents, but it remained a lawless community. The line between those making an "honest" living and those catering to baser instincts was often hard to define. There were two laundries, for instance—one on Queen Street that doubled as a bakery, and a second on Second Avenue that doubled as a brothel. The subject of gold dominated everything. In Joe Ladue's Front Street bar, Bill and the newcomers lapped up tales of unbelievable strikes by miners fresh from the gold fields—a pan of $65 at No. 21 on Bonanza Creek, then a pan of $57 on Claim No. 5 on Eldorado, then upward of $80 nearby, then a pan of $212 on Claim No. 16 on Eldorado. Was it real? wondered Bill. Or was it braggadocio from prospectors eager to jack up the value of their claims?

There was certainly money to be made from all the frenzy. As the population of the trading post and the creeks swelled, prices skyrocketed for flour, salt cod, salted pork, dried fruit, flannel shirts, rubber boots, wood, tents, and, in particular, for land. Bill was thankful that he had stocked up with provisions before the rush. He knew he would have to haul it all up to the creeks by himself because he couldn't afford a dog.

Finally, Bill could stand it no longer. He'd never heard anything like the yields that were being taken from these pans. "Nothing in the history of the world," as he put it to the other fellows in the bar, "has ever been found to equal this." He *had* to find out if he was going to get rich. Leaving directions to his claim for his partner, Joe, Bill stuffed his pack and a sled as full as he dared, crossed the frozen Klondike River, and started the climb toward the creeks. He was carrying and pulling everything he needed to build a shelter, to keep warm, and to feed and clothe himself for several weeks: he had a little tin Yukon stove and tin plates, nails and canned salmon, flour and bacon, thick mitts and a heavy fur robe, a tent, axes, saws, and a large bag of nails. His shoulders ached before he had reached the first summit, but he gritted his teeth and hiked on.

Once on his claim, "I set to work to construct a place in which we could make life endurable for the winter." The logs were green and the ground on which he built his cabin was frozen solid, but Bill thought he did a pretty good job filling the chinks between the logs with moss and mud.

Nothing had prepared the twenty-nine-year-old for the frigid loneliness of winter just below the Arctic Circle. "The snow fell nearly every day, mantling the great frowning hills. It was a scene of solitude, and a time of deep silence broken only by the wailing of the wind." Occasionally, he would see a passing figure, muffled in thick winter clothing and hauling a sled, shuffling along the creek. There were a couple of other miners within half a mile, working their claims. But there was no time or excuse for sociability. The daily routine, as days grew shorter and shorter, was relentless.

Each morning Bill reluctantly emerged from under the cover of his lynx blanket, made from the skins he had bought the previous summer, and stuffed some of his carefully prepared kindling into the stove. Once the fire was lit, he put the kettle on to boil. After a mug of tea, he pulled on mitts, hat, heavy, knee-length woolen stockings, fur socks, moccasins, and a hooded Indian parka made of wolverine fur—over the woolen long johns, undershirt, shirt, wool pants and jacket that he rarely removed—and ventured outside. He spent the day chopping down the pitch pines and building a woodpile that would last him and Joe through the winter. They would need firewood to keep them warm in their cabin and for the nightly fires that would melt through the frozen muck where they dug a shaft. He had to make sure that his clothes and supplies stayed dry, and his face and fingers were free of frostbite—he had already seen too many men missing fingers, toes, and noses. Every night, Bill shaved splinters from a log, to be dried on the Yukon stove for starting the fire the next day. Every day, he melted enough ice for cooking, drinking, and washing. Most days, he just ran a damp rag over his face; he took his clothes off and washed the rest of his body only when the temperature had risen slightly, or the lice, the itching, and his own smell got too much, generally about a couple of times a month. His toilet was an old can, which he had to remember to empty outside before the contents froze solid.

His world shrank to the size of his 500 by 500 foot claim: he had no idea what was going on next door, let alone in Ladue's township or Outside. Some nights, he played solitaire with a greasy pack of cards by the light of a "bitch"—an old meat can filled with a loose wick stuck in discarded bacon grease. Candles were too precious to waste on such diversions. Other times, he allowed himself to daydream about books. Once, travelers' tales, adventure stories, and books about history and myths had fed his imagination. Now, he was starved of reading matter. "A trademark on a pick handle becomes fairly eloquent in that solitude."

Life improved once Joe arrived. Joe was not the chattiest fellow in the world, but at least he was company. The two men got to work at the spot that looked most promising. Each evening they lit a fire. Each morning, when the ground was thawed and loosened, they scraped off the ashes, dug out the muck, and piled it next to the shaft. Every other day, they melted a pan of ice to see if they had reached any color. Days went by—nothing showed up in the pan. As December wore on, the sun's rays glimmered over the horizon for increasingly brief periods, and they grew heartily sick of bacon, beans, oatmeal, canned goods, and salt meats. It was hard to keep the faith.

Joe worked the ground with single-minded determination, while Bill did all the cooking and became quite proud of his baking. "My method was simple. I would take a quart of flour, throw in a couple of table-spoonfuls of baking-powder and about half a teaspoonful of salt, and mix till quite stiff with water . . . Then I would grease the tin with the best grease that was obtainable [and] push the tin into the oven, and in half an hour take out a loaf of bread which, in the ravenous condition of our appetites, would make our eyes water. The only difficulty was that a loaf would disappear at every meal, so that as long as our supply of flour continued abundant I was compelled to bake two or three times a day." It was naked hunger that caused the loaves to vanish. The bread was coarse, leaden, and indigestible. Bill joked that his bread often had a greater specific gravity than gold itself. "A winter in the Arctic, devoted to digging dirt out of a frozen hole, is the only complete dyspepsia cure I ever saw."

By Christmas, the two men were starting to bicker. In the tiny cabin, there was no escape from one another's coughs, smells, habits, snores, opinions. It got so bad they could scarcely communicate. Joe was sup-posed to be the guy who could find gold, but they still hadn't located paydirt. He was snappy and morose, and Bill was losing patience. They knew of other cabins where partners came to blows with a savagery bred of frustration and despair. Bill recognized that they needed a change. He suggested they strap on their snowshoes and tramp down to the mouth of the Klondike to see what was going on: "anything to break the monotony." Bill didn't admit to Joe that he particularly yearned for the sound of a female voice—he rarely saw the two white women who had accompanied their husbands to the creeks. It wasn't sex he wanted (though that would have been welcome) so much as a change of conversational chemistry. The monotony of male company was getting to him.

The trail back to Ladue's townsite wound through a landscape so white and silent that it might have been carved out of carrara marble.

Bill envied miners who could afford a dog team to carry loads from the sawmill to the creeks.

Shapes of men and windlasses stood in black silhouette against the pale skyline. As the men walked, they noted which other claims were being worked, how many shafts had been dug, how big the tailing piles were. There were fewer than four hours of dim light a day, but on a clear night the moon reflected off the snow and they could easily pick out the trail. On cloudy nights, however, it was too easy to lose their way; then they took refuge in the cabins of friendly prospectors. With men whose words they trusted, they compared notes. They avoided blowhards who exaggerated the size of their take. When pressed about their own claim, Joe would shrug and Bill would mutter, "Not yet." They were not having a good time.

There was little action at the trading post on Christmas Day, 1896. The guys in the bar asked anxiously, "Well? Any color?" Their faces fell when they heard the grim answer. Joe and Bill celebrated Christmas in a scruffy "restaurant" located in the front half of a wooden shack, with a couple living and preparing meals in the back. Since turkey, plum pudding, or mince pies were all unavailable for love or money, the Christmas dish was moose. There was no church of any denomination in which to hold a service. The major concern was to keep working and keep warm, so even on Christmas Day Ladue's sawmill was busy. "Outside," recorded Bill, "it was a cold, cold world. The wind howled and the snow fell . . . The thermometer outside registered fifty degrees below zero." The likelihood of an entire new city blossoming on a scrubby few acres of riverbank still seemed remote. Everything depended on what lay trapped within the frozen earth. Was the Klondike strike just another foolish bubble, inflated by hope and desperation? Or would it be the eldorado that people like Joe Ladue and Bill Haskell were banking on? Bill began to wonder how long he could bear to stay in the Yukon. "It is a splendid country to leave whether one has gold dust or not."

Back on the creek, the two men abandoned the log cabin in January because it was too damn drafty. Instead, they pitched their tent in front of it, set up their stove with a metal chimney stuck through the canvas roof, and used the hut as a storeroom for tools and supplies. Snow drifted and banked up and over the tent, protecting the interior from the cutting wind (although whenever one of them lifted the flap, an icy blast penetrated). The thermometer edged above zero for four days in February 1897 but then fell steadily, reaching seventy-two degrees below freezing point on a particularly bitter March day. Until mid-April, the snow did not thaw a particle. The wind blew constantly in frigid blasts, often filled with swirling snow. On the worst days, the men abandoned any thought of digging and focused simply on staying alive: it was far too cold to go outside. On these days, Bill could actually hear his breath strike the air as he rose to light the stove. "There was a sort of crackle when the warm breath met the cold atmosphere, and it was at first painful to draw such cold air into the lungs." When he ventured out to grab some logs off the woodpile, "My eyelids kept freezing together, but I had to be very careful about pulling off my gloves to thaw them apart." Several times his hands nearly froze before he could pull his fur-lined mitts on again.

On and on winter dragged, and the partners were way beyond bick-ering. Most communication consisted of grunts, although occasionally their former camaraderie revived as they lay in their separate bunks at night, recalling some of the colorful characters they had met. But they were weary—tired of Bill's bannocks, tired of hauling up gravel on the windlass and tipping it on the dump, tired of dashed hopes when they tested a panful of gravel and found only a few cents' worth of gold. Since mid-March, the only provisions they had had were dried beans. "We nearly starved, or, at least we thought we did. It would not have been much of a job to get together a million dollars' worth of gold dust along the creek, but such a thing as a good square meal was not to be had."

The chilly darkness rendered Joe almost catatonic: only Bill's contin-ued curiosity about the world around him kept his own spirits up. The sound of wolves howling still sent shivers down his spine; the crackle of the northern lights could still occasionally drag him out of bed. Older miners shook their heads as they saw the young American strapping on his snowshoes and climbing up a hillside to get a better look at the bril-liant reds, greens, and violets swirling across the wide night sky. A true romantic, Bill found them mesmerizing. "The more I reflect on this life and the hereafter, the more I am in doubt as to whether the gold in frozen placers is in itself worth going after. But the aurora . . . is worth seeing, even if you have to live on short rations of bacon and beans for three months and find no gold."

Slowly, the days began to lengthen. In late April 1897, light lingered in the sky until well after ten o'clock, and the piles of muck besides the shafts on each claim formed sizable hillocks. The miners began to prepare for the spring clean-up, when they could wash their piles of paydirt through running water and pan out any gold. It was a time of anxious laughter. Men who had staked near the Discovery Claim were confident that they would do well for, as Bill grimly noted, "the gold fairly stuck out of the dirt." Bill and Joe began to hear of big pans all along the creek: "Clarence Berry took out over three hundred dollars to the pan, James MacLanie over two hundred dollars, and Frank Phiscater over one hundred and thirty dollars." Miners working a claim on Eldorado had found a pan containing $800. But the farther you were from the Discovery Claim, and the shallower your shaft, the less likely you were to pan out. And before you could even start the process, you had to build a sluice box. Since the Klondike hills had already been stripped of timber, this meant a hike down to Ladue's mill to buy lumber at the exorbitant prices he was now charging.

Joe Meeker kept digging. Bill Haskell set off down the trail, now muddy with spring run-off, to buy lumber. Along the way, he heard story after story about men who had been paupers the previous fall and were now millionaires. But he also saw plenty of half-starved men who had toiled all winter long on the creeks and come up empty handed. "The lucky one did not strike the pocket because of his ability as a miner," Bill mused. "Chance favored him, that was all." He still didn't know whether he was one of them. Had he and Joe struck lucky, or had they drawn a blank?

Bill Haskell crested the hill above the Klondike, and looked down the slope toward the Yukon River. He stopped in his tracks. He didn't recognize the vista below him.

CHAPTER 5
Sourdough Success, April–May 1897

BILL HASKELL RARELY ESCAPED the icy claustrophobia of that winter on the creek. "Joe and I have poor luck," is the steady and depressing refrain as he describes those bleak months in his memoir, and only
occasionally does he give readers a glimpse of what was happening in
the wretched mining camp at the mouth of the Klondike. But while
Bill was away, the makeshift trading post that was Joe Ladue's personal
fiefdom had morphed into a town. It had also acquired a new name.

The changes flowed from decisions taken 3,000 miles away. The political leaders of the young Dominion of Canada had noticed that something was happening in their country's vast northern hinterland. Up
until now, the national government in Ottawa had ignored its subarctic
wilderness. It had been tough enough for Canada's first prime minister,
Sir John A. Macdonald, to bind the country east to west with a railroad
in the 1880s. The North appeared to offer no benefits for a thinly populated country scrambling to coalesce into some kind of nation. It was
cut off from the rest of the country for up to eight months a year by ice,
and the possibilities for agricultural settlement (on which the former
British colony relied for expansion) were zero. In the seventeenth and
eighteenth centuries, thanks to the European appetite for hats made
of beaver fur, the North had underwritten the success of two powerful
trading companies, the Hudson's Bay Company and the North West
Company. But by the mid-nineteenth century, beaver hats were out of

fashion and the trading companies' stranglehold on northern development had been swept away. Trapping in the North continued because
there was still a market for arctic fox, moose, lynx, wolf, and beaver. But
Canadian politicians, busy with developing the prairies, had no interest
in taking on treaty obligations with the North's aboriginal peoples.

Then as now, however, nothing fired up Canadians so much as the
suspicion that Americans were encroaching on their territory. In the
early 1890s, the steady flow of American prospectors like Bill and Joe
into a remote corner of Canada caught the attention of the Canadian
government. Missionaries at Forty Mile had complained to Ottawa
that aboriginal people were being debauched by the miners. And if
there really was gold in those godforsaken subarctic regions, it was
Canadian, not American, and Canada should benefit. But the Ottawa
government recognized that, to assert its ownership of the Yukon
creeks, it needed some muscle up there. Muscle, in the Canada of the
1890s, meant the red-coated Mounties. Founded in 1873 by John A.
Macdonald, the North-West Mounted Police had already controlled
American whiskey traders in the West and helped suppress a Métis
uprising on the prairies. The force was a curious blend of uniformed
traditions—deliberately, as Macdonald had specified that it should
be "a civil, not a military body, with as little gold lace, fuss, and fine
feathers as possible: not a crack cavalry regiment, but an efficient
police force for the rough and ready—particularly ready—enforcement of law and justice." In its short existence, it had established an
impressive esprit de corps, attracting recruits from Britain as well as
from well-to-do families in Ontario and Quebec.

In 1895, a detachment of twenty Mounties under the command
of Inspector Charles Constantine was dispatched across the St. Elias
Mountains and down the Yukon River to Forty Mile. Constantine was
a gruff and incorruptible Yorkshireman with the rigid views and lack
of imagination that twenty-four years in uniform can produce. His job
was straightforward but dauntingly large: to assert Canadian authority

(which meant, at this stage in the country's existence, raising the British flag). The various roles of magistrate, mining inspector, crown land agent, timber agent and, by default, Indian agent all devolved onto his portly figure, since his detachment was the national government's sole representative in the region. When Constantine and his men marched into Forty Mile, they spelled the end of random shootings, cardsharping, and rough justice in the settlement. In the spring of 1896, when Bill Haskell watched French Joe being summarily convicted in a Forty Mile saloon of stealing an ounce of gold, he was also watching one of the last (and by then, illegal) miners' meetings held on Canadian territory.

Constantine and his Mounties had been joined at Forty Mile by William Ogilvie, an employee of the Geological Survey of Canada. Ogilvie, a bearded Scotsman who was a great raconteur, was an old hand in the North: he had first traveled there in 1887, with George Mercer Dawson, one of the survey's most senior scientists. Ogilvie had overseen the first official surveys of the Chilkoot Pass and the Yukon and Porcupine rivers. Now, he was the official with whom prospectors had to register any claims made on Canadian territory. When hundreds of men started rushing into his humble log office in the fall of 1896 to register claims on the creeks of the Klondike, he was astonished by the quantity and quality of the nuggets he was shown. He sent word to Ottawa that this strike was the first real whopper within Canadian borders, and it would startle the world. The territory's population would exceed 10,000 within two years, he predicted, and the new mining camp at the mouth of the Klondike would be the greatest yet in the Canadian North. At the time, it was easy to dismiss Ogilvie's predictions as ridiculously inflated—another tremendous tale intended to hook an audience's attention. In fact, they would prove to be accurate. Equally astonishing was that it took two months for his message to travel to Ottawa, and then several more weeks to creep up the ranks of government officials.

In Forty Mile, as winter fell, Charles Constantine and William Ogilvie watched prospectors, saloonkeepers, camp followers, and traders disappear upriver and knew they couldn't wait for politicians in Ottawa to decide what to do. Ladue had already bought his 160 acres, and now other Yankee speculators were applying for similar townsites. The two officials had to move now if they were going to stop a bunch of roughneck Americans from getting out of hand on Canadian territory. Inspector Constantine sent a group of Mounties ahead of him to establish a post at the mouth of the Klondike and start collecting customs duty. He persuaded Ogilvie, in charge of the land registry, to reserve forty acres near the Ladue townsite for "Police and other Government purposes." He had his eye on a wooded area around a slough, so he could use the timber for a police barracks to be erected in the spring. All Constantine's anti-American hackles rose when he heard that the Alaska Commercial Company, the most powerful trading company on the Yukon, had already planned a warehouse on Ladue's land. ACC managers often weaseled out of Canadian customs duties, he snapped. In another message to Ottawa, he wrote (with absolutely no supporting evidence but with the vehemence of rank prejudice) that they were "all Jews and not to be depended on." He insisted that the NWMP do business only with the rival North American Transportation and Trading Company.

William Ogilvie could see that he, too, needed to move fast. Joe Ladue might claim ownership of his 160 acres, but the township needed an official survey before squatters overran the area. Although lots were being snapped up, street lines were still crooked and many had tree stumps in the middle. Moreover, the original staking of the creeks, particularly Bonanza and Eldorado, had been so frenzied that there were regular arguments and fights between neighboring claimants. Claim jumping was rampant, as latecomers tried to take over claims that the owners had staked, then left unworked. In January 1897, Ogilvie arrived at Ladue's site with his surveyor's chain and compass and began to pace out a proper rectangular grid, with the streets intersecting at right angles. The avenues, which ran parallel to the Yukon River, were a conventional

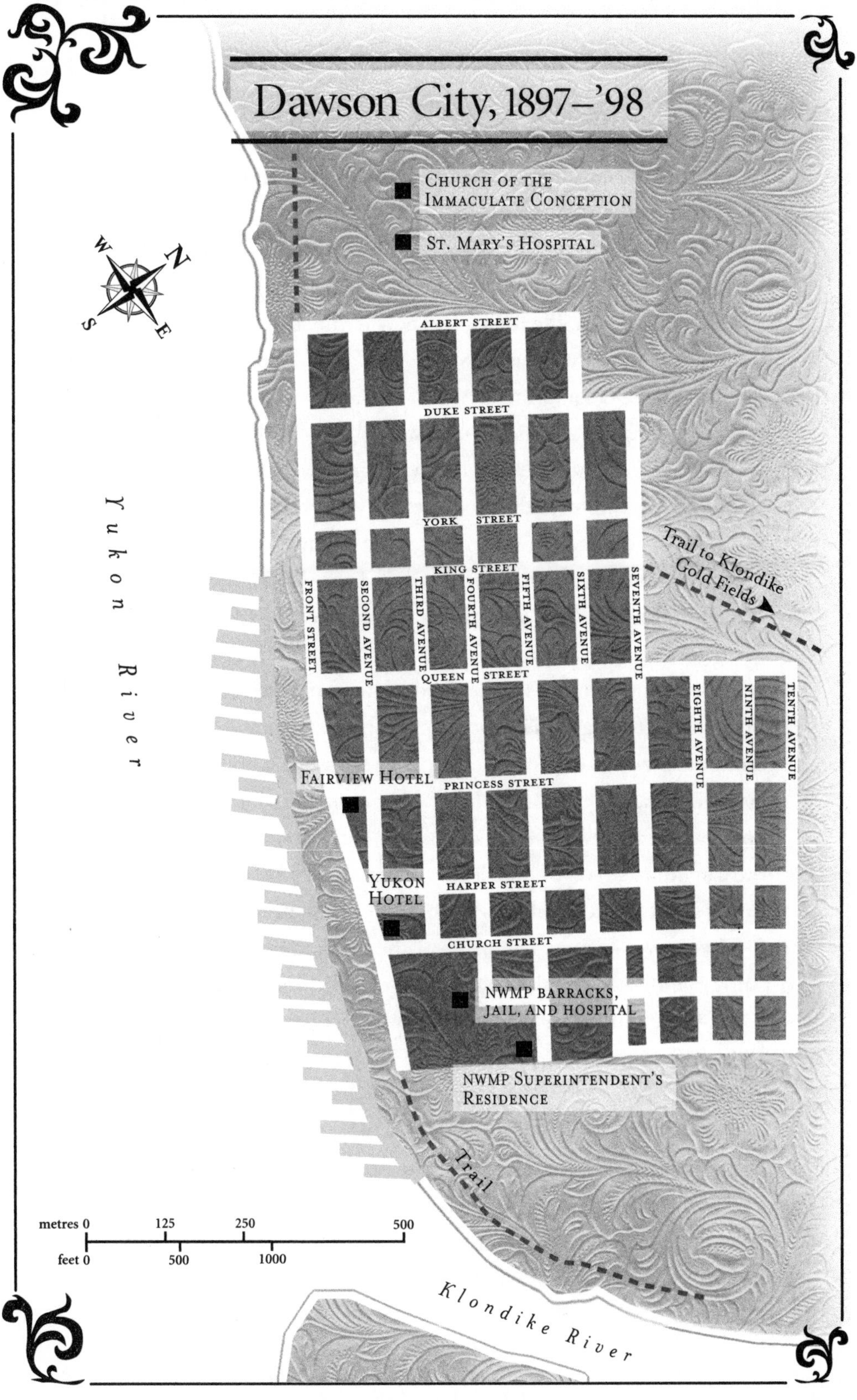

Dawson City, 1897–'98

■ CHURCH OF THE IMMACULATE CONCEPTION

■ ST. MARY'S HOSPITAL

Yukon River

ALBERT STREET

DUKE STREET

YORK STREET

KING STREET

Trail to Klondike Gold Fields

FRONT STREET

SECOND AVENUE

THIRD AVENUE

FOURTH AVENUE

FIFTH AVENUE

SIXTH AVENUE

SEVENTH AVENUE

QUEEN STREET

EIGHTH AVENUE

NINTH AVENUE

TENTH AVENUE

FAIRVIEW HOTEL

PRINCESS STREET

YUKON HOTEL

HARPER STREET

CHURCH STREET

■ NWMP BARRACKS, JAIL, AND HOSPITAL

■ NWMP SUPERINTENDENT'S RESIDENCE

Trail

Klondike River

metres 0   125   250   500
feet 0   500   1000

chain's width, or 66 feet wide, while the cross streets were 50 feet wide. Ogilvie was able to mark out only a few individual lots, measuring 100 by 50 feet, as the snow was thick on the ground. Any unfortunate squatter who discovered he had pitched his tent in the middle of one of Ogilvie's carefully drawn streets was sharply told to relocate.

Ogilvie also gave the townsite a new name: Dawson City, called after his boss, George Mercer Dawson, who had recently been appointed director of the Geological Survey of Canada. Ogilvie followed the practice of naming the avenues common in the West: the closest to the river was Front Street, and behind it ran Second Avenue, Third Avenue, and so on. When it came to the cross streets, Ogilvie couldn't resist reinforcing Dawson City's ownership by giving them decidedly un-American names—King, Queen, Princess, Albert, Duke, and York. There were no drains in Dawson City, and merchants and restaurant owners dumped their garbage on the frozen Yukon, knowing it would be swept away when the ice melted. The squalid reality of smelly outhouses along Princess Street was a delicious contrast to Ogilvie's lofty street names and grand vision of a northern metropolis. But who knew? San Francisco had started from such humble beginnings only fifty years earlier, and was now a wealthy port with a population of over 300,000. Anyway, the Canadian surveyor had done all he could for now, so he tramped off to the creeks fifteen miles away, to sort out the problems there.

The arrival of representatives of the Canadian government brought some stability to the mining community, but it brought only grief to Chief Isaac and the Hän people. By the spring of 1897, miners had completely overrun the traditional Hän fishing grounds on the southern bank of the Klondike River, and had torn down the fishing racks so they could erect their own tents. Chief Isaac had assumed that the newcomers would share the territory's resources in the same consensual way that most aboriginal groups did, respectful of both each other and the land. He quickly realized that they had no interest in negotiations and were destroying the Hän way of life. They brought new diseases with them, like measles, chicken pox, scarlet fever, diphtheria, and tuberculosis, which decimated villages, and they shouldered aside Hän fishermen from their traditional fishing spots. They traded alcohol for food supplies, and respected Hän elders could now be seen stumbling helplessly down Dawson's muddy streets. Worst of all, the newcomers treated all Hän people with unveiled contempt and threatened the safety of women and children. It was evident that southern racism meant the two communities could not integrate.

At first, the Hän tried to relocate to a small plot of land on the Dawson side of the Klondike. But this was the wooded area that Inspector Constantine had already earmarked for the NWMP compound. With his usual gracelessness, Constantine made it clear he didn't want to share his compound with the very people who had peacefully occupied the land for centuries. Although he had spent little time in the North, he shared the widespread prejudice against the Yukon's aboriginal peoples. In an official dispatch to Ottawa, he dismissed the Hän as a "lazy, shiftless lot, who were contented to hang around the mining camps. They suffer from chest troubles and die young." Finally, Chief Isaac negotiated a deal with Constantine and the Reverend William Bompas, Anglican bishop in Forty Mile—representatives of the two most powerful institutions in the Canadian North. Thirty Hän families were moved three miles downstream of Dawson City to a reserve known as Moosehide Village, which was the same size (160 acres) as a standard homestead occupied by one family on the prairies.

A century of misery lay ahead of the Hän. They would never be able to use their ancestral fishing camp on the Klondike again, and their requests for more land were refused out of fear that the land might contain gold. They were not welcome in Dawson except during the long winters, when they could supply meat. But even here they faced competition from non-native hunters, and soon game reserves were depleted. Moreover, since Moosehide Village was below Dawson, the Hän's drinking water was contaminated by Dawson sewage, so dysentery and diarrhea took their toll. By 1904, sickness and starvation were so acute at Moosehide that the Mounties were obliged to distribute food. In the years ahead, the Hān would see their children shipped off to residential schools, and watch their language and their culture gradually disappear.

The dramatic developments in Dawson in a few short weeks meant that an entirely new settlement met Bill Haskell's eyes when he crested the hill overlooking the mouth of the Klondike River in early April 1897. Before he had even crossed the Klondike, he noticed that the Hān dwellings had gone and construction had spread beyond Ladue's original townsite. He saw the rough wooden headquarters of the NWMP, laid out like a military barracks to the south of the town, and heard orders being barked out by a man in uniform. And to the north, next to a large white tent, the first logs in an entirely new, two-story structure had been laid. What was this?

Bill hurried down the hill, across the frozen Klondike, past the Mounties' half-built barracks, and toward the Yukon Hotel, on Front Street. Once outside the saloon, he leaned his sled against the wall, stamped the mud and slush off his boots, pushed the door open, and made his way through clouds of tobacco smoke to the bar. There, his fellow drinkers were happy to answer his questions. The place was now called Dawson City, Bill heard, and Joe Ladue was doing fine: lots were selling for as much as $300 each. It was still a small, dirty settlement, and the only clean water came from a spring in the hillside under the Moosehide Slide. But there were already three saloons—ramshackle canvas constructions that offered rotgut whiskey and faro tables that operated twenty-four hours a day. And that large structure to the north of the town? That was going to be Dawson's first hospital. In January, several stampeders from downriver had overtaken a middle-aged man struggling alone through the snow, pulling his sleigh alongside a single dog. It had been Father William Judge, the

By April 1897, Dawson's building boom had begun. Newcomers roamed the dirt roads, and makeshift stores were springing up along Front Street.

Jesuit priest Bill had seen at Forty Mile, making his way to the Klondike to see if the rumors were true. The priest had taken one look at the boomtown and felt his calling. He purchased three acres at the north end of town from Joe Ladue for $300 and hired men to start clearing ground for St. Mary's Hospital and the Church of the Immaculate Conception. The hospital would be, he prayed, "a means of leading . . . sheep back to the fold."

Bill's informants told him how this scrawny Catholic priest, with a soft voice and intense gaze, had wasted no time in setting up a tent and offering medical care to anybody who was sick. Next thing the denizens of Dawson's saloons knew, the black-robed priest himself was coming around, asking for money to build a permanent hospital. He had raised $1,400 by public subscription for St. Mary's Hospital, and he had promised Dawson that the Sisters of St. Ann, a nursing order stationed in Alaska on the lower Yukon, would come and take charge of it.

But Bill's fellow drinkers were less interested in some crazy priest's actions than in the news from Bonanza. What could Bill tell them about the clean-up on the creeks? Were the claims paying out? Plenty of gamblers were eager to buy claims sight unseen if there was any hint of gold. They planned to sell them to the greenhorns who would arrive once the Yukon River was open. Dawson's future depended on the Klondike region's being a real gold field. If Eldorado and Bonanza lived up to the promise of their names, Dawson City might fulfill Ladue's prediction as the San Francisco of the North. But if talk of big pans turned out to be ill founded, Dawson City could disappear as fast as Forty Mile and Circle City.

Dawson's explosive growth put a new spring in Bill's step. *Surely* there was some foundation for all this optimism. He purchased the lumber that he and Joe needed to build a sluice, and hauled it over the melting snow, back to Bonanza. There, the two men set to work hammering a sluice together, then diverting the creek down it. Every few days, they stopped the flow of water down the sluice and examined the debris caught behind the riffle bars. "It was well towards spring," Bill Haskell recorded in his memoirs, "before our pans began to make any unusual yields." But finally the gold showed up: amid the black sand and gravel the two men saw the seductive yellow glitter of flakes. That long, lonely, cold winter of burning and digging, burning and digging, had paid off. Bill didn't tell his neighbors that he and Joe took gold worth about $50,000 (over $2 million in today's values) off their claim. Many of the miners were close-mouthed about their yields, since they had no intention of paying Canadian royalties on them. But success made Joe and Bill happy—and friends again. All the containers they could lay their hands on—coffee cans, tobacco tins, leather pokes—were soon filled with dust and nuggets, and plugged shut.

In mid-May, Bill and Joe carefully stuffed their haul into their packs. The gold dust weighed them down, it was so heavy, but they just grinned at each other as they shouldered the clumsy canvas backpacks and took the track to Dawson City. They soon found themselves in a crowd of miners heading toward Dawson's saloons. Bill reckoned there were 400 valuable claims stretched along Bonanza and Eldorado, and every digging "was a fabulous mine of gold . . . Men who had stumbled over the rough trail in September, poor and disheartened, disgusted with their condition and sick of the country, came down in the spring as millionaires and threw their gold dust about like so much grass seed." The men greeted each other as "sourdoughs," the nickname for those who had survived at least one brutal northern winter, living on bread made with wild yeast. Like Bill, these tough, emaciated men were clad in the prospectors' uniform of thick wool pants held up with suspenders, heavy boots, worn flannel shirts, and misshapen felt hats. Their eyes, like Bill's, were bloodshot from wood smoke and bouts of snow blindness, and the prevalence of tangled beards and unkempt mustaches made the crowd look like an assembly of Old Testament prophets. And like Bill, they poured into Dawson City, eager to put the bitter winter behind them.

As the torrent of gold hit the scales on the counters of saloons, hotels, restaurants, and a newly established dance hall, spirits soared in Dawson City. Relief and exuberance suffuse Bill's memoir, as he describes how his gamble on Bonanza had paid off and what it felt like to mingle with other successful prospectors. Rumors flashed up and down Front Street about which prospector had sold his claim too early, which rookie had washed out $24,480 in one day, which of the creeks was the most productive. Clarence Berry's wife, Ethel, had poked around the dumps on her husband's claim and picked up $10,000 worth of nuggets. A young fellow from Seattle who had bought a share on Eldorado Creek for $85 the previous November had sold it five months later for $31,000—and he'd never even visited the place!

Everyone gossiped about the brawny, booted men on Front Street, pointing out who was a loser and who a millionaire. One of the first "Klondike Kings" to attract everybody's attention was a tall, stout, crop-haired Nova Scotian called Alex McDonald. Bill reckoned him "a good-hearted working man," although he was also a canny business-man who didn't miss any opportunity to buy up claims, trade shares in particular mines, or sell services such as hauling provisions on his mule train. Tangle-haired, dirty-nailed, his boots encrusted in mud and his pants patched, Big Alex could have been taken for a hobo by a stranger. A fervent Roman Catholic, he didn't drink and he didn't boast about his wealth. In fact, he was unusually taciturn, and when he did speak it was in a voice so soft it was more like a whisper. But he turned up at the Alaska Commercial Company's warehouse that spring with $150,000 worth of gold, including $12,000 in fat nuggets. Bill was also in the warehouse that day, and he watched Alex spill out his riches under the astonished gaze of a newspaper correspondent called Alice Henderson. Big Alex loved business more than he loved gold, and he casually invited Alice, "Help yourself to nuggets. Take some of the bigger ones." When Alice hesitated, wondering what her acceptance might imply, Alex gave her a sweet smile, rubbed his stub-bly chin, and whispered, "Oh, they are nothing to me! Take as many as you please. There are lots more." Alice chose a nugget that weighed ten ounces, worth about $200 back then and perhaps fifty times that amount today.

Circle City and Forty Mile at their heydays had nothing on Dawson, as it exploded with the wealth flowing out of the creeks. It was now big-ger, brasher, and richer than any other mining town in the Yukon valley. It boasted dozens of log cabins, 600 tents with wooden walls, Father Judge's half-built hospital, and the foundations of both the Catholic and a Presbyterian church. The business section of the town was grow-ing faster than the residential section, despite the sky-high costs of labor and lumber and the fact that the only building material available was wood: everything else—nails, window glass, stoves, furnishings, building tools—would have to be shipped in from Outside once the ice on the river finally melted. Most buildings were on shaky foundations,

The Magnet roadhouse on Bonanza Creek was typical of the commercial ventures catering to lonely, thirsty miners.

since the townsite lay within the permafrost zone. Permafrost changed its texture with the seasons: the soil's high water content kept it solid when cold, but once thawed it turned into a glutinous muck that was neither water nor soil. A heated building standing on posts on this base would soon shift as uneven melting and the weight of the structure took their toll.

No matter. The Alaska Commercial Company had completed its huge new wooden warehouse, but the North American Transportation and Trading Company was busy putting up an even larger two-story warehouse, with concrete foundations, covering about 8,000 square feet. Bill Haskell was of the opinion that "never before was there such a place to make money quickly. Gold dust was flying about in all directions." He reckoned the construction cost for such a warehouse would be $93,500 (well over $2 million today), for a building that would have cost about $4,500 (about $120,000 today) to erect in California.

"It is impossible to adequately describe the effect upon Dawson of these revelations of the rich character of the mines when the sluices were cleaned up," Bill Haskell observed. The heavy bags of gold that continued to be carried down from the creeks were, in the words of one old-timer, "stacked up by the cord" in the Alaska Commercial Company's warehouse for safekeeping, ready to be transferred to steamers for shipping Outside. But *when* would that happen? When would the gold start its voyage south and the warehouse shelves be filled with fresh provisions? *When?* The Klondike was already open: clear water gurgled out of its mouth and onto the Yukon's frozen surface, melting the top layer of rotten ice and carving deep fissures in the solid ice below. But the Yukon ice was at least three feet thick, and you could still walk across the river. It would take several more warm days, and more pressure from below, before it began to move. Until the ice went out of the Yukon, Dawson was locked in. Until steamers could make their way upriver from the Bering Sea port of St. Michael, carrying a far greater cargo of supplies than men could haul up the mountain passes, the Dawson diet continued to consist of the three Bs—bread, bacon, and beans.

The longed-for moment arrived on May 17, 1897. On that bright Monday morning, the massive, craggy jam of ice started to move and the cry went out: "Break-up!" Bill ran down to the water's edge, eager to watch as winter finally loosened its grip. First the powerful current by the far bank swept away the ice in its path. Then the slabs whirling along in the icy torrent widened the channel by smashing aside the ice still clinging to the banks.

One of the most appealing passages in Bill Haskell's book is the paragraph dealing with his eagerness to reconnect with the distant world. He had one thing in mind: a square meal. Food, he bluntly admitted, had replaced sex as his most lascivious fantasy. Sure, he was curious to know what had been happening Outside. But after a winter of living on the three Bs, he yearned for the endless supply of milk, meat, and fresh vegetables he had known as a child growing up on a farm. The Yukon's brutal climate, he sometimes thought, was nothing compared to the horrible scarcity and monotony of the grub, which in his opinion required "a strong stomach and the patience of Job." At night, he dreamed of cutting into a juicy red steak and "the awakening," he confessed, "is very painful." It is easy to imagine this big, healthy man, worn down by bad diet and poor results on the claim, sinking into reveries of chickens larded with yellow fat, mounds of crisp roasted potatoes, soft bread rolls dripping with butter, fresh tomatoes smelling of the sun, apple spice cake. He would give every ounce of gold that he and Joe had panned for an oyster stew, a chocolate cake, or a slice of roast lamb. Now the river was open, it wouldn't be long before a paddlewheeler would come puffing upriver bearing supplies of fresh food. Bill watched great chunks of ice spinning slowly in the rush of black water, and he could almost smell grilled beef.

Within a couple of weeks, a handful of roughly built little vessels appeared around the river bend from the south, swept along by the surging current. In the next few hours, an untidy fleet of more than 200 homemade craft followed them and tied up on the waterfront opposite Joe Ladue's log cabin. More and more boats followed, and the excitement of their arrival was intensified by the piercing, non-stop shriek from the steam whistle atop Ladue's sawmill. It had been tied down to welcome the newcomers, and it set the sled dogs howling in a grating chorus.

But these were not the boats that Bill was waiting for. Their passengers had set out for the Yukon the previous fall, before news of Carmack's strike had even reached the coast. They had been lured up by the general rumors of Alaskan wealth that had brought Bill and Joe north; they heard about the big strike on the Klondike only after they crossed the mountains. Then they had had to mark time in a village of makeshift cabins and tents at the south end of Bennett Lake, building boats and waiting for the ice to retreat from the Yukon's feeder lakes. Their arrival immediately doubled the population of Dawson City, but most of these rag-clad cheechakos (as newcomers were known in the Indian terminology adopted by Klondikers) were even hungrier than

A flotilla of homemade craft sailed from Bennett Lake towards Dawson as soon as the river was open.

the Dawson veterans, having exhausted their own supplies during the long winter. Men and women tumbled onto the shore, bone tired and frozen to the marrow, eager to share hellish stories about life on the trail. Bill hardly listened. There wasn't a tale of treacherous mountain passes, raging torrents, avalanches, frostbite, scurvy, bear attacks, or starvation that an old hand from Alaska hadn't heard before. What shocked him was how little most of them knew about either mining or the land. Veterans gaped with amazement as the new arrivals unloaded stuff that was of no use in the North, then asked plaintively, "Where do we start digging?" One guy had even bought a bicycle, for heaven's sake. There were a couple of women clad in men's city suits. How in heck, wondered Bill, would they handle months of living in a crowded, insanitary town alongside cussing, crude miners? Most of these greenhorns had left for the gold fields on impulse. One man who buttonholed Bill "had never seen a gold pan, much less wielded a pick in the diggings. Many were unfit for the work of mining . . . and a still larger number had no idea what was required." Bill listened laconically to their chatter, uttering the occasional "Is that right?" His mind was still elsewhere. At least once a day he muttered to anybody in earshot, "I'd give a hundred dollars in nuggets for a slice of beefsteak!"

Finally, after the downstream rush of homemade craft slowed in early June, Bill heard the sound he'd been listening out for: a whistle echoing up the Yukon valley. Somebody on the waterfront yelled, "Steamboat!" From the opposite direction, the Alaska Commercial Company's tiny *Alice* came churning into view past Moosehide Creek and puffed her way against the current to the Dawson shore. A flat-bottomed, blunt-prowed stern-wheeler, only her smokestack indicated she was anything more than a small barn built on a scow. But she had made her way upstream the hundreds of miles from the mouth of the Yukon River, and was loaded with newspapers, whiskey, fresh meat, potatoes, onions, and the kind of canned goods (oysters, tomatoes, peaches) that Bill hadn't tasted in months. Crowds of sourdoughs, their filthy wool pants held up by suspenders, ran to the river's edge, cheering wildly. Two days later, the North American Transportation and Trading Company's *Portus B. Weare* tooted her way into sight, tied up next to the *Alice,* and unloaded more goodies from Outside.

That evening, Bill Haskell gorged himself on the beef, gravy, and fruit pie that he had dreamed of during the long, hard winter. Next, he lit a cigar and opened the first newspaper he had held for eight months. The pleasure of reading almost beat the first taste of steak. He devoured the news he had missed during the long winter: the election of Republican William McKinley as twenty-fifth president of the United States, America's looming war with Spain over Cuba, plans for the elderly Queen Victoria's Golden Jubilee, the results of the world heavyweight boxing match between Bob Fitzsimmons and Gentleman Jim Corbett. Then he strolled out of the restaurant and sat down on a nearby tree stump, feeling the warmth of the late evening sun on his face and the unfamiliar joy of a full stomach.

The memory of those six grim months huddled in a tent with Joe, dealing with hunger, cold, disappointment, and boredom, melted away. They *had* survived. They *had* found gold. Bill watched yet more unskilled, unprepared newcomers step onto Dawson's crowded wharf, and shook his head. How many of these gold diggers would find what they were looking for? How many of them could even afford to hang around in Dawson City? By the time he had digested his meal, the price of a good Dawson City building lot had risen from $500 to $800, and it was still rising.

PART 2: MINING THE MINERS

CHAPTER 6
Father Judge's Flock, May–June 1897

NOW THAT THE KLONDIKE'S WEALTH was confirmed, Dawson City's population ballooned, new construction supplies arrived, and the first big building boom started. Joe Ladue was no longer content to mention San Francisco: his new town, he bragged, was going to be the greatest camp in the history of mining operations. There was a non-stop racket of sawing and hammering, and two sawmills ran day and night to keep up with the lumber orders for yet more stores, hotels, saloons, and dwellings. Large log buildings, many with Wild West–style square wooden fronts hiding peaked roofs, appeared overnight on the muddy streets. But it was still a squalid, gold-crazy settlement of shacks and tents. Some of the tents looked like misshapen piles of soiled laundry, while half the cabins were so gimcrack that they might have been cobbled together by ten-year-old boys. Buckets, a few ramshackle out-houses, and the woods on the edge of town were the only toilets; there were still no public bathhouses, drains, or health facilities. What's more, as the waters of the Yukon River rose with the spring run-off from its tributaries, and the ground of the mudflats softened in the sun's warmth, flooding was a constant risk. Lots close to the waterfront were soggy underfoot, while rubber-booted residents waded along most of the streets, tracking mud into every building.

Empty lots were in short supply, and newcomers found themselves pushed toward the steep slope behind the mudflats as they looked for

somewhere to pitch their tents. As they shouldered their way through the
confusion of flapping canvas and piles of lumber, many felt as though
they had landed in a jamboree or religious revival meeting. Alongside
the feverish building activity, however, there were plenty of people just
hanging around, staring at the new arrivals. Shabbily dressed, unshaven
miners perched on tree stumps and fallen logs, or swarmed around
the bars, straddle legged, smoking, chewing, and spitting. A handful of
women lounged outside tents, chatting to passersby. They were dishev-
eled and their clothes were worn and dirty: some looked beaten by the
hard life of a northern prostitute, but others radiated a chippy confidence and an earthy humor. Dawson was a rough and bawdy place, but
it throbbed with life and excitement.

North of Ladue's original townsite, Father William Judge took stock
of the situation. The Jesuit was a strange character—ascetic, deeply
religious, guileless, but not naive. Those who met him recognized the
quality of the man. One contemporary described him as having "eyes
widely spaced and most unusually illuminated, a forehead high, chin
firm, mouth straight but full—if ever character was written on a countenance, the writing here was clear." After Judge's death, his brother,
Charles (another Roman Catholic priest), would collect up many of his
letters and write a book about him. The book's frontispiece is a grainy
black-and-white photograph of the priest, clean shaven and neat, thin
and solemn, with wire-rimmed glasses and a black cassock buttoned
tightly at the throat. His shoulders slump, he wears a rosary threaded
through his sash, and he is too uncomfortable before the camera to
allow a glimpse of the humor and compassion that impressed contemporaries. The picture was probably taken in 1886, the year he was
ordained. Did it stand year after year on his mother's dresser in Baltimore, as the earnest young man traveled farther from home comforts
toward hardship and self-sacrifice, his hair thinner and his skin more
lined with each successive move?

The priest was unique in Dawson because he was not obsessed by

Father William Judge was as single-minded as most of his flock, but his quest was for souls rather than gold.

finding, accumulating, and spending gold. But he was not so unusual in the larger world. In the nineteenth century, a huge army of missionaries spread round the globe and scattered through industrial slums, Indonesian jungles, African villages, Pacific islands, and South American mountains. Some 360 Christian organizations, from celibate Roman Catholic orders like the Jesuits to mass membership Protestant bodies such as the Society for the Propagation of the Christian Gospel, maintained an estimated 12,000 Christian missionaries in the field during these years. The Jesuits were among the most well-established missionary forces: Francis Xavier, one of the order's founders, arrived in Goa, in western India, as early as 1542. Since Xavier's successes in India and China, Jesuits had been converting souls on every continent. Three and a half centuries later, there was barely a corner of the globe in which the black-robed figure of the Jesuit missionary, with his biretta and large wooden cross, was not a familiar sight. So it was hardly surprising that such a figure had arrived in the new boomtown.

There was another aspect of Father Judge that made him unusual in Dawson, alongside his lack of interest in gold. In his late forties, he was twice the age of most of the men there. As Bill Haskell had discovered during his bitter winter on Bonanza, prospecting in the frozen North was not for the fainthearted or frail. The Klondike Gold Rush was a young man's game, particularly in an era when most white American men died before their fiftieth birthdays. Yet the unworldly priest had tramped off in late March into the hills, when the sixteen-mile trail was still covered in snow. He was dazzled by the wealth of some claims on Bonanza and Eldorado. "I myself saw one hundred and twenty-three dollars' worth of gold in one shovelful of dirt," he wrote to a fellow Jesuit. But he also realized that "there are far more men here than there are good claims for. Those who are working for wages have been making fifteen dollars a day all winter, which is not bad for hard times; but if, as we suppose, a great many men come in when the river opens, wages will very likely fall to ten dollars and maybe to six, as they were before the deposits on these creeks were found." Judge knew that a crowd of unemployed, disappointed men spelled as much trouble as the town's lack of sanitary facilities. Disease and desperation would sweep Dawson, and he felt a paternal impulse to protect ignorant sinners from the folly of their ways. But the priest also recognized that the dark cloud of overcrowding had a silver lining for him. Now the river was open and men would start pouring north, it would be easier for him to find laborers to work on his church and his hospital.

So far, progress was slow. From his letters, it is obvious that the priest *loved* designing buildings and thinking about how to make them work. He got as excited about placing windows as he did about saving souls, and he spent hours carving the decorations onto his church's improvised altar. His enthusiasm was just as well because in Dawson he was his own architect, contractor, and head carpenter. In a town of cramped tents and one-story shacks, he had drawn up extraordinarily ambitious plans. Both buildings would be fifty feet by twenty-four, with four windows down each long wall. The hospital would have two floors, and the church would have a hexagonal belfry tipped with a wooden cross and containing a small bell. It had been a monumental challenge to raise money, find nine men (he had hoped for twenty) to start construction, and organize the purchase of 5,000 feet of milled lumber for the planned buildings. The logs had had to be rafted down the river or drawn by dog teams to Dawson. Given that no supplies were yet available from outside the region, the priest was constantly improvising. Instead of plaster for the inside walls, he used muslin coated in white lead paint. He tacked more white muslin into wooden frames for windows, since there was no glass available. He used empty boxes for washstands and hammered rough-hewn planks together to make beds. Mattresses were stuffed with dried grasses and sawdust instead of hair or cotton. All the supplies cost outrageous amounts of money, for which the priest was constantly scrabbling. Although the prospectors treated him with respect, with a few exceptions they were a godless lot who regarded him as an oddball. They might toss a little gold dust his way if they were feeling flush, but they had no interest in doing the heavy lifting.

The Jesuit priest was not surprised by the miners' attitude: he had already spent six years in Alaska, and had seen the best and the worst of the North. As he confided in letters to friends, "O, if men would only work for the kingdom of heaven with a little of that wonderful energy [they exhibited on the creeks], how many saints we would have!" Yet if Judge differed from the gold diggers in the focus of his energies, he shared with them the obsessive dedication to a goal.

William Henry Judge was dedicated to a life of piety almost before he was born. A member of a sprawling Irish family from the Roman Catholic–dominated city of Baltimore (besides his brother, Charles, the priest, there were three sisters who became nuns), he was such a sickly child that his parents feared he was too frail to pursue his religious calling. He left school early and went to work in a mill, but at thirty-five he could resist his mission no longer. In 1885, he entered the Jesuit order. His sense of vocation was punishing: despite his ill health, in

1890 he volunteered for the toughest assignment available. He offered to join the newly founded Jesuit mission among the indigenous peoples of Alaska: the newest American territory and the final frontier in the American imagination. "May God grant me grace and strength to do and suffer something for his glory," he wrote to his superior the day before he sailed from San Francisco, bound for St. Michael, close to the Yukon River delta.

Glory was in short supply, but there were plenty of chances to suffer. Yet although William Judge was frail, he was not feeble. In fact, he was as practical as he was saintly. At the mission's Alaskan headquarters at Holy Cross, he constructed an ingenious boiler attached to the kitchen stove so that in the hideous winters hot water was always available. The Sisters of St. Ann, who ran the mission, were captivated by this modest priest who went on to build a bake-oven and take over all the baking for their school. Scurvy was endemic among both natives and non-natives, since there was so little fresh food in the diet. Father Judge invented a system of Turkish baths to alleviate the painfully stiff joints that resulted from the disease. At the same time, he demonstrated a profound respect for the local Indian peoples and their herbal remedies for common diseases—spruce bark for scurvy, for example, or cranberries for bladder infections. He also followed the well-established Jesuit tradition of learning and translating the local language (Koyukuk in this region). He compiled a Koyukuk–English dictionary. The children who boarded at the mission loved the soft-spoken priest who played the flute and made violins for them out of birch wood. And he loved them. He wrote to a fellow priest that the "Indians . . . are fine-looking, fond of work, anxious to learn and very good-natured. I think they would make good Catholics."

For four fulfilling years, Judge did the rounds of Koyukuk and Tanana villages in the interior of Alaska, where he said Mass, taught hymns, prayers, and the catechism, and baptized people of all ages. It was a demanding, exhausting way of life: one winter, the only protein available was arctic hare. That year, he made his congregations laugh by telling them that he felt his ears each morning when he woke to see if they were growing longer. The scattered communities welcomed the solemn man of God, whose blue eyes shone with what they believed was celestial inspiration (but was in fact hopeless myopia). Father Judge shared his communicants' hungers and sorrows, joined their annual feasts, blessed their children, and taught them new songs. His attitude was a welcome contrast to that of coastal traders, who haggled fiercely about prices and devastated communities with alcohol.

Then new orders arrived from the Jesuit superior in Holy Cross Mission, Alaska. Father Judge's heart sank as he learned he was to transfer to the new mining camp of Forty Mile, several hundred miles east of the region he had come to know well. Now the suffering for which he had once prayed really began. He would be the only priest in a community of cynical, tough-talking men; he would have no communication with other Jesuits for almost ten months a year. Most of his work would be Sunday Masses and funerals: he would have little opportunity to officiate over joyful family occasions such as baptisms and weddings. And he knew that miners, as he confided to one of his sisters, "as a rule, ain't no saints . . . I would prefer to remain with my Indians, but I know that what is done from obedience is more pleasing to God." Man proposes, God—and the Jesuit Order—disposes.

Father Judge packed up his meager belongings, and took a steamer up the Yukon River. At Forty Mile, he soon got the measure of his new flock. These men worked hard, drank hard, and despised the aboriginal peoples for whom Judge had developed affection and respect. "A great part of the miners seem to be men who have been running away from civilization as it advanced westward in the States, until now they have no farther to go and so have to stop here." One man had clung so tightly to the frontier as it moved west that he had never even seen a railroad. The priest learned that in mining communities, the best way to start a conversation was to ask, "What's your story?" He met Civil War veterans, British remittance men, criminals on the lam, and runaway wives. He accepted everyone he met as a child of God whom he might lead back to the Lord. Even the most wayward soul warmed to a man who treated everybody equally, listened sympathetically, had no interest in material gain, and who frequently put himself at risk by giving away his own coat, mitts, or boots to those in need.

It is a wonder that the far-from-robust priest survived these years. In January 1896, Judge set off with his dog and sleigh in a temperature so cold that the mercury in his thermometer had frozen. After about three miles, his sleigh broke through the ice and he had to walk up to his knees in the freezing water for about 200 yards. "I pushed on," he wrote to his sister, in a letter that must have made her wince, "trying to keep my feet from freezing by walking as fast as I could. But the sleigh was made much heavier by the ice that formed on it and the snow that stuck to it after it had passed through the water, so I could not go as fast as I ought to have gone." By now the light had gone. Father Judge could not even feel his feet in their sodden boots, and he was dizzy with exhaustion. He thought about stopping, wrapping himself in his blanket, and waiting for divine intervention—even if it arrived in the form of a merciful death. But the dog gave a sudden yap and lunged ahead. In a few minutes, they had reached a deserted cabin on a high bank. The cabin had no floor, no window, no hinges on the door—but there was a stove and a woodpile.

Judge's trial was not over yet. The wood was so cold that he could not light it with a match. This meant he had to go outside and fetch a candle from his sleigh, which he had left at the bottom of the snowbank. He tried to pull on his big fur mitts but discovered that, like his boots, they had got wet, and they were now frozen so hard that he could not get his hands in them. He struggled down the bank on elbows and knees, trying to keep his hands covered by his sleeves, found the candle, then had to haul himself up the bank, once again keeping his hands hidden. Eventually he lit a fire, but "as soon as I started to thaw the ice off my boots, I felt a pain shoot through my right foot, so I knew it must be frozen. At once I went out and filled a box that I had found in the cabin with snow, then took off my boot and found that all the front part of my right foot was frozen as hard as stone . . . I could not make a mark in it with my thumbnail. So I had to go away from the fire and rub the foot with that awfully cold snow, which is more like ground glass than anything else, until I got the blood back to the surface, which took at least half an hour." Finally he was able to crouch near his fire, but it took another hour before his foot was completely thawed out. Judge knew that "with such treatment, no harm follows from the freezing. But if you go into a warm room, or put the frozen part to the fire before rubbing with snow till it becomes red, it will decay at once and you cannot save it."

Such ordeals, in the priest's opinion, were God's way of testing his faith. He offered his Lord humble thanks for delivery, then pushed on with his ministry.

Father Judge watched Forty Mile turn into a ghost town in the fall of 1896, when news of Carmack's gold strike on the Klondike River came down the Yukon. He knew immediately that he must follow his flock. "One would think," he commented wearily, "that gold is the only thing necessary for happiness in time and eternity, to see the way in which men seek it even in these frozen regions, and how they are ready to sacrifice soul and body to get it." After his January scouting expedition to the new camp at the junction of the Klondike and the Yukon, he returned to Forty Mile and packed up his cassock, biretta, flute, demijohn of Mass wine, and limited supply of native medicines. He hauled them upriver to the acres he had secured for his church and hospital, then set about erecting his buildings, cooking for the construction team, and procuring enough provisions.

Father Judge was forty-seven on April 28, 1897, and he felt his age. His hair was thin and gray, his body gaunt and stooped, and deep grooves etched his forehead. In his thirties, despite a weak chest and thin frame, he had been capable of shouldering any amount of lumber and wielding a bow saw for hours at a time. Now, his back ached if he spent too long bent over letters, drawings, or his little stove. "Age begins to show its effects," he admitted in a letter home. Yet he quickly added, "but only at times, and not sufficiently to prevent me from performing all my duties." Besides, wasn't his suffering proof that his life was committed to Christ?

In Dawson he was needed as never before: his faith and his medical knowledge were in short supply. As Bill Haskell noticed, "The excitement of washing and accumulating the gold was so great that many men devoted their time to it when they should have devoted some to cooking, cleanliness and the rest ... Some men lived on barely nothing, and that half-cooked." The priest watched Bill's fellow miners limp in from the creeks, their feet bound in sacking and their hair hanging to their shoulders, suffering from pneumonia, rheumatism, broken limbs, or scurvy. He saw crowds of newcomers arrive with little idea how to deal with frostbite or gangrene. He knew that malnutrition was inevitable since there was still almost no fresh food. And the townsite was filthy. A reporter from the San Francisco *Examiner* noted with dismay this summer that Dawson was a death trap because of "this dripping moss, this putrid water, these dismal swamps, this rotting sawdust, this vileness as to sewage." Sick men lined up outside Father Judge's tent begging for food and shelter, although St. Mary's Hospital was still half finished and he had almost no medicines or bedding. By early June, he recognized the symptoms of typhoid in five of the men he was treating: insanitary conditions were taking their toll. The hospital had been intended as a way to reintroduce Roman Catholics to the consolations of their faith, but Judge now insisted that the sick should be admitted regardless of their religion. At the same time, he began to count the days until the arrival of the Sisters of St. Ann, who were expected at the end of September and would take over nursing duties.

There was little ego to Father Judge, but there was a burning sense of mission that appreciated recognition. As the spring of 1897 wore on the busy priest, in his tattered and mud-splattered cassock, felt his sense of fulfillment blossom as he urged on his builders, bargained for provisions, and celebrated Mass. The merchants and saloonkeepers on Front Street started to tip their dirty felt hats to him and call out friendly greetings. Bill Haskell noted that the hospital did "good work under the greatest difficulties." Women offered shy smiles to the cadaverous figure. Big Alex McDonald, the Nova Scotian who was one of the richest Klondike Kings, made himself known to Judge, assuring him that he was both a teetotaler and a Catholic, and that the good Father could expect to see him at Mass when he was in town. The priest's public image gradually shifted from eccentric oddity to the one person in the gold fields who would give disinterested counsel and spiritual support. People looked up to a man so selfless that he would give the coat off his back and the food off his plate to somebody in worse straits than himself. He became a symbol of nobility in a town where altruism was rare.

Judge's living conditions were still wretched—a drafty tent he shared with two of the men building the hospital. But suffering was good for the soul, he believed, and when the buildings were completed, he would have, he boasted to his brother, "the finest place in town." As Father Judge considered his situation, he had to suppress a sinful spurt of pride in what he had accomplished. He had no interest in finding gold nuggets, but in his life there were other forms of treasure.

While Father Judge was creating a slice of heaven up in Dawson's north end, downtown, entrepreneurs were gleefully flirting with hell. These were the hurdy-gurdy, throw-the-dice, devil-may-care streets that gave this instant settlement the reputation of "the town that never sleeps." Bill Haskell loved this side of the town, and couldn't wait to throw open a saloon's swinging doors as soon as he reached Front Street. "In the matter of iniquity," he observed, "Dawson was not slow in eclipsing all rivals on the Yukon." In the spring months, during the few hours of darkness, there was a dreamlike quality to the isolated community. When lamps were lit inside the canvas shelters, they glowed like diamonds as the music spilled out into the chill northern air. By the summer of 1897, the camp was "the liveliest town imaginable . . . When it was light all the time, the public resorts were wide open every hour of the day."

Harry Ash, who had watched the clientele disappear from his bar in Forty Mile the previous year, had set himself up in a ramshackle canvas structure called the Northern Saloon. Other proprietors from Forty Mile and Circle City had also shown up in Dawson and now ran similar drinking establishments, with names like the Pavilion and the Monte Carlo. They stood open twenty-four hours a day, seven days a week. (Once the Mounties arrived, they were meant to close on Sundays, but the back door was often open.) Along one wall of each of these raucous watering holes stood a long wooden bar, its shelves filled with bottles of what purported to be rye whiskey but was more likely raw alcohol and "tincture of kerosene." Tattered pictures of half-clad women were pinned to the walls. On chilly evenings, the wood stoves glowed red hot, inviting patrons in to warm themselves and play poker, faro, or roulette. Many of the tables were rigged, according to Bill Haskell. "The dealer generally knew what to do when it was necessary to make a certain card win. He who sat down to a promiscuous poker table was either reckless or ignorant . . . The professional gamblers reaped the harvest, and the tenderfeet and the hardworking miners paid the fiddlers." Since saloon-keepers did not have to pay for liquor licenses, their costs were low and their profits sky high.

Bill was no gambler: he had worked too hard on his claim to throw away his earnings. But he loved the spectacle—the backslapping fellowship, warm air thick with blue smoke, long-haired waiters bustling about balancing trays of shot glasses, champagne that cost thirty dollars a pint and tasted like sugared fizz, and the swagger of a man like Swiftwater Bill Gates, who didn't think twice about losing nearly $8,000 of gold nuggets in a single evening. Bill Haskell once saw a fellow known as Shorty try to slip out of a saloon leaving debts unpaid. Shorty "edged toward the door and was about to push it open when the bartender called to him: 'Say, Shorty, haven't you forgot something?'" Bill recounted in his memoirs, still relishing the excitement. There was a sudden flash of flame, a ringing report in that low-ceiled, smoke-darkened room, and as the door swung closed, "it stopped half way and a draught of icy air came in . . . [It] was obstructed by the body of a dying man . . . 'Shorty' was buried the next day." Within weeks, the Mounties had declared that it was an offense to carry firearms into Dawson's drinking establishments. But they couldn't stop the fistfights sparked by claim disputes, drunken insults, or accusations of cheating.

When Bill Haskell tired of watching miners blow their fortunes, he would wander along Front Street and into one of the dance halls. The first dance hall opened when a piano arrived on a steamer that had chugged upriver from Circle City. This hall was a ramshackle, cavernous structure with log walls and a canvas roof, and it soon faced competition from rival establishments. By mid-May, the clamor of construction and howling dogs had been joined by other sounds—the squeaking of a violin, the jingling of the piano, and the harsh voice of the prompter— "balance all," "ladies change," "swing yer pards." The dance halls opened around seven in the evening and, as Bill observed, by midnight would be "crowded with gallant beaux, the most of them having spiked-bottom shoes, broad-brimmed hats, costumed in the regulation mining suits, and with cigars between their teeth . . . They sit around the hall on the benches, smoking and talking and immensely enjoying the relaxation from the hard monotony of the mines." Through the blue haze, a couple of musicians would be visible, fiddling away or banging the keys for dear life, while the dance hall girls were spun around the floor by partners who paid them a dollar a dance. The girls kept half plus any tips: the rest went to the dance hall owner. Every time the door swung open, passersby heard polkas like "The Ashland" or waltzes like "The

Blue Danube." Girls might make as much as $100 a night on the dance floor, but the dawn would find them, according to Bill, "a tired and disheveled lot."

For men, Dawson was a town without boundaries. But it was also steeped in Victorian prudery, and although women constituted a tiny minority (about 200 among the 2,000 residents in June 1987), they found themselves slotted into a rigid hierarchy. Bill Haskell could tell at a glance which ones were respectable and which were "loose." The most respectable women were the wives of prospectors, and he always greeted them politely—unless they were the Tlingit or Tagish wives of old-timers who had been in the North for years, in which case he ignored them. One rung down the ladder were the "artistes" who sang music hall favorites on the stages rigged up at the back of the saloons: Bill tipped his hat to them but was not above tossing a cheeky remark in their direction. Further down the ladder were the girls who made their living twirling around the wooden floors of dance halls with lonely miners. The women that Bill did not mention in his memoir were those on the lowest rungs of the hierarchy: the prostitutes. But on Front Street, he couldn't miss them, in their thick woolen skirts (worn short enough to get them thrown into jail in Chicago), bloomers, and broken boots. Like the men, these women smelled pungent: nobody in Dawson's early days washed more than once every two weeks, or bathed more than twice a year. Their lips were as chapped and their skin as rough as the miners', and most matched the men drink for drink, for the same reason—to anesthetize themselves against cold winds and broken dreams. As an old dog driver recalled years later, "The girls looked beautiful enough to men who had been isolated in this wild environment for months or years, but I guess they would have been pretty terrible compared with any ordinary woman back home." Once the Yukon was open in 1897, they were joined by women from Seattle, San Francisco, and other West Coast cities, whose clothes were cleaner but whose avarice was sharper. In these early days of Dawson, Inspector Constantine and his red-coated Mounties were too busy trying

Prostitutes plied their trade openly in Dawson, and looked after each other in the rough-and-tumble town.

to control cardsharps and violent criminals to worry about prostitutes roaming the streets looking for business.

Bill may have ignored the hookers, but he was friendly enough with the dance hall girls, whom he described as "young and pretty." After all, he was a young man who had just spent a bleak, lonely winter on the creeks with a grumpy partner. He yearned for a girl, and a glimpse of a satin slipper or a silk petticoat was intoxicating to him. But there were so many men and so few girls—with nine men to every woman—that he quickly found himself elbowed off the dance floor. Toward morning, fights often erupted in a dance hall, but as far as Bill was concerned, it was most likely the result of a squabble between two men "to win the hand of some woman for the succeeding dance." A romantic at heart, Bill simply didn't want to believe tales of drunks getting rolled by dance hall girls, and "respectable" women who offered laundry or meal services earning money on the side with sexual favors.

If Bill Haskell turned a blind eye to the seedier side of Dawson, it was because he had a naive view of Dawson as "less vicious and more orderly" than mining camps elsewhere. He clung to his belief that the ordeals of the Chilkoot Pass and northern prospecting kept out desperadoes. The men, he insisted, were "sober and provident" because of "the awful hardships one endures to get rich up there, the dangers that must be braved, and the privations suffered in getting to the new gold fields." He was even more impressed by the wives who made it over the mountains because they showed none of the physical and emotional fragility glorified by the Victorian model of femininity. Women like Ethel Berry, wife of Klondike King Clarence Berry, or Catherine Spencer, whose husband ran a saloon, were good humored, tough, and strong. To a Vermont farm boy, this was "a revelation, almost a mystery." Bill watched these women hitch up their petticoats, discard their corsets, and enjoy themselves, and gradually realized that the North offered all women, not just "loose" ones, "a freedom which is in a way exhilarating." He even shed some of his own chauvinism as he explained how such a woman "has thrown off the fetters which civilized society imposes, and while retaining her womanliness becomes something more than a mere woman . . . She steps out of her dress into trousers in a region where nobody cares."

While Bill slowly adjusted his views of what constituted "proper" behavior for women, the women themselves threw aside conventional expectations. In the macho world of mining camps, the rigors of pregnancy, childbirth, childrearing, or violence pulled them together, whether they were wives, dance hall girls, or prostitutes. Everyone knew and liked Esther Duffie, for instance, a motherly, good-humored woman in her forties who had already spent a couple of years in the North and who had survived on her wits. She had a share of a claim on one of Eldorado Creek's tributaries, but she was also not above turning a trick when necessary, to keep the wolf from the door. "One of the best old hearts God ever put on the face of the earth!" one friend commented. "She was friendly with all the women. They were all her pals."

Bill Haskell's chivalry and wide-eyed enthusiasms made him a favorite of women who had wintered with their husbands on the creeks, or who had established themselves as bakers, dressmakers, and cooks in town. They mothered him, baking an extra batch of bread for him when he made a trip into town from Bonanza. Their attentions reinforced his loneliness and made him ache for decent female company. "A good woman is at a high premium," he reflected. "So long as mines are rich, and millionaires are turned out every season, women who have the courage to brave such hardships as a journey to Alaska entails, and are not too particular about the culture of the eligible men, may marry a fortune." But Bill's cautious nature and $25,000 purse weren't enough to attract the handful of women he tried to court. "The fact is," he regretfully wrote, "that most good women are particular about the men they marry."

On trips to Dawson City, Bill would often stroll down to the wharf to watch the jerry-built boats steering toward the riverbank and their unshaven and half-starved passengers jumping ashore. He thought about the sort of girl he wished he had on his arm—not the whiskey-voiced, tough-skinned type he met in Dawson but the kind he had known back home, with soft skin and coy smiles. But he was back on his claim by June 15, when, as the midnight sun was setting, a short, stocky woman stepped onto the riverbank. This was Belinda Mulrooney, who knew all about throwing off the fetters society imposed. She had come to the Klondike to get rich, and she wasn't going to let anybody get in her way. She shook out her skirts, cast a measured glance at the raucous mining camp, then turned and tossed her last quarter into the river's surging current.

CHAPTER 7
Belinda Mulrooney Stakes Her Claim, June 1897

TWENTY-FIVE-YEAR-OLD Belinda Mulrooney must have wondered what she had come to as she gazed around her. She had been in some pretty dismal camps during her ten-week journey, and could tolerate any degree of discomfort. But as she crawled on hands and knees over the mountain pass or huddled in the bow of a boat, hiding from the Yukon's stinging spray, she had been buoyed by the hope that her destination—the famed Dawson City—would be a *little* more settled than this muddy hodgepodge of flapping canvas and ramshackle lean-tos. "After looking around," she would recall, "I saw there was nothing in Dawson I could buy for a quarter. So I threw my last coin into the Yukon and said, 'We'll start clean.'"

Belinda's gesture caught the attention of the usual crowd that hung around the wharves. They stared at this arresting figure in her calf-length serge skirt, leather boots, and long-sleeved man's shirt. Under a jaunty fedora, her thick brown hair was tied back in a knot, and her square face bore a tight-lipped expression of belligerence. From her self-assured gestures and the deference with which her fellow passengers treated her, onlookers could tell that this was no hooker or dance hall girl. Her voice was deep and gruff, which made her seem even less feminine, although she had a delightful chuckle when chatting with friends. But she didn't have a husband, father, or brother in tow to guarantee her respectability. What was she doing here?

Irish-born Belinda had come to the Klondike, like everybody else she could see, to make her fortune. The gesture of tossing away her last quarter was theatrical and, at the same time, duplicitous. She may have pitched her last remaining piece of legal tender into the river, but she was quite right—coins were not the currency of Dawson. In her baggage were goods that would be much more useful as she took the first steps toward building a commercial empire in this remote northern community that ran on gold dust. First, however, she had to find somewhere to live. The men with whom she had been traveling were eager to get to the creeks, so she asked them if they would sell her the boat they'd been traveling in. What for? asked one of the men. And how would she pay them?

"You wait awhile, and I'll pay you later," Belinda countered. "You have to see the mines and the country. I'll store your provisions if you will give me your help for three days." Then she explained that she needed their skills to take the vessel apart and build a frame out of the lumber. "We used the old tarpaulin from my tent as a roof," she recalled in later years. "There was no floor. There I kept the goods I'd brought in to sell and their outfits." It was a deal that suited everybody. The men tramped off to stake their claims (cheechakos like them were now working their way up a new set of creeks, named Last Chance, Dominion, and Gold Bottom) secure in the knowledge that their goods were safe. Belinda had shelter and breathing space to find her bearings in Dawson City.

Belinda recalled her Yukon experiences in an unpublished memoir she dictated when she was in her late fifties. She minimized the hardships of the Klondike, exaggerated her own successes, and skated over some of the less savory details of her adventures. Her voice comes through loud and clear—blunt, humorous, ruthless, with no trace of sickly-sweet Victorian femininity. Nevertheless, she understood the importance of appearances. That gesture of bravado with her last quarter (which she recalled for several newspaper reporters in later life) set the tone for her Dawson career.

*Belinda Mulrooney rarely dressed in frills and
lace, but she knew their market value.*

Belinda's assessment of the town where she planned to do business was quite different from Bill Haskell's. Each time Bill trudged down from the creeks, he was thrilled to see how Dawson prospered. A new bar, restaurant, or saloon opened every few days. Maybe they were all barnlike buildings with dirt floors and little natural light, but for Bill, they offered some welcome company. In Belinda's eyes, Dawson City's commercial potential was seriously underexploited. She wandered around that first day, avoiding the mud holes, dog excrement, and tobacco wrappings, and noticing the scarcity of stores and animals other than dogs. The waterfront was a tight maze of weather-beaten canvas tents, with hundreds of small boats tied to the shore and banging against each other. Idle men were everywhere—some staring curiously at her, others slumped on the boats, snoring loudly and oblivious to their surroundings. She gave a cursory nod to the gawkers and a curt brush-off to anybody who wanted to talk. She noticed that the shabby shelters advertising themselves as "restaurants," with three or four tables, all offered the same badly cooked fare. The cabins where people lived were no better than hovels. There were few women around, and they were clad in garments hardly fit for a tramp. Belinda had little interest in the drinking and gaming establishments because they were men's business. But everything else interested her. Despite her relative youth, Belinda was already a seasoned businesswoman who knew that there were unmet needs in a place like Dawson.

Belinda Mulrooney's own story was that of a female Horatio Alger. Born in Ireland in 1872, she had spent her early years in a threadbare County Sligo village, cared for by an extended family of grandparents and uncles. Her own parents had emigrated to the United States to escape poverty soon after her birth. She was thirteen before she laid eyes on them again. Meanwhile, she did her share of chores on the small family farm, milking cows, collecting eggs, slaughtering chickens for the dinner table, collecting wood for the stove. Her uncles taught her never to expect any favors and, as she put it, "to know that a woman around men who couldn't do her share was a nuisance and was left behind." Belinda grew up fearless and determined to lead.

On the other side of the Atlantic, Belinda's father, John Mulrooney, was working in the Archbald coal mines near Scranton, Pennsylvania, and he and his wife, Maria, had two more children. They needed a nursemaid, so they sent for Belinda. Their eldest child did not want to leave the green hills of rural Ireland. But her account of her transatlantic voyage is vintage Belinda, all about her appetite for drama. "I loved the sea . . . I loved the wind blowing and the spray . . . A flying fish came up once and knocked me silly. There was something in my blood, something [about] the storm [that] appealed to me."

After that adventure, her new home, in the Lackawanna River's steep, dark valley that stank of anthracite, was a hideous disappointment: "The dirtiest hole in the world . . . I didn't like . . . my family or the dirt and coal dust." She was expected to take responsibility for the housework and look after the younger children, including two more sisters who arrived soon after she joined the household. At school, the other children laughed at the chunky little girl's thick brogue until she was so "boiling mad" that she rammed her fist into a schoolmate's face. "I had only one set idea from the first, to find enough money to get out of there." She realized that her parents had only sent for her to exploit her, and she vowed she would never allow anyone else to take advantage of her.

The combination of natural aggression and a drive to escape made Belinda a terrier. In her oral memoir, she bragged about the way, as a youngster, she had faced fears and smashed taboos as she scraped together a Running Away fund. When the Archbald miners' kids went berry picking for eight cents a quart, she would venture alone into areas infested with rattlesnakes because the best berries were there. If she met a rattler, she killed it. "The rest were afraid of the snake district, so I got two pails to their one." She also persuaded the owner of a coal wagon to try her as a driver for his mule team, although girls were specifically forbidden by law to do such jobs. With her deep voice and the tell-tale long hair stuffed inside a cap, she passed easily for a boy and proved so adept that the coal man employed her on the sly. She hid her earnings in a coffee can buried in the backyard. "I knew the family wouldn't stand for it."

After four years of scrimping, fighting, and brooding, Belinda bolted. She persuaded her mother to send her to Philadelphia to visit an aunt, and as soon as she got there she looked around to see how she could earn her livelihood. Soon she was living in the well-to-do neighborhood of Chestnut Hill, working as a nursemaid in the household of a prosperous industrialist called George King Cummings. She also found a mentor in the person of George's wife, Belle Brown Cummings, mother of her young charge, Jack. Mrs. Cummings admired the verve and ambition of this cheerful, energetic young Irish girl. She taught her how to use a bank, encouraged her to read any book in the extensive Cummings library, and discussed her future with her. "It was the happiest life," Belinda would recall. But it came to a sad and premature end when the economic depression caused George Cummings's business to fail.

Aged twenty, Belinda decided she would be her own boss. The fact that she was uneducated and penniless did not dampen her ambitions. She traveled to Chicago, where she built and ran a restaurant conveniently close to the gates of the spectacular Columbian Exposition held there in 1893. By the time the fair closed and she sold the business, she had accumulated $8,000. Many of the entrepreneurs she had met in Chicago were moving west because the California Midwinter International Exposition was going to be held in San Francisco the following year. Belinda went with them, and built a restaurant and rooming house. But this time she was felled by bad luck: her buildings burned down and she lost all her money.

This must have been a dreadful blow to a young woman with no home or family. But according to her own account, Belinda barely paused for breath. Her successes so far had given her confidence in her ability to survive on her own wits rather than to rely on a man—a confidence that few young women in her period had the chance to develop. In fact, Belinda seems to have convinced herself that she could manage better on her own than most men her age could. She looked around to see where a competent young woman might be employed, and decided to get involved in the shipping business. She planted herself in the office of the San Francisco port steward and told him, "I want to work on one of the ships. I want to work on one going to Alaska." She had seen a poster for Alaska on the dock, and "it seemed far away and new to me." Eventually she wangled a job as stewardess on the *City of Topeka*, which sailed up the North Pacific coast to supply the little towns and villages perched along southeast Alaska's rugged coast.

"There's nothing like being a stewardess to develop your wits when you're just a bit too independent for the job," she later remarked. "I remember an old Englishman who expected me to black his boots. I told him I wouldn't, and I told him if he put 'em outside his door again I'd be thinkin' he was wantin' ice-water and turn a pitcherful into 'em." When she wasn't putting passengers in their place, she was developing a side business as a purchasing agent for Alaska residents. They would give her orders for goods from Seattle, and she would bring them north on her next trip. A particular dry goods store in Seattle "used to look forward to the docking of the *City of Topeka* . . . They allowed me a good stiff commission, but I would not let them charge the Alaskans more than Seattle prices." She quickly learned that despite the harsh climate and rough living conditions, women in the North, both native and non-native, yearned for a few luxuries in their lives—pretty blouses, soft nightgowns. There were also rumors that Belinda peddled whiskey as well as dry goods even though alcohol was illegal in Alaska.

By now, Belinda Mulrooney had learned a great deal. In the Cummings household, she had seen how rich folk lived and how the business world worked. From her Chicago and San Francisco ventures, she had learned how to grasp commercial opportunities, how to read a balance sheet, how to assert her authority over male employees. Most important, she had developed a sixth sense for underlying shifts in the American economy. She could see that America was still in the grip of the grinding depression that had bankrupted George Cummings's factories and sent Bill Haskell north. But she had also felt, particularly at the Columbian Exposition, a renewed entrepreneurial energy. Twenty-two million Americans had been drawn to Chicago to see an incredible phenomenon that would revolutionize modern life: electricity. Belinda had marveled at the exposition's spectacular displays based on this newly harnessed power source: illuminated fountains, an elevated railway, a Ferris wheel with 1,340 colored lights, General Electric's seventy-foot Tower of Light, a movable sidewalk, speedboats, ovens, and vacuum cleaners. It was impossible to ignore the optimistic buzz in the air. Electricity was going to kickstart the next wave of innovations and a new boom in the economy.

At the same time, Belinda had grasped that some investments were riskier than others. Businesses could go bankrupt; buildings could burn down. But one investment seemed rock solid: gold. When the economy took a downturn, gold took an upturn. Gold was always worth having—if you could find it. One of the attractions of the Alaska run was that she was soon hearing rumors of gold strikes. Her curiosity about the vast land beyond Alaska's coastal mountains grew: "I wanted to see what was over those hills." She had already decided to jump ship when, in late 1896, she heard about a fabulous gold strike on a tributary of the Yukon River called the Klondike River. By April 1897, she was climbing the Chilkoot Trail.

A tailor in Seattle had provided her with practical clothes of her own design: "I ditched corsets . . . I had three suits—one of corduroy, one of tweeds, and one of navy serge." Her kit included dried fruit, canned butter, cornmeal, coffee, flour and bacon, and a fox-fur sleeping bag lined with eider quilts. There were also several long and mysterious tin cylinders, the contents of which she refused to divulge. Belinda's physical stamina was tested by the long, grueling journey over the St. Elias Mountains, which she made twenty-three times before she had hauled all her possessions over the Chilkoot Pass. On the final, vertical climb, she just gritted her teeth and focused on each step. But her entrepreneurial instincts never flagged. "Such a small percentage [of those who started] made the Summit . . . They'd make one trip to the top and knew they'd have to relay to get sufficient food for one year. Before they'd make the round trip they'd give up and say, 'Impossible.' I bought their outfits."

Few crossed the Chilkoot Pass alone: the party that Belinda joined included about eighteen people. Once they were en route to Bennett Lake, where they would build boats for the river journey, Belinda made herself useful to the party. She hated cooking, having seen too many women stuck in that dead-end job, but she realized that she was more useful as cook than boat builder so she became camp cook without complaint. She was first up in the morning, lighting a fire, cooking the dogs' breakfast of dried fish and cornmeal, then preparing flapjacks and bacon for the men. She and two men were assigned to get fresh food. "The men were always hunting moose and never found any. There was an abundance of fresh fish." Belinda was adept at chopping a hole in the ice, dropping in a line, and pulling up enough to feed everybody. Then she would fry the fish in bacon fat on the stove and serve it with ladlefuls of beans.

The men learned to respect this forceful, no-nonsense character who snapped their heads off if they cheeked her. "I never got friendly," Belinda recalled. "I held to myself, was nice to anyone with knowledge." Yet she lavished on animals a tenderness she rarely showed humans. She had picked up six dogs from miners who had turned back, "and trained them with little pockets for freight hanging down on each side of them. Poor things! They'd slip and their feet would get full of ice packs. They'd be miserable and cry like children. The sharp ice would cut into the tender part of the foot. I'd take it out and had the Indians make them little shoes out of hide. We'd lace them on. I'd do all I could to protect them, but all I could possibly do was to render bacon and pour grease in the cracks. The salt would smart and the dogs would cry. They'd be ready to bite, snap at me, and then lick my hand [to show] they didn't blame me."

Belinda was captivated by the endless daylight and the sublime scenery of the North. She saw "lots of tragedy" in Miles Canyon and White Horse Rapids, but shattered boats and dead stampeders just increased her determination to beat the odds. The woman who was brisk and short tempered with her fellow travelers revealed a dreamy, romantic streak when she contemplated nature. "The beauty . . . You can't possibly overdo it. It seems to me that every day and every night is different. You just feast on it. You become quite religious, seem to get inspiration.

Or it might be the electricity of the air. You are filled with it, ready to go . . . You couldn't keep your eyes off the heavens." After three weeks on the water, Belinda's party caught sight of the Moosehide Slide around midnight on June 15. A couple of hours later, the tents and saloons of Dawson City swung into view. Belinda listened to the din of dance hall music, took one look at the miners surging through the saloons' swing doors, and decided to build her cabin two blocks south of the busiest part of Front Street: "I wanted to be where I could be by myself." And then she flung her last quarter into the water.

Several people watched this defiant gesture and were intrigued. One of them was Esther Duffie, the motherly woman who had spent years in the North and scraped a living from a handful of menial jobs, shares in various claims, and occasionally selling sex. Esther could see that the new arrival, who was half her age, was probably a kindred spirit—a woman who was nobody's helpmate or victim. She was also curious to see what was in those mysterious long tin cans Belinda had brought with her.

The following day, after Belinda had made herself comfortable in the newly built cabin and strolled around the shabby mining camp, she was ready to set up business. By now, she had introduced herself to Esther (she didn't have much choice, since Esther had plopped herself down on a stump and followed Belinda's every move with curiosity), plus two other women who had strolled past. Like Esther, these two sisters— Catherine, who was married to Harry Spencer, co-owner of the Pioneer saloon, and Lizzie, wife of tinsmith Julius Geise—were longing to know what was in the cylindrical cans.

"I opened one to let them look," Belinda always enjoyed recalling. A long roll of soft, silken fabric fell out, then unfurled like a butterfly. The three women stared at a pile of flimsy dresses, petticoats, nightgowns, and underwear—the kind of luxury goods Belinda had been peddling in Alaska when she was working on the *City of Topeka*. Esther, Catherine, and Lizzie fondled the gorgeous fabrics, rubbing them against their faces. Belinda was delighted. "Girls," she said to them, "I'm going to start a store, and you folks will have to help me. You know the people here and the gold dust. I don't understand gold dust or the right prices to charge. It's all new to me." The women couldn't wait. Esther disappeared and returned with the kind of scales that sat on the bar of every saloon, so Belinda appointed her cashier and head saleswoman. In no time at all, Esther was standing behind a little board counter, yelling, "Next? Who wants a beautiful night dress?" to the women in the rapidly growing crowd in front of Belinda's cabin. Esther refused to open the next tin until she had sold everything that was already unpacked, which added to the sense of anticipation.

Belinda chuckled as she watched Esther. "A lot of things the women bought they didn't know how to wear, but they had been so long separated from luxuries, they just wanted to possess them, to feel 'em," Belinda recalled in her oral memoir. "They didn't care what they paid, either. I just looked on and let Esther run the business." Many of the miners had Tutchone or Tlinglit wives who were just as interested as the non-native women in the delicate garments, and their husbands were soon separated from their money. "I can see those old-timers now," Belinda remembered, "standing around, be-whiskered and dirty, protesting, 'What's that good for?' as Esther would hold up a silk something . . . The squaws would just eat the things up. I remember one old duffer grunting when his squaw came back for more. It was a night gown this time. 'That'll be a fine outfit when the mosquitoes get after you' . . . Things vanished as fast as Esther showed them."

Commerce in camisoles boomed. Belinda could see that Esther was a hard worker and a smart woman, and knew everybody in town. She learned a lot from the dexterity with which Esther traded in gold dust. "She had her little scales, and I don't think she ever changed the weights. After she poured the dust on the empty [pan], she'd pour my share through a funnel into a big sack. How she soaked them, those old-timers!" Belinda calculated that her new friend had netted her a profit of 600 percent on the sale of her goods. But the men's derisive familiarity with Esther, and the implication that she was "easy," bugged Belinda. She could see why the men behaved like that: "When she was drunk, she was a holy terror." Belinda learned to close her eyes when Esther went on a spree. Their friendship also persuaded her to insist that men call her "Miss Mulrooney." Nobody was going to take advantage of her.

Belinda also used these first couple of weeks to explore other chances to make money. She noticed that most of the men, though rich in nuggets, were hungry for a meal that offered a little more taste and variety than the three Bs. So she converted her cabin into a restaurant. (She had already paid off her traveling companions for the boat from which she had constructed her shack.) She hung a canvas curtain toward the back to conceal her own sleeping quarters. Since she disliked cooking herself, she commissioned Julius Geise to make a good stove and hired Lizzie Geise as the cook. The restaurant was open round the clock. Meals cost a flat two dollars, and patrons ate whatever was cooking that day. Belinda solved the problem of inadequate supplies by purchasing in bulk from any supply boat that arrived, and by buying the outfits of any newcomers who pulled up their boats on the bank near the cabin. "I'd see the men come in and tell them if they'd turn over their food and outfit to us, they'd get credit in cooked food in the restaurant. Or they could sell for cash. They were glad to give up their stuff because they hated individual cooking—all that chopping bacon with an ax and the waste, the packing and repacking of supplies."

Soon business was so brisk that Belinda had to hire another girl—Sadie O'Hara, a well-brought-up Canadian youngster with an infectious laugh. "The men used to come in just to see her, as she was handsome, and to hear her laugh." But Belinda stayed firm behind her boundaries: she never palled around with the clientele, and if anybody asked her where she was from she would reply, "It's a long story. I'm awfully busy. Wait until winter and I'll tell you." She dressed in a severe navy shirt and long black skirt, and Lizzie nicknamed her "schoolteacher" because she was so aloof. When one diner complained that she was overcharging, she took him by the collar and threw him toward the door so hard that the whole building shook. Her blood boiling, she yelled at him, "You'll say we are crooks and dishonest?" The poor man stuttered that it was just a joke, but Belinda would not be mollified and told him he had better get out and stay out. Only when Lizzie Geise took the victim's side, and her brother-in-law, Harry McPhee, announced that the victim would now buy a drink for everybody in town, did Belinda calm down. But she never let the man back in her restaurant. Nobody could nurse a grudge like Belinda.

With Esther, Lizzie, and Sadie running the restaurant, Belinda turned her attention to her next venture. By late June, Dawsonites knew there were plenty more gold diggers en route, and Belinda could see that there was nowhere for them to stay. Moreover, many of the men out on the creeks intended to spend some of the winter in Dawson, and they would need somewhere to live. So Belinda Mulrooney turned herself into a property developer. She bought several building lots, organized a team of men to cut lumber for her, and hired a carpenter and two other men to begin construction. The first cabin sold so fast for $500 that she doubled the price for her next sale. Soon Mulrooney cabins were selling for over $4,000 because they had amenities that no others offered. "We'd clean tarpaulins from the packs by tying them to a rope and letting them stay in the Yukon River current," Belinda recalled. "Then we'd take them out, stretch them and dry them. Canvas was useful stuff for lining cabins and making partitions." Belinda had a small army working for her: besides construction workers, it included a young woman to make curtains, two men to make furniture out of barrels and birch poles, and a salesman to drum up business. She was good at details, like hooks to hang clothes on and a little cache for food. "The thing that pleased them most," she would chortle, "was a doghouse . . . We also gave a lot of service. After he bought a cabin, a miner . . . would find the

Belinda, second from left, in carriage, quickly emerged as a sharp-elbowed entrepreneur who held the reins of several enterprises.

first night he was in possession water in the barrel and a meal prepared. We'd send a cook up from the restaurant and give him moose steak."

Belinda Mulrooney had her finger on the pulse of Dawson's development. Raised a Catholic, she had little time for religion. (Later in life, she would tell Catholics she was a Presbyterian, and Presbyterians she was a Catholic.) But she had paid her respects to Father Judge because she admired what he was doing for the sick. She got to know Inspector Constantine. She also secured strategic introductions to Dawson's wealthiest citizens because they were obvious marks for her enterprises. Her most successful catch was Swiftwater Bill Gates, the flamboyant character whose gambling habits had already caught Bill Haskell's attention.

Gates was one of the good old boys who had been in the North before the Klondike strike, having spent the previous spring as a dishwasher in Circle City. His nickname derived not from a heroic passage through the swift waters of the White Horse Rapids but from being too scared to stay on his boat: he had stumbled round the foaming torrent with the women in his party. By mid-1897, however, he had a one-seventh share of a rich claim on Eldorado Creek, was flush with dust, and was a well-known gambler. "When he broke loose," Bill Haskell recalled, "the dust was sure to fly." One night Bill followed him into a saloon, where Gates sat down at the faro table and dropped $7,500 in gold nuggets in just one hour. Bill loved Gates's insouciant reaction to this reverse. Gates stood up, stretched lazily, then announced, "Things don't seem to be coming my way tonight. Let the house have a drink at my expense." Along with the rest of the saloon's customers, Bill Haskell dashed to the bar. "That round cost Bill [Gates] one hundred and twelve dollars." But Swiftwater Bill didn't blink. He lit a dollar-and-a-half cigar and strolled out into the evening light.

When news of Gates's style reached Belinda's ears, she got to work. She had an elderly German man who had been a scenery painter in his past life working for her; she told him to follow Swiftwater Bill around, and sketch him and his dog team. Then she hung a canvas bearing Gates's likeness on the wall of her newest cabin. ("But we had the canvas only tacked on, so we could turn it around if he didn't buy.") This cabin also had linen on the bed, chairs with padded hide seats and backs, and a pail of clean water with a dipper in it. Knowing Swiftwater Bill's interest in dance hall girls, she added a final touch that would appeal to the girls themselves—bedroom curtains made out of silk nightdresses. When Bill Gates returned from his claim and was shown the cabin, he protested that he could have built it for himself in four days. Why would he pay $6,500 for it? But Belinda was a brilliant saleswoman, and Swiftwater Bill bit. The following week, he announced that he wouldn't sell it even if he was offered $10,000.

By the time she had been in Dawson City a couple of months, Belinda Mulrooney had three thriving businesses: a store, a restaurant, and a property development company. She operated on instinct: "The miners never knew how little I knew and I never got close enough for them to find out." But she faced competition: other entrepreneurs in Dawson were eager to mine the miners. The Alaska Commercial Company already had several warehouses near the waterfront, plus a sawmill on the north bank of the Klondike to provide lumber for its store and warehouses. The North American Transportation and Trading Company was establishing and stocking a rival empire. Between them, the two companies imported and sold a wide range of merchandise, and as there was still no bank in Dawson, they often gave miners extended credit.

The summer days were long and warm, and most of the stampeders arriving in Dawson spent only a few days in the town before setting off for the creeks. In her restaurant, Belinda had picked up valuable tips about which new creeks were being staked and which old claims were changing hands. She decided it was time to explore opportunities on the creeks herself.

The latest batch of prospectors had discovered gold where veterans had sworn none could exist—on hills above Bonanza Creek that were now named Gold Hill, Cheechako Hill, and French Hill. These "bench claims" tapped into stream beds that had dried up millions of years earlier, and had proved unexpectedly rich. Ancient waterways that showed up as streaks of white gravel had flowed through these hillsides, depositing nuggets and dust in sandbars on the slopes. In midsummer, Belinda took Esther with her on the trail to Bonanza to explore the hills. But once the two women had hiked the sixteen miles to The Forks, where Eldorado Creek flowed into Bonanza, it wasn't the muddle of sluice boxes, tailing piles, diggings, flumes, and shabby cabins that caught Belinda's eye. She was fascinated by the volume of traffic. The junction of the two creeks was the perfect spot for a roadhouse.

The Grand Forks Hotel was Belinda's own personal gold mine, as miners gossiped about prospects in the bar.

The sight of two women pacing out the bare wedge of land between the two creeks aroused plenty of interest among observers. Most scoffed at the short woman in a long skirt, who announced in a broad Irish brogue that she was going to build a hotel bigger than any Dawson establishment. When Dawson saloonkeepers heard the news, they said she might as well start building at the North Pole. But in no time at all, Belinda was dragging lumber up to The Forks behind an old mule called Gerry, and her Dawson builders were constructing a two-story log roadhouse, with capacious kennels behind it, to which Belinda gave the pretentious name, "The Grand Forks Hotel." According to Frederick Palmer, who was working a claim on Eldorado at the time, a miner walked over from a nearby claim to tell Belinda that she should stick to Dawson.

"Now, that's kind of you," Belinda replied, "and may I ask if you would like something to drink?" The miner was surprised at what he took as an offer, and said he would. Belinda told him sharply that it wasn't an offer. "If you or any of the other boys were hungry or thirsty, you'd . . . walk sixteen miles to Dawson and back for it, wouldn't you? And the boys going over the divide to Dominion or Sulphur, when they break the journey at The Forks would hang up in a tree over night before they'd sleep in a hotel, wouldn't they now?"

The miner stared at this forceful little figure for a few minutes, then grinned. "You'll pass, Miss Mulrooney, you'll pass," he replied. "You kin take care o' yourself all right. With that head of yours, you'll own the Klondike by the time you've been in the country as long as I have." It was a prescient remark.

The Grand Forks Hotel was finished by mid-August. Its bar was immediately thronged with thirsty men in checked shirts and heavy boots. The ground floor of the roadhouse was divided into a bar and a dining room: there were no gaming tables. Upstairs, in one long room, two tiers of wide bunks, each with a blanket and curtain but no sheets, could accommodate any number of exhausted men. One visitor recalled how each lower bunk was wide enough for two: an occupant "might be awakened at any hour by a nudge, and 'Pardner, sorry to trouble you, but I guess you'll have to move over a bit to make room for me.'"

Belinda poured the drinks, served the bacon and eggs (outrageously priced at a dollar for each egg), and listened to the miners' talk. Soon she had to bring Sadie O'Hara up from Dawson to help her. To escape the roadhouse bustle, Belinda had a private cabin built for Sadie, herself, and her closest companion of these years—a huge, good-natured St. Bernard mix called Nero, with a white nose and legs and silky brown ears and head. The dog had been left with her by a destitute miner from England, who had lost his outfit on the way downriver and had no way of feeding the ravenous, lanky puppy he had brought with him. Together, Belinda and Nero became one of the best-known partnerships along the Klondike. She harnessed Nero to a sled for the journeys between Dawson and Grand Forks. All the love and warmth that

Belinda withheld from any man who came too close was lavished on her faithful dog.

The hotel's iron safe filled up with nuggets, and its proprietor heard about gold strikes and grubstaked prospectors before the news had even reached the big trading companies in Dawson City. Soon she was working on her next scheme.

The same week that Belinda Mulrooney had arrived in town, about eighty mud-encrusted Klondike millionaires had left Dawson City for Seattle and points south. Each carried between $5,000 and $500,000 of gold. Clarence Berry was one of them, along with his wife, Ethel, who wore a nugget necklace. Joe Ladue, who had not left the North for thirteen years, was en route to Plattsburgh, New York, to propose to the sweetheart he had left behind. "Professor" Tom Lippy, who had been a YMCA instructor before heading north and acquiring Claim No. 16 on Eldorado, was leaving with a suitcase full of gold that weighed 200 pounds. On the day that the Klondike Kings sailed out of Dawson on the first steamer of the season, the receipts in one saloon amounted to $6,500.

They and their fellow millionaires began the long voyage down the Yukon River on the *Portus B. Weare,* which belonged to the North American Transportation and Trading Company, and the Alaska Commercial Company's *Alice.* The nuggets and dust, packed in jam jars, tobacco cans, leather sacks, caribou-hide pokes, trunks, belts, and bottles, weighed close to three tons, and the steamers' decks had to be shored up with extra wooden props. The little Yukon paddle-wheelers were so heavily loaded that they almost ran aground several times before they reached St. Michael. There, the treasure and its owners were transferred to two ocean-going steamers: the *Excelsior* and the *Portland,* both bound for the U.S. Pacific Coast.

Belinda knew that once the Klondike Kings disembarked, the Yukon Gold Rush would begin in earnest. Dawson City had seen nothing yet—but when the stampede hit, she would be ready.

CHAPTER 8
Jack London Catches Klondicitis,
July–October 1897

"GOLD! GOLD! GOLD! Sixty-Eight Rich Men on the Steamer *Portland*. Stacks of Yellow Metal! Some have $5,000, Many Have More, and a Few Bring Out $100,000 Each . . . The Steamer Carries $700,000."

In Seattle, an enterprising reporter named Beriah Brown had decided to go for broke. When news of the *Portland*'s imminent arrival reached him on July 16, 1897, he was determined that his paper, the *Seattle Post-Intelligencer,* would be first with the story. The steamer was still at sea, so he chartered a tug to intercept the boat as it entered Puget Sound, shinnied up a ladder to the deck, and interviewed as many passengers as he could before the vessel docked. As the *Portland*'s mooring ropes were thrown over the capstans on Seattle's wharf, Brown was already filing his story. Readers learned that some of the passengers were carrying nuggets the size of guinea fowl eggs, and most of the big strikes were "made by tenderfeet." By the time the *Portland*'s gangplank was in place, 5,000 people were standing on the waterfront. The crowd surged closer to see the Klondike Kings, and when the first miner lifted a fat leather satchel to his shoulder and stepped onto the gangplank, a cheer went up: "Hurray for the Klondike!"

In single file, the miners staggered off the *Portland*—unshaven, lean, and ragged. Their faces were lined and they squinted into the crowd. They were weighed down with moosehide sacks and sailcloth bundles:

only a few carried the usual travelers' luggage because most had no personal belongings. Just gold.

In a subsequent edition, the *Post-Intelligencer* printed a quarter-page map of the Yukon valley with the caption "The Land of Gold," and speculation that before the end of the year, $10 million of gold (approaching half a billion dollars' worth in today's values) would be taken out of the gold fields. In the next few weeks, the two Seattle newspapers, the *Seattle Post-Intelligencer* and the *Seattle Times,* did everything they could to promote gold fever. The Klondike never left their front pages. At the end of July, the *Post-Intelligencer* published a "Special Clondyke Edition." (Spelling of the Klondike varied wildly for the next several months.) The *Seattle Times* described the Klondike as a wonderland of "fabled riches." Seattle exploded with excitement. Within days of the *Portland's* arrival, the city's streetcar operators had walked off the job so they could head north, and twelve members of the local police force had resigned for the same reason. Soon, both papers were carrying advertisements for Seattle companies offering complete outfits for anybody who was hurrying north. The Cooper and Levy Company's half-page ad read, "Klondyke! Don't get excited and rush away half prepared. You are going to a country where grub is more valuable than gold and frequently can't be bought for any price. We can fit you out better and quicker than any firm in town. We have had lots of experience, know how to pack and what to furnish."

The Klondike Kings and their treasure ship made great headlines. Privately, most of the reporters recognized that news of the *Portland's* arrival was not really a scoop. Gold from the Yukon basin had been shipped south since 1895, when Bill Haskell had first heard of Alaska gold. Belinda Mulrooney had caught wind of the Klondike strike in the fall of 1896, when she was on the Seattle–Alaska steamers. The first Klondike nuggets, and estimates of the river's wealth, had arrived in Seattle five months earlier and been noted by the local press. What made the *Portland's* arrival in July different was not the amount of gold it was carrying but the collective decision by local newspapermen to spin the news for their own purposes. They wanted to sell this story to the big eastern newspapers and pump up Seattle's economy, which had been in the dumps for too long. Up to now, they had been infuriated at the way their stories—*any* stories—won them little attention beyond the Pacific Coast. Beriah Brown himself had discovered "the insurmountable difficulty which existed in inducing any Eastern newspaper man to take any interest himself, or to believe that the readers of his newspaper would take any interest, in gold discoveries made in such an isolated region as Alaska." But the *Portland*'s arrival was their big chance, and they worked hard to find a hook to snag the attention of New York editors.

The hook turned out to be a simple headline over one of Brown's articles: "A Ton of Solid Gold." By 1897, the depression across the United States had intensified as gold supplies contracted, people began to hoard what they had, and pools of capital available for new businesses shrank still further. In the summer of 1896, when Bill Haskell scaled the Chilkoot Pass, the populist politician William Jennings Bryan had campaigned for the American presidency under the slogan "You shall not crucify mankind upon a cross of gold." He had failed in both his bid for the presidency and his campaign to liberate the value of the dollar from its rigid link to the government's supplies of gold. Instead, the demand had intensified for new sources of precious metals to finance renewed economic growth. Everybody was mad for gold.

This was what Brown and his newspaper colleagues capitalized on. One of them noticed that a New York journal had galvanized Wall Street early in the summer of 1897 with a story about a shipment of "ten tons of silver" bound for France. A buzz of excitement, and speculation about what the French government was going to *do* with all that silver, ran through New York's banking world—until someone calculated that the shipment was worth only $120,000. The Seattle reporters got the message: talk in weight, not dollars. They sent off stories on spec to eastern editors mentioning the weight of the *Portland*'s cargo, rather than its value of about $700,000. The replies were better than they had hoped. Almost immediately there was a demand for the very stories that had been rejected all winter.

The phrase "a ton of gold" appeared in headlines across America and Canada, and Seattle stringers gleefully supplied thousands of words about the new eldorado. News dispatches were followed by a barrage of special articles, telegrams, features, and supplements describing the Klondike's incredible potential and Seattle's advantages as the place to buy an outfit and a ticket. "Klondicitis" swept the continent. By late July 1897, 1,500 people had already embarked at Seattle for the voyage north and nine more ships in the harbor were crowded with "Klondikers" and ready to weigh anchor. Seattle, according to the *New York Herald*, had "gone stark, staring mad on gold," but the city had secured its status as the premier departure point for the Yukon. Four days after the *Portland* had docked, a triumphant *Post-Intelligencer* declared, "Prosperity is here. So far as Seattle is concerned the depression is at an end."

The *Portland*'s sister ship, the *Excelsior,* had landed at San Francisco two days before the *Portland* tied up in Seattle, but it had caused less of a stir. The San Francisco *Examiner,* owned by William Randolph Hearst, gave more attention to another newly docked vessel, the *Annie Maud,* which had arrived from Calcutta carrying several people suffering from bubonic plague. Then the *Excelsior*'s big spenders got to work in the city. One grizzled veteran ordered nine freshly poached eggs and tipped the waitress with a nugget. A group of the new arrivals commandeered a four-horse truck to take their loot to a local smelter. When they tipped out the contents of their sacks, jelly jars, and tobacco tins, the gold lay on the counter, according to one observer, "like a pile of yellowed shell corn." At the same time, the wave of Seattle hysteria rippled down the coast and excitement exploded.

Carefully crafted reports of the *Portland*'s and *Excelsior*'s cargoes triggered an insatiable hunger for information about the town the Klondike Kings had come from—this magical metropolis where the

Tappan Adney, correspondent for Harper's *magazine,*
purchased his snowshoes and Métis sash in Winnipeg.

streets were apparently paved with gold. Correspondents were immediately sent north. Hearst was furious that his San Francisco paper had
missed the biggest story in a year of lackluster news, and now ordered
all-out coverage in all his papers. He chose Joaquin Miller, a flamboyant, black-cloaked character known as the "poet of the Sierra" who was
a veteran of earlier Rocky Mountain stampedes, to represent his chain.
In New York City, *Harper's* magazine commissioned Tappan Adney to
supply both news and photographs of Dawson City and the Klondike
creeks. Since it would take weeks for these men to reach the Yukon valley, some editors resorted to outright fabrication to maintain circulation and reader interest. A special Klondike supplement to Hearst's

New York Journal included the startling information that "there abound reminiscences of the slaughter of innumerable bands of early colonists and explorers. Near by are the ruins of what was once the largest post of the Hudson's Bay Company west of the Rocky Mountains."

Within weeks, printing houses across the United States, Britain, and Canada were pumping out Klondike guidebooks. The Liberal government in Ottawa, warned earlier in the year by Ogilvie of the oncoming stampede, had already rushed into print a set of mining regulations and dispatched north additional officials and Mounties to reinforce Canadian authority in the new gold field. Now the hastily written guidebooks combined copies of the Canadian regulations with plagiarized newspaper features, lists copied from advertisements of items required for an "Alaska Outfit," and dubious maps. In Chicago, E. O. Crewe published *Gold Fields of the Yukon and How to Get There.* In Philadelphia, L. A. Coolidge produced *Klondike and the Yukon Country,* in which one of the miners who had arrived on the *Excelsior* claimed that Dawson had a population of 3,500 and "all the ambitious scope of a bonanza town." The well-known naturalist Ernest Ingersoll, who had never strayed much beyond the forty-ninth parallel, wrote *Gold Fields of the Klondike and the Wonders of Alaska,* in which he described Dawson as "the metropolis of the Klondike country and if not the largest city in the world, it now takes first rank among the liveliest and most thriving."

As gold fever mounted, thousands of desperate people jammed the streets and docks of Pacific ports. Horses, oxen, dogs, mules, and goats set up a cacophony of neighing, barking, and bleating as they were herded onto overcrowded steamers. Many of the horses, according to Tappan Adney, were nothing more than "ambulating bone-yards . . . afflicted with spavin and spring-hat, and many with ribs like the sides of a whiskey-cask and hips to hang hats on." Outfitters and shipping lines watched business soar, as customers snapped up anything—soup, glasses, boots, medicine chests—that was labeled "Klondike." The standard Klondike uniform consisted of wide-brimmed hat, high-top boots, heavy wool socks, thick long underwear, a buckskin shirt, and a suit of coat, overshirt, and trousers made of "mackinaw," a heavy plaid woolen fabric. Then there were all the supplies required to feed, clothe, and house each man for a year, in a region and climate where it was usually impossible to obtain supplies. Yet many travelers, noted Adney, filled their packs with bizarre items. "One man has taken . . . one case of thirty-two pairs of moccasins, one case of pipes, one case of shoes, two Irish setters, a bull pup, and a lawn tennis set." Adney asked the fellow whether he was going to sell the stuff, only to receive the reply that the owner was going "just for a jolly good time, you know."

The stampede was immediate, intense—and suddenly, a source of concern. In Ottawa, Canadian authorities realized that the Yukon summer was already so advanced that most of the stampeders would not reach Dawson before freeze-up. It published a warning that anybody leaving now risked starvation and should wait until spring. On July 28, the Colonial Office in London issued a bulletin advising Englishmen to wait until the following spring before setting out for the eldorado. But the tide was too great to turn: a collective madness had taken hold. Before Tappan Adney had even reached the Pacific coast from New York, he had stopped at the Hudson's Bay Company's store in Winnipeg for an outfit and discovered it was cleaned out of fur coats and hats. He had to make do with a Hudson's Bay blanket coat and a Métis sash, but in the photo he supplied to his employer for his first dispatch he did look incredibly dashing dressed up as a voyageur.

In San Francisco, a restless twenty-one-year-old was gripped by the frenzy. The Klondike Gold Rush was made to order for Jack London, a sturdy young man bursting with muscle and guts. On the wharves of Oakland, across the bay from San Francisco, Jack was already a well-known figure, with his rolling sailor gait and two front teeth missing from a brawl. One contemporary recalled that, with his brilliant blue eyes and open-necked shirt, he looked like a "strange combination of

a Scandinavian sailor and Greek god." Jack was hell-bent on making
his mark on the world, but he hadn't yet settled on what kind of mark
he would make. Insecurity and unrealized ambitions gnawed away at
him. The Gold Rush would change all that. Within a few short years,
Jack London would establish an international reputation as a writer—a
reputation that would long outlast him.

So far, nothing had really worked out for Jack. His frustration and
insecurity sprang from a deeply unsettled childhood, during which his
mother, Flora Wellman, and stepfather, John London, lurched from one
financial crisis to the next and moved house constantly. Flora was a
selfish little woman enthralled by spiritualism; John was a soft-spoken
failed storekeeper. Jack's real father was William Chaney, a blustery con
man who had abandoned Flora when she was pregnant and denied
Jack's paternity when the latter confronted him. The son was permanently scarred by the father's rejection.

Always a keen reader, Jack had been forced to leave school at fourteen
to help support the family. He spent the next seven years holding odd
jobs and rebelling against routine. A nineteenth-century cross between
Jack Kerouac and Ernest Hemingway, Jack London had been a salmon
fisherman, a roustabout on the wharves, a longshoreman, a cannery
worker, a binge drinker. Seeking adventures both inside and outside the
law, he became an expert sailor and used a little skiff to loot the commercial oyster beds in San Francisco Bay. At seventeen, he sailed as far
as Siberia and Japan with the sealing fleet. His raw, animal physicality
and mop of golden curls made him dangerously attractive to women.

When he was only nineteen, he had joined an army of unemployed
men who were marching on Washington (and traveling there by riding the rails of the Southern Pacific Railroad). "I went on 'The Road'
because I couldn't keep away from it," he later told a friend, "because
of the life that was in me, of the wanderlust in my blood that wouldn't
let me rest . . . because I was so made that I couldn't work all my life on
'one same shift.'" His traveling adventures were brutally interrupted in

Tousle-haired and muscular, Jack London was desperate to escape a cramped household and menial jobs.

Buffalo, where he spent one month in jail for vagrancy. Jail was an education for Jack. First, it had the impact that today's promoters of boot camps for delinquent youth like to promote: it scared him straight. But the trip east also exposed this impressionable young man to the appalling poverty and social conditions that existed alongside American affluence. "I had been born in the working class," he wrote later, in his essay "What Life Means to Me," "and I was now . . . beneath the point at which I had started. I was down in the cellar of society, down in the subterranean depths of misery about which it is neither nice nor proper to speak. I was in the pit, the abyss, the human cesspool, the shambles and the charnel house of our civilization." For the rest of his life, however much wealth he accumulated, Jack London vehemently argued against capitalism and in favor of socialist solutions to social problems.

Returning to San Francisco, Jack London decided to return to school and complete his education so that he could make a career as a writer. He wanted to escape from the laboring class, but he also wanted to publicize its plight. Soon he had discovered Karl Marx, and joined the Henry Clay debating society, an Oakland group steeped in Fabian socialism. He poured his personal insecurities into political analysis, running as a Socialist-Labor candidate for the Oakland Board of Education (and polling a respectable, but hopeless, 552 votes). Nothing could shut him up. He made headlines when he was taken to court for challenging a city ordinance prohibiting soapbox oratory, and was then acquitted after an impassioned speech of self-defense.

In the summer of 1897, Jack London had knuckled down to the challenge of writing his way out of poverty. It was a bold ambition for a young man with no money, little learning, and no contacts in the publishing world. But he was obsessed. He holed up in his mother's Oakland home, toiling for up to fifteen hours a day at his self-imposed task. Fiction, poetry, essays, humorous verse—he hit the keys so hard on an old Blickensderfer typewriter, which wrote entirely in capitals, that his fingertips blistered. It did not go well. His creative efforts were overwritten and unconvincing. Rejection slips piled up as fast as debts. He had pawned every single one of his possessions—his books, his clothes, his future—and he felt trapped. Then, at exactly the moment when he was desperate to escape, the *Excelsior* docked in San Francisco. Joining the stampede north was an insane gamble, but the opportunity was irresistible. He told a friend that he wanted to "let career go hang, and [take] the adventure-path again in quest of fortune." In the words of novelist E. L. Doctorow, Jack "leapt on the history of his times like a man to the back of a horse."

Jack left only a few random pieces of personal, unpublished writing about his Klondike adventures—a couple of letters, a journal about his homeward voyage. He makes mention of his year in the North in the two versions of his autobiography he published: *John Barleycorn* and *Martin Eden*. One photograph of him during his ascent of the Chilkoot Pass has surfaced. It shows a slender, short youth with a diffident expression, almost hidden in a party of men who look older, bigger, and more hardened. But several of the people who knew him in the North never forgot him and were happy to reminisce about him in later years, when that slender youth had turned into a world-famous writer. Best of all, Jack himself used and reused his Klondike experiences in the short stories and novels (particularly his masterpieces *The Call of the Wild*, published in 1903, and *White Fang*, published in 1906) with which he made his reputation.

Like Bill Haskell, Jack was not simply running away when he embarked on a ship that took him up the coast. Raised on the myth of the frontier, the Gold Rush spoke to a deeper need in him, which he caught in the work that gave its title to his second book of short stories, *The God of His Fathers*: "True, the new territory was mostly barren; but its several hundred thousand square miles of frigidity at least gave breathing space to those who else would have suffocated at home." Jack wanted to feel like a man, not a cog in a machine. The frontier was where a rebellious young man sick of his own and his nation's prospects could commit himself to unvarnished authenticity and emotional truth. This would be his quest.

Yet how could Jack afford to get there? He had nothing more than the clothes on his back. Within hours of the *Excelsior*'s arrival, he was begging the local newspapers to send him as a reporter. Dozens of other writer wannabes had had the same idea, and celebrity columnists were already en route. Jack's friend the poet Joaquin Miller had boarded ship, as he liked to boast, "with forty pounds on his back and his face to the stars."

Luckily for Jack, his brother-in-law had also been caught up in the collective madness. It is hard to imagine a less suitable stampeder than

Captain James Shepard, an elderly Civil War veteran with a bad heart who had married Jack's stepsister, Eliza. But Shepard was gung ho to go, and offered to grubstake Jack if he would take him along as a partner. The scheme involved Jack carrying all the bags and Eliza Shepard mortgaging their home. But why not? One man's eagerness reinforced the other's: it was Klondike or bust. Charmian London, Jack's second wife and author of *The Book of Jack London,* described the next stage: "Such a buying jamboree Jack had never enjoyed. Eliza's hundreds flowed like water: fur-lined coats, fur caps, heavy high boots, thick mittens; and red-flannel shirts and underdrawers of the warmest quality . . . The average outfit of the Klondike also must include a year's supply of grub, mining implements, tents, blankets, Klondike stoves, everything requisite to maintain life, build boats and cabins. Jack's dunnage alone weighed nearly 2000 pounds."

Jack spent a feverish forty-eight hours assembling the outfit. His mother was appalled by his "awful news." In a letter, she begged him to "give up the idea for we feel certain that you are going to meet your death and we shall never see you again." Her pleas were ignored. On Sunday, July 25, only eleven days after the *Excelsior's* arrival, the Pacific Steamship Company's *Umatilla* left San Francisco with Jack London and James Shepard aboard. In Jack's pocket was a handbook to the North that was already out of date: Miner Bruce's *Alaska.* The steamship, licensed to carry 290 passengers, had 471 on board as it steamed north to Juneau. Over 1,000 people, cheering lustily, waved it on its way.

During the eight-day trip up the coast, on the Alaska panhandle, Jack and Shepard teamed up with three other men for the long trek ahead. Two of these men boasted invaluable manual skills. Merritt Sloper was a cheerful, slightly built forty-year-old who had recently returned from South America and who knew how to build and sail boats. Jim Goodman was a hefty fellow, keen on hunting and mining. The third man, Fred Thompson, had no experience in roughing it, but while he traveled he kept a diary. Fred's diary gives the factual background to several

At both Skagway (above) and Dyea, shallow water and the absence of docks meant that stampeders had to haul their goods up the muddy beach.

of the short stories that Jack would compose, months or years after they had both left the Klondike.

Fred's diary is a laconically written document: most days he simply jotted down the party's progress up the coast to Juneau, from Juneau north into the Lynn Canal to the wretched little harbor of Dyea, and from there toward the dread Chilkoot Pass. "Aug. 2. Arrived at Juneau . . . Aug. 6. Still on our way to Dyea. . . . Aug. 8. Laid in camp all day and purchased boat for 10.00 to carry our supplies to head of Navigation 6 miles up from Dyea . . . Aug. 12. Began to pack our goods on our backs up the trail making our cash [cache] 1 mile further up the river." As the small party pushed north, Fred rarely allowed himself to admit how grueling the journey was. But sometimes he couldn't help himself: "Aug. 19. It is raining now but we still have to keep on the move . . . Aug. 23. Rain and oh the mud . . . trail very bad and are getting up pretty close to snow, it is quite cold tonight."

The Chilkoot Trail swarmed with stampeders this summer, most of whom were city dwellers in no condition for such an adventure. The various stopping points along its seventeen-mile length had become as well known as the Stations of the Cross. In any season it was a brutal hike, but Jack's party undertook it at the most difficult time of year. Bill Haskell and Belinda Mulrooney had traveled in spring, so they could use sleds over the snow and ice for most of the trail as they laboriously hauled their outfits forward in several loads. Jack and his partners faced mud, landslides, endless rain, treacherous fords, flimsy log bridges— and crowds of fellow stampeders jostling on the narrow path. Hundreds of Indian packers were milling around Dyea: men, women, and children from the local Chilkat, Tlingit, Stick, and Tagish peoples. But packers' rates for portaging stampeders' packs over the pass had jumped from less than ten cents a pound to over thirty cents. That worked out to $600 a ton—an impossible price for Jack's party. If they were going to make it, they would have to do as Bill Haskell and Belinda Mulrooney had done: break up their outfits into smaller loads, then pack them over the pass in relays. For every mile a complete outfit was advanced up the trail, a stampeder had to travel thirty-nine miles—twenty of them carrying the pack uphill. Hundreds of stampeders took one look at the prospect before them and abandoned the venture. Captain Shepard couldn't face it. A couple of days into the trek, he simply turned round and headed home, "having got rumatism very bad," in Fred's words. It was a relief for Jack.

From Dyea, Jack and his partners were able to drag or pole their possessions in a boat for five miles, along the Taiya River to Finnegan's Point. The next twelve-mile section of the trail took the heavily laden stampeders across rubble-covered flats, up a dark canyon lined with spruce trees to Sheep Camp, and past overhanging glaciers to the way

In this photograph taken at Sheep Camp on the Chilkoot Trail, Jack London is the youth standing in front of the group in the center, with Jim Goodman on the left and Fred Thompson half-sitting on the right.

station called The Scales. Stampeders were now only a mile from the summit, but as Bill Haskell had discovered, that mile was up steeply pitched, ice-scoured rock where packers climbed with hands and feet. And when Jack climbed, he was in that dark line of stampeders captured in Eric Hegg's photos—a line nobody dared step out of because you would never be able to elbow your way back in.

According to Jack himself in the autobiographical *John Barleycorn,* he thrived. The journey up the Chilkoot Pass and then on to Lake Lindeman, seven miles beyond the summit, was a chance to test his muscles and manhood in a way for which there was less and less opportunity in turn-of-the-century America. "I was twenty-one years old, and in splendid physical condition," he would write. By the time he reached Lake Lindeman, he claimed, "I was . . . outpacking many an

Indian." Consumed by the discipline and willpower required to keep going, stripped to his red underwear, he strode along the trail, heavy backpacks attached by both shoulder and head straps. "The last pack into Lindeman was three miles. I back-tripped it four times a day, and on each forward trip carried one hundred and fifty pounds. This means that over the worst trails I daily travelled twenty-four miles, twelve of which were under a burden of one hundred and fifty pounds." His triumph at the end of the trail made up for the painful tightness of his muscles, the searing ache in his lungs, the sting of sweat in his eyes.

The Chilkoot Trail was more than a physical challenge for Jack London. As adrenaline raced through his body, his eyes were taking in the sheer human drama surrounding him. Gold was what drove him forward, but his literary ambitions still simmered and here was the best raw material that a writer could ever ask for. *This* was what had been lacking when he blistered his fingertips on the old Blickensderfer: unique experiences he could polish into tales of adventure that would appeal to American readers. He stored every vivid detail in his imagination, so that what he wrote in later years might exaggerate the tensions and the tragedies yet remain true to the facts. In *A Daughter of the Snows,* the novel he would publish five years later, he described that awful slog over the mountains: "Time had rolled back, and locomotion and transportation were once again in the most primitive stages. Men who had never carried more than parcels in all their lives had now become bearers of burdens. They no longer walked upright under the sun, but stooped the body forward and bowed the head to the earth. Every back had become a pack-saddle, and the strap-galls were beginning to form. They staggered beneath the unwonted effort, and legs became drunken with weariness."

Just below the summit, while Jack's party was in camp, an early snow squall blew up. The extreme conditions cried out for descriptive hyperbole: "A snort of the gale dealt the tent a broad-handed slap as it hurtled past, and the sleet rat-tat-tatted with snappy spite against the thin canvas . . . A few water-soaked tents formed the miserable foreground, from which the streaming ground sloped to a foaming gorge. Down this ramped a mountain torrent. Here and there, dwarf spruce, rooting and groveling in the shallow alluvium, marked the proximity of the timber line. Beyond, on the opposing slope, the vague outlines of a glacier loomed dead-white through the driving rain. Even as they looked, its massive front crumbled into the valley, on the breast of some subterranean vomit, and it lifted its hoarse thunder above the screeching voice of the storm."

Only two weeks after Jack and his friends passed through this area, a landslide roared down the mountain and wiped out a section of the trail. At least one man was killed and several others were injured, while dozens of tents and outfits were buried under tons of rock and mud.

Jack was particularly affected by the gruesome fate of most horses shipped north by the stampeders. In the summer of 1897, many of the parties headed toward the Klondike had chosen an alternative route over the St. Elias Mountains, across the White Pass. The newly opened White Trail began in Skagway, just down the coast from Dyea, and was longer, but the White Pass, at 2,900 feet above sea level, was lower than the Chilkoot Pass. In theory, travelers could pack their outfits over it on the backs of horses or mules. In practice, almost every single animal died in the struggle. Most of them (as Tappan Adney had noted on the Seattle wharves) had been unfit in the first place, their owners had no idea how to care for them, and there was absolutely no forage on the route. On the northern side of the passes, where the Chilkoot Trail met the White Trail, Jack London and his partners heard how, in the words of Fred Thompson's diary, "there are enough dead horses and mules along the trail to lay them side by side for the entire length so one can walk on horse flesh the entire length of 50 miles." The Mounties would estimate later that 3,000 horses had been killed by abuse, starvation, and overwork on this trail.

In his short story "Which Make Men Remember," published in 1901 in the collection *The God of His Fathers,* Jack London drew on the tales he had heard about the horrors of the White Trail: "The horses died like mosquitoes in the first frost, and . . . rotted in heaps. They died at the Rocks, they were poisoned at the Summit, and they starved at the Lakes; they fell off the trail, what there was of it, or they went through it; in the river they drowned under their loads, or were smashed to pieces against the boulders; they snapped their legs in the crevices and broke their backs falling backward with their packs; in the sloughs they sank from sight or smothered in the slime, and they were disemboweled in the bogs where the corduroy logs turned up in the mud; men shot them, worked them to death, and when they were gone, went back to the beach and bought more. Some did not bother to shoot them, stripping the saddles off and the shoes and leaving them where they fell. Their hearts turned to stone—those which did not break—and they became beasts, the men on Dead Horse Trail."

The London party reached Lake Lindeman on September 8, six weeks after Jack had left San Francisco. Along the way, he and his three partners had joined up with another group of men; together, they started building two boats, the *Yukon Belle* and the *Belle of the Yukon*, which they would sail, paddle, or drag through 600 miles of lakes and rivers to Dawson City.

The days were shortening: the wind had shifted to the north; there was frost or snow on the ground every morning now when the men crawled out of their tents. The fear shared by the men was caught in Jack's story "The One Thousand Dozen" (published in his 1904 volume, *The Faith of Men*): "A great anxiety brooded over the camp where the boats were built. Men worked frantically, early and late, at the height of their endurance, calking, nailing, and pitching in a frenzy of haste for which adequate explanation was not far to seek. Each day the snow-line crept farther down the bleak, rock-shouldered peaks, and gale followed gale, with sleet and slush and snow . . . Toil-stiffened men turned wan faces across the lake to see if the freeze-up had come. For the freeze-up heralded the death of their hope—the hope that they would be floating down the swift river ere navigation closed on the chain of lakes."

By late September, Jack had organized sails and booms for the boats, and the vessels had crossed Lake Lindeman and Bennett Lake. "Weather very cold," noted Fred. All the talk at the campsites was of food shortages in Dawson City as winter approached. Plenty of stampeders had decided the journey was madness, and had turned tail. But Jack and his companions had no intention of retreating. At Tagish Lake, they saw a tattered British flag: this was the newly established Canadian Customs House. Customs officers, supported by a detachment of Mounties, stopped all boats to ensure they had enough provisions and to levy duties on items not purchased within Canadian territory. Jack and his partners somehow charmed their way through. "By scheming," Thompson gleefully recorded, "got off by only paying $21.50 on our outfit—others that were not onto their job had to pay very much more and parties that did not have the money their goods were confiscated by the officers."

The men hurried on as the weather worsened. "Snowing, Blowing and Cold all day, could not stir out," recorded Fred Thompson on October 1. Time was running out. The hundreds of stampeders waiting to cross Marsh Lake all knew that the icy wind presaged freeze-up: they *had* to get across the lake. If they didn't, they would be stuck in the makeshift camp all winter, hoping their rations would last. It took six days for Jack's group in the *Yukon Belle* to get across, but they finally made it and rowed into the upper Yukon River. Now they faced the most feared section of the water journey, Miles Canyon and White Horse Rapids, where Bill Haskell and Joe Meeker had almost lost their lives fifteen months earlier and had watched as most of their outfit was swept away. Since then, Belinda Mulrooney had made it safely through the miles of white water, whirlpools, rock reefs, and sandbars, but at least nineteen large boats had capsized in White Horse Rapids, and no fewer than 200 eager gold seekers had drowned. Graves marked by crooked crosses lined the riverbank.

Jack prepared to steer his heavily laden vessel through the turbulent waters of Miles Canyon, while over a thousand spectators fringed the brink of the cliffs that towered above him. Seconds later, all he could see were "rock walls dashing by like twin lightning express trains." Three miles farther on, but only two minutes later, the menacing white waters of the White Horse Rapids beckoned. Thanks to Jack's nautical skills, the *Yukon Belle* survived the dangers.

Now they could cross Lake Laberge, then float along in the river's swift current, alert for sandbars and ready for the Five Finger Rapids and Rink Rapids. Each day, more slush ice swirled into the Yukon from its tributaries, and the ledges of ice protruding from the bank crept outward.

At three o'clock on Saturday, October 8, Jack London, Fred Thompson, Merritt Sloper, and Jim Goodman arrived at a flat, sandy island in the mouth of the Stewart River, about eighty miles south of Dawson City. There were several old but habitable log cabins here, the remnants of a trading post. Thompson noted in his diary, "This is a good place and we think shall make it our headquarters." They had heard that food, cabins, and fuel were all in short supply in Dawson City, and they realized that once the Yukon was frozen they could reach Dawson more easily over the ice. What's more, the Stewart River itself was reckoned by several old-timers to be a good bet: gold had already been located on a couple of creeks, and there were plenty more to explore. The men unloaded their boat, unpacked their goods, and studied the information about the Stewart in Jack's handbook.

Three days later, Jack London set off with four companions to explore Henderson Creek, a stream that flowed into the Yukon a couple of miles downriver. This was Jack's first experience of panning, but he would quickly master both the techniques and the words with which to describe the thrill: "Earth and gravel seemed to fill the pan. As he imparted to it a circular movement, the lighter, coarser particles washed out over the edge ... The contents of the pan diminished. As it drew near to the bottom ... he gave the pan a sudden sloshing movement, emptying it of water. And the whole bottom showed as if covered with butter. Thus the yellow gold flashed up as the muddy water was flirted away. It was gold-dust, coarse gold, nuggets, large nuggets. He was all alone. He set the pan down for a moment and thought long thoughts . . . It was beyond anything that even he had dreamed" (*Burning Daylight*, published in 1910).

In October 1897, neither Jack nor his companions were sure whether the glittering gravel at the bottom of their pans was the real stuff. But it was good enough, and Jack's head was full of dreams of what lay waiting for him—gold, gold, gold. He was convinced his claim would make him rich. The next step was to register his Henderson Creek claim with the Canadian mining recorder, and that meant several days' journey to the place he hungered to see: Dawson City.

CHAPTER 9
Starvation Rations, October–December 1897

BILL HASKELL HAD KNOWN for weeks that the township was unprepared for winter. He had nothing but contempt for cheechakos who had "made no preparation": in his opinion, most of them "would have difficulty in taking care of themselves anywhere." In Dawson City during the long summer days of the building boom, jobs had been plentiful "so everything looked rosy to many who were so constituted." Newly arrived carpenters relished earning twenty dollars a day when the average wage in American cities was two dollars. Laborers who had scrambled for employment in the flagging economies back home picked up twelve dollars a day, usually in the form of three-quarters of an ounce of gold dust.

It was easy for beginners to assume that survival through the winter would be simple with wages so high. They reveled in Dawson's frontier lifestyle: girls in the dance halls, fish in the river, raconteurs in the bars, game in the hills. Could life get any better? The newcomers had no idea that within a few weeks it would hurt to fill their lungs, and gold would be useless because there would be nothing to buy. But old-timers like Bill thought back to the previous February and shivered as they recalled the sound of wind snarling down the creeks and the bite of bitter cold when they ventured out.

As early as mid-August, Bill started buying provisions for his and Joe's second winter on the claim. He had heard rumors that the two trading companies had got together to work out what Dawson would need to survive the winter. There were about 5,000 people in the town, hundreds more on the creeks, and most had no provisions. In addition, about twenty eager gold diggers arrived each day through September, and still more were heading north across the St. Elias Mountains, or traveling upriver from St. Michael. There wasn't enough food in Dawson's warehouses to feed them all through the months ahead. But the managers didn't increase their food orders to match the expected demand. They certainly didn't reduce their liquor orders to make space for solid provisions, because they made twice as much money on liquor as on flour and beans. In the last few days of the shipping season, 3,000 gallons of rye whiskey were brought in, and the saloons did not run dry all winter. Instead, the merchants raised prices for bacon, beans, flour, and other staples, and tried an informal rationing system. "When the last two steamers arrived from St. Michael, bringing about a thousand tons of provisions," recalled Bill in his memoirs, "the rush to get them resembled the opening of a box-office sale for some great theatrical attraction." Hundreds stood in line for hours around the commercial companies' warehouses, begging for a chance to buy *anything*. One man told Bill that he had waited for three hours before he was able to get his order in, but even after he had handed over his money he did not receive his goods. He was simply told that another steamer would be arriving shortly, and then his order would definitely be filled.

Summer drew to a close, and the birches and aspens on the steep bank behind Dawson turned brilliant yellow. Each morning, fallen leaves were crisp with frost. As the sun lost its warmth, anxious men pulled their shabby coats around them and huddled on the waterfront. "The toot of a steamboat whistle would have brought the whole population to the river bank, eager to welcome the arrival of much-needed supplies," recalled Bill. Yet after the middle of September, the trees were bare and there were few whistles. Plenty of heavily loaded vessels had left St. Michael at the mouth of the Yukon, but the river was unusually low and they were all stuck on the sandbars below Fort Yukon, in American territory. In the Pioneer saloon, Bill watched prospectors quell their fears at the bar. "Men who had been exulting in their success, and were counting upon return-ing [from the creeks] in the spring with sacks of gold, suddenly realized that to remain till then they must run the risk of starvation." Bill and his partner Joe began to discuss their own winter plans. Could they really face another winter digging on the claim? Did they have enough food? Or should they sell their claim and supplies for a tidy profit and walk south once the river was frozen?

Sixteen miles outside town at Grand Forks, Belinda Mulrooney also knew what lay ahead. Like Bill, she had been quietly stockpiling what she might need. Most of her neighbors lacked the means and the fore-sight to stock up, and were likely to crowd into her roadhouse when the going got tough. She and Sadie, accompanied by the faithful Nero, walked down to Dawson City in late summer to see what was going on. Only a thin trickle of water ran through Bonanza Creek, and when Nero startled a ptarmigan in the undergrowth, the women noticed that white plumage was already replacing its brown feathers. Once in town, Belinda strolled down to the riverbank to watch men catching grayling and saw two men poling a small boat against the current. She hailed them to ask what was up. They were exhausted and frustrated, she learned: the steamboat owned by one of the men had given them noth-ing but trouble on the journey upriver, and now it had broken down just beyond the Moosehide Slide. The crew was refusing to refloat it unless the owner paid their wages. But he had no money.

Belinda smelled business. The steamer carried close to $50,000 worth of supplies, and she told the owner that she would buy the lot. She needed a few hours, though: "I can't handle it myself, but I can get people to go in it with me." Then she considered which Klondike King would be a trustworthy partner. Immediately, Alex McDonald came to mind, "Big Honest Alex—so deeply saturated in religion," as Belinda put it, "that everyone looked forward to doing what he did, he was held so high as an example." Big Alex now owned interests in twenty-eight claims (making him, according to Bill Haskell, "rich beyond the dreams of avarice") and had a large workforce that he had to feed through the winter. She sent Sadie off to find the Nova Scotian, and within the hour two figures could be seen locked in negotiation—Alex, the soft-voiced giant, speaking to short, peppery Belinda. "I'll take a third," Belinda told her new partner. "I can't handle all of it, so we'll divide it. You stay right here and I'll go up and get the currency for the owner." Soon she had raised the cash and drafted a crude contract. She had a side deal with the captain that he would give her all the mattresses off the steamer. In return, she would find him enough passengers for the outward journey, "and they'll have their own bedding."

It looked like such a sweet deal. While the steamer's cargo was unloaded into a warehouse, Belinda hurried back up Bonanza Creek to Grand Forks to get more bunks built for the mattresses. On her return to Dawson, she passed several packers loaded with bags of flour and other provisions, heading for Big Alex's claims. But it wasn't until she returned to the warehouse that she realized what her partner had done. Alex had taken all the food staples—the provisions she wanted for her hotel's customers throughout the next six or eight months. All that was left for her were rubber boots, tobacco, underwear, socks, dried onions, a couple of sacks of river-soaked beans, dozens of candles, and fifty barrels of liquor.

Belinda strode up to Big Alex. "Where's my part of the provisions?" she demanded. The miner flinched at her tone. "You have one outfit allowed, and Sadie has one outfit, and there are a couple of sacks of flour," he told her in his quiet Cape Breton lilt, as he rubbed his bristly chin. "Of course, if you run short I'll provide for you, but I have so many men to feed." Outraged, Belinda explained she needed the supplies for her hotel: you couldn't cook rubber boots. But Big Alex was a teetotaler and hadn't been anywhere near her hotel. He probably assumed Belinda wanted goods for her trading post and would be just as happy with boots and long johns as beans. Anyway, he was far too old-fashioned to imagine, let alone approve of, a woman in the roadhouse business. "Hotel?" he said, surprised. "You couldn't run a hotel." Then he stooped, looked into her face, put a meaty hand on her shoulder, and whispered innocently, "You're not mad at me?"

Belinda Mulrooney stared at him coldly. She was absolutely not going to give him the benefit of the doubt. He had cheated her. "No," she snapped, "only you better not let me meet you anywhere after dark." She was as angry with herself as with Alex. She prided herself on being a good judge of character, too smart to let anybody take advantage of her. Convinced that the "big stiff of a Nova Scotian cod fish [had] put something over" on her, she stalked back into the empty warehouse and had a full-voltage temper tantrum. Sadie stared in dismay at the sight of her employer beating her fists against the wall so hard that she knocked a plank askew. When Belinda finally calmed down, she remarked ruefully, "I guess my guardian angel let go of my hand for five minutes . . . I feel as if I had been caught swimming without my clothes on." She started to plan her revenge. But first, like everybody else, she had to get through the winter.

Famine looked inevitable. Fear brought the worst out in everybody. Destitute men started raiding private food caches and the companies' stores. Inspector Constantine decided that the Canadian government must assert some authority—which meant, in practice, he had to act. He had already informed Ottawa on August 11 that "the outlook for grub is not assuring [given] the number of people here," especially because Dawson's population consisted, in his estimate, of about "four thousand crazy or lazy men, chiefly American miners and toughs from the coast towns." In late September he had put the Mounties on half rations; now he swore in special constables to stand guard over the company stores. Superintendent Sam Steele, in charge of the North-West Mounted Police posts at the head of the Chilkoot and White Passes, had already decreed that any stampeder admitted into Canadian territory had to carry a full year's supply of solid food. On September 30, Constantine and Thomas Fawcett, the Canadian government's gold commissioner, posted a notice on Front Street outlining the ghastly truth: "For those who have not laid in a winter's supply to remain here longer is to court death from starvation, or at least a certainty of sickness from scurvy and other troubles. Starvation now stares every one in the face." At the same time, an Alaska Commercial Company official raced through town, telling any men he found loitering on street corners or clumped in bars, "Go! Go! Flee for your lives!"

The warnings had some effect. In the few days before the Yukon River froze solid, a couple of hundred men left town for camps downriver in the same homemade boats and scows they had arrived in. Constantine also managed to evict from Dawson 160 members of what he described as "the unprovided and bum class"—the same slackers for whom Bill Haskell had such contempt. The captain of the steamer *Bella*, the Alaska Commercial Company's paddle-wheeler, agreed to take them downriver on condition the government would pay for any ice damage to his vessel, and the passengers would cut the wood required to keep the *Bella*'s boiler fed and paddles churning. On October 1, under a leaden winter sky, a stubble-chinned army of vacant-eyed, hungry men straggled up the gangplank. Chunks of ice, swept along in the Yukon current, grazed the *Bella*'s hull as the boat cast off and headed north toward Circle City and Fort Yukon. The *Bella* was one of the last boats out of Dawson. Enough people had left town that Inspector Constantine began to hope famine might be averted.

Those who remained hurried about their business. Snow lay ankle deep on the smoothly beaten streets and on the roofs of buildings. Smoke curled upward from stovepipes in the roofs of tents and cabins. Outside every building, dogs lay about sleeping or stood in strings of two or ten, harnessed to sleds piled high with carefully guarded provisions for prospectors on the creeks. There were still crowds of men on the streets, or warming themselves at the stoves in saloons and

By the fall of 1897, all the trading companies were running out of goods.

stores. You could tell sourdoughs from cheechakos by the state of their clothing. Old-timers wore beat-up twill parkas, fur-lined moosehide mittens, mukluks, and shaggy lynx-fur hats; newcomers were clad in mackinaws, leather boots, and heavy cloth caps, as advertised by Seattle outfitters. In the Alaska Commercial Company store, little was on the shelves other than ax handles and sugar, and the shelves of the North American Transportation and Trading Company store were bare. You couldn't buy flour for love nor money, and there were plenty of rumors that the companies were stockpiling stuff in their warehouses for a few chosen customers. Dread stalked the town.

Freeze-up was particularly poignant for Father Judge. After seven years in the North, he had known enough to buy supplies for winter while they were still available. St. Mary's Hospital was now complete, and two large stoves had already been installed in his half-built church to warm the congregation. There were more than enough stampeders either with Irish Catholic roots or from French-speaking areas of Canada to fill the church on Sundays: his congregation often topped 100 people. But the Jesuit priest had longed for the arrival of the three Sisters of St. Ann to help him nurse the sick. The Order of the Sisters of St. Ann had well-established missions in Alaska, at Holy Cross, Akulurak, and Nulato. Their practical aid would be invaluable, but Judge was even hungrier for their spiritual companionship. He had plenty of acquaintances in Dawson—Big Alex McDonald regularly attended Mass, and when Belinda Mulrooney saw the stooped priest on the street, she gave him a respectful nod. But there were no soul mates, nobody to share daily prayers and nursing duties with. He frequently couldn't even find volunteers to help dig graves in the rough ground behind the hospital. When he knelt at the altar he had carved with his own penknife to say his evening prayers, he said them alone. The nuns would create an intimate religious circle within the den of thieves.

The sisters never arrived. With the water level so low in the Yukon River, their steamer had got stuck halfway through the voyage upriver and they had been forced to return to Holy Cross. The priest faced another winter of isolation amid his gold-obsessed neighbors.

But Father Judge knew what was expected of him. In mid-November, after his regular evening visit to the twenty patients in his hospital, he retired to the little cabin that was his personal residence, put another log on the stove, and carefully balanced a small inkpot on top of the stove. Slowly, the warmth of the stove melted the frozen lump of sooty ink. Then he lit a candle, found a sheet of paper, pulled a stump up to the crudely built table, and dipped a steel-nibbed pen into the inkpot. It was time for his regular report to the Reverend Father J. B. René, prefect and superior of the Alaskan Branch of the Jesuit Order.

"Reverend and dear Father Superior: Pax Christi!" he wrote. "I have so much to tell your Reverence that I fear I shall forget at least half of it . . . This morning was the coldest we have had, viz., 20 degrees below zero; but it moderated during the day. The first and most important news is that the Sisters of St. Ann did not get here . . . When I found that the Sisters were not coming, I made arrangements for a permanent staff of nurses, cooks etc., and everything is working as well as could be expected under the circumstances."

The priest wrote about the influx of stampeders through the summer. His report was factual and his tone stoic: he was a loyal servant of Christ. Self-sacrifice was his raison d'être. He described how, each Sunday, he celebrated High Mass and Benediction of the Blessed Sacrament and delivered a sermon. He assured his earthly boss that he was supervising health care in the hospital and keeping the accounts. He mentioned that "there is only one thing spoken of here, and that is 'grub'"; nonetheless, he had enough bare essentials to last the winter. But he couldn't resist hinting at his own exhaustion: "Of late my own health has not been as good, at times, as it might be, but I cannot complain. I had a slight attack of the chills a few weeks ago, but I was not laid up at all. I have not missed Mass a single day, nor have I been prevented from attending to my duties. However, the work here is too much for one priest. I know your Reverence realizes the fact, and that you would leave nothing undone to send assistance . . . If God spares me, I hope to keep everything in good order. Your humble servant in Christ, Wm. H. Judge, S. J."

Then the gaunt priest laid down his pen and prepared to do a final round in his log hospital. As his moccasin-shod feet crunched on the dry snow, he looked up and saw the aurora spread green across the sky while the stars twinkled brilliantly in the arctic night. He felt a chill in his bones, this lonely man, and he wondered if God would spare him.

Jack London had no such gloomy thoughts when, just before the river froze, he arrived in Dawson City in the *Yukon Belle* to register his claim on Henderson Creek. For him, the Yukon was still a great adventure—a test of his own stamina and an escape from his dreary, debt-ridden life

in Oakland. He, Thompson, and two other men had left their companions and most of their outfits at the island at the mouth of the Stewart
River, and brought a tent and three weeks of provisions with them to
the mouth of the Klondike. When they rounded the bend in the Yukon,
they must have been dazzled by the size of the remote mining camp. As
far as they could see, from river rim to mountainside on both sides of
the Klondike, was a carpet of tents, cabins, and warehouses. The riverbank was lined with dories, rafts, canoes, and barges. Eager to explore,
Jack left Thompson with the boat and went off to find somewhere they
could stay. He soon ran into men they had met on the trail, including Marshall and Louis Bond, the Yale-educated sons of a prominent
Californian judge. The Bonds had reached Dawson a couple of weeks
earlier with their large dog and established themselves in a cabin. Jack
pitched his tent nearby.

Jack London spent six weeks in Dawson on this visit. Neither he nor
Thompson recorded their impressions at the time, but Jack was busy
soaking up stories and atmosphere. He explored what was by now the
most famous mining camp in the world but was careful not to draw
attention to himself in this rough town of frightened, and often inebriated, men—most of whom were older and bigger than he. "His face was
masked by a thick stubby beard," Marshall Bond would later recall. "A
cap pulled low on his forehead was the one touch necessary to the complete concealment of head and features, so that that part of the anatomy
one looks to for an index of character was covered with cap and beard.
He looked as tough and as uninviting as we doubtless looked to him."

Jack had always loved animals, and the Bonds' dog was one of his
greatest delights. The large, shaggy black animal, a cross between a St.
Bernard and a Scottish collie, idolized his masters. That winter, dogs
ruled Dawson. Since dogsleds were the main source of transport,
strong, healthy dogs were highly valued. Such dogs were fearless, ferocious, and unscrupulous: many were said to have wolf blood in their
veins. Harnessed into powerful teams, with bells jingling on their yokes,

In the Yukon, Jack London watched dogs save lives, fight for survival, and work harder than many of their owners.

they hauled logs and firewood around town and freighted provisions and supplies up to the mines. But many of the stampeders had brought small, weak dogs with them that were of no use. Now abandoned and starving strays, they were treated with vicious cruelty. The streets rang with barks, howls, yelps, growls, and the sound of snapping jaws as ugly fights erupted. Jack took it all in. A dog's struggle for dominance mirrored, in his imagination, a man's fight for supremacy. A dog's devotion to its human master reflected, he chose to believe, the natural hierarchy of power. The howling of huskies ("an old song, as old as the breed itself") would haunt his dreams for the rest of his life.

Dawson looked bleak that fall: when it wasn't shrouded in a chilly fog, snow or freezing rain fell from a pewter sky. But the bars offered the same welcome that Jack had enjoyed in Oakland's waterfront bars, and besides, the place was stuffed with the kind of personalities Jack loved to talk to. He hung out in dance halls like the Orpheum; he watched cardsharps gambling and big spenders losing their fortunes in saloons like the Monte Carlo and the Eldorado; he strolled round the North-West Mounted Police barracks at the south end of town and Father Judge's hospital and church in the north end. His favorite occupation was talking to stampede veterans. He drank in tales of men driven mad by the cold, corpses frozen to death, gunfights in isolated cabins, noble Indian warriors protecting the helpless. The sight of this yellow-haired youth sauntering round the dirt streets and stopping to watch bar-room brawls and dogfights soon became familiar to Dawson residents. "It seemed to me," recalled Edward Morgan, another stampeder, "that whenever I saw him at the bar he was always in conversation with some veteran sourdough or noted character in the life of Dawson. And how he did talk. London was surely prospecting, but it was at bars that he sought his material."

Jack particularly enjoyed the unexpected contrasts he discovered in Dawson—the strange clash between isolation and convention. For Klondikers like Bill Haskell, this same contrast produced an aching homesickness, but Jack London saw only rough grandeur and a race of American heroes. In his opinion, rugged prospectors who had spent years in the North embodied the primitive modern male. The northern lights were spectacular ("bubbling, uprearing, downfalling . . . this flaming triumph"), the girls were beautiful ("one of Gainsborough's old English beauties stepped down from the canvas to riot out the century in Dawson's dancehalls"), and the atmosphere enthralling:

> The crowded room [at the Opera House dance hall] was
> thick with tobacco smoke. A hundred men or so, garbed
> in furs and warm-colored wools, lined the walls and
> looked on. . . . For all its *bizarre* appearance, it was very
> like the living room of the home when the members of

the household come together after the work of the day.
Kerosene lamps and tallow candles glimmered feebly in
the murky atmosphere, while larger stoves roared their
red-hot and white-hot cheer.

On the floor a score of couples pulsed rhythmically to
the swinging waltz-time music . . . The men wore their
wolf- and beaver-skin caps, with the gay-tasselled ear-flaps
flying free, while on their feet were the moose-skin
moccasins and walrus-hide muclucs of the north. Here
and there a woman was in moccasins, though the majority
danced in frail ball-room slippers of silk and satin . . . A
great open doorway gave glimpse of another large room . . .
From this room, in the lulls of music, came the pop of corks
and the clink of glasses. (*A Daughter of the Snows,* 1902)

On November 5, Jack made his way to the log cabin on Front Street
that was occupied by Gold Commissioner Thomas Fawcett. The cabin
was as dimly lit and grimy as every other building in Dawson. Untidy
piles of official forms were stacked up on a rough-hewn desk, and Fawcett had the air of a man overwhelmed by paperwork. In August, the
government in Ottawa had established a royalty regime on all gold
taken from Canadian territory in the Yukon basin, in order to pay for
its administration. Oblivious to the expenses of getting to and living in
the Far North, Ottawa had set the rate at 10 percent on gross output,
or 20 percent on claims producing more than $500 a day. The min-
ers were furious, and had made plain to the man charged with collecting the royalty their objections to both government regulation and
such an iniquitous tax. Fawcett had developed a profound dislike for
outspoken Yankees—and here was another rude, badly dressed American demanding instant service. The Canadian bureaucrat greeted Jack
curtly and told him how to register his claim. Jack solemnly swore that
he had discovered a deposit of gold on placer mining Claim No. 54 on

the Left Fork ascending Henderson Creek, and paid a total of twenty-five dollars in fees: ten for a mining license and an additional fifteen to file his claim. He received a claim certificate as proof of ownership.

Next, Jack crossed the Klondike River, and walked up Bonanza Creek to see for himself the claims that had triggered the Klondike stampede. This was where men toiled like animals—crowded together in damp cabins, scraping at the frozen earth, surviving on their dreary diet of the three Bs. In London's 1910 novel, *Burning Daylight,* the sweaty, monotonous existence became a scene of Dantesque drama in which men struggled to conquer a hostile landscape: "The hills, to their tops, had been shorn of trees, and their naked sides showed signs of goring and perforating that even the mantle of snow could not hide. Beneath him, in every direction, were the cabins of men. But not many men were visible. A blanket of smoke filled the valleys and turned the gray day to melancholy twilight. Smoke arose from a thousand holes in the snow, where, deep down on bed-rock, in the frozen muck and gravel, men crept and scratched and dug, and ever built more fires to break the grip of the frost. Here and there, where new shafts were starting, these fires flamed redly . . . The wreckage of the spring washing appeared everywhere—piles of sluice-boxes, sections of elevated flumes, huge water-wheels—all the debris of an army of gold-mad men."

Yet Jack never forgot the Fabian socialism that he had embraced before he was swept away by Klondicitis. Sometimes, when conversation in the Monte Carlo or the Yukon Hotel turned from prospecting anecdotes to political issues, he spoke up. One evening, Jack sat quietly beyond the circle of lamplight while others, including Marshall Bond, started to argue about the difference between socialism and anarchism. "Then from out of the shadow," recalled Marshall, "came a quick-speaking, sympathetic voice. He took up the subject from its earliest history, carried it on through a rapid survey of its most important points and held us thrilled by the hypnotic effect which a profound knowledge of a subject expounded by an exalted believer always exerts. Intellectually

By the time Jack saw the hills around Bonanza Creek, the landscape was shorn of trees and scarred by mine shafts, piles of dirt, and sluice boxes.

he was incomparably the most alert man in the room, and we felt it. . . . He was refreshing."

Jack's political convictions shaped his reactions to the whole endeavor of panning for gold in the Far North. Yes, the wild stampedes and frontier camaraderie were intoxicating. But in the end, only a handful of lucky prospectors would make their fortunes, and most stampeders would barely cover their expenses. When he wrote *Burning Daylight* a decade later, his main character saw the cruelty of Bonanza Creek: "It was a gigantic inadequacy. Each worked for himself, and the result was chaos. In this richest of diggings it cost one dollar to mine two dollars, and for every dollar taken out by their feverish, unthinking methods another dollar was left hopelessly in the earth. Given another year, and most of the claims would be worked out, and the sum of gold taken out would be no more than equal [to] what was left behind." What was needed was collective effort—but the Klondike was not about organized labor. Instead, it spoke to an outlaw's drive for individual triumph, or to a writer's craving for epic stories.

Jack London fell in love with the Dawson of late 1897. It was, he would recall, "a Golden City where dust flowed like water and dance-halls rang with never-ending revelry." But in early December, it was time for him and Fred Thompson to leave. The sun's rays edged above the horizon for a mere four hours each day, yet the glittering white of the frozen Yukon and the hard-packed snow on the trails made travel easier. Except for the crunch of their feet and the occasional sharp crack of a branch snapping in the cold, they hiked through a silent, frozen world. Newly fallen snow was different from anything Jack had known Outside. "It was hard, and fine, and dry," he noted. "It was more like sugar. Kick it, and it flew with a hissing noise, like sand . . . It was composed not of flakes, but of crystals—tiny geometrical crystals. In truth, it was not snow, but frost." No birds sang in the relentlessly white landscape that stretched forever under a vast sky. After five days, what a relief to see the wisp of dark smoke from the cabin where they had left their companions in mid-October! In this tiny cabin, measuring only ten by twelve feet on the inside, Jack would spend much of the next five months alongside at least three other men, eating, sleeping, smoking, playing cards, cooking, talking, entertaining visitors from other cabins. There was little hope of privacy for the most basic human functions— and this would lead to trouble.

While twenty-one-year-old Jack looked forward to his first arctic winter, thirty-one-year-old Bill Haskell was wondering if he could take a second hungry, cold winter on the creeks. He and his partner, Joe Meeker, faced a dilemma. Canadian mining regulations decreed that a claim would be forfeit to the crown if it was not worked at least once in a six-month period. The partners did not want to lose their claim, but they were worried that their supplies wouldn't last. Should they tough it out? Could they find anybody to work the claim for them? One evening Bill and Joe sat down by the crackling stove, lit their pipes, and began to talk about the coming months. The logs of the cabin walls had shrunk since Bill had built it, and the men could feel cold drafts whistling through the gaps between them. Joe was still convinced that "there may be millions in those mines," and was prepared to grit his teeth and keep digging. But Bill was weary. He knew there might be only "frozen muck and gravel and hard work," and the men available to work the claim for them had neither experience nor provisions.

Then Bill had another idea, which he tentatively raised. They could probably sell the claim for about $50,000. And there was lots more gold in Alaska—"better diggings, I'm thinking, than these British moose pastures, especially if the government concludes to take a large share of the profits."

Gradually Bill pushed Joe toward the conclusion that a bird in the hand was worth two in the bush: it was time to cash in. They could sell up, travel south over the frozen river to the coast, then return in the spring with a bigger outfit. Joe hated to leave the claim he had poured so much effort into. He stoked the stove and puffed silently on his pipe. The two men held their hands to the brief burst of warmth from their battered little Yukon stove. Then Joe nodded. They would walk south.

The two men left the Klondike in a blinding snowstorm. The mercury in the miners' bottles was frozen solid, which meant the temperature was forty degrees below freezing point. The pack ice on the Yukon River was frozen into humps and bumps "and the only way to maintain a tolerably smooth course was to cross back and forth . . . It was hard, cold drudgery for Joe and me." Every mile felt like ten. Along the way, they encountered dozens of boats that had been locked in the ice when the river froze a few weeks earlier. They met travelers with frozen cheeks, noses, fingers, and feet. They passed injured men abandoned in the swirling, stinging snow by companions who were desperate to leave the godforsaken country. Bill and Joe turned their faces away from these agonized victims of a Yukon winter. They knew the men were too far gone to save and that they themselves must not slow their pace. They left them to die.

"Joe and I, who, by spending a winter on the Klondike, had learned how to prepare for cold weather and rough trails, worked our way along very well over the rough river." Where the river ran swiftly through a narrow gorge, they narrowly escaped plunging into the furious current and sliding under the ice. When walls of ice lay ahead, they crawled upward on hands and knees, dragging their sleds.

Each night, the two men pitched their tent, cut boughs of evergreen to sleep on, lit their Yukon stove, and boiled up beans and bacon. By now they were like an old married couple: each knew what the other was thinking before he opened his mouth. For years they had worked together, suffered together, bickered and argued, and learned to trust each other. Joe's lack of imagination exasperated Bill, and Bill's boyish optimism irked Joe. Yet they had looked after each other and, despite their differences in temperament, they rarely disagreed on important issues. But one night, Bill got a surprise. Staring into the red hot stove, Joe said, "A fellow's life ain't worth much till he gets out of a place like this." Bill shot him a quick glance; Joe wasn't usually so philosophical. Bill reminded Joe what he had said when they first discussed seeking their fortunes in the Yukon valley.

Joe didn't take his eyes off the stove. "Yes," he replied, "It takes grit, but we have made pretty well for two years of roughing it, and I was just thinking that if I ever got out of here I would not be fool enough to return. Colorado is good enough for me. You too. We've got a snug sum, and what we need now is to get it out with our lives."

Bill had never expected Joe to turn his back on their Yukon dreams. What had prompted these remarks? What did they presage? But it was late, and Joe was not inclined to talk further. Tomorrow they had to clamber over the perilous ice shelves alongside the roaring waters of the White Horse Rapids. Ahead of them lay the chain of lakes and the awful St. Elias mountain range. They should reach Dyea in a couple of weeks.

Once again, Bill's mouth started watering for a big, thick beefsteak. He put his companion's comments out of his mind. If Joe didn't want to return to the Klondike, their partnership would work just as well in the Rockies, wouldn't it? Soon the tent was filled with the snores of two exhausted men.

CHAPTER 10
The Pioneers' Show, January–March 1898

ON DECEMBER 31, 1897, the sun's rays reached only the mountain tops around Dawson and its creeks during the four hours of daylight. For five gloomy weeks, the sun had never risen high enough in the sky to shine directly into the valleys. At each end of its brief appearance, there were long twilights, and if there was a half-decent moon during the arctic night, enough light bounced off the snow to allow people to see their own cabins or tents. Beyond them, deep darkness loomed.

The cold was worse than any newcomer had ever imagined. The temperature never rose above minus thirty degrees that bleak New Year's Eve, and it was dangerous to venture outside. White spots of frostbite quickly appeared on cheeks and noses; ice crystals gummed eyelashes together; tightly wrapped scarves trapped the moisture from breath, then froze as hard as wood. Icicles festooned every building, and ice glued doors shut. Most days, Dawson residents spent their time sleeping, drinking, working in the sawmills, or huddling around roaring stoves, occasionally dashing outside to split more firewood. On the creeks, miners kept busy—digging, emptying buckets at the top of the windlasses, cutting firewood, and trying to stay alive and healthy. The only advantage of bitterly cold spells like this was that you could easily split wood for stoves. But if you left a splittinfg ax outside, the handle would split too.

It was now more than sixteen months since George Carmack and his

Hãn relatives had first found gold on Bonanza Creek, and more than five months since news of the Klondike gold strike had blasted across North America. Many of the professional prospectors, like Bill Haskell and Joe Meeker, had scooped up their wealth and escaped. Those early gold diggers were already vastly outnumbered by the gamblers and dreamers—people like Belinda Mulrooney and Jack London—who had flooded into the Yukon valley. The population of Dawson City had grown tenfold in 1897, from 500 in March to over 5,000 by September. Thanks to the famine panic, the population of the town and the surrounding creeks had dropped by the end of the year, but those who soldiered on through the winter grabbed at any chance to get together. Human company around a saloon's roaring stove was a welcome relief for men living in badly heated cabins, weary of their partners' stale smells and staler talk.

Sixteen miles outside Dawson, New Year's Eve was celebrated with particular gusto at Belinda Mulrooney's Grand Forks Hotel. From lunchtime onward, company-starved miners began trudging toward the two-story log building, where lamps glowed in the windows and the smoke from its chimneys settled onto the roof in the icy air. Once the door was shut behind them, the men stamped the snow off their boots, wiped the frozen snot from their noses, and made for the steamy good cheer round the stove. The noise level gradually rose as more men crowded in and Belinda's barman, Andrew, a frail fellow who always wore a white shirt and tie, hurried to keep up with the orders. Between walls decorated with colored lithographs and cigarette advertisements, the air was thick with tobacco smoke and the odor of thawing hair, unwashed clothes, and human sweat.

It was a typical mining crowd: some of the men had been in the North for more than a decade and greeted each other by nicknames such as Tin Kettle George, Handshaker Bob, Windy Jim, Slobbery Tom, Montana Red, Happy Jack, Circle City Mickey, Long Shorty, French Curly, Hootchinoo Albert, or Tom the Horse. Successful miners like

Johnny Lind and George "Skiff" Mitchell paid for their drinks with gold dust; gold-nugget watch chains were strung across the front of their filthy checked shirts and wool vests. Men like these had come close to killing each other in drunken brawls, and they had saved each other's lives in blizzards. Now they listened to braggarts talking about next summer's strikes, and they exchanged anecdotes about the challenges of winter. There were peals of laughter as an old-timer related the story of a cheechako who had made an unpleasant mistake. Freezing temperatures involved a mounting column of human excrement in every outhouse, with no way of dispersing it or digging a new hole. The man had foolishly fired a shotgun in the hopes of destroying the solid column of shit. Instead, he had been peppered by hard bullets of the stuff flying back in his face.

As the clock struck midnight on the last day of 1897, everyone raised their glasses to toast each other and the coming year. Belinda, clad as usual in a prim starched blouse and a long skirt, paused for a minute to join the cheers, before bustling off to check the stove.

Through careful housekeeping, and the purchase of outfits from men who had retreated south, Belinda's food cache was well stocked. The shelf behind the Grand Forks bar, a narrow counter of spruce boards, was laden with bottles. In the dining room, meals were served round the clock on a couple of long tables covered in clean cloths. Customers paid $3.50 for a dinner served on china dishes, or $12 a day for board and lodging. In addition to the inevitable bacon and beans, there was always canned beef, canned mutton, or ham, and on each table a bowl of applesauce (made from dried apples) that the cook refilled regularly. For men hungry for sugar and fruit and at risk of scurvy, applesauce was nectar. From time to time there were even eggs at a dollar each, "at the diner's risk." If the first egg proved too old to be edible, the guest could order another one as long as he paid another dollar. And for special occasions like today, there were unusual delicacies such as moose heart roasted with bacon, or pickled nose of moose.

In its first three months, Belinda's roadhouse had become a trading post, a repository for gold dust, and an informal brokerage center where people could buy and sell claims. When the weather allowed Father Judge to hike up from Dawson, it even doubled as a church. Prospectors would kneel quietly behind rough benches while the priest, clutching his wooden cross, said Mass and spoke about God's infinite love. "Father Judge told the boys they had got all the gold and riches for a reward for their faithfulness under hardships. It was a gift of God for a good purpose." Belinda was always surprised at how the toughest old miner would listen intently to the priest and then debate the sermon long after the cassocked figure had hiked down the hill.

Roadhouse rules were simple: no spitting, no swearing, leave your dogs in the kennels behind the hotel, and always have a word with the proprietor about the latest goings-on. The Grand Forks bar was Belinda's own private gold mine. She heard about every new strike days before the news reached Dawson, making her the best-informed person in the gold fields. "You happened to be in place, and the men were going to stake, a stampede was on. They wanted to exchange an outfit for an interest." The canny businesswoman grubstaked prospectors from her store of axes, shovels, picks, clothing, whipsaws . . . She even had a portable sawmill and a team of dogs so she could deliver lumber to claims. Soon she had three claims on Eldorado and ten claims from new strikes. Along with five other claim owners, she also became a partner in the Eldorado-Bonanza Quartz and Placer Mining Company, which was incorporated in Missouri for the purpose of raising capital to finance heavy mining equipment. The legality of a woman owning a mine was dubious, since mining was traditionally a male industry and in English common law a "person" still meant "male." Belinda simply ignored convention, and nobody dared challenge her.

Belinda continued to maintain her own privacy in the snug little cabin behind the hotel that she shared with Sadie O'Hara and Nero. Keeping her distance from the men increased their respect for her, even if there was speculation about the nature of her relationship with Sadie. In the cabin she was warmed by a blazing stove and the knowledge that she was making money almost as fast as Big Alex McDonald. On days when the north wind dropped and the temperature rose, she would harness Nero for the sixteen-mile trip down to Dawson, to catch up with news and developments there. But most of the time she could be found in the Grand Forks Hotel, giving a curt welcome to any bundled-up figure, swathed in furs against the icy air, who jerked open the door and stumbled toward her.

Stampedes sparked by rumors of a new gold-bearing creek always ignited a hullabaloo of men shouting and dogs barking. One day, Belinda decided to join the fun. She and Sadie wrapped up warmly in parkas, thick shirts, buckskin skirts, long underwear, fur mitts, and moccasins. With a dog team and sled, they plunged off with the crowd for a twenty-mile hike through thick snow across a mountain to Dominion Creek. "We came back that night exhausted and slept in the hotel. That was our one night in the hotel. The place, except for the little room for women, was filled with miners, tired from their long round trip to Dominion and back again. We went in because we didn't want to warm up our own cabin."

Belinda soon discovered she couldn't stand to *live* in her private gold mine. "The lumber of the hotel had shrunk. There were wide cracks everywhere, so you could hear everything." Men of assorted nationalities and types lay elbow to elbow in tight rows, and the stench of filth, tobacco, and human exhalations was suffocating. The blankets were filthy and lice ridden: one traveler complained that a previous occupant of his bunk had failed to remove his boots and had then slept with his feet at the head of the bed, which was now "ornamented with globules of dried mud of varying size and appearance, which adhered firmly to the black blanket." There was an endless chorus of snores, belches, farts, and moans, and the anguished cries of those lost in nightmares. Belinda discovered that "the whole place rocked with the noise." After a couple of hours she shook Sadie awake and announced, "This is surely a man's hotel." Sadie started to laugh, then went into such hysterics that Belinda threw a bucket of water at her.

The only person unwelcome at the Grand Forks Hotel was Alex McDonald. When he asked Belinda if he could use her hotel as the headquarters for his freighting business, she refused: "This is our home, and we have not enough provisions." When he offered to buy it from her, she told him the price was an outrageous $100,000. When he protested that the building was only a log shack, she laughed at him. Belinda understood better than most the ephemeral nature of wealth. "It may be just logs, but what are your claims?" she retorted. "Just dust. It's only a state of mind anyway."

Big Alex began to see he had made a formidable enemy. For the second time in his dealings with this Irish firebrand, he blinked in surprise, scratched his chin, then leaned down and whispered, "You're not mad at me?" Once again, Belinda pretended she wasn't. But she hadn't finished with the Nova Scotian yet.

Miners on more distant creeks didn't have the luxury of a roadhouse nearby. Eighty miles up the frozen Yukon, Jack London's world had shrunk to the handful of log cabins on the small, windswept island that in his stories would be known as "Split-Up Island." (It earned the name because so many prospecting partners split up when they reached this point, unable to stand each other's jokes, tempers or personal habits for another day.) About thirty men had holed up at the mouth of the Stewart River, grimly waiting for spring. In the cabin Jack shared with Fred Thompson, Merritt Sloper, and Jim Goodman, the most important daily duty was to keep logs blazing in the Yukon stove. Even when the sheet-iron was red hot and the faces of the men crouched around it were beaded with sweat, their feet tingled with cold. Anything more than a couple of feet from the stove remained frozen. Chunks of bacon and moose on the meat shelf by the door were rock hard. The walls were covered in a half inch of dry, white, crystallized rime. Frost glistened in the chinking between the cabin's logs, and the frozen moisture of men's breath coated the small square of oiled paper that constituted the sole window. Each day began with one of the men shoveling out the ice that had accumulated on the bough-covered floor.

Most of the island's residents had already decided that mining was not for them. The group included a judge, a professional gambler, a doctor, a professor, and an engineer—though many had rocky professional reputations. An old-timer called "Doc" Harvey, for example, was well known as a drunk. Most had traveled north on impulse and were hopelessly unsuited to hard manual labor. Instead, they spent the time playing whist, cribbage, and chess. Jack's hunger for literature was frustrated by the shortage of light (candles were precious) and books. According to one companion, Jack had carted an extraordinary library over the Chilkoot Pass: Herbert Spencer's *The Philosophy of Style,* Karl Marx's *Das Kapital,* Charles Darwin's *On the Origin of Species,* Ernst Haeckel's *The Riddle of the Universe,* and John Milton's *Paradise Lost.* Once, for lighter reading, he walked seven miles to borrow a copy of Rudyard Kipling's *The Seven Seas* from a man camped upriver. Two of the only recreations available to him were talking and arguing—and he was excellent at both. Soon a visit to his cabin became the favorite break in the monotony of winter for adjacent cabin dwellers. A fellow miner, Bert Hargraves, left a vivid account of such a visit: "I remember well the first time I entered it. London was seated on the edge of a bunk, rolling a cigarette. He smoked incessantly and it would have taken no Sherlock Holmes to tell what the stains on his fingers meant."

Goodman was preparing a meal when Hargraves arrived, and Sloper was repairing a piece of the cabin's primitive furniture. Jack, nonchalantly swinging his legs and smoking, was challenging Goodman's faith in God by insisting that there was no scientific proof of divine existence. Years later, Hargraves would tell Charmian London, Jack's second wife and biographer, how "Jack interrupted the conversation to welcome me. His hospitality was so cordial, his smile so genial, his goodfellowship so real, that it instantly dispelled all reserve. I was invited to participate in the discussion, which I did, much to my subsequent discomfiture."

Jack's cabin appears, from Bert Hargraves's account, to have been a subarctic debating society, with Jack playing the role of devil's advocate in every argument. "He applied one test to religion, to economics, to everything . . . What is the truth? What is just? It was with these questions that he confronted the baffling enigma of life. He could think great thoughts." Hargraves was impressed: "One could not meet him without feeling the impact of a superior intellect . . . He possessed the mental equipment of a mature man and I have never thought of him as a boy except in the heart of him . . . the clean, joyous, tender, unembittered heart of youth."

Another miner, Emil Jensen, told Charmian London that the young Jack "stood ever ready, were it for a foraging trip among the camps for reading matter, to give a helping hand on a woodsled or to undertake a two day's hike for a plug of tobacco when he saw us restless and grumpy for the want of a smoke." Jack even surrendered a precious quart of whiskey that he had carefully hidden from Doc Harvey for use as a painkiller during emergency surgery on a man's ankle. "The doctor and the patient emptied my bottle between them and then proceeded to the operation," he recorded in *John Barleycorn,* the memoir he wrote in 1913 of his drinking life.

But Jack was young and energetic, and hated being penned in for weeks. He must have made at least one visit to his claim on Henderson Creek, several miles away, during which he carved on the back wall of a cabin belonging to a miner called Charles Taylor the inscription "Jack London, Miner Author, Jan 27 1898." He learned all the tricks of northern survival—how to break trail in snowshoes, how to keep biscuits and bacon warm against his skin, how to bake sourdough bread, how to rig up a shelter with a blanket, how to avoid frostbite. Like Bill Haskell and Belinda Mulrooney, he felt both rapture and awe as he observed the immensity of the North and the icy stillness of winter there. He would capture the sense of human inconsequence in his short story "The White Silence," published in the 1900 collection *The Son of the Wolf*: "All movement ceases, the sky clears, the heavens are as brass; the slightest whisper seems sacrilege, and man becomes timid, affrighted at the sound of his own voice. Sole speck of life journeying across the ghostly wastes of a dead world, he trembles at his audacity, realizes that his is a maggot's life, nothing more. Strange thoughts arise unsummoned, and the mystery of all things strives for utterance."

On the opposite bank of the Yukon River lived an intriguing couple: a man called Stevens and a redheaded woman. One day the couple crossed the frozen river and dropped in on Jack's cabin. According to Emil Jensen, Stevens introduced his companion as "Mrs. Stevens," but the woman quickly made it clear that they were not in fact married. Stevens settled down near the stove and began bragging about adventures in the jungles of South America, which featured fierce tribesmen, wanton women, and ferocious animals. Stevens's tales were farfetched, but Jack loved them.

It was stuffy and smoky in the cabin, but even in the dim light Jensen could see that the woman was at least a decade older than Jack and "smoke-tarnished." She was the first non-native woman the men had seen for weeks, and "notwithstanding . . . her bedraggled appearance generally, she was comparatively fair to look upon; besides, she was unreservedly frank, and her voice was soft and caressing . . . and there was music in her laugh." Her presence in the cabin was electrifying, and the men's eyes kept drifting away from Stevens to her. She had a way of meeting their gazes without flinching, and her eyes were full of incitement, full of promise—and yet there was a mocking glimmer in them too, as though she was challenging the men. She was distracting, disturbing, and the smell of her sweat pierced the masculine fug. The men stared as though mesmerized by the sight of her ankles; they groped toward a half-remembered gallantry as they offered tea.

Stevens talked on, but Jensen noticed that the woman's eyes had now fastened on Jack's handsome young face. Then she deliberately struck a provocative pose, throwing her head back and smiling as she lifted her thick curls away from her neck. It was deeply erotic. "Despite the soiled, unkempt apparel, her small, well-rounded figure showed soft and yielding in the tight, dilapidated dress. I remember well her dark blue eyes, the innocent baby-like stare, and teeth small and white gleaming between red-blooded, rather sensuous lips." Jack noticed those lips and breasts too.

When Stevens finally pulled on his parka and made his way to the door, the woman dutifully followed him. Then she turned, and invited everybody to visit their cabin. "Come soon!" she said, speaking directly to Jack.

Jack couldn't resist the invitation. "Baby eyes in a woman of her age spells trouble," Jensen warned the young Californian, but Jack ignored him and set off across the river alone. Once inside Stevens's hovel, he settled down for another dose of blood-curdling braggadocio. But Stevens's welcome cooled when he saw that his "wife" was moving steadily closer to Jack. His mood changed. "Have you ever seen straight shooting, Mr. London?" he inquired. Without waiting for an answer, he took a Winchester rifle from its hook upon the stove and strode outside. He then proceeded to blast ten bullets into a tin target nailed to a tree in the space of a few seconds.

Jack finally realized that Stevens was not a man to tangle with—particularly in a frozen wilderness where many a traveler simply disappeared. Without bidding farewell to the woman, he headed back across the river to his own cabin. There he confessed to Jensen that "it surely was the quickest, straightest, surest shooting that I ever saw . . . That man is afraid of nothing. Of nothing, I tell you, not even the truth." Jack did not revisit the Stevens household. But lodged in his memory were the smoky atmosphere, the woman's looks, the man's fearlessness, and the heady eroticism of male rivalry.

Sometimes it felt as though spring would never come. Tensions developed between the Split-Up Island residents, who were desperate to leave this frozen hell. How many more weeks must they drag heavy buckets of water up from ice holes in the river? How many more arguments about the existence of God would be started by the bumptious youth who smoked too much, quoted Herbert Spencer and Karl Marx too often, and kept asking, "What is the truth? What is just?" Jack would catch the intolerable tensions that built up among idle men cooped up together in his story "In a Far Country," which appeared in *The Son of the Wolf* in 1900: "The intense frost could not be endured for long at a time, and the little cabin crowded them—beds, stove, table, and all—into a space ten by twelve. The very presence of either became a personal affront to the other, and they lapsed into sullen silences which increased in length and strength as the days went by. Occasionally the flash of an eye or the curl of a lip got the better of them, though they strove to wholly ignore each other during these mute periods."

In Jack's story, the two main characters murder each other. In his own life, there was a shake-up between cabins after he had borrowed Merritt Sloper's splitting ax once too often and dulled its edge by using it on ice. Jim Goodman had also grown exasperated with Jack's insistence that visitors stay for dinner, even when their stock of beans and dried fruit was running short. Jack left Goodman, Sloper, and Fred Thompson and ended up with Doc Harvey.

Jack London never lost his sense of wonder at the vastness of land and sky: his friend Emil Jensen would later describe how Jack was "ever on tiptoe with expectancy, whether silent with wondering awe, as on a night when we saw the snows aflame beneath a weird, bewildering sky or in the throes of a frenzied excitement while we watched a mighty river at flood-tide." But as the days lengthened, the toll taken by the bitter, claustrophobic winter showed in the men's dull eyes and shrunken muscles. Lassitude overwhelmed Jack: his teeth loosened, his joints ached, his gums bled. When he pushed his thumb into the puffy skin of his legs, the dents remained. Months without fresh vegetables had produced the first signs of scurvy, or "blackleg," as Klondike stampeders called it because it turned men's legs dark purple with bruises. The miners dreaded it because they knew it was caused by lack of vitamin C and the most effective remedies (lemons, raw potatoes, salad greens) were unavailable. Had Jack's companions been prepared to trust the Hān people, they would have learned to brew up some spruce tea—but they didn't.

All over the creeks in cold, lonely cabins, men who had survived through the winter on beans and bacon were suffering from tuberculosis, bronchitis, or scurvy. Scurvy was the worst. The excruciating pain in their limbs would leave them too weak to get out of bed, and they would lie there until their bodies were bloated and black and they rotted to death. Those who had partners might get a decent burial in the frozen ground, but if the grave was not deep enough, parts of the recently buried body would be seen lying around, dug up by wolves or sled dogs. Scurvy killed more stampeders than accidents on the Chilkoot Pass or in the mines. Doc Harvey knew that he had to get Jack to Father Judge's hospital in Dawson City as soon as it was safe to travel.

For months, men had been struggling down from the creeks to the hospital. One man, brought in by sled, had spent thirty days in his cabin on his back; he survived by mixing sugar and flour in a tin cup and making a paste with ice he had picked off the wall and melted against his body. He was rigid to the hips when a fellow miner discovered him, and his gums had puffed through his lips. "We have had as high as fifty in the hospital, about half of them scurvy cases, and all new men who came last summer," the priest wrote to his brother early in March. Since the hospital had opened seven months earlier, 168 patients had passed through its doors. Nobody was turned away, regardless of their religious views. The Jesuit's days were filled with comforting the dying, burying the dead, overseeing the hospital's extension, cheering the convalescents, coaxing the obstinate, praying with and for his fellow Catholics, planning meals from an almost empty larder, and saying Mass.

The work was endless. There was still no glass in the windows and the shabby blankets crawled with lice, but Father Judge was not discouraged. In fact, his mood was lighter than it had been the previous fall. Fears about the coming winter had proved groundless. "We have great laughs at what is printed in the papers about these parts. Everything is so exaggerated, both the good and the bad." Sure, the temperature had dipped below minus sixty degrees in February, but he had good helpers in both the hospital and the church, and his provisions had proved adequate. There had been music in the church at Christmas, and parishioners had often left hunks of caribou or moose on his doorstep to supplement his diet. His own health had held up. "The papers have us all dead or starving, and yet for my own part, I feel as if I were back in civilization again."

Father Judge's contentment sprang from his careless disregard for his own comfort (lice never seemed to bother him) and from his total conviction that he was doing God's work. "About a month ago we had a beautiful death," he confided to his brother. "A man well known outside was converted while in the hospital by reading 'Plain Facts for Fair Minds.' He received the Sacraments with great devotion, and died most happily." A few days after he sealed the letter to his brother, he sat down in his cabin to write a similar missive to his sister. "The hospital has been the means of leading quite a few sheep back to the fold . . . I am glad that I am here to give some consolation to the great number of Catholics . . . and to sow good seed among the many non-Catholics. I have abundant consolation in all my labors."

There was an additional, worldlier cause for the Jesuit priest's improved morale. More than ever, he was his neighbors' touchstone of integrity, his selflessness a beacon of compassion in a brutal world. His unwavering yet naive faith that the Lord would provide had become a self-fulfilling prophecy because he brought out the best in others. One day he accepted twenty more patients than there were beds in the hospital. Before dark, three bales of blankets were dumped at the door, and the unknown driver hurried off. Another time, in the dead of winter, he had struggled to dig a grave in the frozen ground. He was about to give up in despair when two burly strangers arrived with picks and shovels and did the job for him.

"A saint," the hard-bitten miners called him, grateful for his presence in their uncouth community. The proof of their respect was that they had raised the funds he needed to finish and furnish his buildings. Many of Dawson's most important citizens belonged to the Yukon Order of Pioneers, established some years earlier in Circle City. Only prospectors who had been in the Yukon valley before the 1896 Klondike strike were eligible to join this service club. These veterans guarded their exclusivity jealously, even as they chanted their motto: "Do unto others as you would be done by." (It is a sign of Belinda's forcefulness that she was admitted as an honorary member although she was a woman and had arrived in 1897. Apparently nobody dared refuse her.) In early March, the Pioneers organized a benefit for St. Mary's Hospital in appreciation of Father Judge's efforts to provide medical care. Belinda Mulrooney hiked down from Grand Forks to help run the fundraiser in the newly erected Pioneers Hall. There were dance hall girls, a fiddler, a caller, and the gratifying sense that it was all in a good cause. The miners, giddy at the chance to throw their wealth around, raised over $50,000. "Looking back on the money we made that night," Belinda would recall later, "always made the pickings of the usual church fair on the Outside somehow seem small to me."

Belinda particularly enjoyed the droller aspects of the fundraiser, including a raucous dancing competition and hefty fines for those who danced or talked too much. In the guttering light of the oil lamps, couples twirled around while the thick crowd of men standing against the walls shouted insults at the dancers. According to Belinda, the crowd was roasting the master of ceremonies, saloonkeeper Bill McPhee, "and they were having a lot of fun out of it." But a couple of killjoys thought all this cursing and derision had no place at a benefit for the Roman

Catholic church and went off to complain to Father Judge. "Father Judge came . . . down to look at us," remembered Belinda. The priest, who was at least twenty years older than most of those present, gently admonished the revelers: "Children, children. Just children." But he ingenuously added, "You mustn't *make* people give money." Belinda went right on collecting the fines, reassuring Father Judge that it was just a lot of miners enjoying themselves. "This is the Pioneers' show. They like to stand up and argue."

After the dancing came a raffle. Belinda's employee Sadie had contributed a leather pillow that she had made and stuffed with moss. Sadie and her laugh were immensely popular, and the pillow emerged as the most desirable object in the world. "My Lord!" Belinda loved to recall. "The bidding was a scream." In an attempt, perhaps, to ingratiate himself with Belinda, Alex McDonald was determined to win it: "[He] certainly spread himself that night. I think it was the first time in his life he'd ever had a good time." The bidding war was so fierce that Belinda feared "the damn bit of moss and leather would go to $100,000, or we'd have to pull it apart." Big Alex finally won it for $5,000.

Belinda faced a trickier situation when Esther Duffie pressed into her hands a heavy purse filled with $20,000 of dust, nuggets, and coins collected from Esther's friends among the dance hall girls and prostitutes. What would the holy-rolling killjoys think of this? "I was razzed pretty strong for a little innocent fun," she confided to her friend Joe Barrette, a French Canadian dog musher. "They'll think it dirty money." Joe suggested that they exchange the nuggets and coins for gold dust: "That's clean enough." Belinda gave short shrift to that idea. "It's not that . . . It's where it came from." Joe was all for casting convention to the wind, insisting that the donors were "fine women! Give for churches! Good as anyone! I know it! You know it! Make the rest know it!" Belinda did know it, and usually she had no time for moral superiority either. She had no intention of slamming the door on such well-meant generosity.

Belinda Mulrooney always took a broad-minded view of successful business-women, no matter what the business. Those such as the "Belgian Queen," shown here, had plenty of customers.

But on this occasion, she held her tongue, handed over the purse, and would describe it only as "a gift."

The fundraiser demonstrated more than affection for Father Judge. Dawson's old-timers had had it with the Canadian government, which was eager to squeeze a large royalty out of the Klondike and to impose Canadian law but reluctant to spend a cent on civic improvements. Ottawa had made no attempt to bring any kind of order to the town other than to lay out its streets and send the Mounties. There was no local government, no library, no effort to improve communication with the outside world by telegraph lines or better routes. Dawsonites realized that the town needed better organizations, particularly if its population expanded, and they themselves would have to provide them. Making sure St. Mary's Hospital stayed solvent was only the first step.

By mid-March there were more than twelve hours of sunlight each day, and the hard-packed snow on the trails was turning yellow and slushy on warm days. News began trickling down the trail from Whitehorse. Most of the talk was of the crowds of frenzied stampeders waiting to reach the world-famous San Francisco of the North. At least 30,000 people had crossed the St. Elias Mountains and were now camped at the head of Bennett Lake, ready to launch homemade boats as soon as the Yukon River was open.

But there was also one horrifying piece of news that shook Dawson old-timers. Joe Meeker, Bill Haskell's partner and a man familiar to all the original prospectors on Bonanza and Eldorado, was dead—drowned on his journey to the Outside. In Dawson's bars and saloons, news spread of how Joe had lost his footing while the two men had been inching their way along an ice shelf adjoining the White Horse Rapids. It was a ghastly fate: Joe had slipped into the Yukon's raging current and instantly been pulled under the ice, taking his precious bag of gold dust with him. He was gone before Bill Haskell realized what had happened. For men who had worked alongside Bill and Joe, this was a grim reminder of the river's treachery and the dangers of their lives. They could only imagine Bill's horror—how he had stared at the churning foam and nearly dived in after his partner, how he had forced himself to continue along the trail to Dyea, sick with grief.

When word of Joe's death reached Dawson, many a tired old-timer wondered whether he would ever escape the North with his life. Sourdoughs speculated on Bill's future. Would he return to the Yukon as he had intended, now he had lost his partner? Was the dream of a big payout worth the risks they all took, the hardships they suffered?

Break-up was imminent, Dawson's population was about to explode, and the town was totally unprepared. Belinda attended a meeting of nervous town leaders held at the Alaska Commercial Company warehouse. One pioneer insisted that the townsite must be drained. Another proposed more cabins. Belinda suggested that the buildings along Front Street should all add another story and install bunks. She was furious when the men laughed at her and ridiculed her idea. Jutting her chin forward and standing with arms akimbo, she announced that she was going to build a three-story hotel. "That caused an uproar. They all just screamed. I was boiling. I made up my mind to make the bluff good." A prospector called Bill Leggett with a rich claim on Eldorado bet her $5,000 that she wouldn't get a three-story hotel built by the summer, and "If you ever did get it built, you couldn't get it heated afterwards." Belinda narrowed her eyes, gave Leggett a filthy look, and took the bet.

The Canadian government also began to realize how ugly life might get when the population of Dawson City mushroomed and only a handful of Mounties were there to police it. The triangular mudflat squeezed between river and hills would overflow with old-timers and newcomers, entrepreneurs and gamblers, dancers and sled dogs, crooks and hookers, cardsharps and Christians, the sick and the lame. An official party was sent to oversee the orderly development of Canada's most northerly settlement. The first bureaucrat to arrive was Frederick

Coates Wade, a Canadian crown prosecutor with orders from Ottawa to clean up land ownership in this distant mining camp.

Wade was an outspoken bully of a man, with a big mustache and a bigger ego. He had made his name as a crusading journalist in Manitoba, and he had wangled the Dawson job thanks to his friendship with the prominent Liberal politician Clifford Sifton. Sifton was both minister for the Interior, responsible for settling the prairies, and minister for Indian and Northern Affairs. He regarded the North as a convenient source of patronage for loyal friends. Now Fred Wade focused his energies on controlling what he liked to describe as "these U.S. freebooters." He was appalled by what he found in the township: squatters living along the riverbank without paying rent, no public sanitary facilities, no clear property rights. He made the unilateral decision to find a private citizen—an entrepreneur—who would lease the strip of land along the waterfront and then take over the job of cleaning up the waterfront, erecting decent buildings, collecting rents, and installing three public toilets.

Wade didn't give Belinda Mulrooney a second look: she was doubly disqualified by being both American and a woman. But Alex McDonald was exactly the kind of man Wade had in mind. Describing him to Sifton, his political boss in Ottawa, as "the most responsible man here," Wade gave Big Alex and a partner a sweetheart deal for the property for a mere $30,000—less than the community had raised in one night for Father Judge. Wade did not tell Sifton that he thought so highly of Big Alex that he had offered to act as his solicitor and had therefore got a cut for himself. Conflict of interest was never a problem for Frederick Coates Wade. But it was a problem for Dawson's American residents, who raged at the way Canadian officials ripped them off while acting as if they embodied virtue itself.

As Belinda traveled between Grand Forks and Dawson that March, she noticed the first hints of spring: the gurgle of running water under the ice of the creeks, the slow shrink of snow drifts, and the occasional arctic hare scampering across the trail. It would be weeks before bears came out of hibernation or the jam of people on Bennett Lake could begin the last 600 miles of their journey. Dawson was still small enough for most of its residents to know each other by sight if not by name, but Belinda knew this would change when the new crop of stampeders arrived. More rules and less freedom lay ahead, more "civilization" and less glorious, thigh-slapping, bloody-minded liberty. It made her nostalgic even to think about it. She threw herself into a special celebration held in the Alaska Commercial Company warehouse on March 17 to celebrate St. Patrick's Day.

The sun shone and the air was crisp that day. Everyone was dolled up for the occasion: a handful of women sported summer straw hats, decorated with ribbons. "With winter footwear, mukaluks of hair seal to the knees, fur coats or parkas, and those blessed silly hats stuck on top of their heads, they were a scream," Belinda recalled years later. Somebody hollered out, "My God, a dog race!" and immediately a course was agreed and two teams of huskies harnessed. One belonged to the Mounties, the other to Belinda's friend Joe Barrette. Father Judge arrived to watch the fun. As a shot rang out from a starter's gun, the two teams raced off down Front Street. Onlookers cheered their favorite and the rest of Dawson's dog population barked fit to burst. "It was just splendid to watch those magnificent animals strain all their muscles and fight with their might for every inch of ground," Belinda remembered. "Up to the finish none of us could name the winner—they were neck and neck." When Joe's team beat the dogs that belonged to the North-West Mounted Police, the crowd bellowed with glee.

Next, the fiddles came out for square dances, waltzes, and jigs. "There was an undercurrent," according to Belinda, "of feeling like a big family that dreaded some unknown danger. I think it was covered by an old timer who couldn't sing or dance, but had to make a speech. He asked us all to have a good time while the country still belonged to us. He hoped to the Lord that the mosquitoes would chase the new arrivals back to where they came from, so we could live our own lives and be happy in God's country." The dancing continued until daylight, when coffee and pancakes were served. Then the dogs were fed, and weary miners started up the trail to the creeks.

Hibernian high spirits had not blinded Belinda to business. During the dancing, she had inveigled Joe Ladue onto the dance floor and made him an offer for a piece of land two blocks from the saloons. "I knew as much about dancing as a pet bear, and old man Ladue knew less," but they had cut a deal. Now she was ready to confound her critics and start building her three-story hotel. No question, 1898 was going to be a helluva year in Dawson City.

PART 3: MONEY TALKS

CHAPTER 14
Gumboot Diplomacy, April–August 1898

BY MID-APRIL, DAWSON CITY was clear of snow, and the sun did not set until hours after cities like Toronto and Boston had seen the last of its rays. The white silence of winter had been replaced by a symphony of sounds—the chirp of birds, the rustle of branches in the wind, the creak of ice on the rivers, and the gurgle of melted snow that turned creek beds into rushing streams. Almost overnight, wild heliotrope, starwort, fireweed, and wild roses colored the hilltops on the north bank of the Klondike.

Spring brought a smile to Belinda's square, pugnacious face. The moment had arrived when she could settle her score with Big Alex McDonald. Within days, streets, cabin floors, claim shafts, and paths to outhouses would all turn to mud, and everybody in and around Dawson would shed their winter footwear and be desperate for thigh-high rubber waders. She already had a big stock of gumboots from the cargo she and Alex had purchased in the fall—the cargo from which he had grabbed most of the foodstuffs. Now she told her men to buy up every additional pair of rubber boots they could find. In particular, they should persuade anyone working for Big Alex to give up his boots in exchange for warm wool socks, or a nip of hooch, or *anything* else he fancied. When one of her crew asked why she wanted a pile of old boots, she gave a ridiculous answer: "Because they are the best things in the world . . . to use to start a fire. In the woods if you have just a five inch square of rubber, they make the best fire starter." She also bought up every candle that she could find in Dawson.

"The men suspected something, but they didn't know what. Before long I had every boot in Alex McDonald's outfit." Alex himself had no clue what was happening; he continued to assume he could buy what he needed in Dawson. But when he finally visited one of the trading companies' warehouses, he was told that the town was clean out of gumboots and the only person who had any for sale was Miss Mulrooney at Grand Forks.

As he trudged up the trail to Grand Forks, Big Alex must have rued the day he underestimated Belinda Mulrooney. Sure enough, she had a grin as big as Alaska on her face when he asked how much she was charging for boots. The going rate, he knew, was fifteen dollars, but Belinda had other ideas. "Thirty dollars," she snapped at him, "and if you take one pair, you take cases and cases of these boots." As she recorded in her memoir, "Honest Alex McDonald, the Nova Scotian cod fish, had to buy every one."

Those rubber boots were cheap at the price. With the spring thaw came vivid reminders that Dawson was built on a swamp on top of permafrost. January's ice-hard streets had become black, reeking bogs by April. The mire on Front Street was so bad that anybody who fell off the duckboard sidewalks would sink knee, hip, or even waist deep in the stuff, as floodwater surged through town and the underlayer of frozen ground thawed into sludge. Tappan Adney, the *Harper's* magazine special correspondent, was horrified to watch buildings spring up on the unstable, melting muck "like mushrooms in a night . . . Several buildings of dressed lumber, intended for use as stores, hotels and theatres, were as handsome as one would care to see." News of the crowds now pouring over the mountain passes and building boats at Bennett Lake had prompted speculators like Joe Ladue to accelerate construction projects. Three sawmills, running night and day, were unable to keep up with the demand for lumber, which was selling for $150 to $200 per

1,000 feet. Men stood with dog teams, waiting to take the boards as they fell from the saw. Nails were so scarce that the price had risen from $1 a pound to $6. Big Alex could afford Belinda's gumboot games because he was leasing out for $8 to $12 a foot per month the riverfront land for which he was paying the government only $1 a foot.

Excitement ran high, as builders waited for the rush of newcomers looking for shelter, and miners prepared to sluice their dirt piles and collect their gold. On May 1, Bonanza Creek was clear of ice, so sluicing could begin. But the creek was soon running faster and fuller than anybody had expected. It flooded the cabins on its banks, including Tappan Adney's, and the *Harper's* correspondent discovered that it wasn't much fun "having to wade about the house in rubber boots, fighting mosquitoes, trying to cook a flapjack or make a cup of tea over the stove, and climbing in and out of a high bunk with boots on." He decided to return to town. At the junction of Bonanza and the Klondike River, he watched as a couple of huge ice floes picked up a stout wooden bridge over the Klondike "as if it had been a bunch of matches." With a roar of surging water and splintering timber, the mountain of moving ice destroyed five of the bridge's seven piers.

People started to worry. The previous year, the end of winter had been a much smoother event. In 1897, water had lapped over the wharves, but there had been nothing like the mountainous pile-up of ice that now obstructed the Yukon River. Hundreds of anxious men watched with alarm as the water flowing in from the Klondike rose rapidly behind this ice blockade. They stayed up all night, fearful the river would overflow its banks and sweep the town away. Inspector Constantine strode up and down the waterfront, pulling at his mustache and expecting the worst. He saw one mighty ice floe, forty feet wide, strike the ice barrier, half rise out of the water, then dive under it. A similar monster was not far behind: this one crunched into the barrier with a dull roar and remained there. Every now and then an empty boat sped along in the current, struck the ice jam, and was sucked under it by the river's mighty pull. It was a forcible reminder to onlookers that this was a land where water, wind, and weather could wipe out a puny human settlement in a few terrifying minutes.

But at four o'clock in the morning of May 8, the bridge of ice cracked, groaned, then slowly began to move. The shout finally went up: "Ice-out!" In a few minutes there was nothing but a wide, powerful river, as tons of water rushed onward, pushing cakes of ice as big as cabins out of its way and onto its banks. Nevertheless, the water level stayed high, transforming the streets closer to the river into channels of gumbo.

Not long after the ice had gone out, a roughly made raft with a handful of men aboard swung into view. These were not emissaries of the next crop of stampeders but some of Split-Up Island's winter residents, among them Doc Harvey and a pale, weak Jack London. As soon as Harvey had seen open water in the river, he and his pals had torn down their cabin and built a raft with the lumber. Then they had made the perilous trip downstream, knowing that they could be tipped into the frigid water at any moment if the swirling current or jagged pans of ice upended the clumsy craft. Jack, the practiced sailor, insisted on taking the main oar, or "sweep," although it was hard to grip it with hands crippled by scurvy. He cursed the water, the cold, the current, and the gravel banks with all the obscene ferocity of the oyster pirate he had once been, as the oar was swept out of his hands and the raft nearly capsized. Once Harvey had landed their frail vessel at Dawson, the waiting prospectors surged forward to hear about the state of the river. Was the ice on the Stewart out? Had they seen any boats coming down from Bennett yet?

Jack staggered ashore, wincing when he put weight on his legs. His knees were black and blue from internal bleeding in the joints. As he waited for Doc Harvey to come and help him, he looked around with dismay. Dawson in the spring of 1898 was nothing like the Golden City of the previous fall. Instead, it was "dreary, desolate Dawson, built in a swamp, flooded to the second story, populated by dogs, mosquitoes and gold-seekers." With longer daylight hours had come hotter days, and men wandered about dizzy from heat and sleeplessness. The central part of the town was under from one to five feet of water. A small river separated the Mounties' barracks from the downtown area, and Thomas Fawcett, the gold commissioner, had been forced to relocate from his Front Street cabin to a tent on higher ground. A filthy scum of garbage, logs, human and dog feces, discarded clothing, and old cans floated on the floodwaters. The stench of human sewage was almost unbearable but impossible to escape. Enterprising boatmen were charging passengers fifty cents a head to pole or paddle them down the main street. Some men had been forced to pitch tent on top of their cabins. Tappan Adney's tent was on the steep hillside above Tenth Street and from there, he told the readers of *Harper's,* "I would see a man at, say 11 p.m., push off from shore, pole over to a cabin, clamber out onto the roof, take off his shoes, walk over to a pile of blankets, unroll them, take off his coat, place it for a pillow, and turn in for a night's sleep—all in broad daylight."

Jack London was in no state to care about any of this. There was only one man he wanted to see—Father Judge. The Jesuit's reputation as a miracle worker who cured scurvy and saved lives had spread along every rocky creek and into every filthy cabin in the Klondike region. There were several doctors in Dawson, but they all charged two ounces of gold dust a visit and were, in the words of one miner, "the bummest lot you ever saw." Many were quacks with little training and no knowledge of either the causes or the remedies for scurvy, although the disease was well understood by the medical profession at the time. One insisted that it was caused by lack of sunlight, another attributed it to the consumption of partially decomposed food, and a third swore it was triggered by "thickened and vitiated" blood. Father Judge, the same miner estimated, had saved "mor'n a thousand [lives]. He was the only one of us as had time, or wasn't crazy about gold." Jack London had long ago spent all the money he had brought into the Yukon, but he would be able to pay for any medicine that the priest could give him. Harvey had raised $600 by selling the raft to lumber-hungry builders.

St. Mary's Hospital was overflowing: scurvy patients jammed the wards, the corridors, even Father Judge's own house. More hastily hammered-together beds were lined up in temporary canvas additions. When Jack first limped into the hospital "office," there was nobody in the bare, simply furnished room. He touched a bell on the table, and a tired-looking man with thin gray hair and a care-lined face appeared. Jack looked at his long, dark, shabby coat and heavy boots, then met Judge's gaze and noticed that a wonderful light seemed to shine from his eyes. For his part, Father Judge eyed his visitor thoughtfully, and sighed. The hospital's supplies of lemons, raw potatoes, and spruce-needle tea—the only sources of vitamin C available—were almost gone. But the priest did what he could for the young American, carefully rationing out grated potato and a little lemon juice to him and massaging his inflamed joints. But Judge couldn't give Jack a bed in the hospital. Luckily, Jack's friend Emil Jensen, from Split-Up Island, had pitched a tent nearby and offered him a bed.

Father Judge was more anxious than he had been for months. Jack London was the first, he knew, of the thousands who would appear now that the river was open. The priest was right to worry: 1898 was the year the stampede to the Klondike gold fields would crest at numbers that still, over a century later, seem incredible. Driven by desperation and the dream of instant wealth, over 100,000 people set off this year for one of the most remote, inhospitable places on the globe. Father Judge already recognized that alongside sourdoughs like Jack, who had arrived the previous year and wintered on distant creeks, he could expect all the newcomers who had struggled over the coastal mountains within the past few months. Stampeders were camped for more than sixty miles along the shores of lakes Lindeman, Bennett, and Tagish, impatient for the ice on the lakes to break up.

Judge had no idea of the extent of the human torrent about to hit

Dawson. Estimates of numbers rose daily—would five thousand people turn up? Ten thousand? Thirty thousand? But he did know that Dawson City was about to be invaded by an army of emaciated scarecrows with ragged beards and patched clothing. And many of them, their skin withered and discolored by malnutrition, would be sick. It wasn't simply the shortage of medical supplies that worried the priest. The hospital was deeply in debt. Judge was usually oblivious to financial matters, trusting in the Lord to provide. And he had instituted a system to cover his expenses: he promised any man who gave him two ounces of gold that for a year he would be guaranteed a bed if he needed it at St. Mary's. But the proceeds of this scheme were pitiful, since everybody knew the priest never turned anyone away.

On June 8, 1898, the first boat in the flotilla of new arrivals rounded the bend in the Yukon and steered toward the Dawson waterfront. For the next month, day and night, more and more vessels appeared—a huge armada that would eventually number over 7,000 homemade boats. There were skiffs, rowboats, primitive rafts, slender ten-foot-long canoes, graceless forty-foot freight scows—most fashioned out of green lumber by amateur builders and designed for a single, 600-mile voyage downriver to the Klondike's golden valleys. They tied up side by side along one and three-quarter miles of Big Alex's waterfront, soon forming a floating platform of vessels five or six deep.

Each morning the priest walked down to the wharf to see the motley throng of new arrivals, most of whom were exhausted by their travels, stunned by Dawson's squalor, and too listless to do much more than stare at each other. There were, as Tappan Adney recorded, "Australians with upturned sleeves and a swagger; young Englishmen in golf-stockings and tweeds; would-be miners in Mackinaws and rubber boots, or heavy, high-laced shoes; Japanese, negroes—and women too, everywhere." Some pitched their tents on their scows; others slept in the open on higher ground, under robes or blankets. "The crowd of newcomers," Judge wrote to his brother, "is increasing every day and

*In the spring of 1898, homemade boats formed a floating platform for almost two
miles along Dawson's waterfront. The town was so crowded that new arrivals
pitched tents over their vessels.*

giving our little town the appearance of a large city, the street being
too crowded to be comfortable."

Father Judge was among those bargaining for fresh supplies. At first,
the prices were out of sight because enterprising merchants had raced
ahead of the crowd to get top dollar for their goods. The first case of thirty
dozen fresh eggs sold for $300. Potatoes were $10 a pound. Oranges, lemons, and apples sold for $5 each. All winter, Dawson's millionaires had
had nothing to spend their newfound wealth on. Now they would splash
out on any novelty. One entrepreneur traded kittens for an ounce of gold
each; another made $15 on an ancient newspaper used as food wrap.
Belinda Mulrooney could afford the food prices for her hotel because she
could pass on the cost to her customers. But the desperate, ailing men in
St. Mary's Hospital couldn't afford them. The priest realized he would
have to go "on the beg," as the miners put it, to get what he wanted.

One of his first targets was a young American who strolled into the hospital because he had heard that his friend Henry was sick with scurvy there. Judge met the newcomer and asked him with twinkling eyes, "I don't suppose, now, you've got such things as potatoes with you?" The American was astonished by the question. "Potatoes!" he exclaimed, then added, "I suppose you are hankering for a mess of potatoes after the food famine of the past winter." The priest was equally astonished by this suggestion. "Why, bless your heart, no," he replied. "I don't want potatoes. But I've got a big houseful of fellows here with scurvy, and medicine has been about gone for months. Potatoes would fix 'em though." The visitor had no potatoes, so Judge told him where to find his friend Henry. As the young man started up the stairs, Judge called after him, "You want to cheer him up till I can get some medicine or potatoes for him. We must keep them alive on hope, you know."

The priest's brother, Charles Judge, heard about this encounter from the young man himself, although the latter never gave his name. But he did tell Charles that he found his friend Henry in a small, second-story ward with fifteen other scurvy patients. The walls were untrimmed lumber with moss and rags stuffed into the cracks. The men, clad in shabby, stained underwear, lay listlessly on crudely made beds, covered in patched and soiled blankets. Henry's first question was "I don't suppose you've brought any potatoes?" Once that sad matter was dealt with, conversation moved on to the priest himself. The visitor allowed that Father Judge appeared to be a popular sort of fellow. "Popular!" protested Henry. "Don't use the word 'popular' here. He's the finest man that God ever put a soul into. Where'd we all have been this winter without him, I'd like to know. He's just killing himself trying to take care of everybody."

Henry's visitor, who had no time for the Roman Catholic Church, looked skeptical, but his misgivings were swept away. Henry stated bluntly that religious affiliations were irrelevant. "Why, God bless me, here's a bunch of sixteen of us here now in the room, and not a blessed

Catholic in the lot. But Father Judge is making Catholics fast. Never preaches or talks doctrine or forms of faith, you know, unless you ask him or show him your mind is uneasy on that score. No! He just does all a mortal man can do for you, and evidently wishes he could do more. Then he jollies you along and goes to church, and you feel you'd give one of your two useless legs if you could follow him. Whist! Here he comes."

The young man watched how each patient sat up and lifted his face as the Jesuit walked into the room. "Oddly enough there was a smile on every sick face; only the priest looked dull and old." Father Judge immediately made his way to a bed in the center of the room and began to talk softly to the desperately sick patient who lay there, swollen with scurvy. The newcomer watched the priest's solemn face light up with an inner glow as he spoke softly to his patient: "I've been praying for you. If it is the good Lord's will, you're going to get well. The medicine is beginning to come down the river. Your good old mother is going to see you again if prayers and medicine can avail. Say your prayers, my boy. I'm going down to the chapel again, and I'll leave your case in good hands." The man's eyes filled with tears as Judge stroked his hair from his forehead, and he grabbed Judge's hand and raised it to his lips before burying his face in his pillow.

Judge made his way from bed to bed, rearranging one man's pillow, tucking another man's feet under the threadbare bedding. "I've got good news for you all," he announced. "There's a whole scow-load of potatoes just landed! What do you think of that! Now I do hope the good Lord will not require me to steal them." There was a moment of silence, then a chorus of laughter. Judge assured his patients that he wouldn't steal them: "We'll just pray . . . It's quicker." After another quick tour of the room, "petting the big fellows like great children," he prepared to leave. First however, assuming a Baltimore Irish accent, he said, "Now, don't ye all be after getting down-hearted. The boats do be coming in by the hundreds, and I'm going out now to have them send ye down what's good for ye." His departure was the signal for a flood of stories about him from men who knew the priest was the only barrier between them and death. Years later, the newcomer told Judge's brother, "I have never in all my eventful life listened to such a stream of adulation for a living man."

As people and supplies continued to stream into Dawson, prices of provisions dropped. Soon Father Judge could buy dried milk for $1.00 a can, a sack of flour for $3.00, fruit for $1.00 a piece, potatoes for $0.50 a pound, tinned mutton for $2.50 a pound, and eggs for $3.00 a dozen. The waterfront took on the appearance of a fairground, with market stands for the sale of vegetables, clothing, furs, moccasins, shoes, groceries, meat, and jewelry. "In the brief space of a few days there seemed to be nothing that could not be purchased in Dawson," wrote Tappan Adney, "from fresh grapes to an opera glass, from a safety-pin to an ice-cream freezer."

Suddenly, it was carnival time. The floodwaters ebbed, the saloons restocked, and a cluster of hookers' "cribs" sprang up behind Second Avenue. In Dawson's bars, newcomers were dazzled by descriptions of rich pan-outs from sluicing operations on the creeks. Up at the Grand Forks Hotel, triumphant prospectors arrived from their sluicing operations staggering under the weight of filled leather bags, Bull Durham tobacco tins, and old jelly jars. Despite the punishing efforts required to find the dust and nuggets, the miners were astonishingly casual about their riches, flinging them at Belinda Mulrooney's manager, Walker Gilmer, for safekeeping. "Those gold pokes were the worry of Walker's life," Belinda recalled. He refused to take them unless the miners put their names on so he could tell them apart. "I got sick of the dust—would rather see a pile of cord wood than sacks of gold dust. They were mean to handle—heavy and hard to pack. They were like a piece of lead when you put 'em on your back—would work into your backbone and shoulder." The gold was usually taken out in a batch by mule or dog train down to Dawson. At the start of the season there was no bank in

Dawson, so the Alaska Commercial Company and the North American Transportation and Trading Company continued to accept the sacks of dust and nuggets until they could all be shipped Outside. Unless, of course, the owner of a couple of those sacks decided he had earned a little fling and withdrew his poke from the trading company's safe. In those cases, that particular stash was likely to disappear at the faro tables.

Early on the morning of Sunday, June 5, the giddy high living was sharply interrupted. Cries of "Fire!" rang out—an ominous sound in a town of tents and resinous log cabins. People rushed out of the dance halls and bars as the roar of flames competed with the fiddles and laughter. A column of smoke rose at the north end. Was the hospital on fire? Hundreds of men grabbed buckets and blankets from their cabins and ran toward St. Mary's. It was the Church of the Immaculate Conception, not the hospital, that blazed fiercely—but the two buildings were so close that the latter was in danger. While one work party carried the sick out on beds and stretchers, another formed a line and passed pail after pail of water from the river to those on top of the hospital, who poured it over blankets stretched over the roof to douse any sparks.

At first, Father Judge stood in the flickering firelight, his thin face contorted with anguish like a figure in an El Greco painting. The edifice for which he had labored so hard, the altar he had carved himself, everything necessary for religious services, was gone. And the worst of it was that it was his fault. Late the previous night he had gone over to the church to say Compline, the final service of the day, and he had stuck a candle on a wooden support. In the midst of his prayers, somebody had run over from the hospital to tell him a patient was dying. In his haste to administer Extreme Unction, he had forgotten all about the candle. Now all that was left of Dawson's first Catholic church was a smoldering ruin. "My nice church," he wrote to his brother two weeks later, "in which I took so much pride, all the altar furniture, vestments, flowers, lace curtains, and everything for Mass and Benediction were burned."

Yet before dawn had broken, the priest's expression had improved markedly. "Imagine my surprise," one onlooker wrote afterward, "when, espying Father Judge, I beheld the only gleam of tranquility and unconcern—yea, even mirthfulness—to be witnessed in that entire assemblage. Indeed the dear Father's features seemed radiant with emotions of glad cheer, as he flitted about among the almost panic-stricken [staff] of the hospital and, by words and actions, made light of their intensely anxious concerns."

What had caused this mood change? When asked, Father Judge explained, "I had promised our Lord to erect for Him a more commodious temple, and he probably thought I would fail to keep my promise unless the old and inadequate building were destroyed." Judge's saintly reputation was so pervasive that most people accepted this virtuous explanation, but he was being disingenuous. In the middle of the hubbub of shouts, screams, hissing flames, and falling roof timbers, Alex McDonald had whispered to the priest that he would assume the whole expense of rebuilding. As Judge phrased it in the letter to his brother, "I am building a new church three times as large as the old one, and one of my new friends will pay for it."

The success of the Jesuit mission in Dawson City was sweet reward for "the Old Priest," as he was often called these days. Working alone, he had won the respect of a hard-living, hard-drinking community as he fulfilled God's purpose. He was truly oblivious to the earthly riches that his congregation contributed to the new church, to be called St. Mary's Church—but others weren't. There is nothing like a gold mine for triggering interest and competition. When the richness of the Klondike gold fields had first been confirmed, various Americans had asserted that they lay on American territory. Now that the wealth of Dawson City's residents was established, it caught the attention of other Christian churches and Roman Catholic orders.

The Anglican Church, which had been active in the Yukon for more than three decades, now had six ordained priests in the area, including, in Forty Mile, the redoubtable Bishop William Bompas, who had first arrived in the North in 1865. It also had a small church in Dawson City, which boasted window glass held in place by dough—until the warm weather arrived, the dough rose, and the windows fell out. The Presbyterian Church was busy establishing missions at Skagway, Bennett Lake, in Dawson itself, and on the creeks, and planned a second hospital for Dawson: the Good Samaritan Hospital would open in August 1898. The Methodists and the Salvation Army were also on their way north. But these were all Protestant initiatives. Unknown to Father Judge, within the Roman Catholic Church a turf war was brewing, based as much on financial as on spiritual concerns.

The Jesuits' firm hold on Dawson's Catholic population had started to irritate a smaller, poorer, French-speaking Roman Catholic order, the Oblates. Oblate missionaries were already active among native peoples in the Canadian north, and Rome regarded Alaska as Jesuit territory and Canada as Oblate. When Father Judge first strayed east along the Yukon into Canada, his activities had not aroused much comment because this distant, icy region was thought to contain only an aboriginal population and a few hundred prospectors. But things were different now. As Bishop Emile Grouard, the Oblate superior of the Mackenzie River district in Canada's Northwest and vicar apostolic of Athabasca-Mackenzie, wrote, "Our Mackenzie missions are very poor; the Klondike mines will provide us with plenty of funds." Grouard's archbishop, Monsignor Louis Philippe Adelard Langevin, Archbishop of St. Boniface, made the same point in a letter to the superior general of the Oblates: "The Yukon could provide us with precious resources for our missions in the North if, as I hope, you wish to help them." (Le Yukon peut procurer des resources précieuses à nos chères missions du Nord si, comme je l'espère, vous voulez bien aller à leur secours.)

The first sign of ecclesiastical rivalry for Father Judge came with the arrival of the steamer *Portus B. Weare,* only seven days after his church had burned down. He was just finishing his morning rounds at the hospital when he saw a hesitant younger man in a black cassock walking toward him from the river. This was Father Joseph-Camille Lefebvre, an Oblate who had been working on the northernmost edge of Canada, above the Arctic Circle, in the Mackenzie River delta area. Father Lefebvre had been reassigned to Dawson City by Bishop Grouard because his mission in the Far North had been a spectacular failure. American whalers who had sailed into the Beaufort Sea had undermined his efforts with the Inuit by introducing alcohol and contagious diseases.

As far as Judge was concerned, Lefebvre's arrival was literally a godsend. The newcomer brought with him a traveling chapel, including Communion wine and vestments, so the older priest could once again say Mass. He resumed his regular Sunday services in a tent under the Moosehide Slide. But three weeks later, three more Oblates arrived: Father Pierre Edmond Gendreau, Father Alphonse Marie Joseph Desmarais, and Brother Marie Auguste Jude Dumas. Suddenly, Dawson City had five Roman Catholic priests, but four of them were French-speaking Canadians in a primarily American town where little French was heard on Front Street. It would have been an uncomfortable balance at the best of times, and the fact that the English-speaking American Jesuit was widely regarded as a saint whom the Canadian Oblates wanted to dislodge didn't help. "You would find it hard to believe how delicate and embarrassing our position is," Father Gendreau wrote to Bishop Grouard. (Vous ne sauriez croire combien la position était délicate, embarrassante et embarrassée.)

The next few months were a pantomime of money squabbles dressed up as ecclesiastical dialogue. Father Judge's Jesuit superior, the Reverend Father J. B. René, made the long trek from Juneau, in Alaska, all the way to Rome, to petition the Pope to transfer the whole of the Yukon watershed to the Jesuits' Apostolic Prefecture of Alaska. The Pope refused, so Father René shot off a message to Father Judge telling him to stop all building activity. Then he turned round and traveled 11,000 miles back to North America and north to the Yukon to assert his authority. He arrived in Dawson on July 28, intent on settling accounts and escorting Father Judge back to Alaska. A sharp-elbowed negotiator, Father René announced to the Oblates that the Jesuits were ready to leave as soon as the Oblate mission had assumed responsibility for all debts incurred, finished all building projects, and paid compensation for the land and building work already done. In response, the Oblates pointed out that the Jesuits had not used their own funds for Father Judge's mission: the hospital and the church had been financed locally by both Catholics and Protestants, thanks to Father Judge's personal charisma. But Father René brushed aside the argument that these institutions therefore belonged to the citizens of Dawson themselves. Father Judge, he pointed out, had paid $300 out of his order's funds for the land on which the church and the hospital stood. That land was now worth somewhere between $50,000 and $60,000. Did the Oblates really expect the Jesuits to hand it over for free?

The situation was complicated by the much-anticipated arrival of the Sisters of St. Ann, to help Father Judge in the hospital. Suddenly the north end of town was aflutter with cassocks, habits, and crosses. The black-robed nuns couldn't sleep in their designated hospital wing because their beds were occupied by patients, so they moved into the parsonage that had been earmarked for the Oblates. And Father Judge, with quiet intensity, made it clear to his superior that he was most reluctant to abandon his flock. Dawson was his *vocation*. He had ignored Father René's instruction to stop all building activity, arguing that the latter didn't know that the original church had burned down. Now he mused about whether Big Alex's benevolence would continue if he himself disappeared.

Father Gendreau was a very different personality from Father René. Besides having the Pope (if not God) on his side, the Oblate was by nature a peacemaker. He solved the compensation issue by avoiding it. He requested that the Old Priest be allowed to stay in Dawson as chaplain of the hospital, over which he would exert both temporal and

By 1903, the capacious new Roman Catholic church and the three-story hospital would dominate the north end of Dawson City.

spiritual authority. This allowed Judge to continue administering to his American parishioners and to see the completion of the new church. Father René was not happy to be outsmarted by Canadian Oblates, but he knew when he was defeated. After giving Father Judge firm instructions to begin no new construction, to settle all his debts, and to leave Dawson when the river opened the following spring, Father René returned to Jesuit headquarters in Juneau.

From now on, Father Judge preached and sang Mass every third Sunday. Father Gendreau welcomed him as a colleague, partly because the Oblates had some difficulty communicating with their flock. In Gendreau's optimistic estimates, the Dawson area contained about 15,000 Roman Catholics, half of them French Canadians. He probably exaggerated the numbers, but the Catholics who did turn up for Mass each Sunday were mainly English speaking and couldn't understand a word of the Oblates' French sermons. So the Old Priest's status as the public voice of Roman Catholicism in Dawson remained unchallenged, and his congregations were twice as large as the Oblates'. The younger priests spent more of their time hiking up the creeks, administering to French Canadians within the cramped log cabins on their claims. A fifth Oblate who arrived reported that he had said Mass in one cabin where "sixty miners were packed in, one pressing against another . . . During the whole mass, they were obliged to stay standing or lying on their beds, because they couldn't move."

Perhaps the happiest day in Father Judge's life arrived on August 21, 1898. His superior, Father René had left; his own position within Dawson was confirmed; he finally had medical help in the hospital; and today he was preaching at the opening of his grand new church. A congregation of over 500 people looked reverently at the much-loved figure standing before the new altar. The Jesuit's deeply lined face, with its sunken cheeks and wispy gray hair, radiated piety: his hands, with their broken nails and flaky skin, were clasped so tight that the gnarled blue veins were taut on the surface; his voice, with its Irish lilt audible through the quiet message, was low and steady. He was so gaunt that his black robes almost engulfed him and his vestments hung limply over them. When he preached, he stood erect, hands immobile, and spoke quietly about God's will. "He always said he was no preacher," an observer later recalled, but "every word that fell from his lips sank into his hearers' hearts . . . I do not think the sublime character of the Mass was ever better impressed upon any of us in the grand cathedrals of the States."

On this day, Father Judge had taken as his text "Remember man, the end for which you were created." He knew he had been created to save lives and souls in the Yukon, and nothing would deflect him from that goal. When typhoid broke out that month, he immediately began building a third story on St. Mary's Hospital, notwithstanding Father René's directive that there be no more construction. In order to pay for the extension, he sold a piece of church property—although it was the Oblates', not his, to sell. When Father Gendreau, concerned about the church's mounting debts, proposed that worshippers should pay rent for their pews, Father Judge was so appalled that the suggestion was abandoned. Everybody else in Dawson City was obsessed with accumulating wealth in their lifetime. Father Judge was interested only in spiritual gold. The mission's money problems continued to swell, though as long as the Saint of Dawson was around, they were not allowed to seem important. But would such a frail man survive another arctic winter?

CHAPTER 12
Jack's Escape from the Yukon, June 1898

JACK LONDON WAS STILL only twenty-two, yet scurvy had drained his youthful vigor, destroyed his teeth, and left him as bent and slow as men three times his age. His stubbled cheeks were sunken: his skin was gray with ingrown dirt and malnutrition. He spent the first few days in Dawson close to St. Mary's Hospital, where he chatted with fellow patients and watched Father Judge do his rounds. To his relief, the Jesuit's potato peelings and sips of spruce beer slowed the progress of the disease. Spurts of Jack's irrepressible energy began to bubble, and he was soon strong enough to earn fifteen dollars a day helping Doc Harvey rescue floating logs from the Yukon, then tow them behind a rowboat to a mill.

With improved health came reawakened curiosity. More than twenty saloons lined Front Street these days. At night, the blue-eyed Californian was drawn to dance halls like the Monte Carlo and saloons like the M & M, to watch the latest crop of entertainers and croupiers. Six months of celibacy on Split-Up Island made Jack impatient for female company, the raunchier the better. "How good it was," wrote Charmian London in her biography of her husband, "to see a woman's face again." The women reciprocated by making a fuss of the ailing but still charming young man. So what if his hands shook, his nose constantly bled, his breath stank and his teeth were so loose that he could barely chew meat? He *listened*. He made girls who dealt with male contempt every day feel valued. The women entertained him, as he sat slumped by the bar, surrounded by men he had met the previous November as well as new acquaintances. Edward Morgan, the miner who wrote *God's Loaded Dice*, watched him "saturating himself with the spirit and lore of the Arctic as he caught it from his sourdough drinking companions."

Belinda Mulrooney often caught sight of the young man limping into a bar, on the hunt for drinking buddies. She had no idea he had literary ambitions as he never hung out with newspaper reporters. "London was not received there as one of the writers," she recalled in her memoirs. "He was one of the wrecks of the saloons." On Split-Up Island, Jack had gone for weeks without alcohol, but now he was back in a world he loved: a world of "big-chested, open-air men" where, as he put it in *John Barleycorn*, "drink was the badge of manhood." The lonely claustrophobia of an ice-encrusted cabin was behind him. As a youngster on the Oakland wharves, he had learned the rituals of the drinking life—the need to buy a round for companions to prove you are one of them, the courtesy of buying a drink for the bartender, the drinking songs, the sentimentality of midnight drunks. But Belinda had no time for an almost penniless young drinker, and he had no interest in a woman who dressed like a schoolteacher. For each of them, there were far more attractive companions.

Dawson City came into its own in the summer of 1898 as the wildest, noisiest, roughest frontier town, in the middle of the bleakest landscape on the American continent. A year earlier, Bill Haskell had been astonished to see the population reach 4,000 and saloons spring up along Front Street. By the end of May, the number on the cramped mudflat had swollen to 10,000 and continued its rapid rise. Jack London watched hundreds of people step onto the Dawson waterfront every day. Lots close to the river sold for $20,000 and the cheapest room rented for $100 a week, almost twenty times the price for a room Outside. Most newcomers couldn't afford to stay in one of the newly built log hotels, which hid cramped rooms and primitive amenities behind false fronts and grandiose names like the Criterion, the Pavilion, the Montreal Hotel, the Pacific, the Pioneer, or Eldorado House. Instead, weary stampeders were forced to remain on their boats or pitch tents and build cabins on the other side of the Klondike River (the old Hān fishing camp, renamed Klondike City) or across the Yukon in a sprawling new settlement called West Dawson. Between shelters of every conceivable shape and size, from sketchy lean-tos to circus marquees and cavernous warehouses, there were heaps of supplies, piles of mining equipment and stoves, and great stacks of timber.

The Yukon River had fallen to normal levels once the ice jams downriver had melted, so the floodwaters had receded from Dawson's streets. But Front Street remained a muddy morass, and men, women, and dogs struggled to keep their footing on sidewalks of narrow planking so they didn't plunge into the mire. The main thoroughfare was lined with restaurants, bars, brothels, gambling halls, stores, dance halls, and saloons. Belinda's new three-story hotel, the Fairview, was being hammered together on the corner of Front and Princess. By Outside standards, prices were outrageous: a haircut that cost twenty-five cents in Chicago cost $1.50, while coffee and a waffle that cost a nickel in Seattle cost twenty-five cents in the North.

Jack London quickly learned that Dawson's demimonde had kept pace with the town's growth in size and vivacity. He loved pleasure palaces like the famous Monte Carlo. This season brought a popular pair of dance hall sisters named Jacqueline and Rosalinde, better known as Vaseline and Glycerine. Despite the flood of boulevardiers and good-time girls, etiquette in the dance halls hadn't improved since 1897. Men continued to wear rough mackinaws and rubber boots as they whirled the dance hall girls around. The girls, according to Edward Morgan, were an even rougher bunch than the previous year: "painted, coarse-featured, loud-voiced, brazen hussies." The son of a wealthy New York businessman, Morgan never warmed to the assertive women of the North, who drank, fought, and laughed at his pretensions. "They were

Dawson's streets were paved not with gold but with mud as thick as gumbo.

rouged within an inch of their lives," he noted, "and many of them wore their hair short. Their skirts were abbreviated, their forms uncorseted, their frocks close-fitting . . . Furthermore, they smoked cigarettes unashamedly and tossed off whisky neat with all the ease and *sang-froid* of a he-man sourdough, with a copper-lined stomach. Their badinage and persiflage, the wit and the wisecracks they exchanged with their male companions, were all below-the-girdle stuff."

"Below-the-girdle stuff" was music to Jack London's ears. Jack embraced the low-lifes. He had known poverty and insecurity himself; he had watched women fight to survive in the slums and on the docks of San Francisco. Charmian London, who knew all too well her husband's enjoyment of riotous parties and gregarious survivors, wrote after Jack's death about his admiration for the "grit of women who . . . had entered the frozen territory." He had spent his youth railing against the establishment, so he appreciated women who challenged convention—even if, in many cases, such women were at the mercy of their pimps. One performer who appeared in Dawson this spring was a colorful, tough character called Freda Maloof, who advertised herself as the "Turkish Whirlwind Danseuse." Freda's act consisted of a bump-and-grind belly dance with lots of wispy veils, bare flesh, and suggestive patter. It was based, she claimed, on a performance by an exotic dancer known as Little Egypt at the 1893 Columbian Exposition (the same exposition where Belinda Mulrooney had made her first fortune). A contemporary described Little Egypt as having "more moves in bed than water on a hot griddle, and her gyrations could make a grown man cry," but Freda Malouf's belly dance apparently outstripped Little Egypt's. It was so shocking that even the Mounties, who usually turned a blind eye to outrageous acts, shut her down. Jack London loved Freda's "muscle dance" and relished the dancer's wicked appeal. High-spirited Freda would appear twice as "a certain Greek dancer who played with men as children did with bubbles" in Jack's fiction, but in both stories she is a stereotypical "tart with a heart," who shows greater decency than women of higher status.

As Bill Haskell had noticed, the Mounties paid more attention to gambling halls than dance halls because fights were more likely to break out among gamblers. Owners were instructed that no person under the influence of alcohol should play; players were warned that cheats would be fined or run out of town. This didn't stop miners losing their hard-won fortunes on the turn of a card or a roll of the dice. A man who won might ring the bell over the bar as he announced, "Free drinks all round!" Men would come pouring through the saloon doors. In the saloons, miners fresh from a clean-up tossed nuggets into the cuspidors and laughed as down-and-outers fished them out of tobacco-flavored saliva.

Jack had no money to gamble, but like Bill Haskell before him, he enjoyed the theatricality of the faro tables and roulette wheels. And like Bill, he too enjoyed the sight one evening of cocky little Swiftwater Gates playing pool for $100 a game. Gates didn't stand a chance. He was

In the summer of 1898, dancers like "Snake Hips Lulu" gave Dawson City its reputation as "the town that never sleeps."

playing against a shark who, according to Edward Morgan, "was known up and down the Yukon as one who could charm a pool ball to do his will." Gates lost game after game and was soon down several thousand dollars. But he didn't blink: he was in the limelight and loving it.

Throughout May, Jack London soaked up atmosphere. He picked up the tough, ironic humor of the big guys at the bar, who regarded whiners with disdain. He watched chained-up malamutes and huskies snarling at each other, idle now that spring had come. He heard tales of murder and thievery on distant Klondike creeks. He listened to Father Judge describe the night he spent on the trail, when he had to light a fire and fight off frostbite. At some point during these weeks, his literary ambitions revived and he began to make mental note of anecdotes that he could transform into vivid stories, with the excitement intensified, the terrors embellished.

But there was still not enough vitamin C in Jack's diet to eliminate scurvy, and in early June, Father Judge urged him to leave Dawson.

The lower Yukon was ice free and navigable, the Jesuit argued, and Jack could float with almost no effort the 1,400 miles to St. Michael on the coast, where he would find the fresh vegetables his body craved.

Father Judge's advice was all Jack needed to hear. He had not struck gold, he was impatient to return to writing, and he felt cut off from life beyond the Klondike mud. Like most of the Americans in Dawson, he had been fired up when he heard that the United States had declared war on Spain a few months earlier in support of Cuban liberation. How was the war going? And what about Theo Durrant, the San Francisco medical student accused of two gruesome murders the previous year? Was he hanged? Who was the 1898 heavyweight boxing champion— Gentleman Jim Corbett, "Sailor" Tom Sharkey, or Bob Fitzsimmons, "the Freckled Wonder"? Jack wasn't the only person hungry for news in a town that still had no newspaper of its own. One day he saw a man clad in a dirty red shirt and high rubber boots standing on a wagon and in loud, penetrating tones reading a front-page story about the Spanish– American war from a copy of the *Seattle Times* that was several weeks old. The throng cheered and cheered, while an American began singing the Union anthem from Civil War days: "Marching through Georgia." The newspaper reader then announced that the rest of the paper would be read aloud in Pioneers Hall—admittance, one dollar. In fifteen minutes, the hall was crowded with about 500 men, who patiently stood for an hour while the enterprising owner read to them more war news, accounts of suicides, business announcements, and columns of small ads. The performance was so popular that there was an encore the following day. Jack would use this incident, like so many others, in his fiction. But it reinforced his determination to get out.

Soon large paddle-steamers would arrive in Dawson, and then load up with passengers for the return journey to St. Michael. But Jack couldn't wait that long, and he didn't have the $150 needed for a deck passage to the river's mouth. Besides, he had more than enough nautical skills to navigate a small sailboat in the current of a vast river. So two days after he had watched Father Judge's church burn down, Jack set off in a "home-made, weak-kneed and leaky" little skiff along with two new friends called John Thorson and Charlie Taylor. He had no poke of gold, but he knew he had something more valuable for his literary ambitions—a gold mine of stories. And now, for the first time, he started scribbling notes each day.

"We start at 4 p.m. for Outside," reads the first entry in his diary. "Last words—sailor and miner friends—parting injunctions, 'see so and so, & such a one'—love and business messages—frankly expressed envy of many who had decided to remain—Dawson slowly fading away. Pitched camp at 10 p.m.—no bunk in boat—slight rain . . . broad daylight all the time."

It was not a comfortable journey through the Yukon's slushy, cold waters. For the first few days the skies were gray, then the weather turned unbearably hot. They couldn't buy sugar, milk, or butter in the first few mining camps they passed. But Jack was enthused with purpose: his notes were the basis for an article he would complete as soon as he got home. His account of the voyage would appear in the *Buffalo Express* two years later, entitled "From Dawson to the Sea." According to this article, Jack and his companions "had sworn to make of this a pleasure trip, in which all labor was to be performed by gravitation, and all profit reaped by ourselves. And what a profit it was to us who had been accustomed to pack great loads on our backs or drag all day at the sleds for a paltry 25 or 30 miles. We now hunted, played cards, smoked, ate and slept, sure of our six miles an hour, or our 144 a day." Charlie Taylor was designated cook for the voyage, while Jack and John Thorson shared rotating watches. All three joined in a moose hunt on June 9. Sighting a moose at the water's edge, the men sprang to arms in the hope of bagging some red meat. Since their arsenal consisted of an ax and an ancient blunderbuss loaded with birdshot, it was a vain hope. A gunshot succeeded only in scaring the moose back into the woods.

Swarms of mosquitoes plagued the travelers. Jack's diary is dotted

Jack London and two friends made the 1,400-mile voyage down the Yukon in one of the leaky, single-masted skiffs built by many stampeders at Bennett Lake.

with such entries as "mosquitoes thick," "Mosquitos make a demonstration in force," "Put up netting and fooled mosquitoes," "John driven out of bed by mosquitos," "Evening burned smudges" (smoky fires to drive the insects away), "Bite me through overalls and heavy underwear." The men smeared their faces with clay for protection. In his diary, Jack began to enjoy shaping his experiences into stories: "One night badly bitten under netting—couldn't vouch for it but John watched them & said they rushed the netting in a body, one gang holding up the edge while a second gang crawled under. Charlie swore that he has seen several of the largest ones pull the mesh apart & let a small one squeeze through. I have seen them with their proboscis bent and twisted after an assault on sheet iron stove."

Jack frequently took the evening watch. Drifting down the river at midnight in broad daylight, he listened to the song of robins, the drumming of partridge, the croak of ravens, the cries of loons, plovers, geese, and seagulls. He made notes of which incidents might be developed into articles for such publications as *Outing* magazine and *Youth's Companion*. He rehearsed descriptions of the scenery (trees "stand stretching their bleached limbs heavenward, mute witnesses to the Ice God's wrath") and catalogued the birdlife ("killdeers, plover, ducks . . . martins, owls, hawks").

Most days, the men saw evidence of other humans. On the riverbanks were prospectors' huts, ghost towns like Forty Mile and Circle City, and as they traveled closer to the Bering Sea, abandoned Russian settlements. On the river were more vessels than the Yukon had ever seen before, all heading toward Dawson loaded with stampeders, building supplies, provisions and, in one case, six tons of whiskey. ("Hot time in Dawson as a consequence," Jack predicted.) Some of the boats had set off for Dawson City the previous fall and been caught in the ice. About 1,800 stampeders had allowed themselves to be persuaded that this "all-water" route from Seattle to the Klondike via St. Michael was feasible, but only fifty had reached the gold fields before freeze-up in 1897. The rest had paid for their gullibility with a winter nightmare— iced in, starving and helpless, on the lower Yukon.

Still, for hours on end the voyage seemed little more than a blur of swirling currents, piles of driftwood, and distant hills. For a rookie writer, itching to shape experience into adventure, there was little to note. The only excitement came when the men caught sight of Indian settlements on the riverbank. The Yukon flowed through the territories of Gwich'in, Tanana, and Koyukuk peoples, and Jack scribbled journal entries about "children playing, bucks skylarking, squaws giggling and flirting, dogs fighting etc . . . Banks lined with birch bark canoes, nets in evidence everywhere, everything ready for fish." Salmon weighing as much as 110 pounds were being pulled in, then immediately gutted and hung over smoking fires.

At a Tanana camp called Muklukyeto, the three men waded through sprawling babies and fighting dogs to the entrance of a large log structure where a celebration of the spring salmon run was being held. Jack later described in his *Buffalo Express* article how "the long, low room was literally packed with dancers. There was no light, no ventilation, save through the crowded doorway, and, in the semi-darkness, strapping bucks and wild-eyed squaws sweated, howled and reveled in a dance which defies description." It was a scene made for an explorer hungry for exotica, and Jack relished the idea that he was one of the first non-Tanana people to see the spectacle. To his chagrin, he wasn't. Through the smoke and heat, he caught sight of another intruder. In his journal, he recorded his irritation at seeing "the fair, bronzed skin & blonde mustache of the ubiquitous adventurous Anglo Saxon, always at home in any environment." When he described the same incident in the *Buffalo Express* article, he admitted to "disappointment on discovering that even here, 1,000 miles beyond the uttermost bounds of civilization, the adventurous white man already had penetrated . . . A glance demonstrated how thoroughly at home he was." Elsewhere, he noticed "traces of white blood among the papooses everywhere apparent."

In a Koyukuk village, Jack bargained for some beadwork with a young woman. In his journal he described her as a "squaw three quarter breed with a white baby (girl) (2 yrs.) such as would delight any American mother. Unusual love she lavished upon it. An erstwhile sad expression. Talked good English." She told Jack that her child's father had deserted her; Jack flirtatiously offered to be her man and bring her flour, bacon, blankets, and clothes from St. Michael. The young woman was more honest—and realistic—than the young, sex-starved Californian. Her response was unequivocal: "No, I marry Indian, white man always leave Indian girl." Jack revealed his fundamental insensitivity toward such a woman when he expanded the incident for his *Buffalo Express* article. Striving for solemnity (and overdoing it), he noted, "In the course of trading with natives, one soon learns much of the sickness and misery with which their lives are girt . . . In the most cursory intercourse, one stumbles upon pathetic little keynotes that serve as inklings to the solemn chords of heartache with which their lives vibrate."

Jack London was not an Indian hater like Bill Haskell, but he shared the assumption of Anglo-Saxon superiority common among his contemporaries. During those long, cold weeks in the icy cabin on Split-Up Island, Jack had enjoyed Rudyard Kipling on the British Empire, Charles Darwin on evolution, and Karl Marx on the oppression of the working classes. Now, during the endless, light-filled evenings floating down the river, he attempted to filter the intense experiences of the past twelve months through the perspectives he had absorbed from these writers. He had the self-taught man's weakness for (in E. L. Doctorow's words) "the idea that Explains Everything," and managed simultaneously to embrace two mutually exclusive ideas—egalitarian ideals and white supremacy. He scribbled in his Yukon journal, "Indian seems unable to comprehend the fact that he can never get the better of the white man," and the following year would write to a friend, "The Teutonic is the dominant race of the world . . . The Negro races, the mongrel races . . . are of bad blood." Yet he also harbored the idea of the "noble savage" from a previous era. He took note of aspects of Indian culture that had allowed the different peoples to survive a harsh climate and unforgiving land: their respect for elders, their warrior instincts, their strength and resilience. Although he never identified with them, he sympathized with the challenges met by peoples who had lived for centuries in the North.

Eleven days after leaving Dawson, the three men arrived at a little town called Anvik. By now, Jack London was in terrible shape: "Right leg drawing up, can no longer straighten it, even in walking must put my whole weight on toes . . . almost entirely crippled . . . from my waist down." A local trader offered fresh potatoes and a can of tomatoes; Jack almost wept as he gulped them down. "These few raw potatoes & tomatoes are worth more to me at the present stage of the game than an Eldorado claim—What wots it, though a man gain illimitable wealth & lose his own life?" He felt strength return to his body and the ache in his joints diminish. He recognized that the gift of potatoes was a generous gesture from his hosts: "Quite a sacrifice on their part. White through and through."

The following day, the travelers reached the Holy Cross Mission, the Jesuit headquarters where Father Judge had begun his Alaskan mission. They watched a group of Indian girls playing in a schoolyard and others weaving nets, tanning leather, making rope out of bark, and sewing mukluks out of buckskin. "Indians have better appearance—always do around missions," Jack scribbled. The next challenge was to locate the correct passage through the vast wastes of the Yukon delta. The men took no guide, and if they had chosen the wrong channel through the thousands of islands, they could have lost days and risked their lives. "Threading the maze, keeping to the right," Jack jotted in his journal, as he navigated the 126 miles to the delta's northernmost outlet at Kotlik. "No signs of human life. No white man since Holy Cross Mission." He did manage to catch a final "beautiful king salmon, with cool, firm flesh from the icy Yukon." At last, the travelers felt the "smack of old ocean" and fell asleep in sight of the open sea.

But there were still eighty miles to go to St. Michael. To reach the old port that was the departure point for southbound ocean steamers, Jack and his companions had to travel along the Alaskan coast on the open ocean in their shallow, flimsy skiff. It took five hair-raising days. "Midnight—southeast wind blowing—squally, increasing, splash of rain. Dirty sky to southward. Quite a task of running boat out through surf."

The dangers were exacerbated by the presence on board of a fourth man: a Jesuit priest whom Jack had picked up when he saw him attempting the same perilous trip in a flimsy little three-hatch kayak. Jack was fascinated by Father Robeau, a beefy, bearded loner who had spent twelve years in Alaska. Multilingual and incredibly resourceful, the priest had devoted much of his time to compiling an Inuit dictionary and grammar. As a bitter wind blew and the men huddled together in the little sailboat as it scudded through the pounding waves, Jack

questioned the Jesuit about his life and listened to his bellows of fearless laughter as he described his dealings with the native people. Jack
couldn't help contrasting Father Robeau with Father Judge back in
Dawson. Where the Irish-American Father Judge was fragile, ascetic,
and saintly, Father Robeau was "an Italian by blood, a Frenchman by
birth, a Spaniard by education . . . and his whole life was one continuous romance." Exuberant and energetic, with his "tanned skin and brilliant black eyes," he demonstrated a "vivid play of emotion so different
from the sterner, colder Anglo-Saxon." When the Jesuit finally left Jack's
boat and paddled off alone, Jack noted in his journal, "Never heard
of again—lost in some back slough most likely." But the dedication
of Catholic missionaries in the North enthralled Jack, whose single-
minded intensity as a writer could match a priest's commitment to his
vocation. Father Robeau would live on, under his own name, as a principal character in the title story of Jack's first book, *The Son of the Wolf.*

   "Our last taste of the Bering Sea was a fitting close to the trip," Jack
would write in his *Buffalo Express* article. "Midnight found us wallow-
ing in the sea, a rocky coast to leeward and a dirty sky to windward . . .
Removing the sprit and bagging the afterleech, we shortened to storm
canvas and ran before it." Jack London, Charlie Taylor, and John Thorson reached the harbor of St. Michael on Wednesday, June 28, twenty-
one days after they had cast off the lines at Dawson and less than a
year since Jack had joined the Gold Rush. They quickly found a steamer
heading south to Victoria, British Columbia, from where Jack would
continue home to San Francisco. The last entry in Jack's Yukon journal reads, "Leave St. Michaels—unregrettable moment." Jack probably
worked his passage by shoveling coal into the ship's furnace: in *John
Barleycorn,* he described "eight days of hell, during which time we coal-
passers were kept to the job by being fed whisky. We toiled half drunk
all the time. And without the whisky we could not have passed the coal."

   The Klondike had nearly finished Jack London, but Jack hadn't finished with the Klondike. The Gold Rush gave him the felt experience—

the thrilling mix of endurance and exuberance—with which he would make his name. He returned to San Francisco in mid-July with a few flakes of gold from his Henderson Creek claim, and vivid memories. "It was in the Klondike I found myself," he later mused. "There . . . you get your true perspective."

CHAPTER 13
Rags and Riches, May–June 1898

DAWSON CITY'S GROWTH was meteoric. When Bill Haskell arrived there in late 1896, a few hundred people huddled on the mudflat. By June 1898, there had been a fiftyfold increase and 20,000 people crowded onto the same site. And it was still growing.

The summer of 1898 saw the peak of the Klondike Gold Rush: the Mounties counted more than 7,000 boats setting off across Bennett Lake, and hundreds more people appeared via different routes. Dawson's extraordinary growth had made it the largest city west of Winnipeg and north of Seattle. There were roughly 8,000 Americans, 8,000 Canadians, and the rest were drawn from every other corner of the world. There were still nine men for every one woman. And there were almost *no* services, except for those required to answer basic needs for food and shelter. The place stank and the streets were filthy. Yet thousands of people had willingly made the dangerous, exhausting, miserable journey to reach Dawson's overcrowded squalor, and thousands more were on their way.

Belinda Mulrooney could handle any amount of deprivation as long as she was making money. She was determined to be ready for the human flood coming down the Yukon River, as she supervised construction of her new hotel, the Fairview, on the Dawson waterfront. She boasted that the Fairview would rival the finest hotels in San Francisco, Chicago, or Seattle. With characteristic ruthlessness, she bribed the sawmill operator to divert scarce lumber her way and promised big bonuses to her workmen if they finished the three-story building by midsummer. She was hell-bent on making Bill Leggett pay the $5,000 bet, and her foreman, Harry Cribb, was so keen to confound his boss's critics that he told her, "I'll put that blame hotel up if I have to tie it together with wooden pegs." By late June over 30,000 people had faced death in the mountains in the frantic race to get rich quick, and the building project gave Belinda a grandstand view of the surge of newcomers.

Dawson's expansion may not have surprised Belinda, but despite being a connoisseur of human incompetence, even she was amazed by how few of the newcomers knew what they were doing. Stricken by gold fever, they had made the nightmare journey without any plan beyond reaching the subarctic Xanadu. They staggered off the boats like zombies. Confronted by the cold, hard facts that Dawson's streets were not lined with gold, that all the best creeks were staked, and that gold mining in the North was a brutal occupation, the great mass of stampeders milled around helplessly. Hundreds sold what was left of their outfits for anything they could get, without ever seeing a sluice box or a rocker, and retreated home.

There were other novel sights on the streets these days—horses (skeletally thin after the cruel trek), steers (slaughtered on arrival and sold to restaurants), a cow that produced fresh milk for thirty dollars a pail, even a few youngsters. Even so, Belinda would recall, "children were so scarce they were like a zoo [animal] or a regular work of art." And among the throng were characters who were frankly out of place on the frontier, men with soft hands and city manners, who stared in wonder at the grimy shantytown. Belinda realized that Dawson was evolving before her eyes and these were the people who would nudge the frontier town toward semi-civilization. The Klondike had already caught the attention of church organizations, eager to save souls and fill coffers. Now, secular institutions were on their way. Thanks to those soft-skinned city types, Dawson would soon acquire two features essential for any self-respecting community in late-nineteenth-century America: newspapers and banks. Belinda couldn't have been happier: this was the professional class she wanted to attract to the Fairview Hotel.

Newspapers arrived first. Up until now, Klondike prospectors had made news but had had limited opportunity to consume it. A slight, sharp-faced Seattle newspaperman called Eugene C. Allen was determined to be the first to give Dawson a weekly dose of news. Gene Allen was an indefatigable busybody, for whom joining the Gold Rush stampede was both "a corking adventure" and a chance to "clean up the gold faster than those boys dig it out of the ground." He and three friends had hauled a heavy printing press plus a year's supply of paper stock over the White Pass. The three-month journey had dampened some of Allen's enthusiasm. "It sure seems a lifetime since we left home," he confided to his diary. "That former existence is something out of another life, while we have the feeling that we have always been mushing along the snow-bound trail into the teeth of this awful Arctic wind, with the thermometer 25 to 35 degrees below zero." Allen's distress was compounded when he heard that he wasn't the only newspaperman careering north. G. B. Swinehart, editor of Juneau's *Mining Record*, was ahead of the Seattle gang on the trail to the gold fields, with a superior printing press. Not to be outdone, Allen arranged to travel in advance of his friends so he could get established and start news gathering in the mining community before either of the two printing presses was finally unloaded. He reached his destination in mid-April with barely a cent in his pocket.

Allen weaseled his way onto a small, empty lot near Father Judge's hospital, where he pitched his tent before setting off to walk the sixteen miles up to Bonanza and Eldorado creeks and figure out the gold-mining operations. He discovered several old friends from Seattle, most of them working as paid employees of claim holders and eager to greet a familiar face. Allen was a sponge for the latest stories:

who had struck paydirt, who had started a fight, who was reckoned to be pulling far more of the yellow stuff out of the ground than he was admitting. He heard how the "bench claims," staked on hillsides above the creeks, were proving as rich as claims along the creek bottoms. Best of all, a Seattle friend with a rich claim tossed him a small leather sack about the size of his thumb that contained $100 of gold dust. Back in Dawson, Allen could finally afford a decent meal, plus his first haircut and shave in months. Before that, he joked in a memoir, a couple of sourdoughs had mistaken him for an ape man.

Gene Allen was eager to rush into print, but his printing press was still hundreds of miles away. Undaunted, he bought enough lumber from Ladue's sawmill to make a bulletin board, and erected it in a prominent position on Front Street. Then he sat down to compose, on a borrowed typewriter, the first issue of the *Klondike Nugget*. As he finished each page, he tacked it up on the bulletin board.

The very first page read:

THE KLONDIKE NUGGET

Vol. 1. No. 1. Dawson City, North West Territory. May 27, 1898

THE FIRST NEWSPAPER TO BE PUBLISHED IN DAWSON

Until our plant arrives items of interest which may come under our notice will be bulletined from day to day. It is hoped that we may be of some benefit to the greatest mining camp in the world, and that the venture may prove of slight benefit to the publishers.

E. C. Allen, Business Manager

G. E. Storey, Chief of Staff.

(Allen had run into Storey, a former colleague from a Seattle newspaper, in Dawson and immediately appointed him manager of the composing room, even though there was still neither room nor presses to compose on.)

In his own view, Gene Allen had won the race to publish a newspaper in "the greatest mining camp in the world." The nature of the *Nugget* was clear from the get-go: pornography and corruption would sell papers. The first issue included items about the Mounties confiscating photographs of "an obscene and immoral character," the muddle about competing claims on Dominion Creek, and speculation about an issue that Allen would make a meal of in the months to come: the royalty that the Canadian government was trying to levy on the miners. Maybe Dawson's first weekly newspaper was only a single copy of a badly typed gossip sheet, containing more brio than facts. No matter. As Allen himself had predicted, it was an instant success. Crowds of people gathered around the bulletin board to read about sin and scandal. Once the water began to rise in the horrendous floods that year, entrepreneurs started offering boat rides over to the board to read the news. "Venice hasn't anything on us!" crowed Allen. Soon he had found a site for the *Nugget*'s offices on Third Avenue, close to Dawson's business section but on high, dry ground, and persuaded a local lawyer to finance a structure that would house the press.

Ten days after he had tacked up his first page, Allen had erected a canvas tent over a wooden frame and was ready for the rest of his gang. He had also signed up 400 subscribers, charging each of them an ounce and a half of gold dust. This was more than twice the price of an annual subscription for most newspapers Outside, but Allen grasped that Dawson economics bore no resemblance to any normal town's because both demand and quantities of gold dust were apparently limitless. "Money was cheap. I saw at once that an ounce and a half, or $24 a year, could be had just as easy as $10." He also started gathering classified ads ($1 a line), orders for regular advertising ($10 an inch), and orders for printing jobs. Three weeks after he first set foot in the place, there wasn't a Dawson businessperson or official who didn't recognize this bouncy little hustler with beady eyes, a jaunty step, and a corncob pipe, who never stopped asking questions, cracking jokes, and exuding the confidence that he was a player in this booming town. Although he was $4,000 in debt, he reckoned he had $15,000 worth of business lined up.

To Allen's horror, the Juneau printing press arrived before his Seattle press reached town. His rival, G. B. Swinehart, cranked out the first, eight-page issue of the *Yukon Midnight Sun* on June 11. Swinehart's opening editorial pulsed with lofty intentions: "It is with no small pleasure that with this issue of the *Yukon Midnight Sun* we see fulfilled our repeated promises to furnish the people of Dawson a weekly newspaper ... The *Yukon Midnight Sun* will be a clean, bright sheet, free from domination by any class, clique or organization. It will be conscientious in the effort to be reliable on all subjects at all times, reflect the social and business life of the city and be an intelligent exponent of the great mining and other valuable interests of the Yukon valley."

The *Klondike Nugget*'s printing press arrived soon after the *Yukon Midnight Sun*'s. The *Nugget*'s first four-page issue announced its noble mission: "The outside world is anxious for authentic information concerning the Klondike gold district. The miners and other residents of this region are equally desirous of learning what is going on outside, as well as of home occurrences. Hence the publication of the *Klondike Nugget*. We have no higher ambition than to satisfy our readers."

Both papers then rose to the challenge of supplying readers with every whiff of scandalous behavior, every rumor of a new strike, every detail of gruesome murders and thefts, and each overheated notice of a newly arrived entertainer that their skimpy reportorial staffs could accumulate or invent. Lugubrious accounts of lives lost upriver as stampeders continued to pour over the passes were interspersed with poetry, jokes, and classified ads for cooks, waitresses, and dogs.

Vicious rivalry between the two papers erupted. Allen regarded the *Yukon Midnight Sun* as Canadian government propaganda, particularly since Swinehart promised to publish a "Guide to Dawson and the Yukon Mining District" that would include government regulations for mines and lumber and tables of weights for gold dust. Swinehart

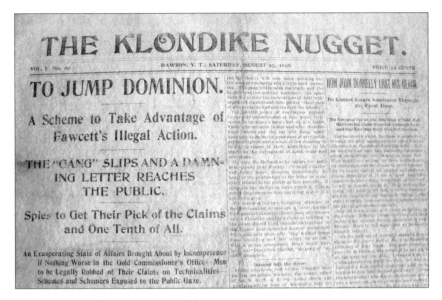

The Klondike Nugget, *Dawson's first newspaper, announced that it had "no higher ambition than to satisfy our readers."*

regarded the *Nugget* as a scurrilous rag, since Allen was soon whipping up resentment against the royalty regime among the miners in his avowed mission to "protect their interests."

In this remote frontier, both newspapermen embraced the outspoken, combative journalistic standards of late-nineteenth-century New York City. Buccaneering proprietors there, like Joseph Pulitzer and William Randolph Hearst, fought ruthless circulation wars characterized by sensationalist headlines, messianic campaigns, and a careless attitude to facts. Allen and Swinehart were eager disciples of the yellow journalism barons, although they were handicapped by Dawson's lack of a telegraph link with the outside world. They depended on dogsled teams to deliver slow doses of Outside news. But Allen, at least, was not going to let this cramp his style. "We're going to hit at some of the dirty deals which miners have been getting at the hands of the government," he explained with Hearst-like bluster to a recently recruited editorial team. "Dig up everything that you can that looks rotten . . . Be sure

you've got your dope straight. Then shoot your wad for all its worth."
Journalism Hearst style could be over the top, but Allen's copy was also
bold and entertaining.

The no-holds-barred competition between the rival publications
suited businesspeople like Belinda Mulrooney fine. Both newspapers
recorded comings and goings at the waterfront, so she could find out
which Klondike Kings were taking their new wealth out of town and
which newcomers sounded like possible clients for her various enterprises. "Ellis Lewis, half owner of No. 23 on Eldorado . . . left yesterday
on the *Bella,* for California," read an item in the *Yukon Midnight Sun* of
June 27. "It is hinted that he carried out about fifty thousand." At the
same time, the *Klondike Nugget* carried in its personal column the following news: "Among the passengers on the steamer *Columbian* were
Messrs. W. H. Miller, David W. Jones, Wm. Neville and Jacob Edholm.
The two first named brought with them a large shipment of liquors
amounting to in all 3000 gallons. They have secured a cabin on First
Avenue, and for the present leave their goods in storage." And two
weeks later, the *Nugget* noted that "Otis Beverstock, an Ohio man who
represents considerable Ohio capital, is in the city and looking up profitable investments."

Newly founded businesses rushed to tout their services. There were
advertisements for laundries, doctors, restaurants, real estate brokers,
hotels ("The Dominion Hotel: Finest Brands of Wines, Liquors and
Cigars") and stores selling "Klondike Hats" and "Gent's Pumps." Some
advertisements are harder to parse today. "Marie Riedeselle, Leading
Professional Masseuse, From 121 West 111th Street, New York City," frequently appeared, selling "Massage Treatments and Baths, Scurvy prevented and cured by new method. Low vitality restored." The *Klondike
Nugget* was particularly good at the kind of sensationalist human interest stories that fueled bar talk. A young man from Seattle called Billy
Byrne had spent the winter in a camp upriver after falling through the
ice and contracting frostbite in both legs. Gangrene set in, but luckily

there was a physician in a cabin only twenty-five miles away. Billy's condition had required the doctor to amputate both legs below the knees—without, of course, the aid of any anesthetic or disinfectant. Somehow Billy had survived this horrendous ordeal, and had now been bought to Dawson to be loaded, legless and broke, onto the next steamer to St. Michael. "Young Byrne Recovers," boasted the *Nugget*.

The two newspapers did more than sell subscriptions and ads. There was a subtle sense of self-congratulation about them: they reminded readers that anybody who had made it to Dawson was a gutsy survivor. The implication of all those disasters and deaths on trail and creek was that if you were left standing, you were a pretty fine fellow—and Dawson was full of fine fellows. Just as Hearst's mass circulation dailies catered to the tastes of blue-collar workers in burgeoning American cities, the *Nugget* deliberately cultivated Dawson's collective sense of itself. Allen understood that even the crustiest old prospector admired local heroes like Father Judge. By now, an average of seven sufferers from scurvy and dysentery were turning up at the Catholic hospital each day, and the *Nugget*, regretting that "the kindly Father has had a great deal to contend with," extended to him "the hand of sympathy and encouragement." It also backed the Jesuit priest's quiet crusade to remain in Dawson despite the Oblates' challenge: "The city of Dawson will be unanimous in lamenting the departure of Father Judge, if such should be deemed the wisest course. Alaska is really his own territory, but in Dawson's need and owing to the numerical weakness of the Canadian contingent, he came forward and has done noble work indeed."

At the same time, Allen recognized that most of this year's crop of stampeders wanted reassurance that they had landed in more than a rough frontier town. "A gasoline launch is among Dawson's latest acquisitions," read an item in the *Nugget*'s "Local Brevities" column on July 2. "We shall soon be as metropolitan as Victoria or Seattle." But Allen also liked to remind readers of the magic that had lured them north: "There

is no color like the glitter of virgin gold, no music like the tinkle of nuggets falling upon a gold scale, no place where eye and ear alike can be so
thoroughly satisfied as in the Klondike diggings."

Both the *Midnight Sun* and the *Nugget* threw themselves into campaigns for local improvements. They agreed on the easy targets, such
as the need for better sanitation and more law enforcement. But the
Sun's style was more restrained. Earlier in the summer, two prospectors working the McClintock River near Marsh Lake were shot—one
fatally—by Tlingit. The wounded man managed to reach a Mountie
detachment and report the murder: four Tlingit men were arrested and
charged. The men were found guilty and three were sentenced to be
hanged. The fourth was a boy. The *Sun* favored commutation of the
sentence on the grounds that the murderers were "alien to the ways
of civilized society." In contrast, the *Nugget* played shamelessly to the
worst and most ignorant prejudices of its readers:

> *The Treacherous Instincts of the Aborigines*
> *Will Get Their Necks Stretched With Hemp*
> *Probably in Dawson—Villainous Savages*
> *In the Toils.*

The campaign that galvanized the whole town this summer centered
on the enforcement of Canadian laws in the Yukon. Dawson was still run
like a colony of Ottawa: the Yukon Executive Council was appointed by
the federal government, yet Dawsonites had no voice in the capital. Both
papers lobbied for representative government and reform of the mining regulations. Both papers protested the 10 percent royalty levied on
all gold mined in the Yukon. "The excessive burden of the royalty tax
has been a lodestone [presumably he meant 'millstone'] on the mining
industry," thundered the *Yukon Midnight Sun*'s Swinehart. "The small
extent of mining ground sufficiently rich to meet this tax is only found
on the richest claims of Eldorado."

Four Tlingit involved in the murder of a prospector faced the full force of racist rage.

But Swinehart did make allowances for governmental shortcomings. The *Yukon Midnight Sun* acknowledged the remoteness of the region and the fact that most miners were non-Canadian and bent on making their fortunes and getting out. The *Nugget* showed no such forbearance. Allen penned furious editorials, denouncing the federal authority as the ruthless exploiter of the miner, on whom the whole economy of the region depended. On the creeks and in Dawson's bars, his fellow Americans had complained loudly to him that they couldn't get a fair deal from the Canadian gold commissioner, Thomas Fawcett. So Allen decided to make Fawcett the issue on which his newspaper would emerge as the people's champion. Before the first edition of his *Klondike Nugget* had even been printed, its editor had decided to go to war on the hapless, overworked Fawcett and provoke a clean-up of the gold commissioner's office. As the *Nugget*'s campaign heated up, Gene Allen noted with satisfaction that the paper "began to ride on the crest of a tide of popularity." Sales increased, and one night a bunch of roughnecks in the Monte Carlo saloon lifted

the diminutive editor on their shoulders and toasted his health amid
lusty cheers.

Banks were not far behind newspapers. Almost two years after Carmack's gold strike, the two American trading companies, the Alaska
Commercial Company and the North American Transportation and
Trading Company, were still the major repositories for prospectors'
gold before it was shipped south for processing. However, among the
first display ads that appeared in Dawson's papers were several for Outside banks, eager to catch the attention of Klondike Kings once they
arrived back in the United States. First National Bank of Seattle announced, "Gold Dust Bought at Assay Value. If dust or drafts are sent
us, proceeds credited to account or remitted to any part of the world."
The Scandinavian American Bank of Seattle gave the same undertaking,
adding a further lure: "Railway and Steamship Tickets to all points East
and Europe. Alaska tickets sold via fast and commodious steamers." But
these two American banks were barred from operating within Dawson
because only British and Canadian banks were entitled to function on
Canadian soil. Moreover, American banks were state regulated, which
meant they were hamstrung when it came to reaching across boundaries to new frontiers.

Canadian banks were already well on their way to being the banking
industry we know today: robust, careful, national in scope, and quietly
ambitious. Regulated by the national government rather than individual
provinces, within the fifteen years leading up to the Yukon Gold Rush
eleven chartered banks had opened dozens of branches throughout
western Canada. These banks had proved far sturdier in surviving the
depression of the early 1890s than their American counterparts, and
had allowed capital from central Canada to flow west and finance rail-
ways and other commercial enterprises in newly settled areas. Canadian
bankers knew how to handle frontier towns. Despite his starched collar
and waxed mustache, a Western Canadian bank manager was a force-

ful and adaptable character who routinely carried a revolver. Now the more ambitious banks looked at business opportunities in the Yukon and found them irresistible. Over $2.5 million of dust and nuggets were said to have been extracted from the permafrost in 1897, and the output this year was rumored to be four times that much. Ten million dollars' worth of gold was a stunning sum in a year when Canada's federal budget was little over $50 million. Just as Dawson had acquired two newspapers this year, so it would now acquire two banks. Rivalry between the banks was politer than the competition between newspapers, but just as cutthroat.

The first bank on the scene was the least prepared for Dawson conditions. Staff from the London-based, Canadian-chartered Bank of British North America raced north in the spring of 1898, with flamboyant manager David Doig swathed in furs and blankets and riding on a sled behind a dog team. He proudly set up for business on May 19 in a tent on Second Avenue, with an advertised capital of $202,000. A couple of days later, he moved operations to the ground floor of the Victoria Hotel on Front Street, between Princess and Harper, but was promptly forced to cease business for a week when he found himself ankle deep in filthy Yukon water. Doig, a shrewd Scot, had already got the measure of Dawson's leading citizens. As the spring flood rose, he marched off to the north end of town to see his new friend, Father Judge. He persuaded the priest to store the bank's books, furniture, and paperwork on the second floor of St. Mary's Hospital until he had found some better premises. Next, Doig negotiated with Big Alex McDonald, who shared his love of Scottish ballads, for a building lot on the corner of Second Avenue and Queen Street. The gray-flannel-suited Scotsman and the scruffy, slouching Nova Scotian agreed that Big Alex would build a decent cabin on the lot for the bank. In the meantime, Doig and his team reverted to operating out of a mosquito-filled tent.

Like the good bank manager he was, Doig's first concern was for the safe accommodation of the six tons of supplies his team had brought in, including a large box that contained $1 million in unsigned bank drafts.

He stopped worrying after he poked his head into the warehouse of the North American Transportation and Trading Company and saw open shelves laden with tins, sacks, and bottles of gold dust.

The Toronto-based Canadian Bank of Commerce arrived in Dawson three weeks after the Bank of British North America. Its manager, H. T. Wills, had planned its northern expedition carefully and traveled at a more stately pace, smug in the knowledge that the Commerce's Dawson branch would be a much bigger deal than its rival's. The Canadian Bank of Commerce had been appointed by Ottawa as the federal government's agent in Dawson and the Yukon Territory. This meant that it would receive commissions for collecting gold royalties and paying wages to police and government officials, and would work hand in hand with the North-West Mounted Police. The last point was reassuring for the bank's Toronto managers, who were concerned about bank robberies in a wide-open town like Dawson. They didn't realize that a bank robber would have a tough time making his getaway from a community forty bleak miles from the nearest refuge.

Wills's arrival in Dawson was far less flashy than Doig's. A big man weighing over 300 pounds, he was stricken by swollen legs and a sore throat and lay retching at the bottom of a Peterborough canoe as his colleagues paddled toward the waterfront. But once ashore, he installed his team in better premises than those of the Bank of British North America. The Canadian Bank of Commerce opened for business on June 14 in a small, windowless shed sheathed in galvanized iron. The shed had problems—it stank of the dried-fish dog food that had previously been stored there; it became impossibly hot in the midsummer heat; the tiny airless loft under its sloping roof was accessible only by ladder. But it was on dry ground. The five staff members (including a cook and a messenger) all slept in the cramped, sweaty garret, while Wills took himself off to some smarter digs. Inside the shed was a long counter across its width, on which to do business. Outside, nailed to a frame, a brave little canvas sign proclaimed

THE CANADIAN BANK OF COMMERCE
CAPITAL PAID UP SIX MILLION DOLLARS

The two banks were rushed by clients as soon as they hung their shingles. People lined up outside to find out how they could get funds forwarded to Dawson, whether there were any letters for them, if they could lodge documents with the bank in escrow, or simply who was inside these shelters. The Commerce staff had put up a mess tent next to their shed, where Tommy, the cook, could prepare their meals. But so great was the crush at the counter on opening day that the tent was abandoned and both Tommy and the messenger were pressed into service as clerical assistants, labeling gold sacks, writing receipts, and ensuring order. Although the official exchange rate was nineteen dollars for one ounce of gold, most clients were so eager to exchange their awkward, heavy little bags for paper currency that they sold their gold for fourteen dollars an ounce. If the depositor was prepared to take a note promising full payment at a later date, the exchange rate was sixteen an ounce. Once a client had gold stored with the Commerce, the bank would accept as legal tender from him any form of currency, including Confederate notes, bills on the defunct Ezra Meeker Bank, and—on one occasion—a three-dollar check written on a spruce plank.

One early visitor to the Commerce's Dawson branch was a plump, highly rouged, and gaudily bedecked woman who asked, "Have you got my tights and slippers? I'm Caprice." With impeccable manners, the teller referred her to Mr. Wills, at the other end of the counter. Mr. Wills looked her up and down, and haughtily informed her that she was in a bank. Caprice gave as good as she got. "Sure," she replied, "the Bank of Commerce, isn't it? Joe Brooks told me he'd send them here." Joe Brooks was a packer on the Skagway Trail, and after a search it was discovered that Caprice's tights and slippers were stuffed into a sack of bank notes. A week later, a bank employee went to a Sunday concert at which "living pictures" drawn from the Scriptures were presented. The curtain rose on a tableau entitled "Rock of Ages," which featured Caprice in all her tawdry, tight pink glory, in a fleshy embrace of a huge cross.

The biggest challenge for the two bank managers was to decide which clients in this freewheeling community of adventurers and gamblers were good credit risks, when almost none of them even had documents to verify that they were who they said they were. Doig and Wills took chances that would have given some of their eastern colleagues apoplexy. The line-up for loans snaked round both bank branches as soon as prospectors discovered that they were offering loans at 2 or 3 percent a month. What a steal! These rates were a far better deal than the 10 percent a month charged by private lenders in Dawson, although they were well over the rate charged Outside. (The Canadian Bank Act—not applicable to the Yukon—restricted the rate of interest banks could charge to 7 percent a year.) Doig told his boss in London that he was getting applications for loans of $5,000 to $20,000 every day, "but have not seen my way to entertain them." He simply didn't know whom to trust. Nevertheless, within a few days of opening, the Bank of British North America had made over $1,000 in commissions. At the Canadian Bank of Commerce, Wills learned to rely on an extremely shrewd teller who was a Mason and, by some mysterious method that none of the rest of the staff could fathom, was able to gauge a man's trustworthiness. The Mason's gut instinct became the credibility test of first resort. By the summer of 1899, Bank of Commerce bills worth $2 million were in circulation in Dawson, and (as the bank proudly recorded in its official history), "the bank incurred no losses through this channel of prolific possibilities."

Banking in Dawson City was unique. During the endless daylight that summer, both banks were open for twelve to fifteen hours a day—double the banking hours Outside. From early morning, a crowd milled around the door, and the bank tellers had just finished recording one transaction in the deposit ledger when the next customer was clamoring for attention and waving his poke of gold dust around. Horses, mules, and dogs loaded with gold dust frequently stood outside both banks for hours, swishing their tails against the swarms of blackflies and relieving themselves on the boardwalks. The Commerce would finally shut up shop around eight o'clock in the evening, when the crowd was drawn away by the blare of cornets, the pounding of drums, and the strident and far-reaching tones of the "caller-off" in the dance halls. Once the doors were closed in the hot, windowless little hut, tellers would light a couple of candles and in the smoky fug try to write up the day's work. They would store cash in an old, unlocked tin biscuit box and sacks of gold dust worth hundreds of thousands of dollars in an iron-lined wooden chest. But they were frequently interrupted by revelers. One night, an indignant drunk threw a rock at the canvas sign, and shouted, "I'm from Missouri, and you have to show me where they have six million dollars in that bum little shack." Another time, a customer pounded on the door at four in the morning, determined to cash a check. When told that the bank would open at eight, he grumbled, "That's a hell of a time to wait for a drink."

In addition to being Ottawa's agent, the Canadian Bank of Commerce had another advantage over its rival. It had brought with it the plans, fire bricks, and chemicals required for an assay plant to test the purity of gold dust, and three staff trained in assaying techniques. Two weeks after Wills had set up shop, he decided the bank should start assaying some of the dust and nuggets it had already accumulated. Much of the "commercial dust" in circulation in Dawson was laced with black sand. Now many of the customers who had received advances on their gold dust, intent on traveling Outside for the summer, wanted to find out what their gold was worth and get the rest of their cash. A melting furnace was constructed, the acids, fluxes, delicate Troemner balances, and all the other paraphernalia of an assay department prepared, then the charcoal was lit. The theory was that the gold dust would melt down, the dross could be scraped away, and the molten mass of pure gold would then cool in a brick mold and be weighed. But the Commerce's

Weighty bags of gold were loaded onto men, horses, and dogs all summer, as tons of dust and nuggets were brought in from the creeks.

first attempt at an assay was a disaster. When the furnace was opened after forty-eight hours, Wills found a lumpy mass that could neither be returned to the customer nor assayed.

Knowledge of this disaster would damage the bank's reputation, as well as making it the laughingstock of its rival bank's employees. Bank officials agonized about what to do as their customers grew impatient. The bank staff tried to placate them, and conceal the mess, by taking them to the Monte Carlo for a drink. It was in the bar that the problem was finally solved. One of the Commerce's tellers bumped into an Austrian called Jorish who had studied at Vienna's School of Mines and was looking for work. Jorish spoke only a few words of English, but as soon as he was ushered into the room where the furnace sat he saw the problem. With a big grin, he took a chisel and knocked out a couple of fire bricks to increase the draft. Wills promptly hired him as stoker

The last gold shipment of the year weighed 1.5 million tons. It left Dawson City
on September 14, 1898.

for fifteen dollars a day—little more than the going wage for Dawson
laborers but far more than his trained tellers were paid.

Despite the free-for-all atmosphere, the long hours, the tellers'
chronic fatigue, and the lousy accommodation, both banks had a very
profitable summer. At the end of June, the *Yukon Sun* recorded that
three stern-wheelers, the *Portus B. Weare,* the *Bella,* and the *Hamilton*
had left for St. Michael laden with no fewer than nine tons of gold—
much of it in sealed wooden boxes banded with iron, belonging to
the banks. In Dawson City itself, the scales on every store counter and
saloon bar began to disappear, as paper money slowly replaced gold
dust. Not everybody appreciated the switch. Dishonest miners had
often "stretched" their gold dust with brass filings. Unscrupulous bartenders had embraced the fashion for keeping their fingernails long
and their hair greasy. When they were on duty, they ran their fingers

Gold scales were still features of Dawson's bars and stores, even after the introduction of paper money.

through their locks after weighing out the dust; once they got home, they would filter gold dust from the sink in which they washed their hair. But for merchants, traders, and hoteliers like Belinda Mulrooney, Dawson's gradual transformation into a respectable community with a professional class could only be good for business.

Maybe some of the Gold Rush magic disappeared along with the unruly pioneer ways, but the new boom meant even more opportunities for making a fortune. Both Wills and Doig had approached Belinda about giving them some of her business. She had no time for the pompous Chief Wills, as she called him, who one day announced to her in a portentous tone of voice that "my credit was good at the Bank if I wanted to do any buying." Belinda, who had always operated on barter and partnerships, snapped, "What could you buy at a bank?" Anyway, she had already decided that David Doig might be more useful to her. Doig enjoyed whiskey, cigars, and women, and made a habit of drinking a pint of champagne for breakfast. A shipment of Mumm's extra dry had recently been assigned to him, but Belinda decided it would be more appreciated at the grand opening she was planning for her nearly completed Fairview Hotel. "There were eighteen cases of champagne in the lot. I told the bank to take it out of my account."

CHAPTER 14

Flora Shaw, "From Paris to Siberia," July 1898

ON JULY 27, the three-story Fairview Hotel, which towered over the tents and shacks round it, opened its doors. Belinda Mulrooney had won her bet with Bill Leggett, who now gritted his teeth and handed over $5,000. Leggett wasn't the only prospector who had bet and lost against Belinda's hopes of finishing her hotel. The twenty-six-year-old businesswoman and her crew made over $100,000 on wagers against the completion of the Fairview. (The hotel cannot have cost much more than $100,000 to build, so Belinda's bets went a long way to covering her expenses.) On the ground floor was an elaborately furnished bar with painted canvas walls and a dining room featuring starched damask table linens. Dawson's other hotels offered overnight accommodation in one common sleeping room with tiers of bunks, like Belinda's Grand Forks Hotel, but the Fairview was incomparably grander. The second floor had individual, wallpapered bedrooms—too cramped to contain more than a bed but boasting Brussels carpets, brass bedsteads, and lace curtains. Only residents realized that the elegant wallpaper was glued onto sheets of canvas nailed to wooden studs, which meant that the slightest whisper could be heard in the next room. The top floor was left open for the first night's dance but would soon be partitioned into equally tiny bedrooms.

Belinda had thought of everything. The basement furnace (built by her old friend Julius Geise) was circled with wires on which miners

The Fairview Hotel was the first three-story building in Dawson City, and the ultimate proof (if any was needed) that Belinda Mulrooney always won her bets.

could hang wet socks. There was a side entrance for ladies, to protect them from having to walk through the bar. There were electric lights, thanks to a steamboat tied up to the riverbank in front of the Fairview that generated electricity with its paddle wheel. There were telephones, connecting the Fairview with other Dawson establishments: a network of telephone wires had been strung up in town and around the creeks a month earlier, and Belinda had had the foresight to offer a room in the Fairview as the telephone switchboard. There was even a bathhouse, constructed on two barges lashed together in front of the Fairview. This was particularly popular because two of the attendants spoke only German. "The miners . . . used to follow them around . . . asking them over and over, 'Where do you work?' just to hear the boys answer, 'In de bad house.'"

A few details were still missing—this was the Yukon, after all, where it took three months for goods ordered from Outside to arrive. Muslin was tacked over the bedroom windows to keep the bugs out because as yet there was no window glass, and there were no bedroom doors. The legs for the dining room chairs had been left on the dock at St. Michael, so a local carpenter was hurriedly cobbling together new ones. Belinda did not let these trivialities handicap her. Ecstatic to have been proven right, she went all out to flaunt her success on opening day.

The tone of Belinda Mulrooney's memoir as she describes her big bash is shamelessly gloating. This was the culmination of all her efforts, all her dreams. Throughout her life, she had been out to prove that she was smarter, better, tougher than the men around her, and the Fairview Hotel was the undeniable evidence. She had turned herself into a successful businesswoman in an era when such a type was so unusual that the term was most often used as a euphemism for a brothelkeeper. With success, another Belinda emerged. She was still a lot of fun, and loyal to those who were loyal to her, but a nasty streak surfaced. She became a bit of a bully, with no time for losers.

First, however, came her hotel's grand opening. "The opening of the Fairview was an immense thing," she recalled. "For the boys who had built the hotel in such a short time it was one big potlatch ... Bill Leggett was pretty sore. It took him until 12 o'clock to loosen up." Belinda organized a barbecue for her crew of workmen and served them a washtub full of punch on the porch. For Dawson's "society," she served an elaborate menu prepared by a chef from San Francisco. A sense of social inferiority still lingered in Belinda's tough persona, so she took particular delight in the way that *everybody* wanted to be at her opening. Dressed in her usual forbidding uniform of navy blouse and dark skirt, and with her unruly dark hair pulled back into a bun, she personally welcomed Colonel James Domville, a member of the Canadian Parliament from New Brunswick, government officials like Frederick Coates Wade, who was now land commissioner as well as crown prosecutor, and "the boys from the bank." A handful of these professionals had even persuaded their wives to make the grim journey north, and these women flocked to the Fairview. The sense of feminine style that had prompted Belinda to bring gorgeous, flimsy silk undergarments to sell in Dawson made her appreciate the women's "doll rags which were all new to us and brought a touch of the Outside." Sadie, Belinda's loyal employee with the infectious laugh, took their wraps, and the society wives either didn't know or didn't care that the motherly woman serving their tables was the notorious Effie, with her checkered past.

Even the *Klondike Nugget*'s Gene Allen was impressed with what he described in the next edition of the paper as "an immense affair." He was too busy tucking in to take detailed notes of what he was eating. "The spread would make your mouth water to give an account of it in detail," he reported. "Suffice it to say that the menu was equal to anything produced in the centre of a more pretentious civilization, while the wine list was an eye opener to those who suppose the principal convivial drink of Dawson to be 'hootchinoo.' Mumm's extra dry flowed freely."

The only person who didn't enjoy himself was Harry Cribb, Belinda's foreman, who had built the Fairview in less than eighteen weeks. The miners had taken over the third floor and dragged up a fiddler, an accordion player, and a harmonica player for a hoedown. Once the dancing started, Cribb kept running a finger around his collar and looking anxiously at the ceilings. "God, I hope the place [doesn't] fall down," he muttered. The celebration lasted until six or seven in the morning. When they left, half the guests said to the proprietor, "Put up another hotel and make it six storeys next time."

Belinda's timing was impeccable. She had opened her spiffy new log palace just as a new class of visitor was arriving in Dawson City. In the previous year's stampede, almost all of the cheechakos had been dirt-poor prospectors, escaping the depression that still held North America in its grip. Men like Bill Haskell and Jack London were penniless dreamers and gamblers, ready to risk everything in the hope of striking paydirt. Many had already returned south—a few, like Bill, with bags of dust and nuggets, far more, like Jack, with nothing but a body wrecked by hardship and a head full of memories. Most of those who remained in the Klondike gold fields had little time for the damask napkins or silverware in the Fairview's dining room, and couldn't afford the $6.50 a night that Belinda charged for one of her stuffy little second-floor bedrooms.

But this year, the human avalanche included a scattering of a different kind of cheechako. Alongside bank managers and newspaper proprietors were wealthy thrill seekers looking for comfortably upholstered adventures. Although most people in the 1890s were still suffering from the sting of economic depression, this was also the Gilded Age, in which the rich were getting richer. On New York City's Fifth Avenue, the Astor family was busy building the world's largest (and most prestigious) luxury hotel, the Waldorf Astoria. In Newport, Rhode Island, Cornelius Vanderbilt had just completed his seventy-room mansion, The Breakers, at a cost of more than $7 million. At the bottom of the social pyramid, a weary army continued to toil in the shipyards, railroads, workshops, and department stores of the new industrial age. But between the two extremes of super-rich and wretched poor, enough shrewd investors were making money from the country's rapid industrialization to expand their own horizons.

Publicity about Klondike Kings and Dawson's dizzy bar life fired the imaginations of Americans with wanderlust. "Dawson is gold, whisky and women in a riotous whirl," wrote Edward Livernash, a Hearst reporter paid to gush hyperbole. In the *New York Journal* of October 6, 1897, he had compared the Yukon settlement to the camps of previous gold rushes: "Not Leadville in vermilion heyday, nor Tombstone with the lid off, nor San Francisco in the flush of '49, had more picturesqueness than this camp has today . . . Front Street never sleeps." In the spring of 1898, such shameless exaggerations had drawn north travelers who never dreamed a year earlier of steaming up the Yukon. Many took the easier all-water route, a 3,000-mile voyage from Seattle to St. Michael followed by the 1,400-mile journey up the Yukon River to Dawson. Weather permitting, the entire trip took about forty days. In 1897, only five paddle-steamers had made the Yukon leg of the journey, but between June 8 and September 20, 1898, thirty-eight steamers paddled from the Bering Sea to Dawson City and back. Fifteen made the round trip twice and three made it three times.

The very same day that Belinda's Fairview Hotel opened with such fanfare, the S.S. *Leah* tied up at the waterfront after a twenty-one-day voyage from St. Michael. On board was a diverse collection of sightseers, including fifty-year-old Jeremiah Lynch, a debonair figure in suit and polished leather shoes who was a published author and a former president of the San Francisco Stock Exchange. Lynch had made the trip with a vague plan to buy a gold mine and a firm determination to see what all the fuss was about. As Lynch would write in his 1904 narrative, *Three Years in the Klondike,* his fellow passengers were a motley crowd. They included a former U.S. senator from Arkansas intent on opening a law office, a widow and her "*piquante* daughter Georgie, of good old Virginia stock," an elderly German couple from Sacramento called the Wichters, and "two ladies of mental and physical altitude."

The two women of altitude and, as Lynch remarked, considerable girth were Mrs. Mary Hitchcock, widow of a U.S. naval officer, and Miss Edith Van Buren, niece of the former U.S. president. This commanding pair liked to explore exotic locations each summer, preferably in picturesque outfits. Their gold-mining garb consisted of blue serge knickerbockers, striped jersey sweaters, large sombreros, and heavy cartridge belts to which were strapped fearsome handguns. Lynch marveled at their baggage: "Two gigantic Danish dogs, a tent that would entertain seventy-five people . . . a collection of pigeons and rare fowls, boxes and boxes of *pâté de fois gras*, truffles, sardines, *olives farcies*, several kinds of musical instruments, and a bowling alley." Mrs. Hitchcock, a grande dame with a sharp tongue and hot temper, was furious when told she had excess luggage, and refused to be parted from her Edison motion-picture projector, her ice-cream freezer, her air mattresses, or

Two thousand miles from the nearest city, surrounded by wilderness, Dawson's Front Street was crowded night and day with men looking for entertainment, gold, work—or a way home.

a single one of her birds (several canaries, two cages of pigeons, and a parrot).

Most of the *Leah*'s passengers, including the two fat ladies, the U.S. senator, and Jeremiah Lynch, stepped ashore once the vessel docked at the waterfront and joined the crowds on Front Street. But compared to the glittering city of gold described in newspapers, the bawdy reality of Dawson City was a ghastly shock for others. The Wichters announced that they were not leaving the *Leah*. Frau Wichter, who weighed over 300 pounds, remained planted on the large chair outside her stateroom. "From this upper deck I can see the town pretty well, and I am afraid," she confided to Lynch. "It's no place for us, with all these men and bad women. I don't know why we came here."

Despite the Fairview's electric lights and the Canadian Bank of Commerce's assay plant, Dawson remained a dauntingly crude society. There were still only three public latrines on the waterfront. Private scavengers had been contracted to carry refuse outside town limits, but they could not cope with the tide of garbage in the streets. The water from the Yukon River was undrinkable, and although the floods had receded, the dusty streets were lined with pools of stagnant water. A typhoid epidemic had broken out a couple of weeks earlier, and word on Front Street was that about 120 people were dying every week. An undertaker named Charlie Brimstone advertised on a canvas sign: "Bodies embalmed and shipped to the 'outside.'" And Mrs. Wichter wasn't mistaken about those "bad women." A whole new crop of prostitutes were openly touting for business on the streets. Mattie Silks, a famous Denver madam, had just arrived with eight of her "boarders" and set up shop in a big frame building on Second Avenue. When she hustled her girls south three months later at freeze-up, she would take $38,000 with her.

Jeremiah Lynch wandered along Front Street at ten o'clock one night, when it was still broad daylight. Through the open doors of cavernous saloons, a low hubbub of men's voices and fiddle tunes escaped alongside the mingled stench of sweat, tobacco, vomit, urine, beer, and whiskey. Lynch stuck his head into one saloon, in which hundreds of people were "pushing and jostling around the faro and roulette tables, some to play and some to see." He caught sight of a Mephistophelian figure in shirtsleeves and suspenders, who sat silently in front of a huge pair of gold scales "and was ever busy weighing, from the sacks of golddust handed him by the gamblers, quantities of dust in value from 50 to 1,000 dollars, for which he gave them ivory chips to bet with." Professional gamblers, nicknamed "Coal oil Johnnies," ruthlessly and relentlessly shifted the chips from the punters' side of the table to their own. Lynch shuddered: "The whole environment of the place was that of another and a worse world."

Ironically, by the time that Lynch, the Wichters, and the Hitchcock–Van Buren duo reached Dawson City, the American press's infatuation with the San Francisco of the North had already faded. In the spring of 1898, New York proprietors had a sensational new story with which

to sell their papers: the American war with Spain over Cuba. Carib-
bean naval battles knocked Klondike gold strikes off the front pages.
But on the other side of the Atlantic, the Klondike Gold Rush was getting more attention than ever—not for colorful anecdotes about death
on the Chilkoot Pass but for analysis of the mining prospects in the
gold fields. What was fact and what was rumor? Which of the American press articles was sheer boosterism? Would modern technology
increase output? Where could anybody discover reliable information?
In 1898, the *Times,* the *Manchester Guardian,* the *Daily Graphic,* and
the *Illustrated London News* all sent correspondents to the Dominion of
Canada. These writers provided more sober commentary on the northern Xanadu than any of the Hearst boys had done.

By far the most important and influential of the reporters who
arrived in Dawson City this summer was the *Times*'s emissary. Within
the macho gold-mining world, "the Thunderer's" choice of reporter
was also the most surprising. The colonial correspondent of what was
then the world's most influential paper was a petite forty-six-year-old
single woman called Flora Shaw. Flora shared with Belinda Mulrooney
a stamina and ambition that left most of their male competitors in the
dust, but in every other respect these two Yukon pioneers could not
have been more different. Belinda had made the hideous journey to
Dawson City to improve her own fortunes. Flora made the 8,000-mile
journey from London with a much more ambitious goal: to strengthen
the British Empire. She wanted to see if this inaccessible, ice-bound
gold field was a good investment for British capital. Her visit would be
crucial for the future of gold mining in the Yukon.

Wherever she found herself, Flora Shaw never forgot that she was a
representative of the largest empire in the history of the world, which,
in 1898, comprised nearly a quarter of the land mass of the earth and a
quarter of its population. Today, "empire" is a word with negative asso-
ciations, and it is hard to stomach the aggressive patriotism of many of

the British Empire's subjects, including those in British North America, a hundred years ago. But for Flora Shaw's contemporaries, that splash of pink across the globe had a sense of inevitability about it. The previous year they had celebrated Queen Victoria's Diamond Jubilee—sixty years on the throne—and 50,000 troops, from all corners of the earth, had marched up the London Strand. It was a vivid illustration of the comment of British historian James Morris: "The nineteenth century had been pre-eminently Britain's century, and the British saw themselves still as top dogs."

The British Empire had been acquired in a fairly haphazard fashion through the previous century, but by the 1890s it had achieved almost the status of a faith. The New Imperialists, of whom Flora Shaw was one, assumed that it was not merely the right of the British to rule a quarter of the world; it was their duty to spread British values, laws, political institutions, and social habits. At the same time, it was the obligation of Britain's overseas possessions and partners to send an endless flow of goods—furs, food, fruit, skins, wool, cotton, tea, minerals, rubber, wines, diamonds, and gold—back to the imperial capital to ensure the prosperity of the Empire. Now London travel agencies were arranging passages to the Yukon for adventurers, and the *Daily Chronicle* had printed a Gold Rush ballad:

> *Klondike! Klondike!*
> *Libel yer luggidge "Klondike"!*
> *Theers no luck dawn Shoreditch wye,*
> *Pack yer traps and be orf I sye,*
> *Au' 'orf an' awye ter Klondike!*

Spurred on by this vulgar interest, Flora Shaw had suggested to her editor that perhaps the newspaper should investigate what was going on in the Empire's most northerly regions. After all, the *Times* was practically the mouthpiece of the Empire. As the paper's official history puts it,

Flora Shaw, correspondent for the Times *of London, was "as clever as they make them . . . and talking like a* Times *leader all the time."*

"For *The Times,* Imperialism, by which the paper meant the Union Jack and what it stood for, had by 1890 taken rank before all other considerations." The paper of record should see if this new gold strike could be an important imperial asset. And Flora Shaw insisted that she was the writer to send.

Unlike Belinda Mulrooney, Flora Shaw began life with certain advantages. Born in 1852 into a talented Anglo-Irish family, Flora had access to a good library and a network of family friends. Life was not easy: her mother died when she was young, and she had to help raise several younger siblings. She was also enmeshed in Victorian restrictions on women's behavior. But Flora was one of those tough-minded women in late-nineteenth-century Britain whose stiff spine and starched manners hid a will of steel. A slim, self-possessed young woman with neatly dressed auburn hair and intelligent, dark eyes, she listened carefully to what people said, then quietly made up her own mind on issues. She had published five novels before the age of thirty-four, and she undertook social work in London's East End. The overcrowding and poverty she saw in the slums and the insufficiency of private charity appalled her. Unlike many contemporaries, she didn't argue that the problems should be fixed by economic and political reforms at home. Instead, her exposure to industrial poverty in Britain inspired a passionate belief that the answer for her country's poor and destitute masses lay overseas—in Britain's colonies. This sparked the zeal for Empire that infused her later journalism. In "distant lands," she noted in her diary, slum dwellers could "pass from sin and dirt and misery to space."

Thanks to family connections, Flora Shaw traveled extensively outside Britain. She made friends with important people such as Rudyard Kipling and Cecil Rhodes, whose views coincided with her own. She particularly admired Rhodes, the bull-necked South African diamond magnate who was the prime minister of South Africa's Cape Colony from 1890 to 1896; she shared his conviction that it was the destiny of Britain to spread through the heart of Africa. In fact, she was half in love with Rhodes: she was mesmerized by muscular imperial heroes and would eventually marry one. Flora regularly sent reports to London publications from her foreign travels. Her big break came in 1890, when Moberly Bell, the newly appointed assistant manager at the *Times,* offered her a regular column under the title "The Colonies." A couple of years later, he sent her off on a year-long tour of Africa and Australia, returning by way of the United States and Canada. In the Transvaal, she visited the gold fields that had been discovered on the Witwatersrand in 1886.

In 1893, Flora Shaw was appointed colonial editor at a salary of £800, or $4,000. She was the first woman on the staff of the *Times* and among the highest-paid women journalists of her day. It helped that her enthusiastic belief in the British Empire as a civilizing force echoed her employer's editorial line. In the 1890s, Flora wrote over 500 articles, columns, and leaders for the *Times* promoting British imperial interests.

Flora's views were definite and her influence was considerable, but part of her success was thanks to her calculations about which conventions to challenge, and which to observe. She never rocked the boat in the gentlemen's club that constituted the *Times*. She was rigidly proper: she always wore black, and in later years would join the Women's National Anti-Suffrage League alongside Gertrude Bell. Her articles were written in the same cool, lucid tones as those of her male colleagues, and when her byline first appeared it was simply "F. Shaw." This approach was quite different from the florid style adopted by most late-nineteenth-century women writers; one editor complained that she never wrote anything "to bring a lump to the throat." But Moberly Bell applauded her disdain for emotional appeal. "You don't seem even to have mentioned anything about the Dominion on which the sun never sets," he chortled about one of her pieces. "This will never do!" Her contemporary Mary Kingsley, another fearless woman traveler who deliberately dressed like a maiden aunt, observed that Flora was "as clever as they make them, capable of any immense amount of work, as hard as nails and talking like a *Times* leader all the time."

Government officials treated the *Times*'s colonial editor with such awe that they regularly invited her to private briefings on matters of state. On occasion her close relationships with on-the-ground sources (especially Rhodes and his cronies) got her into trouble. In 1897, she was accused of having prior knowledge of the Jameson Raid in South Africa, in which one of Rhodes's lieutenants led a raid into the Boer Republic of the Transvaal, aimed at instigating an uprising and seizing the gold-rich Transvaal for Britain. The plan failed, and Flora was called in front of a select committee of the British House of Commons to explain her role. With icy dignity, she parried MPs' questions. "It is not possible," wrote the *Times*'s historian, "to doubt that Miss Shaw used her woman's wits rather to conceal than reveal."

Like any good reporter, Flora Shaw was always on the lookout for a solid story that would burnish her professional reputation and imperial ideals. She was well aware of the value of South Africa's gold fields and diamond mines to the British Empire: once in production, the Rand mines (two-thirds of which were owned by British stockholders) would provide a quarter of the world's supply of gold and make the Transvaal government the richest in Africa. As soon as she heard the first rumors of gold strikes in the most remote corner of the British Empire, Flora plunged into research on the Yukon. Were British interests at risk? "If the Yukon is really as big a thing as it promises to be," she wrote to Moberly Bell in early 1898, "I think it is important British as well as American capital be encouraged to flow into the gold fields." In a diffident response, Bell raised the possibility that Flora herself might make the arduous trip to this bleak and distant corner of the Empire. She grabbed at the chance, and made appointments with the Canadian high commissioner, various senior bankers, and several mining authorities to prepare for the assignment.

On June 22, Flora settled herself comfortably in the dining car of the London and North Western Railway train, bound for Liverpool docks and the White Star Line's steamship *Britannic*, on which she would sail to New York. At London's Euston Station, she had waved goodbye to her sister Lulu and a "circle of dear kind faces on the platform"; now she was finally able to relax and enjoy the railway company's idea of a "Light luncheon—consommé printanier, curried mutton. Roast beef, beans, potatoes, fruit tart, lemon jelly." Afterward she returned to her compartment, opened her leather writing case and began a short note to her sister. "Dearest Lulu, I love you all. I believe that is chiefly what I want to say." Tucking the luncheon menu into the envelope, she gazed out of the window at the smoky industrial towns and gently rolling countryside of the British Midlands. Ahead of her, as she traveled to Dawson City by way of New York, Montreal, Winnipeg, and Vancouver, lay far more dramatic and magnificent vistas—and also the opportunity to escape the stifling British expectations of a "lady" and to chase a good lead.

During her Canadian trip, Flora would write four "Letters from Our Colonial Correspondent" that appeared in the *Times*. They were

well-researched, sober accounts, weaving together information about
the gold fields, the Dominion's economic prospects, and the shortcomings of Canadian officials. But she also wrote far more reveal-
ing letters to her younger sister, Lulu, consisting of several sheets of
onionskin paper covered in her elegant, slanting script. In the inti-
macy of this private correspondence, Flora did not muffle her strong
opinions or disguise her snobbery. During her previous travels in
North America, she had confided to Lulu that San Francisco's streets
gave her "the disagreeable impression of having got hopelessly astray
in one vast servants' hall from which there is no escape." Now, as soon
as she was settled into a large deck cabin on the *Britannic,* she took
the same line in a quick note to her sister. She declared her fellow
passengers to be chiefly American "of I fancy a distinctly second rate
order but it is early to have opinions of a sweeping character." She
didn't think much of the dining room, either. "Dinner was served in
the American fashion which to English tastes is unseemly, all of it
being apparently ready at once and everybody ordering that part of it
which they preferred. My neighbour was at strawberry ice when I was
still eating underdone roast beef."

What Flora's fellow passengers thought of her is unrecorded, but
they were probably intimidated by the well-spoken English woman,
with her patrician profile, flawless complexion, and polished remoteness. Neatly dressed in well-tailored black suits or elegant gowns, she
had the direct gaze and firm chin of a bitingly intelligent schoolteacher.
In a later era, she might have played a leading role in the kind of events
about which she wrote—as an imperial administrator, or elected politician. As a journalist, she was always hungry for facts. On the *Britannic*
she quickly buttonholed a Mr. Monroe, a badly dressed, noisy passenger
who would never have met her exacting standards had he not recently
returned from the Klondike. Flora and Monroe spent hours together,
heads bent over Flora's maps as Monroe described what lay ahead.

"His accounts of the hardships to be encountered are at first somewhat staggering," Flora wrote to her sister. "The bedrock of ice melting constantly under the summer sun turns the ground into one sea of mud through which you have to wade. The mosquitoes are such that a strong man could not live for two hours and a half if exposed to them without protection in the bush. You are always foot sore, bruised and cut with falling over logs and stones. The food is insufficient because everything has to be carried on men's backs and at night there is no rest but such as you can make for yourself when you are dead tired by cutting boughs and heaping them upon the damp ground." After this recitation of horrors, Flora had asked Monroe how much personal luggage she should take. The grizzled old prospector hooted with laughter and told her she didn't need any. Flora blenched and asked about a change of linen. "Change?" replied Monroe. "You won't want to change the clothes you stand up in till you get out of the country again!"

The idea of dirty underwear didn't bother Flora as much as Monroe's guffaw at the very idea that she could make the trip from Montreal to Dawson City and back in sixty days, as she had planned. It would take at least three months, he told her. She was also stunned by the supplies he said she needed. In addition to provisions, she would have to arrange for the carriage of numerous articles: "A small cotton tent, a camp stove and utensils, a waterproof sleeping bag and a revolver, with two complete changes of [outer] clothes and two pairs of blankets makes up the rest. I add a further 101 lbs of luxuries chiefly condensed soups, candles, matches . . . and a few necessary drugs." But the *Times* special correspondent had no intention of letting standards slide: "I suspect my Klondyker of being of a pessimistic temperament and much inclined to make the worst of things."

Flora assured her sister that she would enjoy a daily sponge bath, wear a flannel nightgown for bed, and would wash her feet with alum each night. And she planned to pack a few extras: a costume like a bee-keeper's outfit to shield her from the mosquitoes, a small tin kettle and spirit lamp in a canvas satchel so she could "make a cup of tea whenever

I feel so disposed," split peas, haricot beans, rice, and a bottle of curry powder. "When I am tired of eating boiled bacon and pease pudding I shall eat curried bacon and rice with haricot soup made from the scraps and bones for a third variation . . . It will only amuse me to do my own cooking and washing." Finally, Flora assured Lulu that she would not take stupid risks. "What *The Times* has sent me for is to send them good letters . . . They have not gone to the expense of my journey for the purpose of leaving my bones in Canada."

Flora sent a similar letter to Moberly Bell, but she included a comment from Monroe that she hadn't told Lulu. "Now I am an old Klondyker," her fellow passenger had said, "and you take my advice! Never draw out your revolver till you need it and when you draw it out *shoot quick*!!" Flora confessed that she had never fired a gun. Monroe shrugged. "Well, when you get in the woods I guess you'll have to practice some." Flora confided to her boss: "A reflection on the state of the woods in which other equally inexpert persons may be 'practising some' does not tend to reassure me."

The *Britannic* docked in New York and Flora Shaw took the train to Montreal. As soon as she reached Canada, she was welcomed as though she were the personal ambassador of Queen Victoria herself. Senior members of the four most important institutions in the country— the federal government in Ottawa, the North-West Mounted Police, the Hudson's Bay Company, and the Canadian Pacific Railway—did everything in their power to ensure that the Thunderer's representative crossed the continent in record time. Although Canada had achieved Dominion status in 1867, it still had a distinctly colonial mindset. Most Canadians spoke of the "Mother Country" and celebrated Queen Victoria's birthday with feverish enthusiasm. On her previous visit to Canada, in 1893, Flora had been as unimpressed by Canadians as she had been by Americans. She described them to Lulu as infused with "ineffectual and sentimental loyalty" to the Empire, satisfied with "imperfect achievement," and lacking "the democratic self-reliance of Australia and the executive High Toryism of South Africa." This did not "promise well for the making of a new country," Flora suggested to Lulu, adding that Canada's "general laxity and . . . semi-good-natured incapacity" to tackle economic problems was a recipe for government corruption. Five years later, she carried this preconception westward with her as she was ushered across the continent. Nevertheless, she appreciated the royal treatment, particularly the offer from the Canadian Pacific Railway to telegraph her dispatches to the *Times*. "All goes admirably," Flora wrote to Bell in early July 1898. "I travel like an Indian rubber ball, only the better for it the further I bound."

As soon as Flora arrived at the west coast, she went straight to the Hudson's Bay Company's store in Vancouver. The lower floors of this establishment were filled with household gadgets, gastronomic delicacies, and the latest fashions for ladies and gentlemen. Ignoring such distractions, Flora took the elevator to the top floor—a journey that a contemporary described as "a trip from Paris to Siberia"—where busy clerks sold, packed, and shifted enormous piles of goods while anxious stampeders jostled for their turn. Flora was shown to the front of the queue, and the store manager himself helped her locate everything on her list, including the tent, stove, sleeping bag, beekeeper's outfit, and mosquito netting. Then he arranged for it to be loaded onto the little steamer on which she would head north.

Ahead of Flora lay the voyage up the Inland Passage of Canada's west coast to Skagway, the jumping-off point for the route over the St. Elias mountain range via the White Pass. From the deck of the coastal steamer, Flora gazed out at the unfamiliar northern panoramas, then wrote a huffy little note to Lulu: "If only there were colours it would be lovely but the weather is permanently grey and the whole scene in half-ghostly, dove-coloured tones, grey sea, grey sky, grey hills, dark at the base, which is generally crowded to the water edge and white on the snow-capped tops."

On July 12, 1898, twenty-one days after she had left London, Flora disembarked from the steamer at the American port of Skagway, three miles south of Dyea at the head of the Lynn Canal, and got her first taste of Gold Rush culture. This settlement had barely existed until July 1897, when the first stampeders had opted to land here, instead of Dyea, so they could attempt the White Pass. Since then, it had swelled to a muddy town of 5,000, filled with shacks, tents, gambling houses, and makeshift saloons with names like the Mangy Dog, the Nugget, the Home of Hooch, and the Blaze of Glory. On first glance, an observer might assume little difference between Skagway and Dawson City, a few hundred miles north. But Skagway was lawless and, in the words of Sam Steele of the Mounties, chief law enforcement officer on the Canadian side of the northern border, "about the roughest place in the world . . . little better than a hell on earth, [where] the hard, cracked voices of the [dance hall] singers wailed amidst the shouts of murder, cries for help, and the sharp staccato crack of gunfire." Exhausted, penniless men begged in the filthy streets, or earned enough for a meal by digging graves in the overcrowded cemetery for victims of an outbreak of spinal meningitis.

Until four days before Flora's arrival, Skagway had been under the control of a ruthless thug called Jefferson Randolph "Soapy" Smith. There was no hospital or civic government, only a deputy U.S. marshal who supplemented his income by befriending Soapy Smith and sharing in his loot. When pressed to establish a police force, the marshal had responded, "Other cities are over-governed, but Americans, when left to their own resources, are disposed to do the right thing." Soapy had proved him wrong: Smith's gang of thieves, scoundrels, con men, and shills had dominated this miserable settlement, where murder was commonplace and justice unknown. Saloons, bars, brothels, gaming halls, and hotels all paid protection money to Soapy because if they didn't, their businesses would suffer. Unwary prospectors were steered into crooked card games, sold non-existent goods, or fleeced of their savings. Soapy had even established a bogus Skagway Telegraph Office. Despite the fact that there was no telegraph line to Skagway, newly arrived stampeders were persuaded to send a reassuring message home, for the price of five dollars. Soapy's telegraph operator ensured that an answer would arrive within a few hours. It always came collect.

Smith's crime spree in Skagway had come to an abrupt end on July 7. A returning Klondike miner had been foolish enough to get into a game of three-card monte with three of Soapy's henchmen. They persuaded him to stake his sack of gold dust, worth $2,800, which he promptly lost. When he protested that the game was fixed, they grabbed the sack and ran. A local committee of vigilantes, who had been trying to drive Soapy Smith out of Skagway for months, demanded that the gold be returned. Soapy just sneered at them. The following night, in a shoot-out on the waterfront, both Smith and a guard named Frank Reid were fatally wounded.

A couple of days later, the steamer's captain carefully escorted Flora off the ship. As soon as they were on dry land, Flora heard about the whole affair. Blood stained the wharf; Smith's sidekicks were crowded into the log jail ("as full as it could hold of wickedness"); the towns-folk exuded overwhelming relief that they were rid of such a crook. The Wild West tenor of the tale amused the Londoner, and in a light-hearted letter to Lulu, she bestowed an aura of revolutionary grandeur on the criminal by referring to him as a "Robespierre of the name of Soapy Smith" responsible for a "reign of terror." Once her own luggage had been unloaded, she watched the vigilantes march some of Smith's associates, including the U.S. marshal, onto the boat under an escort of rifles. "The interest of watching these irregular proceedings delayed me for some hours, and I did not get away with my pack train until seven in the evening."

Nevertheless, the story of Soapy Smith's crimes was more evidence, in Flora's view, of the inferiority of American society. She was appalled by the "American principles" of vigilante justice on which the town seemed to be run. In Canadian territory a few days later, Flora watched the Mounties deal with the four Tlingit whose story had attracted the vindictive headlines of the *Klondike Nugget.* The men were on their way to trial in Dawson. At one stage, Flora found herself eating dinner in the Mounties' tent alongside two officers, the four suspects, and a man they had tried to kill. Flora behaved as graciously as if she was joining her friend the Duchess of Sutherland for dinner. Her fellow diners, she noticed, were even more gracious. At one point, one of the suspects could not reach the dish because he was in handcuffs. The man they had attacked, whose arm was still in a sling, pushed the dish toward him, saying, "Want some more beans, boy?" Suffused with pride in standards of British justice, Flora wrote to Lulu, "When murders are committed on our side of the border we don't require the citizens to rise in raucous indignation to avenge them. We simply give notice to the police. The offenders are promptly arrested and sent down securely ironed to Dawson where they will be well and truly hanged."

Despite the fact that she was at least twenty years older than most of the other travelers and corseted in ladylike skirts and a tight-waisted jacket, Flora Shaw hardly broke into a sweat as she tackled the forty-five-mile uphill switchback of the White Trail. The long days and the July sun meant less mud and more warmth than stampeders in previous months had known, although "it was not an altogether pleasant experience because of the number of horses that have been killed by the steepness of the way and whose bodies no vultures are here to remove." The smell at the notorious Dead Horse Gulch, she told Lulu, "is not to be described." But this was a passing phase; during the three-day hike to the summit she reported, "the scenery was magnificent and, but for the dead horses, the journey would have been delightful." Perhaps it was so easy to keep chin up and cheerful because she had to make the journey only once, she was not carrying her own baggage, and she had powerful protectors. The Mounties were *so* obliging. While she sat on a log, boiling her kettle for a cup of afternoon tea, "the nice comfortable police are putting up my tent." This allowed her to scribble another note to Lulu, in which she described how the climate reminded her of an English summer and the scenery of the Scottish Highlands.

In the sprawling tent city at the head of Bennett Lake, Flora Shaw did *not* blend in with the crowd, and certainly had no interest in doing so. One young woman, Martha Munger Purdy, stared in surprise at this lady who was so "different from the usual type coming into the country. She was wearing a smart-looking rain cape and a tweed hat, and as she turned, I noted that she was not so pretty as clever-looking." Martha was from an affluent, well-connected Chicago family and had the self-assurance to make her way over to where Flora was watching men building boats, and introduce herself. Flora explained that she had been sent to the Klondike by the London *Times* and was exasperated by the length of the journey. To both their satisfaction, the two women found they had a mutual acquaintance, "which proves," Martha would later write, "that the world is really small." But there was no time for stampede small talk. The nice, comfortable police had found a stern-wheeler to take their VIP through the chain of lakes to Whitehorse, and a second steamer on which she could complete her journey to Dawson.

Flora's only complaint about steamer travel was the diet of bad fish and stewed tea. She maintained her standards despite the black bilge water swirling round her feet, the lack of passenger cabins, and the smell of oil, freight, and sweat. "I have borrowed a galvanized iron pail and a tin basin from the cook and can just manage to shut myself in so as to secure privacy for a wash." She did find that being "over the boiler the heat is almost unbearable. The woodwork is hot to the touch and one's clothes smell of roasting."

The water level of the Yukon River was gradually falling and the White Horse Rapids were not as fearsome as in earlier months, but Flora's sangfroid was tested when the stern-wheeler repeatedly got stuck on sandbanks. She spent a day in the pilot box, talking to the crew as they steered the vessel round various hazards. She even began to unbend. "The good humour and kindliness of all these rough people is remarkable. The captain tells me that they pride themselves out West upon their great Western hearts and so far as I am concerned I find everyone ready to be kind and helpful . . . It is rather touching to me to find nearly all the men frankly lonesome for their wives and children."

On July 23, 1898, the *Times*'s colonial editor arrived at her destination. It was only thirty-one days since she left London, and despite her shipboard friend Mr. Monroe's claim that she couldn't possibly reach Dawson from Montreal in less than thirty days, she had done it in fewer than twenty. She had no intention of slowing her pace. She wanted to get the measure of the gold fields on which Bill Haskell and Jack London had pinned their hopes, and the community that Father Judge and Belinda Mulrooney were nudging toward civility.

CHAPTER 15
"Queer, rough men," August 1898

WHEN FLORA SHAW ARRIVED in Dawson City, a reception committee of prominent citizens, including the senior police officer, was waiting for her on the crowded wharf—not because she was a woman but because she was from the *Times*. A *Times* report on the Klondike would inevitably have a big impact in London and Ottawa, and would influence British investors. It was important that she get the "right" impression.

The Dawson authorities hustled their distinguished visitor through the crowd of loafers and layabouts hanging around the wharf, giving her no time to see the ramshackle, false-fronted buildings on Front Street, Belinda's Fairview Hotel among them, or to hear the cries of croupiers escaping from saloons. The Bennett Lake–Dawson steamship company had arranged for her tent to be pitched alongside the log cabin of its Dawson agent, above Eighth Avenue on a steep hill covered in silver birches and alders. Here, close to a source of clean water, log cabins and tents were scattered through the woods overlooking Father Judge's hospital. The company had also found a handyman, called James Short, to look after her, making Flora one of the few people in town other than proprietors of hotels and brothels who employed a domestic servant. Given that Short charged Flora four dollars a day at a time when the average wage in Dawson was ten dollars, he was probably subsidized by the authorities.

If so, the strategy worked. The day after her arrival, she settled herself outside her tent to write to Lulu. "I had a long sleep last night and this morning a bath and clean clothes and feel much refreshed." She had expected Short to be "the equivalent of an English charwoman" but was pleased to discover that he was more like "a knight errant . . . He knows apparently everything there is to know about American woodcraft and brings all the resources of his knowledge to bear upon my comfort." Short provided fresh brushwood on which Flora could spread her sleeping bag, new spruce boughs for the floor of the tent, and hot water for her daily wash. Flora had an upper-class Englishwoman's culinary limitations, and cooed with delight when, after her wash, Short settled her at a crude table and served the most appetizing meal she had seen for days. "Hot cakes of infinite varieties appear at breakfast, buttered toast, porridge, sort of omelette dishes made with crystallized [dried] eggs, bacon cooked in batter, bacon in sandwiches of hot rice cakes, bacon curried, bacon with a thick white gravy." Pies, curries, hashes, and stews were conjured up out of the only two kinds of meat available, bacon and tinned corned beef. Short also produced "a wonderful series of sweet dishes from evaporated fruits and prunes and farinaceous stuffs."

Although Flora was no cook, she was an energetic hiker and gardener. Her first morning, she walked up the hill behind her tent to take in the magnificent view of the Yukon River, snaking silently between hills now clad in emerald-green alder and plum dark spruce. Only the snow-capped mountains in the distance hinted at the frozen bleakness of the same landscape in winter. As she retraced the steps to her tent, she picked a bouquet of lupines, Jacob's ladder, and purple fireweed, then arranged the wildflowers in an empty condensed milk tin in the middle of the table. She was fascinated by the way her neighbors' vegetable gardens flourished during the brief growing season, thanks to the never-ending sunshine. In late July, a full month after the summer solstice, light lingered in the sky until well after midnight. Lettuce, peas,

Behind the wooden buildings of Dawson's commercial district, a sea of canvas stretched over the hillsides.

and beans flourished on the sod roofs of cabins. "I could not resist the temptation to sow mustard and cress and radishes around my tent."

Flora's positive impressions were also reflected in the first paragraphs of the "Letter from Canada" that would appear in the *Times* on Monday, September 19, 1898, under the byline "From Our Special Correspondent." Her description of the Gold Rush town was very different from the "dreary, desolate Dawson" that Jack London had left only five weeks earlier, when he disappeared down the Yukon River. Dawson City, according to the *Times*, seemed well on the way to becoming yet another little colonial town, far from the center of power but proclaiming its allegiance with a bravely fluttering Union Jack. Flora had seen such towns all through Africa and Australia; now she envisaged Dawson developing into a subarctic version of Rhodesia's Salisbury or Tasmania's Hobart.

"Dawson City has stretched itself across a little cove of river-wash which forms a hundred acres or so of the flat land in the sweep of a bend made by the Yukon just after it has received the waters of the [Klondike River]. The main street of Dawson follows the river bank. Behind it tents are thickly studded on the flat, and as the town stretches up the encircling hills log cabins, in some cases tastefully constructed with little balconies, verandahs and projecting porches, stand in rows among the uncleared copse. In the south-eastern suburb of the town, which mounts high over the hill dividing the course of the Yukon and commands a view of both rivers, a broad road has been cut through the spruce wood. Here cabins built of white peeled logs succeed each other on either side in little clearings of about half an acre, and form in their setting of aromatic scented wood an original and charming suggestion of a boulevard which only needs the advent of women and the house life which they will bring with them to the town to realize its possibilities." Nobody had talked about aromatic-scented wood, balconies, and verandas before, or suggested that Dawson had suburbs.

Privately, Flora was much more critical. She wrote to Lulu, "Few people permit themselves the extravagance of a servant but do everything for themselves washing included. The natural result follows that everything on occasion is left undone, and the universal dirt is one of the worst features of the situation." Swirls of brown dust rose from the dried mud streets and lodged in every crease of skin and fabric; Flora's skin itched in the dry, grimy air. The town itself, she told her sister, "is hideous." Streets that only two months earlier had been quagmires were now rock hard, with ankle-twisting crevasses. "All the refuse of the town of tents flung out of doors, no order of a sanitary kind pursued and the so-called main street along which wooden warehouses and hotels are rapidly closing up in a continuous row is a mere lane of mudholes and dust heaps where you feel you are breathing poison all the time you walk. I only go down on business and am always glad to get back to the hillside."

While Short whipped up curried bacon and washed Flora's napkins, Flora got busy. Within five days of her arrival in Dawson, she had walked all around the town and spoken to most of its more respectable citizens. She was looking for answers to two related questions. How much gold was here? And was there enough to continue to draw people to the district for a period of years sufficient to achieve, in her words, "the permanent and civilized settlement of the country"?

Finding the answers involved polite but relentless grilling of Dawson's prominent citizens. She made appointments with both the affable David Doig of the Bank of British North America and the thin-lipped Mr. Wills of the Canadian Bank of Commerce, so she might learn how much gold had been deposited in their tin chests. Knowing that the trading companies acted as repositories for miners' pokes and as lending institutions for prospectors needing a grubstake, she walked into the offices of Captain John Jerome Healy, general manager of the North American Transportation and Trading Company, and Captain J. E. Hansen, general manager of the Alaska Commercial Company. She spoke to Mike and Sam Bartlett, who ran the largest packing business in the city, about the amount of gold their mule trains carried down from the creeks. She questioned the NWMP commander about how much gold was being circulated in the town.

One of Flora's most important interviews was with Thomas Fawcett, the gold commissioner whose office was now even more cluttered with piles of paper than when Jack London had met him. Flora questioned Fawcett closely about official and unofficial gold production statistics. How much gold was evading the royalty fee? The *Klondike Nugget*'s campaign against Commissioner Fawcett was going full bore while Flora was in the Yukon. A week before she arrived in Dawson, editor Gene Allen had accused Fawcett of favoring certain claimants in a recent stampede up Dominion Creek and displaying utter incompetence in fulfilling his duties. "The Rottenest Piece of Business and Rankest Injustice the Gold Commissioner's Office Has Yet Perpetrated" read the *Nugget* headline. A few days after Flora arrived, a *Nugget* editorial entitled "How Long, Oh Lord?" thundered, "We . . . have never before run across a public officer so universally condemned for vacillation, incompetence and disregard of the individuals composing the public." The *Klondike Nugget* also fulminated against the royalty regime imposed by the Canadian government, pointing out (with justice) that this was taxation without representation, since the Yukon had no voice in Ottawa. According to the *Nugget*, the offensive royalty was throttling the development of the creeks. In vain did Fawcett point out that the royalty was the government's only means to reap any benefit for Canada before the gold disappeared into the States. The large number of American prospectors shared the *Nugget*'s indignation, and *Nugget* sales soared: "Uncle Andy," the sixty-five-year-old paperboy in charge of street sales, was sold out before he had finished his cry, "The *Nugget*! The *Nugget*! The dear little *Nugget*!" The *Nugget*'s huffing, puffing tone of outrage would not have appealed to the *Times*'s correspondent, but Flora Shaw certainly heard the message.

Between business meetings, Flora picked her way along the wooden sidewalks of Front Street, noting a mob of about a thousand men idly staring at boats tied up at the wharves, wagons driving up and down the street, or any other passing show. "They appear to be for the most part in the prime of life, sturdy, well fed, and in a rough sense, well dressed: they also appear to have nothing in the world to do." She was puzzled by their lassitude in the midst of such a buzz of activity: the ceaseless whine of sawmills, the yells of stevedores unloading freight, the hammer blows of builders erecting yet more false-fronted buildings, the shouts of hustlers drumming up business. A man might easily find work, so why were so many slouching around with their hands stuck in their pockets? She also told the readers of the *Times* that there was scarcely a woman to be seen, although this was not strictly true. As she made her way down Second Avenue, she would not have been able to avoid prostitutes, wearily soliciting clients, outside their cabins ("hutches" or "maisons de joie" in Dawson lingo). But Flora had developed that essential characteristic of a Victorian lady, the ability to remain oblivious to "fallen women."

One night, between midnight and two o'clock, Flora went with a male escort (almost certainly a police officer) on a tour of some of the twenty-two gambling salons and music halls operating in the town that summer. These were the dives Jack London had loved—music hall melodies bashed out on honky-tonk pianos, bottles lined up behind the long mahogany bars, the warm light of coal-oil lamps reflected in gilt-framed mirrors. But it was not Flora's world. She cast a cool eye on the professional gamblers, the blowsy hookers, the long-nailed barmen with their sleeve garters and bowler hats, and the throng of boozy miners. As she reported to the *Times,* "The gaming tables are habitually crowded and are piled with counters representing substantial sums . . . Some calculations put it at hundreds of thousands of dollars a night . . . The price of liquor ranges from half a dollar for a glass of beer to forty dollars for a bottle of champagne; but everybody drinks." Her escort pointed out to her several men who regularly spent $5,000 to $10,000 at a sitting, treating their friends. She noted how, despite the Canadian Bank of Commerce's bills, gold dust remained the universal currency and "every house of business has its gold scales."

In the *Times,* Flora reported her observations without comment. To Lulu, she wrote of her night on the town, "It was not a pretty sight, but it enabled me to form a more complete estimate of the miner's life. It was the miner at play. I shall probably respect him more when I see him next week at work."

Flora Shaw was all business, judging by her *Times* dispatches and letters to Lulu. She had no time for the lives of those not directly involved with gold production. There was no mention of the Hän people, struggling to maintain their Moosehide community a couple of miles downriver. She was too busy writing up her notes to socialize with the handful of Dawson residents who might have approached her social standards. Every steamer from St. Michael brought in more affluent tourists, and they were changing the look and feel of the isolated town. There was even a whiff of sophistication. Miss Van Buren and Mrs. Hitchcock

The decks of little Yukon steamers had to be reinforced to take the weight of gold when it was shipped out at the end of the summer.

had established themselves in West Dawson, the new settlement on the western bank of the Yukon River, safely removed from Dawson's typhoid epidemic. They had pitched their huge circus tent and were serving anchovies, mock-turtle soup, roast moose, pâtés, stuffed olives, and peach ice cream to the *gratin* of Dawson. Their guest of honor was often Big Alex McDonald, gussied up and uncomfortable in a starched white shirt and stiff collar for the parties. Belinda Mulrooney's Fairview Hotel was thriving; Mary Hitchcock had visited it and widened her eyes with astonishment when she read a menu that began with "oyster cocktails." Father Judge was delighted to discover among the newcomers a fellow Baltimorean, a physician, with whom he could play chess and discuss philosophy.

None of these notable characters appeared in Flora's account of her subarctic sojourn. The only hint of conversations with strangers beyond official circles is a reference in her third *Times* letter to a handful of women who had wintered in Dawson. When asked if Dawson was dreadful in January, they assured the fastidious Londoner that "winter is the pleasantest season." One, more outspoken than the others and sounding suspiciously like Belinda, had retorted, "Why, we get a great deal more daylight than you ever see in London in the winter." If this was Belinda, Flora never mentioned her by name, and probably treated the fiery little Irish-American woman with her customary crisp sense of superiority.

The only person Flora felt on equal terms with was the husband of a distant English acquaintance, whom she had met on the street. She invited him to supper in her cabin, and her handyman, Short, managed to rustle up a four-course dinner featuring mulligatawny soup. As Flora told Lulu, her visitor marveled at the sophistication of Flora's quarters, regarding them as "luxurious" because, as Flora remarked, "I happened to think of bringing half a dozen dinner napkins with me and I have one put in the middle of my [packing case] table." Flora herself had no interest in accepting invitations to dinner in cabins where "people sit on packing cases for chairs and dinner is served on tin plates which you wash as you use them."

After five days in Dawson City, Flora set off to visit the gold-bearing creeks. The stamina of this forty-six-year-old woman, accustomed to English mansions and Westminster pavements, was impressive as she set out alone to see things for herself. She pulled on canvas leggings under her skirt and a seasoned pair of leather boots and headed out of town for four days. It rained for two. The mud was terrible, and she frequently found herself wading through streams or balancing on tree trunks that had fallen across them. Nevertheless, her letters reveal that despite the hardships she was exhilarated by the midnight sunsets and "the sensation of immense solitudes the very moment you are out of sight of occupation. One realizes the newness of it too by the tameness of the birds . . . They don't appear to have learned yet to be afraid of man and the wild canaries and other birds will almost perch on your head." In common with many women who went north, Flora enjoyed the chance to strike out on her own, unshackled from the stifling social conventions of life back home.

Flora Shaw was as shocked as Jack London had been the previous fall by the desecration of a landscape now buzzing with activity. Valleys that had once been carpeted each summer with soft green moss and wildflowers were glistening expanses of black mud, through which creeks snaked. The miners' insatiable need for timber to build cabins, windlasses, flumes, and fires had stripped the hillsides naked, making the scenery, in Flora's word, "monotonous." A network of sluice boxes, elevated wooden tubes, threaded its way from creek mouth to canyon. Rockers, boilers, winches, and trestles littered the ground in every direction.

An army of gold diggers worked like horses and lived like dogs here. Their homes were filthy, surrounded by lines of soiled, flapping undergarments drying in the summer sun, and a debris of rusty old cans. Sled dogs roamed free, and the primitive outhouses attracted flies and mosquitoes. Flora was grateful for her beekeeping veil. Inside the cabins, sheds, and shacks, furniture was makeshift and minimal, dirt floors unswept, and spittoons filled with evil-looking tobacco juice. But where Jack had seen exploitation of the working man, Flora saw business potential: "It was extraordinarily interesting to see the gold being taken at every point out of the ground." Nobody could hope to cover in four days the hundreds of square miles around Dawson where between 4,000 and 8,000 miners were working, but Flora Shaw did her best. On the first day she walked sixteen miles from Dawson along the lower stretch of Bonanza Creek to Grand Forks, where Belinda Mulroney had established her roadhouse. Flora stayed in this boomtown, which was home to almost 10,000 people this summer, for the next three nights. She spent the day after her arrival exploring the mines on the upper section of Bonanza Creek, the next visiting the claims on Eldorado and Hunker creeks, and returned to Dawson on the fourth day. Altogether, she walked at least seventy miles and probably saw most of the 165 claims on Bonanza, the 56 claims on Eldorado, and several of the 90 claims on Hunker Creek.

Throughout the Klondike Gold Rush, these three creeks ran through the busiest and most productive valleys in the whole district. Their bare slopes were criss-crossed with flumes bringing water down to sluice out those great piles of paydirt. Flora watched thousands of men digging into mounds of gravel and muck, then tipping spadefuls into the running water with the same sense of crazed urgency as if they were digging for bodies under a recent mudslide. There were so few weeks to find gold before winter set in again and everything froze. But when the miners saw this imperious Englishwoman striding along the creeks in her veil and leggings, they paused, open mouthed. Flora herself was relentless. At several claims, she pulled out her notebook and had a long chat with the men about what they were doing and how much gold they were finding. She soon grasped the system—how land was staked, how the miners spent the winter deep underground, excavating muck, gravel, and paydirt until they reached bedrock, how the paydirt was shoveled into sluice boxes or rockers in the spring, and how running water then washed away the dirt, leaving the gold behind.

The almost fabulous wealth of the creeks stunned Flora. On one claim, she watched a prospector collect the gold from the bottom of the sluice boxes after only two days of sluicing. "I stopped for a few minutes, and while I stood there they took, besides nuggets, 500 ounces, or close upon £2,000 worth of gold-dust from the open boxes." The yield from that clean-up in today's terms was close to $500,000. On another claim, she heard that $400,000 of gold (over $20 million in today's terms) had been taken in the previous weeks. She was staggered to see how the men casually threw gold scrapings from the bottom of the sluice boxes into shallow pans that were "as carelessly exposed as if the yellow heaps they hold were so much sawdust or brown sugar." Throughout the diggings she inspected, "Gold might be seen spangling the ground, and there were places in which gold dust and nuggets might be scraped together with a spoon." She also marveled at the amount of gold coming from the bench claims overlooking the creeks, where ancient, dried-up river beds were proving immensely productive. Flora told *Times* readers, "On French Hill and on Skookum, overlooking the El Dorado and Bonanza Valleys, I have myself picked up nuggets and seen gold washed as freely as in the phenomenal river-beds two or three hundred feet below."

Flora had expected to hear appalling language and was even prepared for disrespectful attitudes. But her decorum quelled obscenity. Her new acquaintances, she noted, seemed determined "that 'the lady' would be spared any unnecessary acquaintance with the coarser side of life." When asked for their views on the gold fields, many gave her an earful about the 10 percent tax that the Canadian government demanded on what they took out of the ground. When Flora apologized to one man for her indiscreet inquiries, he guffawed: "Oh, you can ask me anything you like! When I don't want to tell you, I shall lie. That is how we manage. The Government has made perjurers of us all in this country."

Flora Shaw also discovered that not all the hobnail-booted miners were laborers or "foreigners," despite living conditions that would shock a working-class Englishman. Some she might even have met in London, although they were well disguised in their filthy shirts, bushy beards, and battered felt hats. ("No-one cleans their boots in this country and there is no blacking," she told Lulu. "I have had a pot of Trumpers complexion cream which I have shared daily with mine.") On Hunker Creek, she stumbled into the smoke-filled cabin of a man called McFarlane, who, she discovered, "is the sort of man who in London would probably belong to one or two good clubs and enjoy all the luxuries of civilization." There wasn't a book, decanter, newspaper, or piece of silverware in his shack. Instead, three or four of McFarlane's friends were seated on packing cases drinking weak tea and gulping down corned beef off tin plates. Despite the down-at-heel surroundings, McFarlane treated Flora with the utmost courtesy. "I've just had a clean-up at the

Flora was astonished at the careless way prospectors stored their treasure. This man had $1.5 million of gold stacked in his cabin.

mine," he remarked. "Would you like to see my gold?" When she said she would, he casually put two gold pans in the middle of the dirty floor and emptied his leather sacks into them. There was about a thousand ounces—worth, according to Flora's calculations, over £3,500.

In other cabins, she saw rows of old tobacco canisters and apricot tins filled with gold, lined up on windowsills. Nuggets were stored with as little security as peppermint candies. "It is extraordinarily curious," she confided to Lulu, "to see the contrast between all the piles of wealth which lie about in the most careless manner and the extremities of poverty in which everybody lives." Successful miners rarely carried their own harvest back to Dawson, since gold was so heavy. Instead, they sent it down on pack trains that regularly moved up and down the creeks. "One little pack train of three mules brought down a few days ago £24,000 worth of gold in common sacks . . . tied at the mouth with common twine," Flora noted. The mule driver had the foresight to fasten some sailcloth over the sacks to prevent them getting ripped open if a mule fell or they were snagged by an overhanging branch.

Throughout her tour of the creeks, and despite the miners' reticence to tell her their total yield, Flora was busy assessing the output of the mines. One of the firms of packers, which handled about one-third of the total business, told her that their pack trains had brought down from Bonanza and Eldorado around 45,000 pounds in weight in the previous two months. Flora made a rough calculation that the output so far in 1898 of the creeks she had seen was around £2 to £3 million, or $10 to $15 million in 1898 values.

On the strength of these calculations, Flora decided that "this subarctic province," as she described it to Mr. Buckle, the *Times*'s business editor, was more interesting than she had expected. She knew she was not alone in her conclusions: Close Brothers, a London bank, had recently plunged into an extraordinary engineering venture: financing the construction of the White Pass and Yukon Railway, which would transport stampeders from Skagway to the summit of the White Pass.

Flora sent Buckle a locally printed map: "I think the business world might be glad to have a map of the Klondike district in which the principal creeks should be marked." And she tried to convey her own sense of the region's potential by mentioning, "Capital is beginning to come here. Rothschild and others have experts on the spot." The previous January, the Ottawa government had enacted new regulations that allowed the gold commissioner in Dawson to approve twenty-year dredging leases to large corporations. Flora had already heard that at least two companies were interested: the English mining promoter Arthur Newton Christian Treadgold and the Guggenheims, the wealthy mining family from Philadelphia.

The same positive note crept into the third of her letters to appear in the *Times*. "Impeded as the work has been by the exceptional difficulties of climate and position," she told readers, the gold field's 1898 output "is in itself remarkable enough to deserve the attention of the business world." She pointed out that costs were high because everything was done by hand. Flora had learned enough about the mining industry in South Africa to know that, with some capital investment, the digging, shoveling, drilling, and sluicing could be mechanized. Hauling the heavy dredging equipment out to the creeks would be expensive, but once it was installed a successful claim would need a workforce of three to five men, instead of between twenty and forty. Not only would labor costs drop sharply but so would the incredibly high bills for packing provisions and supplies out of Dawson to the creeks.

After twenty days in Dawson City and on the creeks, Flora Shaw decided she had enough material. Her notebooks were full, she had purchased a small gold nugget for each of her sisters, and she had already eaten the mustard and cress she had planted around her tent. The brief northern summer was drawing to a close, winds were icy, the sky was filled with geese flying south, and she was impatient to escape. On August 11, she embarked on the stern-wheeler *Anglian*, steaming upriver. The journey home was rougher than her trip north. The *Anglian* was more comfortable than the steamer she had taken downriver—she even had her own cabin—but she was traveling upstream now, and the journey to Whitehorse took eleven days instead of six. The boat had to stop almost daily to collect wood for its furnace from the cordwood piles located at regular intervals along the bank. Then the boilers broke down, causing a day's delay. Next, supplies ran out: "We had practically nothing but beans, but we found ourselves coming in contentedly like horses to their mangers to eat them three times a day." Flora had developed a grudging regard for men who had fought their way north to chase their dreams of gold. "I lived on deck and slept with the cabin windows open, and did nothing but talk to the miners—queer, rough men, who put themselves at once on a footing of complete equality and were very kind and even chivalrous in their own way. One learns a lot about human nature on a trip of this sort."

From Whitehorse, there was still a lot of ground to cover. Desperate to get out of the Yukon, Flora was too impatient to wait for comfortable transportation. She crossed four lakes huddled under a tarpaulin in a scow, climbed the northern side of the Chilkoot Pass in a baggage train, scrambled on hands and knees over the summit, then slithered down a glacier on the other side. At Dyea, she staggered onto a Victoria-bound steamer only two weeks after she had left Dawson. Despite the pessimism of Mr. Monroe, her shipboard adviser, she had completed her journey in and out of the Yukon in fifty-three days. It was only ten weeks since she had waved goodbye to Lulu in London.

Our Special Correspondent telegraphed her final two letters about the Klondike gold fields to the *Times* from Victoria, on August 29. She had been overwhelmed by the potential of the fields and the amount of gold that was being hauled out of the ground by primitive windlasses. Her calculations about the impact of mechanization were prescient: within a couple of years the pick-and-shovel prospectors would be replaced by well-funded corporations with steam-driven equipment.

But Flora Shaw also had her scoop—although it was not the story that she had expected to bring home. Her fierce criticism of what was going on in Dawson City would not endear her to her hosts.

CHAPTER 16
Scandal and Steele, September–October 1898

AFTER REACHING VANCOUVER, Flora Shaw made her way slowly east as a guest of the Hudson's Bay Company. In the new pioneer settlements of Alberta and Saskatchewan and the booming city of Winnipeg, she took copious notes about agriculture, climate, the fur trade, and the lumber industry for future "Letters from Our Colonial Correspondent" for the *Times*. She was still on a campaign to export Britain's excess population to distant colonial corners, and wrote to her sister Lulu that the land would benefit from an influx of "poor clergymen's and soldiers' and sailors' daughters as well as sons."

Yet her Yukon adventure had widened her horizons. With her main objective accomplished, she was more open to new sights and people— especially the Indians she met. Impressed by the Hudson's Bay Company's Cree and Métis employees, she questioned the Indian wife of an HBC officer extensively about her people's religion and customs, and a few days later, in northern Ontario, she admired the quill- and beadwork of a "pretty and graceful . . . young squaw." Relentlessly intrepid, in late September she took a ten-day canoe trip with an HBC factor and two Ojibwa guides in the Rainy River region north of Lake Superior to study the sturgeon fishing industry. She was captivated by the dramatic, rocky scenery, and she visited an Indian camp where she was intrigued by a way of life so remote from her own. But her attitudes were colored by the self-serving assumptions of government and HBC bureaucrats and the romantic novels she had read as a child, particularly those by James Fenimore Cooper, author of *The Last of the Mohicans*. She swallowed the conventional wisdom that Canada's indigenous peoples belonged to a "rapidly-dying race."

As Flora traveled east, she quietly speculated on the impact that the four letters she had so far telegraphed to London would have on both editors and readers of the *Times*. She knew that the first two letters would not cause a fuss. The first had appeared on August 27, 1898, with the dateline July 12, and was accompanied by a quotation from Virgil's *Aeneid*: "Quid non mortalia pectora cogis, Auri sacra fames?" (To what do you not drive human hearts, accursed craving for gold?) The editor introduced the letter with a preface: "It is not so long ago that Canada was regarded by a certain class of politicians as a troublesome dependency of no great value to the British Crown. Did such an idea linger still in the minds of Englishmen, it would be dispelled by such an account as we publish today."

Both this letter and the next one, which appeared on September 10, were thoughtful travelogues. But the next two letters were written and telegraphed after Flora had left the Yukon, and they covered her Dawson experiences. She had already written to Lulu that "the corruption among the Canadian officials is a shock to my faith in British institutions for which I was not prepared. It is absolutely scandalous but I trust that an end will be put to it when it is exposed." Flora had seen government corruption in the Transvaal, but in her view it was nothing compared to what was going on in the Klondike. Government officials, she told her sister, "sell everything down to the right to enter a public building and poor men cannot get their gold claims recorded unless they give a part interest to the officials." Flora's imperial pride was outraged, and she was going to set things right. The third and fourth letters, published in London on September 19 and 23, respectively, each occupied an entire page of the *Times* and sparked both thundering editorials and correspondence.

Flora was as forthright in the Thunderer as she had been to Lulu. The potential of the gold fields thrilled her, but "to put the position as plainly as it is daily and hourly stated on the mining fields and in the streets of Dawson, there is a widely prevalent conviction not only that the laws are bad, but that the officers through which they are administered are corrupt . . . It is impossible to talk for five minutes on business with anyone on the mines or in the streets without some allusion occurring to the subject, and it is a painful experience for Englishmen proud of the purity of the British system of government to be compelled to listen to the plain-spoken comments of Americans and foreigners."

What exactly was Flora Shaw talking about? Until her letter was published in the *Times,* most of the tales out of Dawson had been a combination of horror stories about conditions and climate and good-old-boy anecdotes about the brotherhood of prospectors and the incorruptible Mounties. Now here was this woman from London, who had only reached the Klondike thanks to the Canadian government, the NWMP, the Canadian Pacific Railway, and the Hudson's Bay Company, writing that more than just the townsite stank. She was arguing that Dawson City was a moral blot on the map of the British Empire.

Flora's accusations focused on two particular issues. The most important was the behavior of Canadian government officials. They were on the take, charged Flora. The gold commissioner's office deliberately dragged its feet on recording claims, surveying mining districts, and publicizing areas available for staking in order to facilitate bribery. "A half or a quarter interest is frequently quoted as the price at which good claims can be recorded," she wrote. The post office was just as bad. "Scarcely a day passes in which some fresh story does not become current of the number of dollars which it has cost to obtain letters." A delivery of mail to the post office, located in a log cabin on Front Street, could produce a line-up to receive longed-for letters that stretched along the wooden sidewalk for several blocks.

With no system for sorting mail at the Dawson City post office, the line-up outside would stretch for several blocks and last for days.

The second issue was the royalty of 10 percent on gross output that Ottawa had imposed on the mining industry a year earlier. The *Times* was not the first major newspaper to protest the royalty, but Flora backed up the argument with facts. She recounted conversations with miners about the economics of their claims: she had come across one prospector who had spent $26,000 on a claim that had yielded gold to the value of $21,000 in the same period. "The owner under the law was not only the loser of $5,000: he remained the debtor of the Government for $2,000." Some mine owners had told her that they were leaving their dumps of paydirt unwashed, "thinking it a better investment for their gold to remain in the ground than to be taken out to pay ten percent to the Dominion Government." The excessive royalty, Flora wrote, would drive away capital and slow the development of the region.

The prospectors were also riled by a recently announced regulation that the government should be allocated every alternate claim on creeks currently being surveyed. "For the law to halve the rights of the public only in order to take the whole amount so saved for the Government is resented as a gross injustice to the local prospectors who have borne the burden and heat of early development."

Flora's style was more elegant than Gene Allen's in the *Klondike Nugget,* but she shared his indignation. She had heard the complaints on the creeks, where American prospectors resented the Canadian government's attempt to regulate their freewheeling world. (Most of them ignored that on the American side of the border, a non-American was not allowed to stake or own a claim at all.) Flora also made a more fundamental point about a town that was now two years old and had already remitted to Ottawa a substantial revenue. It was "ineptitude and inattention," she charged, "on the part of responsible officers . . . that there are as yet no roads, no trustworthy mail arrangements, no sanitary organization of any kind, and no clear distribution of streets and town lots in a town of nearly 20,000 inhabitants." Ottawa was treating Dawson City as a cash cow. "The Yukon district feels itself to be corruptly administered and badly governed."

In her final paragraphs, Our Special Correspondent sounded a more optimistic note: "A change is at hand which renders it unnecessary to labour the subject of the need for political reform." The Ottawa government had recently announced the appointment of William Ogilvie to the post of commissioner of the Yukon. A member of the Geological Survey of Canada, he had done the surveys twenty months earlier of both the Dawson townsite and the creeks. Flora had met Ogilvie in London the previous spring and considered "his name . . . as the synonym of disinterested integrity." She also suggested that most of the loafers on Dawson's Front Street would leave town as soon as they had run out of provisions. And once a telegraph had been installed, capital from Outside would be attracted to the rich gold fields. "There seems no reason why the Yukon district should not soon be counted among the pleasant and prosperous centres of British settlement."

In Britain, Flora's descriptions of the wealth of the Klondike gold fields had the desired effect: British investors turned their attention to the gold fields in Canada's remote North. But Canadians were thin skinned about British criticism, and her articles caused a sensation. Flora's final letter from Dawson was given additional punch by an accompanying editorial in the *Times* about "our Correspondent's grave allegations." After repeating the assertion that nothing got done in Dawson City "unless some official's palm is greased," the Thunderer roared that "the iniquitous burden of corrupt exactions and obstructions should be immediately removed" before the Klondike fields would look inviting to investors. Both editorial and article were reprinted in several Canadian newspapers, including the Toronto *Globe* and the *Winnipeg Daily Tribune,* both of which were usually bastions of support for the Liberal government in Ottawa. The *Tribune*'s front page on October 5 was an avalanche of headlines about Flora's report: "Thunderer has spoken. Leading newspaper of Great Britain on the Reported Scandals in the Yukon—Result of the Investigation by Its Special Correspondent. A Discreditable State of Affairs in Officialdom. The Toronto Globe Pays a Tribute to the Writer. An Investigation must take place."

In Ottawa, Flora's accusations spelled trouble for the Liberal government of Sir Wilfrid Laurier, prime minister since 1896. The cabinet minister responsible for the Yukon was Clifford Sifton, Minister of the Interior and Superintendent General of Indian Affairs. Sifton, a Manitoba lawyer, was the chief political organizer of the Liberal Party and a master of machine politics and patronage. Sifton immediately telegraphed the *Times* demanding that it publish a retraction of Miss Shaw's statements. But huffing and puffing was not enough; he was an agile enough politician to know he had to defuse the scandal. He immediately launched an official inquiry into the charges of "official malfeasance" made by the special correspondent of the *Times* and announced that Fawcett would be replaced as gold commissioner. The *Times* could not have been more unctuous as it reported Sifton's action and took credit for the initiative: "This inquiry . . . will assuredly act as a warning

to officials of doubtful integrity, and we receive with not a little satisfaction the testimony that this is due in no small measure to the coura-
geous intervention of our Correspondent."

Flora was comfortably settled in a first-class carriage on the eastbound
Canadian Pacific Railway train when the local Hudson's Bay Company
manager handed her a bundle of newspapers containing her fourth
"Letter from Canada" and accounts of Ottawa's reaction. The headlines
in the *Manitoba Free Press* on October 8 read, "Searching Enquiry to Be
Made into the Administration of Yukon. Mr. Fawcett Replaced. The Minister of the Interior Acts Promptly." As the train pulled out of the station,
she must have felt a surge of pride in both her journalistic coup and the
power of her employer. But as she gazed out of the carriage window at
the dry autumn stubble of farmlands and the steely gray waters of rapidly
chilling lakes, she must also have wondered what lay ahead. In Ottawa she
was scheduled to stay at Rideau Hall, home of the governor general of
Canada, and she planned to interview several cabinet ministers, including Mr. Sifton.

The visit to Ottawa started badly. Flora's train was scheduled to arrive
in the mid-morning, but it was delayed by an accident on the line. Flora
was too self-disciplined to allow a note of panic to creep into her voice
as she repeatedly asked the conductor what was happening, but she was
worried. Governor General Lord Aberdeen and his wife had organized
a dinner in her honor at Government House, at which she would meet
those whom she had sharply criticized. The gown she intended to wear
was in storage at the Ottawa rail station. She had shipped most of her
bags directly to the Canadian capital several weeks earlier, after hearing
from Mr. Monroe about Dawson's social life. Before she left London, all
her smartest clothes had been sewn tightly in canvas bags to keep out
the dust. How could black silk taffeta be anything but a crumpled rag
when she finally unlocked the trunk, cut open the canvas, and shook
the dress out?

The train finally pulled into Ottawa's station at eight in the evening, and the Governor General's carriage was waiting to take Miss Shaw the half-mile to the viceregal residence. "You can fancy the comfort," Flora wrote to Lulu, "of unpacking and dressing under the circumstances in less than half an hour." Lady Aberdeen's personal maid rose to the occasion, and Flora appeared only a few minutes late at the dinner table, looking calm and unruffled. The guests stayed talking until after midnight. Though Flora drooped with exhaustion, she managed to speak coherently and intelligently despite feeling quite ill after the wine and rich food. Afterward, she took the time to write to Lulu, "I am at Ottawa resting in the luxuries of Govt House sleeping in sheets, having a bath, wearing an evening dress, and submitting to the same ordering of my ways which prevails in an English country house."

The following day, several interviews with ministers had been arranged. But first Flora found herself dragged off in a carriage by the impossibly bossy Lady Aberdeen to inspect all her viceregal projects. Our Special Correspondent had to visit women's organizations and nursing homes before escaping her imposing hostess's firm grasp. At last Flora sat down with, among others, Clifford Sifton. "You may have gathered," she wrote Lulu, "that my Klondike letters have been the occasion of somewhat animated controversy here." She disclosed that the minister of the Interior felt "very sore," and he and his cabinet colleagues "would all have been glad if they could have had fair grounds to prove my account inaccurate or exaggerated." In a phrase with a wonderfully modern ring, Flora and Sifton had "some long frank talks." Flora wouldn't budge an inch: she catalogued all the horrors she had seen in Dawson and the rumors she had heard about the amount of bribery in government offices. She gave the names of both the accused and their accusers. The tone of the conversation was "fair and courteous," but Flora found the meetings disagreeable. The following day, she told Lulu that the members of Laurier's cabinet expressed "horror and surprise at the facts which I have been able to lay before them," but it all struck her as a bit of playacting. Sifton's assurances and newly appointed inquiry did not impress her. "They have left me more doubtful than I like to be of the desire of the government to take effective steps."

But Flora Shaw had done her best. She was anxious to leave Canada, visit friends in Boston, and then catch the White Star Line's S.S. *Cymric* from New York for the nine-day voyage to Liverpool. She would return to England almost exactly five months after she had left on her fact-finding mission.

Was Flora right? Were Our Special Correspondent's conclusions about the sleaze in Dawson City justified?

There was undeniably official graft in Dawson City, as the local papers loved to point out. The most serious offender was Frederick Coates Wade, the crown prosecutor and land commissioner, who continued to act as both crown agent for land sales and solicitor for Big Alex McDonald and Roderick Morrison, two of the biggest landowners in Dawson. Wade was the most corrupt senior official, but junior clerks in various government offices also had ample opportunities to supplement their pay with a few extra dollars or a well-stuffed gold poke from a grateful client. In the mining recorder's office, where claims were recorded, checked, and transferred, a surreptitiously purchased scratch of the pen might wipe out a man's claim or insert a prior claim on a newly registered statement. A sharp speculator could hire a dance hall girl or a prostitute to wheedle her way into the office on his behalf, and then register a claim that some poor sucker farther back in the line had laboriously staked for himself. And a savvy miner could learn from friends in the mining recorder's office if any prospectors had staked claims on new creeks because they had found "color." A quiet word in the right ear could result in friends and colleagues staking a nearby claim before news of the next big strike triggered the inevitable stampede out of Dawson's saloons.

Similarly, much of what Flora had said about the post office was true. Mail delivery in Dawson was a shambles, since mail bags arrived not in a steady stream each week but on only a handful of occasions during the year, in a vast and unpredictable avalanche. There had been no mail at all from October 12, 1897, until the end of the following February. Then a dog sled had brought in 5,700 letters in a single batch, and as there were no mail deliveries or boxes, every hopeful recipient turned up at the post office in the hopes of a letter from Outside. There was soon an auction for places near the front of the line-up outside the two-story log house on Front Street, conducted by quick-witted entrepreneurs who had anticipated demand. Anyone else might have to stand in line for as much as four days. Mailing a letter out of Dawson in 1898 was even more difficult. The supply of Canadian stamps was so inadequate that the police, who took over the handling of mail in October 1897, slapped a limit on them of two per customer per transaction.

Why had the government allowed such chaos to explode? Because the top-hatted legislators in Ottawa could not believe that a gold rush in the country's most remote and inaccessible corner could possibly last. Their sole goal was to get as much in royalties as possible out of the region, in a "clean up and clear out" campaign. Only now were they beginning to think that the gold might last for several years, making it worth investing in Dawson's future.

Flora Shaw had arrived in Dawson City at the very moment when Ottawa's policy looked most shortsighted. The Gold Rush was at its peak in the summer of 1898 as thousands poured over the White and Chilkoot passes. (The Mounties had already counted 27,000 before Flora crossed, she told Lulu.) Hundreds more arrived from St. Michael or by one of the three other land routes—the Stikine River route, the Dalton Trail, and the all-Canadian overland route from Edmonton—that were even tougher than the two mountain pass trails. The population of Dawson was somewhere between 18,000 and 30,000, and several thousand more people were encamped on the creeks, though it is hard to arrive at accurate figures with so much coming and going. These numbers completely overwhelmed the cramped townsite and its hopelessly inadequate infrastructure. Moreover, the number of claims to be

registered had rocketed. In June 1897, there were 800 claims on record
in Dawson; by January 1898, there were 5,000; and that number had
jumped to 17,000 by September 1898.

But change was on its way. Four weeks after Flora Shaw left Dawson,
two men arrived to clean up the rowdy, overcrowded town. Both were
familiar faces. The first was the incorruptible William Ogilvie, who as
Flora had already noted had succeeded James Walsh, a Sifton crony, as
commissioner of the Yukon. Earlier in the year, the Laurier government
in Ottawa had passed the Yukon Act, changing the district's status from
a distant corner of the vast North-West Territories administered from
Regina to a separate territory controlled directly by Ottawa, 4,000 miles
away, with Dawson City as its capital. Ogilvie was now authorized to
establish an executive council, plus the kind of administrative structures Dawson needed desperately: a board of health, a fire department,
a sanitation department. Ogilvie would supervise the grading of streets
and the construction (at last!) of drainage ditches to deal with Dawson's
appalling flood problems.

The second new arrival was Superintendent Samuel Benfield Steele,
who took over from Inspector Charles Constantine in Dawson when
he was given command of the 250 North-West Mounted Police in the
Yukon and British Columbia. Sam Steele would become a Klondike
hero, with a nickname—the Lion of the North—straight out of a juve-
nile comic book.

Born in Ontario, Sam Steele was a tall, heavily built man who came
from a long line of defenders of the Union Jack, and by 1897 he was
already a legend. His British-born forebears had cropped up at all the
great battles of the previous century, including Waterloo and Trafalgar.
As a broad-shouldered twenty-four-year-old, Sam had been the third
man to be sworn into the newly formed Mounties in 1873, as a sergeant
major. The new Canadian force was more than a police force but less
than a militia, and its distinctive uniform reflected its purpose. It combined the red jacket of a traditional British regiment with the breeches

and boots of a frontier ranger. The navy serge pants had a distinctive yellow stripe down the outside, and northern lawbreakers always referred to the police as "Yellow Legs." So far, in the force's short history, there hadn't been a Mountie triumph in which Sam Steele hadn't featured. He had been on the Long March west in 1874, helped to negotiate with Sitting Bull after the Battle of Little Bighorn in 1877, supervised construction of the Canadian Pacific Railway across the prairies in the early 1880s, maintained peace on the prairies as immigrants swarmed in, and pursued Big Bear during the 1885 Rebellion in Saskatchewan. (Because he had been under the army's command in 1885, he was often called "Colonel" Steele. Although this was a courtesy title, it was used interchangeably with "Superintendent.") His reputation had spread across the continent. In 1890, he married Marie Elizabeth de Lotbinière Harwood, daughter of an influential Quebec landowner who sat in the Canadian Parliament as a Conservative MP. When the newlyweds went to New York City on their honeymoon, the New York Fire Department greeted Steele of the Mounties with a parade of sixty engines.

Sam's men respected him because there was nobody who worked harder than their boss, and they feared him because he was a bit of a bully. "Gruff and bluff, and absolutely fearless of everybody," as a colleague put it, Sam was up at dawn and hard at it until nearly midnight. His official diary captures his unbending military demeanor. In British Columbia's Kootenay Ferry, where he was stationed at the time, he jotted a terse note on January 11, 1888: "Annual flogging administered to whores, adulterers, drunkards and gamblers." But under the red serge and bullying manner was a devoted family man who wrote long, affectionate letters to his wife, Marie, almost every day when they were apart. His writing was often illegible, and he rarely bothered with punctuation, but the letters resonated with his dependence on Marie as the emotional center of his life. In photos, Marie Steele appears thin lipped and prim—hardly a figure to attract such passion. Nevertheless, Sam adored her and his lengthy epistles

Sam Steele, North-West Mounted Police hero, wrote almost daily to his wife, Marie Elizabeth de Lotbinière Harwood Steele. Under his brass buttons, braid, and love of ceremony was a devoted family man.

home always included pages of sentimental endearments. "My darling Marie," he wrote in bold cursive in a typical letter from Bennett Lake, at the headwaters of the Yukon River, in May 1898, "How I long to clasp you in my arms, my own love, how I miss you. You are in my mind day after day." Photos of Marie and their three small children, Gertrude, Flora, and their only son, Harwood, rarely left Sam's breast pocket.

The public side of Sam Steele, along with his walrus mustache and fierce blue eyes, was already familiar to many Dawson residents because he had spent the previous winter in charge of the Canadian police posts from the summits of the White Pass and Chilkoot Pass to Dawson. In theory he had been subordinate to Ogilvie's predecessor as commissioner of the Yukon Territory, James Walsh. In practice, Colonel Sam Steele had run the whole show on the trail to Dawson. Part military dictator, part sheepdog, he chivvied the army of stampeders along the route and made sure that none of Soapy Smith's villains from Skagway strayed onto his territory. The Mounties had hauled a couple of Maxim machine guns to the top of the passes and set them up there, pointed at American soil, to show they meant business. Sam made up rules and regulations as necessary. First, he insisted that every homemade boat, scow, canoe, and raft had to have a serial number painted on the bow, and the occupants had to register their vessels, their own names, and their next of kin before they set off to face the river's foaming rapids. The boats were checked through each police post (over which Union Jack flags fluttered) as they went downriver. If one disappeared, Steele's Mounties went after it. Next, he ordered that every person who entered the Yukon must carry one year's supply of provisions. Those orders were blatantly illegal (as Steele admitted himself) but thanks to his unilateral pronouncements and muscular authority, dozens of tragedies were averted. He had done everything he could to ensure Flora Shaw's safety and comfort as she traveled into the Yukon over the White Pass and left via the Chilkoot Pass. No wonder Flora was so enthusiastic in her letter to Lulu about "the nice comfortable police."

Sam already knew that Dawson was, as he wrote to Marie, "orderly—but apart from that simply a hell upon earth, gamblers, thieves and the worst kind of womankind." On her journey out of the Yukon, Flora Shaw confirmed his fears when she told him that "she does not envy me my task and that she could not have believed that such things could exist under the British flag. That is pretty blunt talk." Sam was no saint: he lurched into drinking binges when he was bored, much to his wife's consternation. But he was no libertine either, and he was disgusted to hear what was going on along Dawson's Second Avenue. In a letter from Bennett Lake, he confided to his wife that "a coloured woman . . . went through to the south with $25,000 that she saved, and a dance hall girl had eight thousand. It is a tough place indeed." He did not share Flora's sympathy with the miners' fury about the 10 percent royalty. "What on earth right have a few thousand foreigners to take out of the country what there is in it? . . . Perhaps ten percent is too much, but judging from the fact that all are willing to come out with sacks of gold—more money than they could earn in forty years or one hundred—they are not so much oppressed by the royalty."

Steele had been angling for command of all the North-West Mounted Police in the Yukon for months, and in July he heard that when Ogilvie replaced Walsh, he would be given officially the title "superintendent" and the position he had filled informally since January. Two months later, stampeders at Bennett Lake watched Superintendent Steele board a boat for the journey down the Yukon River, in the company of William Ogilvie. Alongside supplies that the two men would need to set up their offices in Dawson were an iron bedstead with wire springs for Sam ("I want to be comfortable when I am in barracks") and a new-fangled "graphaphone" (an early record player) for Ogilvie. As the party steamed north, Steele selected twenty sites for additional police posts along the river. Each would house five officers and two dog teams.

Back in Ottawa, Clifford Sifton was trying to improve the Yukon's hopeless mail service. In September, a dozen new employees for the post office arrived in Dawson. But mail service remained erratic. As one of those new employees, a keen young Ottawa man called Benjamin Craig, noted in his diary, they sent the first mail after the freeze-up to the Outside on November 15, but "they went through the ice and the mail was lost." The same month, Thomas Fawcett, the gold commissioner, left his post. ("Goodbye Fawcett!" gloated the headline on the *Klondike Nugget*.)

Most of Dawson's citizens were happy with the improvements, but they were unwilling to give Flora Shaw much of the credit. Her articles in the *Times* had done damage to the town's growing sense of itself as a little atoll of civility in an icy wilderness. As the population of Dawson had mushroomed, so had the self-importance of its more distinguished citizens. The new professional class, and particularly the wives of the professionals, had not appreciated the way that Flora treated them when she was in Dawson, and now they took umbrage at Flora's negative portrait of their community as a crude boomtown. They wanted Dawson City's reputation to rest on its wealth and sophistication rather than its wide-open gambling tables and corrupt officials. How dare this imperi-

Red jackets, shiny leather boots, and a military demeanor made the Mounties both feared and popular in Dawson City.

ous Englishwoman, with her fancy accent and beekeeper's outfit, flit in and out of their bustling town thanks to the support of Canada's police, railroad, government, and largest commercial enterprise, and then pass judgment? Their resentment was best expressed by the Toronto journalist Alice Freeman or, as she was better known to readers of her articles, Faith Fenton. Faith, a former schoolteacher in her early forties, had been encouraged to visit Dawson by William Ogilvie. She was at a stage in her life when she was hungry for change (she had just lost her job as a magazine editor) and worried about her future. Ogilvie, a jovial raconteur always happy to exaggerate the Yukon's potential, assured her that Dawson was now thoroughly respectable and brimming with marriageable men. The prospect was irresistible. Faith arranged to send regular articles about the booming mining town back to the Toronto *Globe,* and headed north. She arrived in Dawson in August 1898, a week after Flora Shaw had left, and was quickly captivated by the exuberant atmosphere of the town. She became the darling of Dawson's officer class.

Faith Fenton reflected the pique of her newfound friends in the North when she took a swipe at Flora in a column in the *Globe* in January 1899. "There are difficulties of administration," Fenton wrote, "that even Miss Shaw, with all her ability, could not possibly comprehend within the limits of her two or three weeks' stay in the territory."

But Faith Fenton and her fellow residents didn't need to worry. That same January, Flora gave her address on the Klondike gold fields to members of the Royal Colonial Institute in the Whitehall Rooms of London's Hotel Metropole, a substantial brick building close to Trafalgar Square. A striking figure in her tightly corseted black gown, Flora was introduced by Lord Strathcona, High Commissioner for Canada, who had done much to facilitate her travels. Standing next to a large map of western Canada, she spoke for nearly two hours. After repeating much of what she had written in the *Times,* she mentioned recent improvements in Dawson City's administration, for which she and the *Times* were happy to take credit. Next, she suggested that the appetite in Dawson for hookers and hooch would abate as soon as more women arrived. Men wasted time and money in Dawson's saloons because they all yearned for a home life. "In noting the contrast between the splendid qualities exercised in the effort to acquire gold and the utter folly displayed in the spending of it, it was impossible to avoid the reflection that in the expansion of the Empire, as in other movements, man wins the battle but woman holds the field."

Flora Shaw predicted that if British capital and British enterprise were prepared to invest in the Empire, the communication difficulties would be eased and "there will be no more difficulty in going to the Klondike than in going to the Rhine." She ended her talk on a note that must have thrilled all those institutions and organizations that had hosted her visit to Canada's Northwest the previous year. "I went a skeptic," she announced. "I returned convinced that though much that is temporary there is bad, the permanent conditions are very good." She might have added that, officially, gold to the value of $10 million had been taken out of the Yukon in 1898, at least half as much again would leave in 1899, and that those estimates were reckoned to understate real production by at least 25 percent. And only a month after Flora's London talk, on February 18, 1899, the twenty-one-mile, narrow gauge White Pass and Yukon Railway reached the summit of White Pass. By the end of July, it had completed the entire 110-mile overland section— Skagway to Whitehorse—of the Gold Rush route. Over 35,000 men had worked on the project, and the mountainsides were so steep that workers had been suspended by ropes to prevent them falling off while cutting the grade. Thirty-five men had died during construction. The final cost of the project was over $12.5 million—but it was British capital that had financed the most northerly passenger train on the American continent, and the railroad was soon channeling revenues back to Close Brothers, the London merchant bank that had financed it.

Flora Shaw's brief sojourn in the Yukon and her exploration of the gold-bearing creeks helped to secure the future for Dawson City. She had justified the Klondike gold mines as an attractive investment because the huge dredges that large corporations could take north would collect gold from the gravel piles discarded by the individual gumboot-and-gold-pan prospectors. A. N. C. Treadgold, an English mining promoter who had already spent a summer in the Yukon, would find some well-heeled British backers. The battle between businessmen for control of great swaths of the creeks had begun in January 1898, when Ottawa permitted large mining concessions, but now it would be in full swing. And as a *Montreal Herald* reporter wrote in an 1898 column that would be reprinted in the *New York Times*, "It may be said of Miss Shaw without exaggeration that she has not been by any means the least of the forces working for the unification of the empire . . . [She] is certainly one of the remarkable women of the age."

PART 4: ORDER AND EXODUS

CHAPTER 17
"Strong men wept," October 1898–January 1899

IN THE FALL OF 1898, two years after Carmack's strike, Dawson was still like no other place in the world. It had outgrown its roots as a frontier mining camp, but it was no collar-and-tie, kid-glove city. The town boasted four churches, two hospitals (the Presbyterians had just completed their Good Samaritan Hospital), two banks, three newspapers, several theaters, and twenty-two saloons. Yet it lacked amenities enjoyed by every self-respecting North American town in the late nineteenth century: sewers, street lighting, horse-drawn tramcars, railway links to neighboring cities, and a solidly built town hall. Even the basic necessities of civic life were missing—an elected city council, schools, paved roads, or a fire service. There was no telegraph or telephone to the Outside.

It was a town of paradoxes. Some of its residents dined on oysters and caviar, while others scraped by on stale bread, lard, and tea. You could buy a penny postcard but it would cost you a dollar to mail, and if the dogsled carrying the mail broke through the ice, it would never arrive. A dinner of tough roast beef and soggy apple pie that cost fifteen cents in Seattle would set you back $2.50 in Dawson. Mink capes, diamond rings, champagne, and chamois leather underskirts were stocked by Front Street stores, but there were no shopping bags to take them home in. In fact, there was no paper to wrap anything. A physician from Baltimore known to all and sundry as Dr. Jim was shocked when, after buying a thick moose steak, he watched the butcher spear it on a sharp-ened stick, then politely hand him "this meaty lollipop." Dr. Jim walked home "carrying my frozen steak at the far end of that stick, valiantly warding off scores and battalions of hungry dogs with the other arm—and with both feet!"

No wonder that as daylight had begun to vanish, tourists hurried away. After eight weeks of roughing it in the North, in late September Mrs. Hitchcock and Miss van Buren sold their tent and movie projec-tor, spent a night at the Fairview Hotel, then scrambled onto one of the last boats steaming downriver. Several hundred disappointed stamped-ers left too, unable to face the ordeal of working on somebody else's claim during a cruel winter. Those who intended to stay made their preparations for eight months of icy isolation—stocking up with provi-sions, chinking cabins and, if they were men, finding their razors. Many miners let their beards grow as bushy as they liked during the summer, and even suave city types sported luxuriant mustaches and sideburns, partly as protection against mosquitoes. In the words of the *Klondike Nugget*, "The approach of winter marks the period when the Yukon crop of whiskers is harvested . . . The knowing resident of this arctic clime sheds the hairy facial ornaments as soon as winter's chilling frosts begin to convert his mustache and beard into a combination of frost and icicles."

The coming winter would not be as harsh as last year's season of starvation—but it wouldn't be as much fun, either. The town's popula-tion was now so large that strangers outnumbered old-timers on the streets. Racial and class discrimination was shattering the camaraderie among those who previously had clung together for survival. The small Jewish community found itself sidelined by British immigrants: "I eat with the Japs," a lonely New Yorker called Solomon Schuldenfrei wrote to his wife, Rebecca. The "bad women" whom poor Mrs. Wichter had noticed in July were impossible to ignore. You could no longer leave your cabin unlocked or your food cache unguarded: crime filled the columns of the *Nugget,* the *Midnight Sun,* and the new *Klondyke Miner and Yukon Advertiser.* Gold pokes went missing, drunks were rolled outside the bars, inebriated miners enraged neighbors by firing off illegal firearms at night. The line of prostitutes' hutches, bearing signs proclaiming names like "Saratoga," "The Lucky Cigar Store," and "Bon Ton," stretched for three blocks along Second Avenue. There would often be line-ups for the most popular (and cheapest) girls: as one customer emerged, buttoning his fly, the next one would be ready with his two dollars. Some of the women continued to exude the businesslike cheerfulness of long-time northerners like Esther Duffie, but most had been brought in by pimps and madams in the spring and looked faded and exhausted in daylight.

Was this high-spirited circus on the brink of becoming a thieves' kitchen? Would a Soapy Smith emerge to become (as Flora Shaw had put it) the local Robespierre and turn Dawson into another Skagway?

Not if Superintendent Steele had anything to do with it. Sam Steele arrived in Dawson determined to burnish his reputation there, so from the start he exaggerated the wickedness he discovered while publicizing his own achievements. Soon after Steele and Ogilvie arrived in Dawson in September 1898, Sam reported to Marie that "we have our hands full . . . There will be a general clean-up . . . The state of affairs is bad and could not possibly be worse but those who have the task of restoring credit to our country will spare none who have displaced it." One of his first actions was to tighten up the discipline of his own troops. On his arrival in Dawson, Sam was appalled to discover Mounties gambling, falling asleep on guard duty, accepting bribes, and consorting with sleazy dealers and "loose" women. He confided to a friend that if he had had any say in selecting men for service in the Yukon, he would have called for volunteers and then taken only those who declined. "Tried Corporal for being drunk," a typical entry in his official NWMP diary for September reads. "Fined thirty days pay and reduced to ranks." At the same time, he also improved his men's living conditions by building

Goddesses of Liberty, Enlighting Dawson. Y.T.

In the cribs of Paradise Alley behind Front Street, "soiled doves" plied their trade openly.

a hospital, latrines, offices, and a quartermaster's stores, and ordering adequate supplies for the coming winter.

The police were heavily outnumbered: only thirteen Mounties were assigned to the rip-roaring boomtown itself, plus a further thirty to patrol the fourteen creeks that had been identified as gold bearing. How could so few Mounties be expected to keep the peace among so many toughs, let alone develop the community relations on which the force prided itself? Sam reckoned at least a hundred police officers were required for the job, and asked for a fresh contingent of Mounties. He was not happy to learn that the government was sending to Dawson from Fort Selkirk, 150 miles upstream, fifty members of the Yukon Field Force, which had none of the training and esprit de corps of the NWMP. When the fresh-faced military contingent arrived, according to Belinda Mulrooney, "the miners thought they were awfully pretty [in their] nice little red jackets and a fried egg on their heads for a cap . . . but they didn't know what they were there for." One old-timer said to her, "Gee, they look awful cute. They'd make nice ladies' men if only we had the ladies." But the militia contingent, and Sam's smartened-up Mounties, had their effect. A veteran prospector, known as Nigger Jim on account of his southern drawl rather than his skin color, stared at the two light fieldpieces that accompanied the force and the military swagger of the marching soldiers. Then he sighed, and remarked to a Bank of Commerce employee, "I guess this place is getting too damned civilized for me. I'd better be moving on again to the frontier."

Next, Sam Steele got tough with what he described in his memoirs, *Forty Years in Canada: Reminiscences of the Great North-West,* as the "loose characters who had come into the country to prey upon the respectable but, as a rule, simple and unsuspicious miners." At least half of Dawson's 16,000 winter residents, in Sam's private opinion, had at some time in their lives been on the wrong side of the law, so he proceeded to rule with an iron fist in a chainmail glove. "Many of them have committed murders, 'held up' trains, stage coaches, and committed burglary and theft in the United States." He built thirty-four new jail cells—part of an ambitious construction program that saw sixty-three new buildings at the force's twenty Yukon posts and outposts in the fall of 1898. He tightened an already existing rule that saloons, dance halls, theaters, and business houses must be closed one minute before midnight on Saturday and were not allowed to reopen until two in the morning on Monday. From now on, the only music to be heard on Dawson's streets on Sunday was from the Salvation Army band: there were no more lubricious "sacred concerts," at which the likes of Caprice, in the pink tights she had rescued from the Bank of Commerce, would cling like a modern pole dancer to a large wooden cross in a Sunday tableau vivant. And on his own authority, Steele raised the fines imposed by the police court on anybody convicted of public drunkenness, cardsharping, possession of a firearm, assault, breach of the Sunday curfew, or brawling.

Concerned about the rising incidence of syphilis in the town, Sam ordered a round-up of "loose women." His forces arrested 150 women (there were as many as 400 prostitutes working the streets that summer), and fined each of them fifty dollars and costs. Each prostitute was ordered to undergo a monthly medical inspection. (The hookers loved Steele's rules; they were released as soon as they had been fined and inspected, so resumed business on the assumption that the certificates of good health, for which they paid five dollars, were licenses to operate.) Sam also announced that all saloons, dance halls, and roadhouses where liquor was served would have to buy licenses. A hotel owner was charged $2,000 for a license to operate and a saloonkeeper $2,500—prices that "would make a Montreal hotel keeper stare," admitted Sam. The NWMP rapidly collected more than $90,000 from fines and licenses, "a large and useful fund," in Sam's words, "every cent of which was devoted to the patients in the fever-crowded hospitals."

Sam quickly realized that his job was not just to enforce the law; he also had to change the culture of Dawson. "The villainy, wickedness, robbery and corruption that took place last spring are simply beyond belief," Sam told Marie. He had been hearing all about Walsh's regime in Dawson, when "Her Majesty's representative and staff [were frequently seen] in a dance hall box with common prostitutes on their knees and spending easily." But those were the bad old days. In Steele's Dawson, corruption would not be tolerated, and no wicked act would go unpunished. "I know lots of the hucksters . . . will hate the NWMPolice and probably try to eject us, but it will never succeed. We have right on our side and our motto, 'Maintiens le droit,' will prevail," Sam insisted.

Prisoners were put to work collecting refuse, washing dishes, and shoveling snow—saving the NWMP hundreds of dollars in wages. One of Sam Steele's most effective tactics was his embrace of the woodpile. The quantities of firewood burned in the stoves of hotels, saloons, cabins, and tents through the Yukon winters were huge, but nowhere was more fuel consumed than in the government offices, the newly expanded jail, and the Mounties' barracks, which had also been enlarged to house the militia. According to Steele their stoves used "nearly 1000 cords, equal to a pile of fuel almost 8,000 feet long, 4 feet high and 4 feet wide." The timber was cut on distant hills, floated down the Yukon, and delivered to the barracks by lumber companies, but it then had to be sawn into stove lengths. This was the prisoners' job: wrongdoers were given the choice of leaving town or working on the woodpile. "They hated the 'wood pile,' if possible, more than they hated their escorts," he would chortle. The woodpile kept fifty or more Dawson delinquents busy every day, even when the temperature sank forty degrees below the freezing point. Sam Steele put his toughest NCO in charge of the operation. Corporal Tweedy was "a terror to all evildoers and, no matter how they boasted of what they 'would do to him,' one glance of his keen eyes or a grip of his well-skilled hand was sufficient." (One imaginative convict, according to Steele's biographer, Robert Stewart, "got his revenge by spending three months sawing every log he handled exactly half an inch too long for the stoves.")

Belinda Mulrooney liked the way that Superintendent Steele took command of Dawson. As she wrote of the Mounties, "They themselves were part of the country and capable of taking care of trouble. But no trouble ever came up . . . Colonel Steele had a splendid bunch of men." Whenever she saw Steele's imposing figure, brass buttons twinkling and leather boots gleaming, striding along Front Street, she pressed him to enjoy a quick drink in the Fairview Hotel. Sam studiously avoided her. Belinda did not like being snubbed, but she decided to ignore his behavior. With her husky voice, abrupt manner, and air of authority, she was now such a local celebrity that it was hard to believe she was still only twenty-six. Most of her customers called her "Mom" and referred to her as "the Queen of the Klondike." Her hotel had become the hub of Dawson activities, which meant she knew everything that was going on. "There wasn't any better blood in any man's country than that around the Fairview Hotel." The two bank managers were fixtures of the Fairview bar. Any entertainers hired to perform at the new Opera House always began their run with a show in the hotel saloon. The Yukon Order of Pioneers held all their special celebrations in the dining room; Belinda's chefs were good at inventing dishes like Arctic Trout à la Klondike River, Cheechako Potato Salad à la Yukon Bank, and Ptarmigan on Toast au Dome. And having the telephone switchboard next to her office was a master stroke: there wasn't a deal going down that she didn't know about. (The arrangement had its drawbacks: "Every joker who owned a phone liked to play with it. They would get me up in the middle of the night . . . I got rid of them. I charged them ten dollars after the first minute.")

Belinda was particularly amused by the British remittance men who stuck around after the rest of the summer tourists had fled. "Of course those Englishmen after they landed wouldn't look at the mines, the country was too beastly for them, no-one to wait on them, no flunkeys, no body servants, people they could order around. Those Johnnies hung around Dawson [and] took to the dance halls like ducks to water." The Englishmen had one unconventional talent. "It was the wonder of the miners and all western people how they could get full as lords with an eyeglass [monocle] in one eye, drape themselves around a woman and dance. Those foolish miners would hang around for hours watching for the eyeglass to fall out. They would try everything in their own eyes, little round pieces of tin or glass, [but] if they would walk out or move it would drop."

These were good times for Belinda: there were so many ways of making a buck. She still owned her original roadhouse up at Grand Forks, and she was active on her various claims on the creeks. When she first arrived in the Yukon she had cultivated a prim, matronly image. But it was a sham, and now she was an established multimillionaire, a coarser, more hard-boiled Belinda emerged. One of those Englishmen she scorned, Neville Armstrong, would never forget the sight of the "short, dark, angular, masculine [woman who] could swear like a trooper," standing by a mineshaft in a calf-length skirt and knee boots,

Sam Steele used his immaculate military attire to set a standard. He studiously avoided Belinda Mulrooney, whom he considered a corrupting influence in town.

issuing orders. Another of her employees was shocked by her language. "When one of the men came out of the bushes, she asked him where he had been and what he had been doing. He replied, 'A man has to relieve himself once in a while.' Her response was 'You have been there long enough to jerk off. Get your pay and get out of here.'"

The growth of Dawson offered Belinda new commercial opportunities. Typhoid was the big killer after scurvy in Dawson, and dysentery was endemic, thanks to a water supply contaminated by raw sewage. So Belinda put together the Yukon Hygeia Water Supply Company, which offered boiled and filtered water, and in December 1898 issued stock valued at $8,000. She brusquely circumvented anti-American feeling by starting this venture with two Canadian partners. Within a few months, she had knocked out her competitors in the clean water business and established a monopoly for her company. "How much was I making?" she asked herself in her memoirs, then refused to answer her own question because she knew she would sound like a fool "to tell how much [I] made—and then lost."

In the north end of town, these were good months for Father Judge, too, despite the typhoid epidemic. Sam Steele's arrival was particularly welcome to the Jesuit. He was happy that the Sunday closing of casinos was now strictly enforced, and he was even happier because St. Mary's Hospital was a direct beneficiary of the new regime. The *Klondike Nugget,* no friend of Canadian authorities, noted, "We are very pleased to have occasion to chronicle the fact that the government has come forward with a donation of $3000 [to St. Mary's] . . . By reason of excessive charitable work, the hospital had got behind in its books not much short of $30,000."

In the memoirs of Klondikers, there are so many references to "the Old Priest" that it comes as a shock to realize that Father Judge was only forty-eight—by today's standards an age still considered the prime of life. Yet he had lived through nine winters in Alaska and the Yukon, and each of those bitter seasons had carved new lines on his face. One evening in October, the Jesuit settled down at the table in his little room in St. Mary's Hospital to write to his family. Behind him was a washstand, a small bookcase full of religious books, and a rough recliner on which were two neatly folded blue blankets. All Father Judge's worldly possessions were hidden away in a wooden drawer under his bed. He still had no interest in looking after himself: he continued to give away his own clothes to anyone in need, and he often forgot to eat dinner. Yet although the priest was as gaunt as ever, he was more serene now that he shared his work with the Oblate priests and the nursing sisters. Today, he was in an upbeat, count-your-blessings frame of mind. "The doctors all agree that we are having unusually good success in the hospital," he wrote to his brother. "We have five or six hundred at Mass every Sunday . . . I have a telephone in my office, not only for the town but also to the creeks. They are preparing to give us electric light." With a benefactor like Big Alex McDonald, Father Judge was enjoying an unfamiliar sense of security. His latest project, for which he had *not* asked the approval of the Reverend Father J. B. René, was a chapel for the hospital. He was once again enjoying the challenge of being architect, contractor, and interior designer for the building.

This fall, the river froze in mid-October. Father Judge always enjoyed winter, when the entire landscape was shrouded in snow. "This part of the world," he liked to tell parishioners, "is so beautiful in its mantle of purity." He was happy to see the incidence of typhoid and dysentery plummet alongside the temperature, but concerned by the number of people still living in tents. Over a game of chess, he confided to Dr. Jim, "Soon the trees will be cracking like guns in the frosty woods. But these children will not take care of themselves . . . [They] eat half raw, soggy pork, heavy beans, and leaden soda biscuits. Then they will either go back to bed again, or loaf away a night gambling and drinking in some saloon or dance hall. These are the men who get scurvy . . . They are not bad little boys, but lazy little boys . . . So I have to spank them and put them to bed at St. Mary's—I and the good Sisters and our thirty-four helpers."

As arctic winds cut through Dawson like a scalpel through flesh, he continued about his daily business in the most threadbare garments. Some of his friends decided he deserved more, and ordered a warm, well-made suit for him that would "better become the dignity of his calling." All Judge's Jesuit training rose up in revulsion at such indulgence; he refused to see the tailor sent to take his measurements. His friends shrugged and told the tailor to do the best he could. On a cold December evening, Father Judge returned to his room at St. Mary's to discover the suit, plus a long sealskin coat, cap, and gloves, laid out on his bed and a handful of men eager for thanks. "Father Judge was much moved by their thoughtfulness," his brother later recorded, "but he told them that he could not accept the gift, that being a Jesuit priest he could own nothing." He was finally persuaded to accept the outfit because most of the donors were Protestants, who didn't see why God's work should involve frostbite.

The sealskin coat was yet another sign of Father Judge's starring role in Dawson City's self-image as a community that could pull itself together. Tackling the predicament of St. Mary's Hospital was another. Since the hospital was still mired in debt, the Jesuit's friends decided to organize a minstrel entertainment as a fundraiser. Minstrel shows, in which white actors put black boot polish on their faces and strummed banjos, were all the rage Outside, and Dawson merrymakers jumped on the trend. The nightly rental for one of the town's false-fronted halls was usually between $300 and $400, but Joseph Cooper, owner of the Tivoli Theatre, offered his place at no cost. Tickets were sold at five dollars each for Sunday, December 25, when men on the creeks would come into town for Christmas. (The prohibition on Sunday entertainment did not apply to such a worthy event.) Organizers then asked for volunteers to appear on stage. By now, as reported in the local papers, an appetite for "respectable" theatrical performances had developed in Dawson, and despite the Fairview proprietor's severe reputation, Belinda Mulrooney was in demand. She had appeared in a play called *Three Hats,* performed in Pioneers Hall in mid-October, and a month later she performed in a masquerade ball to benefit the newly formed Dawson Fire Department. (She teamed up with another woman to play a husband and wife: the *Klondike Nugget* strengthened the widespread suspicion that this tough businesswoman was a lesbian when it reported that "Miss Mulrooney made a dapper little husband, in regulation broadcloth and silk hat.") Now, she agreed to appear as one of twenty Dawson women in blackface on behalf of St. Mary's Hospital.

On Christmas Eve, the day before the show, a large crowd sat in Father Judge's church, waiting to celebrate midnight Mass on the Yukon. The Oblate priests, sensing the town's mood, had agreed that the Jesuit would conduct the service. Outside, it was thirty-five degrees below freezing, and even with the stove blazing and so many warm bodies, the chill didn't leave the air as a small reed organ played, supplemented by several violins. Then the choir began singing "Adeste Fideles," and Father Judge appeared at the back of the nave. An observer called Charlie Higgins would later recall, "Something seemed to illuminate his countenance as he advanced towards the altar and moved to the Gospel side." The priest read the Gospel, preached a sermon on God's benevolence, then "drew a vivid picture of the loved ones of his hearers in their widely-scattered homes, where the vacant chair was their one anxiety that day." It was a stab to the hearts of most participants, whose brutal labors on the creeks were often accompanied by desperate longing for distant parents, wives, and children. They stared at the skeletal figure in holy garments, as he raised his arms to the heavens and blessed them. "Strong men wept," remembered Higgins.

After the high holiness of Christmas Mass, the priest was reluctant to attend the minstrel show, particularly as it was on a Sunday. He was finally persuaded and luckily, as Charlie Higgins recalled, "the show was clean": neither the song lyrics nor the performers' outfits would cause anybody to blush. At the end, Father Judge himself appeared briefly on stage in his new suit to thank everybody for their generosity. The show raised $2,000 for the hospital. It was the only time anybody saw the priest wearing his new clothes.

A few days after his Christmas triumph, Father Judge celebrated Mass in his new hospital chapel. But a week later, he started coughing, and soon he was too feeble to stand. A tremor of apprehension ran through the community; in the past, no matter how frail he had seemed, the Jesuit had always officiated when required. Father Judge's telephone never stopped ringing and the most unexpected well-wishers turned up to check on his health. The manager of one of the trading companies, who had never set foot in the Catholic church, sent up a case of champagne. "The town seemed as if some calamity were about to fall on it," remembered Charlie Higgins. But each day, the sick man's condition deteriorated. He had pneumonia, and lay on his rough bed, wrapped in blankets, shivering and struggling for breath, but still greeting fellow priests, friends, doctors, nurses, and the Sisters of St. Ann. Hän men and women, whom he had always treated with respect, tiptoed in to see him. George "Skiff" Mitchell, who had first met Father Judge in Forty Mile and who had since then made a fortune on Bonanza Creek, knelt by his bedside and wept. The priest opened his eyes and asked, "George, why are you crying?" Skiff whispered, "We can't afford to lose friends like you." Father Judge managed a smile. "George, you have got what you came for. I, too, have been working for a reward. Would you keep me from it?"

Those closest to him were in denial that they might lose their leader. Surely such a saint was immortal? One of the nursing sisters assured him, "Father, you are not going to die; we shall pray hard, and you will not die." He gave her a weak smile: "You may do what you please, but I am going to die." He was right. After receiving Last Rites from the Oblate priest Father Desmarais, Father Judge passed away on the afternoon of Monday, January 16, 1899.

Father Judge's death triggered an explosion of mourning. The headline in the *Klondike Nugget* read: "Rev. Father Judge is Dead. He Yields Up His Life Surrounded By Many of His Friends. His Splendid Work in Dawson. His Ruling Motive. A Good Man's Work. A Living Faith." Elaborate plans were made for his funeral, and it was decided that the priest should be buried not in the Catholic cemetery up the hill but in St. Mary's Church itself, on the Gospel side of the altar. In the January cold, it took two and a half days to dig the grave in the frozen, packed-earth floor of the church, but there was no shortage of volunteers.

Early on the morning of January 21, in the stygian gloom of the Yukon winter, groups of mourners started walking toward the north end of Dawson to attend the funeral. All businesses were closed for the day. Sam Steele jotted in his diary, "Father Judge buried," and although he himself was too busy to attend the service, he noted, "gave leave to the men to go." The church overflowed with people several hours before the service was due to start. Dark fabric draped the sanctuary's wooden supports and walls, and dozens of wax tapers threw a flickering, smoky light. In the middle of the aisle stood the priest's open coffin; the congregation was mesmerized by the corpse's peaceful expression. One of the nursing sisters remarked that he looked as though he had "fallen into quiet, restful repose." Father Gendreau performed the requiem Mass, assisted by his two Oblate colleagues, Father Desmarais and Father Corbeil, and spoke about the Jesuit's extraordinary service in the North. Then, as the choir sang "Nearer My God to Thee," the congregation filed up the aisle, past the coffin. Finally, the coffin was lowered into the grave.

The death of the gentle Jesuit marked the end of an era in the Yukon. He had traveled north to minister to the Indians, whom he loved wholeheartedly. He had come to the Klondike valley before it became a blackened, treeless landscape of mineshafts, and had seen Dawson City when it was nothing more than a handful of grubby tents. He had saved individual souls and lives, and inspired collective efforts to build a hospital and a church. His ear was always open and his door was never closed. As the *Klondike Nugget* put it the day after his funeral, "There is scarcely a man in the entire community who, at sometime or other, has not come into personal contact with the work of that noble priest."

The priest had been such a familiar figure on Dawson streets, as he peered shortsightedly through his wire-rimmed glasses at passersby and held their outstretched hands between his shabby mittens, that even men who had never bothered to acknowledge him now felt his loss. "Now that this work of love was finished," wrote his brother, Charles, in the biography he published eight years later, "men realized how beautiful, how sweet, his charity had been." In 1899, there were several other "sky pilots" (as church men were called by the miners) in Dawson, but they competed for congregations and none had Judge's quiet grace. "There is no one here," suggested the *Klondike Nugget,* "who can take up the Father's good work with the disinterestedness and unselfishness of Father Judge, or can, in less than a decade, win such individual trust as all felt for this physically feeble, yet charitably strong man." No other representative of the Church had the moral authority of the dead Jesuit. Now it was up to the legal authority of Superintendent Sam Steele of the Mounties to provide Dawson City with a moral compass and some semblance of civilization.

CHAPTER 18
A Cleansing Fire, February–April 1899

RESIDENTS OF DAWSON CITY could set their watches by Superintendent Sam Steele as he did his inspection rounds. Beginning in the frozen darkness of the early morning, he checked the North-West Mounted Police station on Front Street, then the cells in the Mountie prison, and then the Mounties' own hospital, before settling into his barracks office. Sam was in his element, and hard work and ambition made up for his lack of either imagination or humor. He kept record books up to date, filed long reports, and carefully noted in his official NWMP daybook any initiatives taken.

Sam's control of Dawson was tantamount to martial law, and he didn't care if he rode roughshod over the rights of non-Canadians. A handful of disgruntled Americans grumbled to James McCook, the plump and jolly U.S. consul, that they were being persecuted on account of their nationality. When McCook stormed into Sam's office, the policeman listened skeptically to the consul's rant, then coolly announced that these were "petty complaints" and that at least 200 Americans in the area ought to be in jail. "Blatant American fool!" Sam commented to Marie, privately confirming American protests. Most Dawson residents, he was confident, appreciated his regime. When he tramped along the frozen Klondike on crisp, twilit winter afternoons, looking like a big brown bear in his raccoon coat, cabin dwellers along the riverbank shouted greetings. On the rare occasions when he stepped into the Monte Carlo or the Dominion, a respectful hush spread rapidly through the smoky bar while any malefactors melted quietly into the background.

The police chief could not entirely eliminate Dawson's more sinful side, and the *Klondike Nugget* continued to record it in vivid detail. In early February 1899, a twenty-eight-year-old Welsh wrestler named Dave Evans shot his mistress, a forty-five-year-old dance hall girl called Libby White, because of her "promiscuous tendencies," then turned the gun on himself. A few days later, nineteen poker players were arrested in a Sunday police raid on "the Green Cloth Resorts": each was fined fifty dollars plus costs in police court the following day. Mlle Hermine Depauvv, described primly by the *Nugget* as "a typical representative of the tenderloin society," accused a French miner called Emil Rodenbach of stealing from her the sum of $10,700, which she had accumulated during her "thrifty and festive career." Over the course of the winter, the *Nugget* reported the suicides or attempted suicides of at least six prostitutes, including nineteen-year-old Kitty Stroup from Oregon, who ate strychnine four days before Christmas after her boyfriend, a bartender at the Pioneer saloon, dumped her for another woman. And there was a dismal catalogue of thefts, drunkenness, unpaid debts, assaults, and—most poignant—dead babies discovered hidden under rocks or in garbage heaps. But Steele's rules were having an effect. Dawson was no Skagway.

The town's opinion leaders were eager to curry favor with Steele. They had little success. Sam was not particularly gregarious, so didn't enjoy the camaraderie of the saloons, and he knew the advantages of keeping his distance. Unable to inveigle Sam into the Fairview while he was doing his daily rounds, Belinda Mulrooney invited him to a select little dinner. Again, he declined. "She is sharp," he wrote to Marie, and what's more, "mixed up with certain officials in the way of money-making. I am not going to make myself cheap." He barely greeted her when they passed in the street. The *Klondike Nugget* ran numerous articles praising the police force because editor Gene Allen wanted to interview the man in charge. Sam refused. He regarded the *Nugget* as "a rag of a newspaper," he told Marie, because it made "unjust attacks on the council and others of the officials most of whom are pretty good men."

The honor of the force came first in Sam's book. He was determined to project the right image, so he insisted on lots of spit 'n' polish and formality in the officers' mess. Sam admired his colleague Commissioner Ogilvie, who told colorful stories about the early days in the North. Ogilvie humanized the stark, dark, log barracks where both he and Steele lived: his rooms often resounded with the roar of male laughter, as senior personnel joined him for cigars and a singsong around his graphaphone. But Ogilvie's easy manners, and the way he would talk to "any Tom, Dick and Harry" who dropped into the commissioner's office, appalled Steele. "Ogilvie is too simple in his habits," he confided to his wife, and the commissioner's official dinners were shabby affairs, prepared by "a poor cook" and served with "a hasty lot of drinks. This has a bad effect." At NWMP mess dinners, nobody could smoke until after the toast to the Queen, and the plates were changed between courses. "Thank goodness we hold up our end and act as particularly as if in Ottawa or London."

Sam Steele did allow himself a limited social life, with the two bank managers, a couple of Scottish businessmen, and Mr. and Mrs. Davis, the collector of customs and his wife. Sam was also prepared to talk to Faith Fenton, the Toronto journalist who had arrived in Dawson the same month as he, and who in a column in the Toronto *Globe* had contradicted Flora Shaw. Fenton was quite besotted with the red-coated Mounties, and Sam found her respectful attention flattering, although he reassured his wife that although "Faith Fenton and I are quite friendly ... you need not fear a flirtation for she is the plainest [woman] I have met for some time." Faith was smart and demure; more important, she provided Sam with a pipeline to an influential Liberal newspaper.

Perhaps that was why, the previous November, Superintendent Steele had done Miss Fenton a big favor. One of the first stories she sent her newspaper from Dawson was about the four Tlingit prisoners whom Flora Shaw had met on the trail in July. Since then, three of the men had been sentenced to be hanged. Faith knew this was the kind of raw northern drama that Toronto readers would love, but the dogsled carrying mail left for Whitehorse before the hanging was scheduled. So she "prewrote" the story and gave it to the carrier. Then the hanging was postponed, to the exasperation of Sam Steele, who was eager to make an example of the murderers. While he was venting his irritation to his junior officers, a frantic Faith arrived in his office, begging for help. Steele promptly dispatched one of the Mounties' crack dog teams on a fifty-mile chase along the slushy banks of the Yukon River to retrieve Faith's premature report. The "distressed damsel," as Sam Steele called her, saved face.

Mail to the Outside was one of Sam Steele's biggest challenges. As Flora Shaw had noted, the service was appalling. In July 1898, Ottawa had subcontracted it to an American company in Seattle, which sent the mail bags up the coast but did nothing to ensure that Dawson-bound mail crossed the mountains into Canadian territory, or that outgoing mail left Dawson. The North-West Mounted Police had stepped into the breach, and informally provided a mail service two or three times a month up the Yukon to Whitehorse and over the White Pass while the river was still open. Once winter arrived, Sam Steele decided that this arrangement should be formalized. He decreed that NWMP dog teams would carry mail into and out of Dawson on the first and fifteenth of every month, and he arranged to have the trail cleared and fresh teams of dogs at every detachment post. After the disaster of the first mail outfit, which went through the ice on November 15, the service went smoothly. Between 500 and 700 pounds of letters were carried each way, and the police mail carriers vied to set the record for the 600-mile journey. Despite the rocks, snowdrifts, icy swamps, and treacherous slopes, one team had even managed the incredible feat of completing it within seven days.

Sam loved the excitement of the race, and made claims for Mountie sled dogs that smack more of police pride than canine character: "The dogs were the well-known Labrador breed, very fierce, and they had the remarkable reputation of having at one time killed and devoured their driver." By the end of the winter, in horrendous weather conditions, NWMP mail carriers had logged 64,012 miles—the equivalent of about two and a half times round the world. (This was the kind of statistic that Sam loved to collect; he was probably the first member of the force to insist that mileage records for horses be kept. Such punctiliousness would have been unthinkable for similar forces such as the Texas Rangers.) Sam also reorganized the sorting of the mail in Dawson: under his watch, 1,600 mailboxes were constructed at the Front Street post office. However, both the post office itself and the wall of mailboxes were completely inadequate to service a community that numbered well over 30,000 when the miners on the creeks were included.

Sam had a personal interest in getting the mail running on time. He was desperate to hear from his wife. When the Steeles parted in January 1898, they had assumed that Marie would remain for only a few months at the Mountie barracks in Fort Macleod, Alberta, where her husband had previously been posted. Sam planned to bring his family to the NWMP post at the head of Bennett Lake as soon as he had built a decent house and settled in. At first, Marie was happy with the plans, and they regularly exchanged affectionate notes. "My own darling Sam," Marie wrote in August, "Your dear letters of the 15th, 26th, 28th and 30th all came to me on Friday afternoon and needless for me to say what a very warm welcome they received." But with three young children and Sam's transfer to Dawson, Marie's enthusiasm for northern challenges shrank. Instead, she joined her mother in Montreal, and started to dread a winter without her devoted husband. Once the Yukon River froze, mail would be infrequent. "When I think the time is fast approaching when you can write back [only] twice a month," Marie wrote, "I feel as if my heart would break!"

For months, Marie Steele failed to reply to her
husband's letters. Sam became increasingly agitated.

In Dawson, Sam kept scribbling, but after mid-November no letters from Marie arrived. At first, his plaintive missives described how his heart ached to see her. "Oh my dear how I long for the sight of your dear kind face and of the dear little ones but I will not have that pleasure I fear for a long time now . . . It may be possible that I shall God willing be able to go on leave one year from now." As winter stretched on, Sam grew increasingly anxious for a letter from Marie. "I am longing to hear from you my own dearest pet my own darling wife," he wrote in early February. "I have no letter of a later date than September last yet I have written you at least once a week." Sam's reports to the NWMP comptroller in Montreal reached their destination, so he knew Marie was receiving his letters. "It is bad enough to be separated but separated without letters is worse."

By mid-February, Sam was getting tetchy: "My dearest wife . . . I shall indeed be glad when I begin to get letters from you. I have not had one since the first you wrote after the time you arrived in Montreal. I know there are none in the Yukon anywhere; all is cleared up from Skagway to here, and no excuse for any delay . . . You should write me weekly my darling if you *have any regard for me left.*" By late February, he was pleading: "My dearest, I got another mail yesterday but no letter from you although every particle of mail has been sent through up to the 24th of January. I hope I shall soon get a letter from you my dearest wife for I am heartbroken on account of not having got one from you. I had such a happy life with you and our dear little ones that I naturally have my thoughts turned towards you all." Sam's outward demeanor remained as brusque as ever, and he was even tougher on any junior officers who did not make the mail run in record time. But privately, an aching loneliness afflicted him as he tramped along the frozen Klondike. His men learned to fear the arrival of sacks of mail. Their commander would sift frantically through letters addressed to him, then storm wordlessly out of the mailroom.

Finally, in early March, a twelve-page letter from Marie arrived. She had plenty of excuses for not writing: the move to Montreal, ill health, and her struggle to find accommodation, nurses, and a cook had exhausted her. But her letter was a litany of grievances about lack of help from her husband's colleagues, her own relatives, and her household staff. When she and Sam were under the same roof, he probably either dealt with the problems or let the chatter flow over him. Now that they were apart, Marie poured out her complaints on paper. Subsequent letters captured the aggrieved tones of a woman who knew that her husband, for all his fine words, would always put profession before family. "It seems so long since I wrote and since I heard from you that

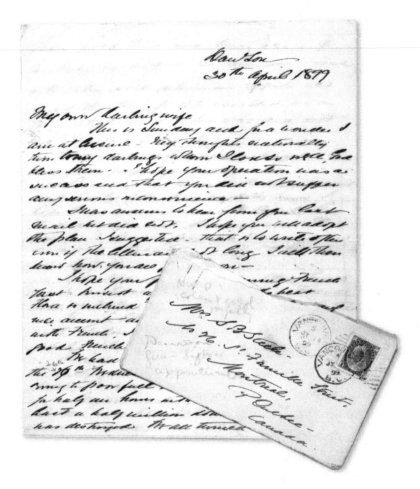

Sam's letters spelled out his love for his family in Montreal. He urged Marie to "write often even if the letters are not long."

your letters are like a ray of sunshine shed on my life from time to time," Marie wrote on February 13. "I am delighted to hear you are so comfortable but fear you may feel less inclined than ever to return to the little wifie and birdies who so anxiously await your return."

Sam Steele was overjoyed to hear that Marie and the children were safe and his marriage solid. He assured Marie that everything was fine, urged her to buy a new gown, and sent a list of new clothes he required.

From now on, his wife's letters infused renewed vigor into his daily routine. He brushed aside her hints of loneliness and did not pick up on her sense of being hard done by. "I am so sorry that you miss me my dear," he explained to Marie. "There is so much to do here and it affects my reputation so much that I must stay for a considerable time." Marie Steele was right about her husband's aspirations. Sam harbored the hope of one day becoming commissioner of the force to which he had dedicated much of his life. Success in the Yukon would improve his chances immeasurably.

All in all, Superintendent Steele thrived in those first few months in Dawson. He reassured Marie that he was far too busy to fall off the wagon. "Liquor has not passed my lips since I have been in the Yukon nor will it do so. I have no desire for it." As his fiftieth birthday approached, he took particular pride in his increased fitness. He had always been a vain man, who loved standing ramrod straight in his uniform for studio photographs—sometimes, he even added a little padding on his torso to achieve an extra-manly chest—but over the years some of the Mountie muscle had turned to fat. Now, his letters home included include regular updates on his weight. He had been 232 pounds when he arrived in Dawson; the following July he announced that he weighed 214 pounds, had not had a drink for thirteen months or a smoke for six months, and was "as active as a cat." The only problem was that his red coat was now too tight on the shoulders and too loose at the waist—please could Marie send an *urgent* note to the tailor, ordering a new uniform. There was also the matter of a pair of pistols he had ordered from Hicks and Sons in London. Where were they? And could she find out what had happened to the ribbon for the North West Canada Medal that he had been awarded a few years earlier but had never received?

Just after seven in the evening of April 26, 1899, a thin red flame like a serpent's tongue shot out of a bedroom above the Bodega saloon at

223 Front Street. Soon the Tivoli Theatre, on the north side of the Bodega, and the Northern restaurant to the south, were in flames. Panic
swept through Dawson City. It was nearly a year since Father Judge's
church had been destroyed by fire, and there had also been a devas-
tating conflagration the previous fall. On that occasion, a dance hall
girl called Belle Mitchell had left a candle burning in her bedroom at
the Green Tree Inn, and as a result, reported the *Klondike Nugget* in
October 1898, forty buildings were completely razed, $500,000 worth
of property was destroyed, and "a number of men lost eyebrows and
mustachios from the burning heat."

Now another, much more powerful inferno threatened. But citizens
hoped that this time they were prepared. A year earlier, a fire engine had
been purchased in the States for $18,000 and hauled over the moun-
tains. It had sat in its crate for months because the government refused
to pay for it, but the October fire encouraged Dawson business leaders,
including Belinda Mulrooney, to take some responsibility. A fund was
established to pay for it, a fire chief and stoker were appointed, a volun-
teer fire department was created, and a hundred men were recruited as
firefighters. In April, when the cry of "Fire!" arose, the "gallant fire boys"
(as the *Nugget* named them) dragged the engine a half mile down to the
riverbank, where it could pump water from the Yukon River.

It was an unusually chilly night, yet the firemen sweated as they unrav-
eled the hoses, then directed the nozzles at the flames while they tugged
them toward the burning buildings. They waited for five minutes for
water to spurt out . . . then another five minutes . . . But their colleagues
were still hacking their way through ten feet of ice to the flowing water
of the Yukon River, and the fire chief could not light the boiler because
it was too cold. For an agonizing thirty minutes, the steam pump failed
to operate and the only source of water was a bucket brigade. The fire
raged out of control. Fanned by a stiff breeze, the flames on Front Street
consumed seven stores, three saloons, a hotel, three restaurants, and the
large Northwest Trading Company warehouse. At the same time, the

fire ripped along the waterfront, destroying a laundry, two more restaurants, and nine more stores, including the Pioneer barber shop and Anderson Brothers' sign and paint shop. Spreading in every direction, it made short work of Dawson landmarks such as the Opera House, the Bank of British North America, the Ottawa Hotel, and numerous bawdy houses.

At last, the frenzied efforts of the men at the fire engine sent water through the frozen hose from beginning to end. A great cheer went up through the fog and smoke as a small stream of water trickled from the nozzle. But the air temperature was forty-five degrees below zero and the line of hose was 400 feet long, lying exposed on river ice. The steam engine was not strong enough to keep the water flowing. The water in the hose turned into solid ice, ripping its length as if with a giant razor blade.

As darkness fell, frantic figures passed buckets of water or dashed around trying to save possessions. Ramshackle wooden buildings began to smolder and collapse, and barrels of liquor were thrown into the street, where the liquid gelled instantly into mini-glaciers. Rescued furnishings, clothes, and goods were piled into the streets, blocking firefighting efforts. People clambered over buildings, vainly trying to protect them by draping wet blankets on roofs and walls. Screams reverberated as scantily dressed hookers and dance hall girls fled into the streets. Belinda Mulrooney was torn between helping friends and ensuring the Fairview Hotel was saved. She ran up First Avenue to Bill McPhee's Pioneer saloon before it was consumed, to get the bags of gold dust out of his safe. "For heaven's sake, Bill," she yelled at her old rival, "Help us with the gold, to get it down to the Fairview." But Bill had other priorities: the enormous moose antlers that he had brought from Forty Mile and nailed above his bar on opening day, two years earlier. "To hell with the gold dust," he replied. "Save my moose horns." Belinda never forgot how he "looked up at them as wistful as could be. They spread right across the bar and were the pride of his life." The proprietor of the Fairview had no such sentimental attachment to animal relics. She ignored him and turned to the dance hall girls.

More than fifty women "were running in every direction crazy in their light pink silk underclothes—some in bare feet, some in slippers, with not enough clothes on to wad a shotgun." Many had frozen feet; all had lost everything they owned. Belinda shooed them down to the Fairview Hotel, which was a couple of blocks south of the inferno. There was a large coffeemaker in the hotel kitchen, "and I dumped into it a lot of rum or brandy for the men fighting fire and had a cup poured for each girl. I took a cup myself and it nearly knocked me silly. After the boys tasted the coffee they all wanted to save the Fairview . . . The place had caught fire a couple of times on the roof. After the coffee the men stood around all night and threw buckets of muck at the hotel where it didn't need it. We had to ask them to stop." Meanwhile, Belinda organized mattresses and bedding for the wretched women, and instructed them to sleep on and under the tables in the Fairview's dining room.

Sam Steele raced from the police encampment to the town center as soon as the alarm was sounded, and quickly took in the disaster—the ferocity of the flames, the absence of water, the public hysteria. There was only one way to kill the fire: to destroy the buildings in its path so they could not fuel the flames and spread them farther. "I personally directed the removal of buildings," he noted in his daybook. His officers organized teams of volunteers to tear down some buildings and dynamite others. When the dynamite charges exploded, the noise was intense. The ground shuddered, the ice on the river creaked, onlookers screamed, log walls and tin roofs cartwheeled through the smoke. Fragments were scattered far out on the frozen Yukon. Sam noticed several of Dawson's undesirables guzzling rescued whiskey and looting burning buildings instead of joining the bucket brigade. He issued orders to arrest men who avoided bucket duty and to close the hotels at midnight "because there was a sign of drunkenness going on all the time and there might have been a riot."

In the early hours of the morning, the fire was contained. A somber sight met Sam Steele's eyes as he patrolled the streets at dawn. The business section of town was a smoking ruin. One hundred and eleven buildings had burned down, and fifteen more had been torn down. Goods and furnishings rescued from the flames still stood in untidy piles in the middle of streets, destroyed by smoke and mud. There were also piles of ice, which had been cut and transported from the river only weeks earlier by several hotels and restaurants for summer use. The wooden buildings in which they had been stored had gone, but the ice remained intact. Belinda Mulrooney's hotel—one of the few commercial buildings left standing—wore a glistening, coffee-colored sheath of frozen mud.

Men coated in soot crouched in the wreckage of saloons, cabins, and stores, panning for gold dust in the cinders. David Doig, the flamboyant manager of the Bank of British North America, was standing white faced in the empty crater where his bank once was. The previous night, as the fire roared toward the corner of Second Avenue and Queen Street, he had promised $1,000 to anybody who could save the building. Nobody snapped up the offer. As flames engulfed the bank, its steel "fire-proof vault" had exploded in the searing heat and the contents had spewed out—nuggets, gold dust, gold watches, chains, rings, bracelets, diamond brooches. Golden sovereigns had been flung twenty feet away, like confetti. Much of the wealth scooped from Bonanza paydirt or bestowed on dance hall girls was now fused into one ugly block of blackened gold. But the three steel safes within the vault were intact. When they were opened, paper money worth hundreds of thousands of dollars was found unharmed. Doig wearily set up a temporary bank headquarters on the second story of the Fairview Hotel, above the impromptu dormitory of hookers.

Before the ashes were cool, the price of lumber had doubled and rebuilding had begun. Belinda was running a soup kitchen. "We served meals in the Fairview from a long table in front of the kitchen stove.

The Bank of British North America's "fire-proof vault" (right) exploded in the April 1899 fire. Scavengers were soon busy in the mud and wreckage.

People just took food up in their hands . . . The hotel was crowded . . . In my office and my room, all you could see was bare feet sticking out. The place was lined with mattresses." At the same time, Gene Allen was furiously putting together a special edition of the *Klondike Nugget*. "DAWSON IS ONCE AGAIN IN ASHES," read the headline, "Queen Of The Yukon Is Once More Attacked By Her Old Enemy! The City's Loss Will Be Fully A Million Dollars!" In the next few weeks, it became evident that even the *Nugget*, with its penchant for hyperbole, had underestimated the losses. Dawson had suffered at least $2 million of damage.

But Sam Steele was the man in charge. He ordered the men who had been arrested and jailed during the fire to appear in police court, then fined several for drunkenness and two for not assisting the fire brigade. He enforced an order from Commissioner Ogilvie that no new structures be built on the waterfront. He moved the dance hall girls down to the barracks from the Fairview Hotel, before they could resume business in Belinda's bedrooms. Then he authorized an inquest into the cause of the fire.

A jury led by Captain Harper of the NWMP questioned the porter at the Bodega saloon. The porter accused Helen Holden, the dance hall girl who lived on the Bodega's second floor, of leaving a candle burning in her bedroom. Miss Holden angrily denied such a charge, and counter-charged that the fire had begun in the Bodega stockroom. The jury was not sympathetic. Reported the *Nugget*, "One of the jurors seemed to entertain the belief pretty firmly that the fire started in Miss Holden's apartments for he asked her if she smoked cigarettes. A titter went through the audience as she replied rather vehemently that she did not, and it was repeated when Captain Harper asked if she curled her hair. Miss Holden, however, didn't see anything in the question to laugh at, and she answered very seriously that she did not—that her hair did not require curling, thanks to Mother Nature."

The previous fall, Sam Steele had promised Marie that he and Commissioner Ogilvie would clean up Dawson, and as far as he was concerned, the fire had done some of his work for him. Across North America, the temperance movement was in full swing, campaigning for a clean-up of red-light districts in major cities. Members of the Women's Christian Temperance Union, like Nellie McClung in Canada and Frances Willard in the United States, were busy handing out abstinence pledge cards to men who promised to give up alcohol. Ottawa politicians, keen to demonstrate that they were as shocked by moral turpitude as anyone, had decided that Dawson's reputation as Gomorrah on the Yukon needed attention. An order to prosecute the prostitutes had been sent north.

Two weeks before the Dawson conflagration, hookers who plied their trade on and behind Second Avenue had received police notices that they must vacate their premises by May 1. "No longer may the woman in scarlet occupy the choicest city lots and flaunt her crimson colors on Dawson's crowded streets," reported the *Klondike Nugget*.

"No longer may the seductive window tap beguile the innocent prospector or hurrying man of business. The reign of the scarlet letter is on the wane, and one of the institutions most cherished and nourished in the halcyon days of yore is about to be degraded." The *Nugget* suggested that there were about 300 "soiled doves" (in the paper's exquisite euphemism) in the tenderloin district, who charged, according to one old sourdough, from two dollars to four ounces of gold "for a very hurried entertainment."

Thanks to the fire, the women were now homeless. Most were pathetically grateful when Colonel Steele told them they could occupy two blocks bounded by Fourth and Fifth Avenues, just west of the Mounties' headquarters and well away from the business district. "The New Tenderloin," announced the *Nugget,* would be ready by June 1. Sam Steele was priggish about prostitution, but he was also a realist. He didn't believe that it was possible to eliminate prostitution in a mining town with so many single men, and he certainly didn't want to spend all his time chasing hookers out of Dawson. "These girls seem to be in the eyes of the majority of the community a necessary evil," he reported to the commissioner of the NWMP in Ottawa in May. Besides, the regular fines for unruly behavior and fees for medical inspections were a useful source of revenue. So Dawson prostitutes continued to be tolerated in a way that was by now unthinkable in the rest of North America.

Each week, in Montreal, Marie Steele pasted into her scrapbook any cuttings that mentioned her husband. Many came from Sam himself. On May 28, he sent his wife some copies of the *Nugget* along with the instruction "Please paste the good ones in your scrap book, the children may need to have it after a time, and it is part of my record."

The family was particularly proud of a widely reproduced dispatch written by Faith Fenton, which was guaranteed to buttress the Sam Steele legend. It read, in part, "Col. Steele should be given a special vote of thanks by Parliament. No man ever deserved it more. Besides having his men under such a remarkable state of discipline he has done wonders in many

Sam Steele didn't see his three young children, Harwood (left), Gertrude (center), and Flora (right), for eighteen months, but they saw his picture in the papers.

other ways. We are now having a weekly postal service . . . He has located nearly every crook in Dawson . . . He is always looking ahead, always planning ahead. That is the kind of man required in a country like this."

American newspapers also carried articles on Steele of the Mounties. Seattle newspapers published accusations from disgruntled American prospectors about dictatorial officials and government corruption in the Canadian gold fields, but these did not find their way into Marie Steele's scrapbooks. Instead, she gave a whole page to a clipping from Chicago's *Sunday Chronicle* of May 14, 1899: "Colonel S. B. Steele . . . is a whole army unto himself. He was born to rule in a country where he must become dictator for he is . . . far away from assistance, from advice and from supplies." Sam was well on his way to becoming that rare phenomenon—an icon in a country that distrusted celebrity.

CHAPTER 19
Stampede to Nome, Summer 1899

IN THE SPRING OF 1899, the outside world was catching up with Dawson. "Yukon Breaks Its Icy Fetters" proclaimed the *Nugget* in mid-May: "Thousands of people cheer in unison with the tooting of steam whistles and the baying of malamutes." For the third consecutive year, two armadas of vessels appeared, the first from upriver, then a few days later a second paddling against the current from St. Michael, at the river's mouth. A crowd of prospectors in shabby wool pants and greasy slouch hats milled around the riverbank in the spring sunshine. As usual, they pestered newcomers for news about everything that had happened Outside in the previous six months. The sourdoughs had specific questions, about boxing champions, Derby winners, government scandals, and imperial wars. Was Queen Victoria, now aged eighty, still alive? (She was.) Had Britain crushed the pesky Boers and their truculent leader, Paul Kruger, in the Transvaal? (They hadn't.) Would the French government finally release Captain Alfred Dreyfus from jail? (Not yet.) Had Spain and the United States made peace? (Yes, the previous December Spain had ceded to the United States control of Cuba, the Philippines, Puerto Rico, and Guam. But since then there had been an uprising in the Philippines.) A couple of British toffs wanted to know the results of the Oxford and Cambridge Boat Race.

Yet as newcomers and old-timers mingled on Front Street, Dawsonites sensed that life south of the St. Elias Mountains was changing. The economic depression that had sent many of them north was lifting: steel rails were criss-crossing North America, bread lines were shrinking, prairie farms thrived, and there was talk of a canal in Panama to link the Atlantic and Pacific Oceans, financed by the American government. As the millennium approached, cracks had appeared in the stifling conformity of the Victorian era. Women were agitating for the vote and working men were flexing political muscles. The first horseless carriages were being seen in larger towns, swarms of bicycles took off into the countryside every weekend, and there was even the astonishing suggestion that in future people might fly through the air in airships held aloft by hydrogen. Drinkers in the newly rebuilt bars along Front Street heard about weird new trends such as dances with names like the "Cakewalk" and paintings made up of colored dots. The new railroad from Skagway up the White Trail had now almost reached Bennett Lake and would soon link Whitehorse to the coast. The journey in and out of the Yukon was becoming incomparably easier. Miners who had not made a nickel since they arrived in Dawson City began to dream of going home. Belinda Mulrooney and the Klondike Kings, who had bags of cash, fantasized about flaunting their wealth among the high rollers of San Francisco, Chicago, and New York.

The outside world was catching up with Superintendent Steele, too. Throughout the winter, while Dawson City was cut off from communication with Ottawa, his word had been law—and as Faith Fenton had reported, it had been an effective law. There was still no telegraph wire linking Dawson to the Outside, but with spring ice-out, dispatches now took only a few days between Ottawa and Dawson instead of up to two months. Sam could no longer ignore stresses facing his own men or orders from Ottawa.

The most immediate tension, which had been building for months, was that government salaries were pathetically low in a community where gold nuggets were playthings and prices ranged between two and ten times the level of those Outside. A Mountie constable was paid

Dozens of paddle-wheelers converged on Dawson City during the Yukon River's five ice-free months.

$1.25 a day; a laborer in the mines could earn the same amount in an hour. Bank clerks were in the same bind as officials. In the hope of recruiting new clients, a Bank of Commerce officer had strolled into a saloon called Tammany Hall when he first arrived in Dawson the previous spring. There a new acquaintance introduced the banker to some old-timers, among them Skiff Mitchell and Johnny Lind, who were drinking champagne that, in the words of the banker, "came thick and fast." Soon it was the newcomer's turn to buy a round. He was horrified to learn that it would cost him $120—small change for a miner fresh from clean-up on the creeks, but more than a month's pay for a banker. He had just enough in his pocket, but "prudence induced him to see in the crowd an imaginary individual he 'simply had to speak to.' He went to his bed and for some time thereafter sought business in less exciting circles."

Belinda Mulrooney professed pity for men who "couldn't live and meet their expenses in Dawson on their salaries." Compassion didn't stop her exploiting their predicament. When Frederick Coates Wade first arrived in Dawson in February 1898, he had ignored Belinda and settled on Big Alex McDonald as the man to buy the Dawson waterfront. But Belinda realized that Fred Wade was for hire, since he combined his government responsibilities with a private practice. She recruited him as her "legal adviser," probably with a retainer. By the spring of 1899, Wade was crown prosecutor and Belinda was full of admiration for his cavalier behavior as "judge, lawyer and everything else—if he did not want a fellow to go to court next day, he'd take him out and lick him or get him drunk so he wouldn't show up." By then, she was also describing him as her "business partner" because she had set him up in some lucrative mining deals. Under her own name she also purchased shares in claims for other officials, including Captain H. H. Norwood, Inspector of the Mines. She insisted that the deals were all legitimate and her clients "were square shooters, lots of the property they picked up was worthless, but they picked up enough good ones to make it worthwhile." It was worthwhile for Belinda, too. In return for her help, "I had lots of favors from the officials."

Sam Steele knew that an open system of kickbacks flourished in the allocation of timber rights. He knew that in the gold commissioner's office crooked officials schemed with powerful mining interests to buy up individual prospectors' claims by fair means or foul. He read the *Klondike Nugget* story on May 3, 1899: "The country abounds in snakes of all kinds. The most venomous, which poisons the public peace and pollutes even the stream of public administration, is known as the 'Voracious Clerkibus Intolerens.'" But Sam's hands were tied. Clifford Sifton, the Liberal minister whom Flora Shaw had met in Ottawa the previous October, continued to regard the Yukon as a rich source of patronage and to give Dawson jobs to men who were more interested in lining their own pockets than establishing good government.

The weekly meetings of the six members of the Yukon Executive Council in the NWMP barracks were a covert battleground. Superficially, they were relaxed get-togethers for men who were far from home and trying to bring order to a rough-and-tumble town. Commissioner Ogilvie presided at the head of the table, puffing away at his pipe and inclined to digress into anecdotes about the bad old days. But of the six men, only Steele and Ogilvie were not making money on the side: the other four, including Fred Wade, were all Sifton cronies. At a meeting in March, Sam voted down a motion that council members should give themselves a hefty salary increase. He told Marie that he was particularly exasperated because Commissioner Ogilvie offered only "half-hearted opposition" to the idea of voting himself a raise: the commissioner was finding Dawson hard on the wallet.

These issues were especially difficult for straitlaced Sam because he himself was strapped financially. In the early 1890s while posted at Fort Macleod, he had accumulated debts that would come due within months. All his NWMP salary was paid directly to Marie Steele in Montreal; in Dawson, he survived on the fees he earned for supervising police courts (about $200 a month) and because he got free board and lodging in the police barracks. At some point in early 1899, surrounded by Klondike Kings, he had succumbed to temptation and bought shares in a couple of new claims on Sulphur Creek and one on Bonanza. He was not the only Mountie to take a flyer on a gold claim; his friend and subordinate Inspector Bobby Belcher had done the same thing.

When Steele and Belcher acquired the shares, it was not officially illegal for government officials to own property on the mines, but that changed in April 1899. In Ottawa, the government published an order-in-council prohibiting the staking or recording of mining claims in the Yukon by officials in their own or any other names, or securing any interest in any claim, or acting as agent for anyone in regard to any claim. Sifton's pal Fred Wade—by now land registrar, clerk of the court, crown prosecutor, adviser to the gold commissioner, and member of and legal adviser to the Yukon Executive Council—was specifically exempt from this regulation. The *Edmonton Bulletin* noted that Wade was told "there was nothing in the mining regulations to prevent [him] from staking a claim in his own name." Sam Steele was not mentioned, but there was a tacit understanding that government officials already in the Yukon were exempt from the new rules. Sam continued to acquire claims, writing to his wife in August that "Belcher is working the claim and we are going to get a share on 66 below Sulphur and on 18 above further north at the rate of fifty percent of the proceeds. One alone might pay our debts all right and have a good margin."

But Sam Steele knew that his own holdings might stain his reputation with the new regulations in place, and then the Ottawa wolves would circle. As he strode through Dawson, he ruminated on the challenge of staying "clean." On the evening of May 28, when daylight lingered in the sky until nearly midnight, he penned a hurried note to Marie: "My dearest, I have just thought that you had better get a miner's certificate in Ottawa even if you have to go up there for it. I cannot hold mining property but you can. Send also a power of attorney made out by Auguste [Marie's brother, a lawyer] so that I can act for you."

Sam Steele was right to worry. An unholy row was brewing in Ottawa about corruption in the Yukon, and every official in Dawson risked being sideswiped in the melee. The Conservative opposition in central Canada was on the attack. They were genuinely shocked by what was going on in Dawson, now regarded as a Babylon of bribery. They were also eager for Sifton's head. In April 1899, the formidable orator Sir Charles Hibbert Tupper, son of a former Conservative prime minister, took the Tory lead. Tupper alleged that "if Mr. Sifton had been given the Yukon District to exploit for his own personal gain, he could not have left anything undone that he did, acting in the capacity of the Minister of the Crown." Tupper demanded a commission of inquiry into Sifton's shenanigans that included, he charged, "taxes and royalties that would make Oom Paul [Paul Kruger, president of the Transvaal during the Boer Wars and a wildly unpopular figure within the British Empire] blush, the appointment of corrupt and incompetent officials, favoritism in the granting of licenses, leases and contracts, gross mismanagement of transportation, and neglect of all sanitary precautions."

Stirring stuff. But the attacks didn't bother Sifton himself one whit, as he continued to hand out contracts to cronies. Sam Steele tried to hold the line: he refused to allow a Sifton pal to receive the contract to supply meat to the Mounties, challenged several other appointments, and insisted that mining royalties should be collected by Mounties, not civilian officials who were Sifton appointees. A showdown between minister and Mountie was inevitable. Despite all Sam's efforts and self-promotion, throughout the spring of 1899 rumors of his impending transfer out of Dawson rippled through the Yukon. The strain began to tell on Sam, who stopped bragging to Marie that he had not touched a drop of liquor. On July 15, he noted at the back of his diary that he had bought two bottles of Scotch, at six dollars each—$120 per bottle in today's values.

Sam Steele was not the only person about whom rumors were swirling that spring. Belinda Mulrooney was also attracting gossip—and not the sort she liked.

The previous summer, an intriguing new figure had stepped off a steamer from Whitehorse onto the Dawson waterfront. At first glance, Charles Eugene Carbonneau seemed entirely out of place in the Arctic boomtown. In his tailored suit, patent leather shoes, spats, and kid gloves, he strolled around Dawson, cane in hand, speaking politely to people in a cultured French accent and creating an impression of wealth and sophistication. His calling card identified him as Count Carbonneau, a representative of Messrs Pierre Legasse, Frères et Cie, well-known wine merchants of Paris and New York. He let drop that he had important connections in Ottawa (although there was no evidence of this). The dapper aristocrat moved into the Fairview Hotel, and immediately complained about the price of a bottle of wine.

In truth, Carbonneau was simply a better-dressed version of a type

well-known on Dawson streets: the con artist. Yet his act was so polished that Belinda was taken in. At first, the Fairview's proprietor didn't
think much of a guest who flaunted his title and challenged her prices,
but she soon found herself drawn to this "dashing sort of chap [who]
wore good clothes," as she would remember him. "His eyes were large
with a sort of sleepy, gentle look some Frenchmen have, and he had a
heavy moustache." Besides bedroom eyes, there were other attractions.
Belinda's dog, Nero, who usually had no time for anybody except his
mistress, "was fond of Carbonneau, liking him better than anybody else
excepting me."

Ostensibly, Carbonneau had traveled to the Yukon not to sell French
wines but to represent a group of London investors interested in Klondike gold. He bought some claims on Bonanza Creek from an old-
timer called Thomas Pelkey. After his August 1898 visit, Carbonneau
returned to Europe to establish the Anglo-French Klondyke Syndicate
and to find more investors. He returned to the Yukon in January 1899,
after braving the winter trails and temperatures as low as forty below
zero, and moved back into the Fairview. Belinda was awed by his outfit.
"He . . . had magnificent furs and other equipment—tents, spirit lamps,
steaks and other fine food stuffs. The ordinary tent wasn't good enough
for him. He had to have silk tents. His cot—you know the rest of us put
down pine boughs and would think them a great luxury, but he had
some blessed thing that knocked down and was padded especially with
curly hair." Carbonneau, now the Dawson manager of his mining company, dined with Belinda whenever she was available. She "found his
conversation restful and interesting, especially his description of life in
Europe." She also noticed that her chef "had more respect for him than
for me. I never bothered, took what they gave me . . . [Charles would]
get into the kitchen and show him if he knew he couldn't cook."

They made an unlikely twosome. Tough little Belinda, with her prickly
manner, sharp tongue, and prim collars, was beguiled by a Frenchman
who was "immaculate in dress, appearance and table manners" and

courted her with flowers. She didn't care that many of the old-timers dismissed him as a dandy and a phony. She refused to listen to gossip that far from being a French nobleman, he was a French Canadian who had been either a baker or a barber on Rue St. Denis in Montreal. Carbonneau got along well enough with Belinda's professional pals, like Fred Wade and the bank managers, but the miners didn't warm to him and he turned up his nose at them, complaining that the men on the creeks never shaved. But Belinda liked Charles. She softened in his company and giggled when he flirted with her. Once or twice, he even made her blush. She was amused by what she saw as "an eternal childish quality" in her beau, who was fifteen years her senior.

How did Carbonneau penetrate Belinda's defenses? Perhaps she feared that if she confined her friendships to tough old boys in the Fairview's bar, she would spend the rest of her life as one of them. Maybe she was tired of insinuations that she preferred women to men. Perhaps, now that she was acknowledged as the richest woman in the Klondike, she had lost the widespread (and justified) female dread that once a man possesses you, he assumes power over you. At twenty-seven, she may have felt the first stirrings of a desire for a different life, with a gallant husband and perhaps some children. Maybe all those snubs from Superintendent Steele had stung, stirring memories of the humiliation she had felt in Pennsylvania when other children laughed at her thick Irish accent. The respectability of marriage to a dignified and titled Parisian would confer a status that, up to now, she had never thought she needed—but something must have changed.

Carbonneau was a cunning suitor. He did what no man had ever done to Belinda: he treated her like a beautiful woman. He returned from one of his frequent trips Outside with a trunk full of elegant gowns. Belinda's first reaction was fury. "I blew up like a balloon! He thought I'd be tickled to death with them. He thought he'd done something wonderful for me when he opened the trunk and showed me those clothes. I was shocked." Belinda's atavistic instinct to beat men at their own game surfaced. How had he so misjudged her? Did he think she was a woman who could be bought with finery? Was he trying to tell her she should dress in a more feminine style? They had a furious row, and Belinda said she would give the gowns to Sadie. But Carbonneau knew what he was doing—he had played on her insecurities and longings. Somehow, the trunk stayed in her room. When she was by herself, Belinda would hold the lacy blouses and long, sweeping skirts against her body. She fondled the delicate fabrics, rubbing them against her cheeks. "I wouldn't wear the things, but they were tempting enough at that . . . It was fun to feel the silks and satins, the beautiful hose."

The flirtation bubbled on as winter turned into spring, and Belinda and Carbonneau pursued their businesses. Belinda promoted her new water company, Hygeia, and regularly visited her claims on the creeks, where she watched the introduction of steam pumps to speed up the thawing process. Carbonneau was buying and selling claims, on at least one occasion borrowing from Belinda when he needed capital. Carbonneau also entered into a contract with her to build an extension to the Grand Forks Hotel and to buy 50 percent of the value of her inventory. He insinuated himself into a deal in which Superintendent Steele was involved, and was soon on the easy terms with the Mountie that Belinda had never achieved. In March, Belinda and Carbonneau hiked up the trail to Grand Forks together. Belinda, arms swinging and small feet fairly dancing along the rutted path, outpaced her portly and panting suitor. Finally, Carbonneau grabbed her arm and exclaimed, "For God's sake, stand still long enough, I want to talk to you." He told her that he had been offered a government post. Belinda asked him why he didn't take it, and recalled in her memoir that he replied, "A man loses his influence if he takes a job. I make more money as it is now. Besides, I feel as if I'd have to be a miner or a sourdough to get you interested in me and I want to get married."

Belinda was not surprised by Carbonneau's declaration and, she admitted, "I knew long before that I was interested." Carbonneau made it clear that he was in a rush. Belinda began her side of the negotiations. "I told him I had no knowledge of a home, or of caring for a house. He told me he would never think of his wife doing house keeping. I told him, 'That suits me.'" Even as she sorted out these domestic details, Belinda knew there were more dangerous snags. By law, married women could not own property: if she and Carbonneau wed, he could have the right to claim ownership of her hotels and mines. In her memoir, she never acknowledges that perhaps this was what her suitor was after. The woman who had bested Big Alex refused to admit that her judgment was not always flawless. Instead, she equivocated on the grounds that disentangling her businesses would be complicated. "I had so many partners. I had to dissolve so much before I ever thought of marrying anyone." She suddenly remembered the parents and siblings she had left behind in Pennsylvania almost a decade earlier. "There was my duty to be discharged to my family, which I wanted to do." But Carbonneau had given Belinda a glimpse of the world beyond the gold fields, where he was comfortably at home and to which he would give her an entrée. "We decided to be married in the fall of 1900 and go abroad after that."

Belinda insisted that their engagement remain secret. She was not ready to shock the insular little society of Dawson with the revelation that the redoubtable Miss Mulrooney had succumbed to her debonair suitor. She knew that old-timers would "resent my marrying a man who carried his steaks in a portable ice box and had his own brand of toilet water." At the same time, she stealthily began to wind up her properties, selling the Grand Forks Hotel in May and making plans to sell the Fairview, too. (Eventually, she would lease it to a man called Fred Kammueler at $1,200 a month for three years.) It was a good time to sell property. Dawson City was booming, as scars left by the April inferno were quickly erased in a flurry of new buildings. Wooden sidewalks snaked along the unpaved streets, and this year there were no spring floods. The *Nugget* relished the way that "the Klondike is rapidly taking on the airs and mannerisms of the effete East." Belinda was less impressed. "Society had hold of Dawson very strong. The ladies were dressing elaborately and there was a different atmosphere. The amusements had changed. Dawson was absolutely in the hands of the Outside." She was too much of a go-getter to yearn for the good old days. Who in their right mind would return to the rough-and-tumble times of dysentery outbreaks, frostbitten fingers, and dog excrement all over the streets? But if she was going to live an Outside lifestyle, she wanted the real thing.

Besides, aspects of the new Dawson irked her. Flora Shaw had loftily suggested in her Royal Colonial Institute speech that the place needed more women to civilize it: "Man wins the battle but woman holds the field." In Belinda's view, women were ruining the place. Intense rivalry erupted between Americans and Canadians about whether May 24, Queen Victoria's birthday, or July 4, American Independence Day, was the more important holiday. In the past, both days had been celebrated with parades, speeches, and parties. "They gave us two days of fun instead of one," recalled Belinda. "We were as happy in one as in the other." But now that the wives of many officials and miners had arrived, "If the [British] flag was an inch higher than the American, the women got into each other's hair."

On Queen Victoria's birthday in 1899, bands played on Front Street, and large crowds gathered to watch such Scottish diversions as caber-tossing, shot-putting, sword-dancing, and a bagpipe competition. There were sack races, running races, a packhorse race, and a chopping contest. Sam Steele noted in his NWMP official diary, "Feu de joie by the YFF [Yukon Field Force] and a salute with the Maxim by the police force. New sports of all sorts and all orderly. All hands busy. Canoe races." Belinda told a different story. A Canadian woman tore down the Stars and Stripes, so a furious American woman retaliated by tearing down the Union Jack. "There was an awful mess as the husbands took sides," according to Belinda. She had organized a tug of war, with a

Queen Victoria's birthday, on May 24, was celebrated with races and a bagpipe competition. Hän women and children from Moosehide Village came to watch (lower right).

Fairview prize of $500 for the winning team, but the sourdoughs abandoned the whole event. "It was the rottenest 24th of May we ever had." Belinda began to plan a triumphant return to her family in Pennsylvania and a visit to her grandmother in Ireland. She commissioned a local goldsmith to fashion gold from her claims into several small cigar cases. Most were gifts for her family, but a couple were for friendly officials in Dawson. The one intended for Frederick Coates Wade had his initials picked out on it in emeralds and diamonds.

Charles Carbonneau was several steps ahead of his fiancée. He had already announced that he would leave Dawson on one of the first steamers out in early June. He purchased a ticket on the *Victorian,* and Belinda, along with half the town, went down to the boat to wish him bon voyage. She was demurely shaking his hand when the Frenchman grabbed her and pulled her toward him. A master of manipulation, he then pressed his lips against hers. A ripple of shock ran through the

Americans celebrated Independence Day on July 4 with a fervor that reflected their exasperation with Canadian rules.

crowd. Carbonneau's fellow passenger H. T. Wills, manager of the Bank of Commerce, grinned from ear to ear. Fred Wade, who was waving goodbye to the passengers, found the sight hilarious. Belinda was "stunned, gasping. It was a good thing the boat was ready to pull out. I was never so embarrassed in my life."

She stomped back to her office in high dudgeon, furious that the whole town now knew her business. Before Wade could say a word to her, she snapped, "We're engaged to be married." Wade remarked, "He seems a nice enough fellow, but he is a man of the world. There isn't much in common between you. You are North and he is Europe." Belinda had reinvented herself so many times already that she resented being stereotyped like this, but her fiancé's gesture had infuriated her. She began to rethink the engagement. "It will disturb the peace of mind of my partners," she admitted to Wade. Her "business partner" gave a knowing smile. "I think that's what he did it for," he said.

Fred Wade promised to make a few inquiries about Count Charles Eugene Carbonneau. He proved a poor sleuth. He never heard about Carbonneau's riotous night on the town as soon as he hit Vancouver. The *Province,* Vancouver's leading newspaper, reported on July 25 that "the rich and titled Frenchman, whose prodigious spending proclivities, likewise his convivial habits, are well known" had spent the night with a woman called May Evans, then accused her of stealing $3,300 from him. When May Evans was arrested, she protested that she had taken only $650, and the evidence seemed to bear her out. Neither the police nor the local paper thought much of the high-living count. Although not prepared to condone theft, the *Province* editor noted that "'Count' Carbonneau . . . is a debauchee and a libertine" and deserved little sympathy. But Belinda knew none of this. She booked passage to Whitehorse on a little steamer called the *Flora,* scheduled to sail on October 5.

Sam Steele's diary and letters through the summer of 1899 kept up the rhythm of "Fine weather. Busy day." He organized the execution, finally, of the three Tlingit men who had been convicted the previous summer of murdering a prospector and had spent a year in jail. He dealt with a delinquent officer, Sergeant Harper, who had lost his head to a notorious dance hall girl called Diamond Tooth Gertie and subsequently been spurned by her. (Sam told Marie that Harper had "spent hundreds of dollars a month on her and she didn't care a scrap for him." Sam reported his errant officer to Mountie headquarters, because the "hundreds of dollars" had come out of fines levied in the police court.) He tried to ignore reports from Ottawa that the Canadian capital seethed with talk that Steele of the NWMP was undermining his boss, Minister Sifton, by speaking out about maladministration in the Yukon.

A sword was hanging above Sam Steele's head. It fell on September 8. That was the day a momentous event occurred in the Yukon Territory. The first telegraph message, which had traveled over a newly strung line from Bennett, was received in Dawson. Suddenly, the town's total

In the midnight sunshine of June 21, 1899, Sam Steele (left) allowed himself to be photographed in civilian dress, with friends.

isolation from the rest of the world evaporated. And just as suddenly, Superintendent Steele's regime ended. One of the first telegrams to be received over the wire was a message from the minister of the Interior to the chief of the North-West Mounted Police in the Yukon. Sam was tersely informed that his Yukon command was terminated. He was to report immediately to Regina, the Mountie headquarters in a region then known as the North-West Territories, and that would soon be the separate province of Saskatchewan.

Sam had seen it coming, but nobody else had. He noted in his diary, "Great deal of dissatisfaction in the district during my move into the N. W. Territories. I am told steps taken, hope not." Steps were indeed being taken. Dawson now had three outspoken newspapers: the *Klondike Nugget,* the *Dawson Daily News,* and the *Yukon Sun* (successor to the original *Yukon Midnight Sun*). As a general rule, the three rags were vicious rivals, but they were unanimous in reflecting popular fury that Sam had been sacked. The *Daily News* insisted that Sam's departure would damage the community. It declared that "Lieutenant-Colonel Steele has proved himself the miner's friend." Under the headline "Wrong is Triumphant," the *Klondike Nugget* described Sam as "the most highly respected man on the Yukon today," and let rip at "the nefarious schemes of the Sifton gang of political pirates." The editor of the *Sun* took advantage of the new telegraph line to send a telegram to the prime minister, Sir Wilfrid Laurier: "For the good of government beseech you to suspend order removing Colonel Steele from command here. Will be terrible blunder."

A public meeting was held in the Criterion Theatre on Saturday, 16 September 16, chaired by a well-known prospector called Joe Boyle. Boyle proposed a motion to be sent to Ottawa expressing "the feelings of dissatisfaction of the entire population of this Territory at this, the removal of our most popular and trusted official . . . It would be a direct injury to the Territory should he be taken away." Five hundred miners, many of whom had walked in from the creeks, listened solemnly, then raised calloused hands in the air to approve the motion.

Sam's professional mask, as a solid soldier, never slipped. "Busy all day, paid off all my outstanding accts.," he wrote in his official diary on September 21. He issued a public statement: "On no account would any influence induce me to remain unless I were ordered and then it would be against my will." On his final day in Dawson City, September 26, he signed his official report and tried to slip away. But Dawson's grateful citizens—the gamblers and the drinkers, the hookers and the miners, the piano players and the prospectors—would not let their hero slink out of town. They streamed down to the dock where the police paddle-wheeler was moored. "Ladies waved their handkerchiefs . . . whistles blew on all steamers," noted Sam in his diary. Alex McDonald had been chosen to present Sam Steele with a bag of dust and nuggets to take to Marie Steele in Montreal. Big Alex was also supposed to deliver a parting address, but at the last moment he was tongue tied. Finally he whispered, "Here Sam—here y'are. Poke for you. Goodbye."

The vessel steamed upriver to Whitehorse. As it passed each of the twenty-six police posts that Sam had established, the officer in charge dipped the Union Jack in Sam's honor. But nothing assuaged Sam's private hurt at being "treated in this very shameful way after working hard and honourably for the people of the Dominion and the honour of the government of our country." In his diary he wrote, "Curse the day I ever served such a country."

Yet despite the hurt, Sam had found gold in the Klondike. The reputation for integrity he established in the North stuck with him to the grave and beyond. He would later serve in the Boer War in South Africa, where he was involved in a nasty scandal. But the scandal would soon be forgotten while Steele would always be remembered because, as the *Yukon Sun* noted on October 3, "He did not come here for money, and no money in the Klondike could buy him."

Sam's departure was a shock to Dawson City, but the northern eldorado itself was being quietly undermined by larger forces. Old-timers who had seen both Forty Mile and Circle City develop from empty moose pastures to booming mining camps and then to ghost towns could almost hear the wheel turning. These were restless men like Bill Haskell, driven not by a determination to "civilize" the North but by the hunger for gold and the taste for adventure. They didn't care one whit for new sewers or the Sunday curfew; they hankered after the adrenaline rush of the stampede's early days. For months now, they had heard whispers of gold strikes elsewhere, in remote Alaskan locations with Indian names like Koyukuk and the Kotzebue Sound. In the spring of 1899, they began to hear about an unexpected gold strike on land as far to the west as a man could travel in North America.

Buried in the sands of Cape Nome, an isolated knuckle of land jutting out into the Bering Sea from Alaska toward Siberia, pockets of gold dust were discovered in 1898. At first, Dawson boosters denounced the Nome rumors as a scheme of St. Michael shipping companies to trigger a stampede and create business for their vessels. But in June, a

Seattle newspaper brought in from Outside confirmed the strike. The impact was immediate. When the steamer *Sovereign* pulled away from the Dawson docks on the sun-filled evening of June 10 and paddled off downstream toward the Bering Sea, it was crowded with men and women heading to the new gold field. Gene Allen tried to sound a note of caution when he saw the *Klondike Nugget's* subscribers disappearing downriver. "It was a rarely edifying sight to see a steamboat load of people leaving the Klondike on a 2,000 mile stampede with little, if anything, more tangible in the way of information than the story of a sensational newspaper in Seattle."

Nome was the new Klondike (although it was nowhere near so rich). At the very moment when isolated Dawson was finally connected to the Outside, the world had moved on. There was still gold in the Klondike but its lure was lost, its luster gone. The exodus from Dawson City gathered momentum all summer, as grizzled prospectors surged to the new frontier. Hot on their heels went the whole colorful jamboree of saloonkeepers, prostitutes, restaurateurs, professional gamblers, bakers, ironmongers, dance hall girls, and churchmen. Within a few weeks, the editor of the *Klondike Nugget* would himself disappear downriver, leaving large debts. At the same time, Sam Steele and Belinda Mulrooney were on their way south. Before freeze-up that fall, the population of Dawson City was halved.

After three years of feverish activity, the Yukon Gold Rush, which had brought so many strange, intrepid characters to the Klondike gold fields, was over, and the giddy days of the San Francisco of the North were gone.

CHAPTER 20
Mythmakers

DESPITE THE 1899 NOME STRIKE, prospects continued to look promising for the Klondike gold fields in the early twentieth century. As Flora Shaw predicted, large mining operations such as the Guggenheims' Yukon Gold Corporation and the Canadian Klondyke Mining Company Limited arrived to reap millions on the creeks with large-scale hydraulic methods and immense floating dredges. The army of gumboot miners had vanished to Nome, but gold production continued to rise—to a value of $16 million in 1899 and $22 million in 1900. The total payout between 1896 and 1909 was nearly $120 million.

Meanwhile, the Canadian government started to take the mines' potential seriously and invest in Dawson's future. Thomas W. Fuller, an Ottawa architect, designed six government edifices, including a commissioner's residence, the territorial administration building, a courthouse, and a post office, plus homes for government employees. The plans were shipped north, and when they arrived in the Yukon a few weeks later, Fuller's splendid neoclassical buildings were quickly built from milled lumber. When the town became an incorporated city in 1902, officials and businesspeople began for the first time to consider it as a permanent home rather than a treasure chest to be looted. Journalist Faith Fenton, who continued to entertain Toronto *Globe* readers with breathless accounts of Dawson's "airs of a metropolis," made a personal investment in the expansion of the new "metropolis." On

New Year's Day, 1900, aged forty-two (but admitting to thirty-nine), she had married John Brown, a genial physician seven years her junior. Brown was both the Yukon's territorial secretary and its medical officer of health. Faith was soon holding "at homes" every Wednesday and being described as one of Dawson's leading hostesses.

It was all wishful thinking. Edwardian Dawson's pretensions to greatness could not last. In the end, the Klondike Gold Rush never yielded as much gold as feverish gold rushes elsewhere. Nor did it have much long-term impact on the Yukon, although it helped boost the economies of Seattle, Vancouver, Victoria, and Edmonton. The 1849 California Gold Rush had hastened the arrival in the West of the telegraph in 1861 and the Union Pacific Railroad in 1869. The 1851 Australian Gold Rush effectively doubled the country's population. But the Klondike Gold Rush was, literally, a flash in the pan, in a region too inaccessible and too hostile. Dawson City's very isolation protected it from pandemics: in 1918–1919, it was one of the few places in the world beyond the reach of Spanish influenza. When the gold dried up, so did the number of residents. From its dizzy 1898 peak of 30,000 people, the population had already sunk to 5,000 in 1902 when Dawson was incorporated. By 1920, fewer than 1,000 people lived there, the forest had reclaimed Ninth and Tenth Avenues, and the Fairview Hotel was boarded up.

The stampede north did not change world history, but it drew attention to the hidden mineral wealth of Canada's North—although it would be half a century before that wealth once again attracted national interest. The stampede also exemplified an aspect of Canada's resource-based economy that remains unchanged: a dizzying boom-and-bust cycle. Finally, it illustrated a vivid difference between Canadians and their southern neighbors. The presence of the red-coated Mounties had brought a sense of order to Dawson that was unknown in American frontier towns. Corruption among officials might be widespread, as the *Klondike Nugget* and Sam Steele had discovered, but participants in the Klondike Gold Rush came away with the indelible impression that Canadians were more law abiding than Americans.

Many stampeders, like soldiers returning from war or mountaineers who have scaled Everest, came to believe that they had been part of something bigger than themselves. Fired up by the temptation to get rich quick, they had pitted themselves against the elements and survived. As the first residents of a wild frontier town, they had felt both the exhilaration of achievement and the terror of the unknown. They had packed a lifetime of experiences into the briefest of spans and seen sights that they would never see again—the northern lights, the midnight sun, gold glinting in creek beds, and nuggets piled high on blackjack tables. It is these elements that have continued to resonate down the years, rather than the grubby rush north and the squalor of the frontier town. The last great gold rush generated its own mythology of heroism and greed.

Dozens of the men who had scaled the Chilkoot Pass struggled to record the experience in memoirs now long out of print and forgotten. But three professional writers did capture the magic and nurture the Klondike's mythology.

The first and greatest of these storytellers was Jack London, whose life was dramatically affected by his year in the Yukon. His meteoric rise to fame began only five months after his return from the Klondike in August 1898—but those were five long, wretched months. In California, he returned to the same challenges he had faced in 1897: how to get food on the table and his foot on the literary ladder. While he was in the Yukon, his stepfather had died and his mother, Flora, was raising a grandchild. At twenty-two, Jack was head of the household, with no visible means of support. His only physical mementoes of the Klondike were a bad case of scurvy and $4.50 in gold dust. He recovered his health with remarkable speed (although one pressing expense was a new set of teeth, since most of his own had fallen out), but despite all his efforts he failed to find full-time work. He pawned his watch, bicycle, and a raincoat that was his father's sole legacy to him, and he applied for a position in the postal service. However, it was the Klondike that would deliver him from poverty, because he began to shape his adventures of the previous year into articles and stories.

All that fall, Jack spent his days hunched over a rented typewriter, drawing deeply on hand-rolled cigarettes as, by trial and error, he learned the craft of writing. To improve his style, he studied the work of successful writers. Rudyard Kipling became his model: he copied out Kipling's stories until he had internalized the older author's vigorous rhythm and clipped voice. The rejection slips kept coming—forty-four by December—and the young writer grew increasingly despondent. His account of the voyage down the Yukon River was returned by the *San Francisco Bulletin* with the comment "Interest in Alaska has subsided in an amazing degree." He also tried mailing out some of the essays, poems, and stories he had completed before he went to the Klondike, but by now, according to one account, the pile of rejection slips was five feet high. Thanks to a few odd jobs mowing lawns or cleaning carpets he could afford the postage, but his patience and his supply of stamps quickly dwindled. The abandoned claim on the Stewart River began to look more promising than a literary career. He wrote to a friend, Ted Applegarth, "My partners are still on the inside and it all depends as to what they write me whether I go back in February or not."

Finally, in early December, Jack sold his first story, to *Overland Monthly*, a Western magazine originally edited by Bret Harte, the master storyteller of the California Gold Rush. Jack's story was "To the Man on Trail," and it featured Malemute Kid—a rugged sourdough with a heart of gold who would appear frequently in Jack's Arctic tales. Malemute Kid was a composite character based on Jack himself and the men he had met on Split-Up Island. The story throbbed with the camaraderie of survivors in a cruel land: "Malemute Kid arose, cup in hand, and glanced at the greased-paper window, where the frost stood full three inches thick. 'A health to the man on trail this night; may his grub hold

out; may his dogs keep their legs; may his matches never miss fire.'"
All the captivating details Jack had absorbed during his Yukon sojourn
were there: the crunch of a sled on snow, the snapping jaws and wolfish
snarls of sled dogs, the moose-meat fry-ups, and the "barren struggle
with cold and death."

Although publication thrilled Jack, he was crestfallen to learn that
Overland Monthly would pay only five dollars for the story. But his
confidence in a literary future was restored, especially when the same
month he received forty dollars from a less prestigious publication, the
Black Cat, for a piece written a couple of years earlier. This was a third-
rate horror story entitled "A Thousand Deaths," but the fee allowed its
author to pay off some debts and keep writing.

Soon Jack's northern stories were appearing regularly in *Overland
Monthly.* The magazine raised its rate to $7.50 a piece and gave Jack's
name prominence on its pages. By October 1899, he had caught the
attention of New York editors, and he sold a Yukon story to the *Atlantic
Monthly* for $120. Jack churned out stories at a gallop, averaging 1,000
words a day without fail. His labors paid off. In 1900, ten more Klondike stories appeared in New York–based magazines with higher rates,
larger circulations, and more readers than *Overland Monthly.* There
were seven more Klondike stories in 1901, nine more in 1902, and four
(including *Call of the Wild,* a novella) in 1903. His first book, *The Son of
the Wolf,* appeared in North America in 1900 and Britain in 1901, and
contained nine Klondike tales that had already appeared in magazines.
Soon he extended his range beyond the gold fields, turning to Marxism
and to South Seas adventures for material. But his reputation was built
on the "Northland stories" he had gathered in the Yukon.

Three years after Jack London left Dawson City, he was known as
the Kipling of the Klondike, and he had become the most highly paid
short story writer in North America. With his square jaw, tousled hair,
and laughing eyes, he was a celebrity—the most popular young author
of his day. Newspapers reported breathlessly on his marital adventures,

sailing expeditions, and speeches promoting socialism. He loved being in the limelight, playing to the gallery with outrageous public behavior. But his success rested on his storytelling ability, and his stories resonated with readers because, in an era of rapid cultural change, he embodied both old ideals and new ideas. His rags-to-riches career, a paradigm of the American myth of success, meshed with one of the most dramatically turbulent periods in American history. These were the years when the Jeffersonian dream of an agrarian republic gave way to the harsh reality of an industrial superpower. The frontier was closed, yet it still exerted a powerful appeal. And Jack combined nostalgia for an era when men were men with a progressive sympathy for the underdog.

The underlying theme of Jack's books is a curious, often contradictory concoction of values taken from the books that had seen him through that long Yukon winter. ("Forty days in a refrigerator," he later quipped.) Like many self-taught individuals, he had cherry-picked the ideas that had an intuitive appeal to him, from writers as diverse as Kipling, Darwin, and Marx. Evolution and dissolution, survival of the fittest, the supremacy of the white race, atheism, determinism, and individualism—a blend of ideas current during his lifetime underpins many of his stories. He admired Indian peoples and sympathized with their sufferings, yet he clung to his belief that Anglo-Saxons were superior. He preached that only collective action could improve conditions for the working man, but he also glorified the rugged individualism that characterized the ethos of America's pioneer past. As he put it in his own words, he raged "through life without end like one of Nietzsche's blond beasts, lustfully roving and conquering by sheer superiority and strength."

Jack's contradictory beliefs, racism, and patronizing treatment of female characters might have irritated some readers had they not been swept along by his unvarnished realism. It was such a welcome contrast to the saccharine prose of much Victorian literature. Jack London's characters speak in dialect, frequently swear, and face horror and loneliness.

The tough-guy modernist style that characterized later authors, including Damon Runyon and Ernest Hemingway, is foreshadowed in Jack London's tales. Jack wrote from experience: his best fiction was created out of real people and events, and these are often clearly identifiable. Swiftwater Bill and Father Robeau both appear under their own names; a "padre" closely resembling Father Judge makes sporadic appearances. Hoary old anecdotes from Dawson's bars, such as the hustler who hiked over the mountains with twelve dozen eggs, or the entrepreneur who arranged public readings from an out-of-date newspaper, are dramatized and embellished. "I never realized a cent from any properties I had an interest in up there," he later wrote of the Klondike. "Still, I have managed to pan out a living ever since on the strength of the trip."

Jack London's best-known work, which was an enormous commercial success and brought him a readership that was loyal to him throughout his life, was his novella, *The Call of the Wild*. The book is a parable about the thin veneer of civilization and about individual self-realization in a mythic wilderness. The hero is Buck, a sort of Nietzschean superdog who is stolen from his Californian home and ends up as a sled dog in the Yukon. As London biographer Franklin Walker has pointed out, a dominant theme in the book is Buck's adaptability, resourcefulness, and courage as he learns to defend his rights and become a pack leader. "With no more training to make him a good sled dog than London had to be a writer," suggests Walker, "he uses brains and brawn to win his way." In the end, Buck (a cross between a sheepdog and a St. Bernard) joins a wolf pack to live in the forest and howl under the stars for the rest of his life. Buck's return to the wild reflected Jack London's escape from the confining elements in society.

Jack was not the only Klondike storyteller of his day, but he rose above the competition because he understood the market. This was the golden age of the magazine: new printing techniques and inexpensive paper, combined with a more literate public, had transformed the magazine industry from a genteel diversion serving a well-to-do female readership into big business serving a mass audience. Aggressive editors such as John Brisben Walker of *Cosmopolitan*, George Horace Lorimer of the *Saturday Evening Post*, and Frank Munsey of *Munsey's Weekly* were hungry for adventure stories. Their literary demands were straightforward. In the words of Munsey, "Good easy reading for the people—no frills, no fine finishes, no hair splitting niceties, but action, action, always action." During the first decade of the twentieth century, hardly a month passed without an action-packed London story appearing in the *Saturday Evening Post, Cosmopolitan,* or *Century. The Call of the Wild* was originally published in four installments in the *Saturday Evening Post,* before it appeared in book form in 1903. Jack's omnipresence in print, combined with his larger-than-life personality, gave the Klondike Gold Rush a literary glamour that was never part of the reality. He created, then fed, an appetite across North America and beyond for stories about survival in the cruel North.

Jack was only forty when he died of kidney failure after years of drinking and overwork. By then he had published over fifty books, yet the impulse that had sent him over the Chilkoot Pass was undimmed. Just before his death he bragged, "I would rather be ashes than dust! I would rather that my spark should burn out in a brilliant blaze than it should be stifled by dryrot. I would rather be a superb meteor, every atom of me in magnificent glow, than a sleepy and permanent planet. The proper function of man is to live, not to exist." No wonder this self-made millionaire attracted such media attention. Emperor Franz Joseph I of Austria died the night before Jack London did, on November 22, 1916, but the American press gave far more space to the loss of the author who had romanticized a get-rich-quick event than the demise of a monarch who had presided over the vast Austro-Hungarian Empire for over sixty years.

Jack's style seeped into every subsequent account of the Klondike Gold Rush, particularly into the ballads written by his immediate successor in the Klondike myth-building business, Robert W. Service. Like

London, Service had an unconventional upbringing. Born in Lancashire in 1874, he was shipped off to Scotland to be raised by his grandparents in a tiny Ayrshire village. Also like London, he never finished his education. Service emigrated to Canada when he was twenty-one and then, like Jack, spent several years on the road, mainly in California. For both men, Rudyard Kipling was a hero. Robert Service would later write, in a poem called "A Verseman's Apology,"

> The classics! Well, most of them bore me
> The Moderns I don't understand;
> But I keep Burns, my kinsman, before me,
> And Kipling, my friend, is at hand.

Yet in appearance and personality, Service and London could not have been more different. Jack was strong featured and broad shouldered, with a boxer's build and a way of getting himself noticed. He threw himself into adventures and burned with literary ambition. Robert Service was a slim, sandy-haired man with cold blue eyes who easily blended into the background. His two volumes of autobiography have been called masterpieces of obfuscation, but he never hid his own misanthropy. "I have never been popular," he wrote. "To be popular is to win the applause of people whose esteem is often not worth winning." Service made few friends, he deliberately lost contact with his family for fifteen years, and he denigrated his own work. The second half of "A Verseman's Apology" continues his praise for Burns and Kipling with a caustic comment:

> They taught me my trade as I know it,
> Yet though at their feet I have sat,
> For God-sake don't call me a poet,
> For I've never been guilty of that.

Robert Service arrived in the Yukon thanks to the banking industry. Before he crossed the Atlantic, he had worked for several years in the Commercial Bank of Scotland as a clerk, and carried with him a testimonial from that bank. In 1903, when he could stand the life of a hobo no longer, he used the letter to get himself a job with the Canadian Bank of Commerce. A couple of years later, he was sent to the bank's branch in Whitehorse.

These were the days when a piano stood in every parlor, and get-togethers in private homes featured acts by each guest—usually in the form of sentimental songs, jaunty piano pieces, or amusing rhymes. Since his Scottish childhood, Service had loved the world of music hall songs and melodramatic doggerel, and he was soon leaning against mantelpieces at various Whitehorse gatherings, reciting "Casey at the Bat" and "Gunga Din." He had already published some verse in Scottish newspapers, and fired by his social successes he now decided to write an original ballad himself. One night he walked past a bar and heard sounds of revelry within. "The line popped into my mind," he wrote in the first volume of his autobiography, *Ploughman of the Moon*. "'A bunch of the boys were whooping it up,' and it stuck there. Good enough for a start." A few days later, he completed "The Shooting of Dan McGrew," the rhyming story of a brawl between two sourdoughs:

> *A bunch of the boys were whooping it up in*
>   *the Malamute saloon;*
> *The kid that handles the music-box was hitting*
>   *a jag-time tune;*
> *Back of the bar, in a solo game, sat Dangerous*
>   *Dan McGrew,*
> *And watching his luck was his light-o'-love,*
>   *the lady that's known as Lou.*
> *When out of the night, which was fifty below,*
>   *and into the din and glare,*

Robert Service wrote his most famous ballads years after the Gold Rush and before he set foot in Dawson City.

There stumbled a miner fresh from the creeks,
    dog-dirty, and loaded for bear.
He looked like a man with a foot in the grave
    and scarcely the strength of a louse,
Yet he tilted a poke of dust on the bar,
    and he called for drinks for the house.
There was none could place the stranger's face,
    though we searched ourselves for a clue.
But we drank his health, and the last to drink
    was Dangerous Dan McGrew.

The woman who had precipitated the brawl, "the lady that's known as Lou," immediately entered Klondike mythology.

Malamutes and moonshine. "The Shooting of Dan McGrew" echoed both the tone and the tenor of Jack London's Northland stories, already huge bestsellers throughout North America. As Service's reputation as a Klondike troubadour spread, a Dawson mine manager decided to suggest another subject to him. Robert described the encounter in his memoir: "Portly and important, he was smoking a big cigar with a gilt band. Suddenly he said, 'I'll tell you a story Jack London never got.' Then he spun a yarn of a man who cremated his pal." The poet liked to pretend that as he strode away into the chilly night air, the first line of the new ballad popped into his head: "There are strange things done in the midnight sun." In fact, he worked hard at pruning and polishing his rhythms (including altering names, like that of Lake Laberge, to fit a rhyme). Nevertheless, it was not long before "The Cremation of Sam McGee" was finished:

> There are strange things done in the midnight sun
>   By the men who moil for gold;
> The Arctic trails have their secret tales
>   That would make your blood run cold;
> The Northern Lights have seen queer sights,
>   But the queerest they ever did see
> Was that night on the marge of Lake Lebarge
>   I cremated Sam McGee.

Robert Service wrote his two most famous ballads before he even set foot near a gold field. It was not until 1908, a decade after the peak of the Klondike Gold Rush, that the Bank of Commerce transferred him to its Dawson City branch. By then, "The Shooting of Dan McGrew" and "The Cremation of Sam McGee" were already in print, and had earned Service a nickname, the Canadian Kipling. They were included in Service's 1907 collection, entitled *The Spell of the Yukon and Other Verses* in North America and *The Songs of a Sourdough* in England, which sold hundreds of thousands of copies. City bankers, shop clerks, and soldiers across the English-speaking world were already rolling up their sleeves, leaning against mantelpieces, and reciting the stories of Dan McGrew and Sam McGee to pre-television audiences hungry for thigh-slapping entertainment. Service had found his market with the same agility as Jack London had found his readers.

Service fans did not always realize the gulf between the poet and his creations. When the trim young bank clerk finally arrived in Dawson, he was overwhelmed by his reception. "Hail to the lousy Bard," yelled his new bank colleagues, as he pushed open the mess hall door. In vain Service protested that he was not the rip-roaring Dan McGrew type they obviously expected. "You've got me wrong, fellows," he protested. His objections were brushed aside and he was obliged to whoop it up with a bunch of the boys.

In 1909, Robert Service published a second volume of verse, *Ballads of a Cheechako*, which was filled with characters like Pious Pete and Hard Luck Henry, and stories taken from real events. One of the poems was titled "The Call of the Wild" (a title already famous, thanks to Jack London's story published three years earlier), and it included London's popular phrase, "the Great White Silence":

> *Have you known the Great White Silence, not a*
> *snow-gemmed twig aquiver?*
> *(Eternal truths that shame our soothing lies).*
> *Have you broken trail on snowshoes? mushed your*
> *huskies up the river,*
> *Dared the unknown, led the way, and clutched the prize?*

Ballads of a Cheechako was another astonishingly successful publication. "It succeeded," Service suggested in his autobiography, "because it was sheerly of the North. It was steeped in the spirit of the Klondike. It was written on the spot and it reeked with reality." With his reputation as a writer of humorous ballads established, he resigned from the bank so he could write a novel about the Gold Rush. When his boss asked him why he had given his notice, he explained that his salary was $1,000 but his annual royalties were running around $6,000. The bank manager gasped; his teller was making more money than he was. Robert Service remained in Dawson, in a small log cabin on Eighth Avenue, working on a novel he titled *The Trail of Ninety-Eight: A Northland Romance*.

Service went on to publish dozens more books, including novels and verse collections with alliterative titles (*Rhymes of a Rolling Stone* in 1912, *Rhymes of a Red Cross Man* in 1916, *Bar-room Ballads* in 1940). The Gold Rush novel was not a success (although it was made into a movie), and none of his subsequent books sold as well as his Klondike ballads. He left his little Dawson cabin in 1912 and never returned to the North. When he died in France in 1958, he was bitter that his reputation still rested on Dan McGrew and Sam McGee despite all his subsequent work.

Just as Jack London mythologized the Klondike Gold Rush in his fiction and became a millionaire on the strength of them, so Robert Service became a millionaire on the strength of his Klondike verses. Like London, Service caught the atmosphere of constant, feverish excitement that dominated Front Street during the years when men arrived from the creeks loaded with nuggets, and more fortunes were lost and won in saloons than in the gold fields. He transformed the icy hardships faced by stampeders into romantic struggles, and his mock heroic tone ennobled the Gold Rush.

No matter that his most famous ballads, "The Cremation of Sam McGee" and "The Shooting of Dan McGrew," have all the subtlety and literary gloss of pulp fiction. Throughout the twentieth century, thousands of Service fans on both sides of the Atlantic learned them off by heart. In fact, these two poems caught the experience of stampeders with such accuracy that a handful of Gold Rush veterans started to claim they had known Service while they were in the North, and had been present when Dan McGrew was shot or Sam McGee burned. Decades later, at a Sourdough Convention in San Francisco, a stampeder with a better memory decided to call a particular blowhard on this piece of nonsense. The audience would have none of it. They shouted down the man who wanted to correct the record because they preferred their version of events. Robert Service had plumbed the "emotional truth" of the Klondike Gold Rush, and that was good enough for the participants.

The third Klondike myth builder was the most important writer of popular history in twentieth-century Canada: Pierre Berton. Born in Whitehorse in 1920, nearly a quarter of a century after the Gold Rush, Berton was the son of a Klondike stampeder. He spent the first ten years of his life in Dawson, in a small house across the street from Robert Service's cabin, and as a student in Vancouver spent his summers working in mining camps in the Klondike. He made his career as a journalist, but always felt a strong affinity for the landscape and history of the Yukon. By the 1950s, when he was managing editor of *Maclean's,* the largest circulation Canadian magazine, Berton had begun to tap into his readers' collective hunger for stories about their country—a former colony in search of a national mythology. In particular, there was a renewed interest in the vast territories north of the sixtieth parallel, which had been neglected for too long. The country's industrial needs created increasing demand for gold, nickel, lead, zinc, and uranium, all of which had been discovered in the North. And the Cold War agreement with the United States to position a string of radar stations from Alaska to Ellesmere Island triggered concern about Canadian sovereignty in the attic of the continent.

Berton, a tall, gangling man with a shock of red hair and an irrepressible sense of humor, would write over fifty books before his death, aged eighty-four, in 2004. But among his greatest was the book that blended his own love of the North with the national mood. Entitled *Klondike*

Pierre Berton revived the Klondike legends for a new generation, and added to the excitement with melodramatic recitations of Service's ballads.

in Canada and *The Klondike Fever* in the United States, and subtitled in both countries *The Life and Death of the Last Great Gold Rush,* it appeared in 1958. (A revised edition was published in 1972.) Berton did extensive research for his book, mining vast numbers of personal accounts, interviewing old-timers across the United States and Canada, and even tracking down Belinda Mulrooney, then in her late eighties, in Seattle. The book was a huge success throughout North America: in the United States, it was selected for the Book-of-the-Month Club and in Canada it won the Governor General's Literary Award for non-fiction.

Pierre Berton described the brutality of the journeys into the Yukon with chilling accuracy, and did not minimize the incredibly hard work of mining on the creeks. And yet there was a "good old days" undertone: *Klondike* reverberated with the exuberance and sweaty machismo that Berton enjoyed in London's stories and Service's ballads. Berton used the same anecdotes from Dawson's saloons that London had reshaped into fiction, and there are echoes of London's stories in Berton's taut depictions of loneliness and horror. Berton's own boisterous personality gave the book added momentum. At the drop of a hat, the author would reinforce the grandeur of the experience with energetic and theatrical performances of "The Shooting of Dan McGrew."

Berton had revived and polished legends of the Klondike for a new generation of readers in the late twentieth century. Like his two predecessors, he celebrated physical courage and manly strength in a period when such attributes were less valued. He also brought a new element to the story: the idea, in his own words, that the Klondike experience was about "man's search for himself as much as for gold." Like London and Service, he transformed the muck and misery of the Klondike Gold Rush into literary gold. Thanks to Jack London, Robert Service, and Pierre Berton, Klondike mythology endures.

Although the gumboot miners had left, residents of Dawson City in 1899 were optimistic that the gold creeks would continue to guarantee them a prosperous future.

Keir. Photo-

What Happened to the Six Gold Diggers?

IT IS NEARLY A CENTURY since his death, but Jack London lives on in his Northland tales, which are regularly reprinted and capture his personality better than any biographer could. He was, as E. L. Doctorow described, "a great gobbler-up of the world, physically and intellectually, the kind of writer who went to a place and wrote his dreams into it, the kind of writer who found an Idea and spun his psyche around it." What Doctorow calls "the cooler, more sophisticated voices of Modernist irony" may dominate literature these days, but Jack London's vivid descriptions of the most intense year in his life remain powerful and compelling.

Prospector Bill Haskell has enjoyed no such immortality. After retracing his steps over the Chilkoot Pass in late 1897, Bill dragged himself onto a southbound steamer and sailed down the west coast. He was numb with grief after losing his partner, Joe Meeker, and vowed he would never return to Dawson. When he reached Outside, he was staggered by the Klondike frenzy he encountered. Everywhere he went, he heard people planning to head north.

Bill was appalled. "To one who has just returned from a two-years experience in the gold regions of the Yukon, who has seen death and suffering as an incident of everyday life, who knows what mining in Alaska or in the Klondike means ... and who has seen his dearest friend swept away under the ice by a raging river which can count its victims

by the score, these preparations for rushing for fortunes into those frozen mountains appeared like madness." He was also horrified by the
misinformation about the Klondike gold fields that was circulating, so
he decided to set down on paper his own experiences in the hope of
persuading people to stay away from the North. Published by a company in Hartford, Connecticut, *Two Years in the Klondike and Alaskan
Gold-Fields: A Thrilling Narrative of Personal Experiences and Adventures in the Wonderful Gold Regions of Alaska and the Klondike* appeared
in 1898, only months after the author had left the Yukon. It is one of
the very few contemporary accounts of the Klondike Gold Rush written
by a humble prospector. Even as the author tried to describe the hardships and disappointments, he could not stop himself whetting readers'
appetites for adventure.

What of Bill himself? Despite bitter memories, he found himself
drawn back to Dawson: he appears on a town registry in 1901. Then
he vanishes. There is no evidence from Yukon registries that he staked
another claim, or bought a house, or even died in Dawson. Perhaps he
took off to Nome, or drifted south again. Perhaps he took the hard-won
gold from his stake on Bonanza and returned to Vermont. Perhaps he
was one of the Klondike veterans who volunteered for the trenches of
France in World War I. Men who had spent a subarctic winter during
the Gold Rush were said to deal with the horrors of trench life better
than any other group.

We will never know. Bill's trail went cold.

Entrepreneur Belinda Mulrooney, in contrast, was in the spotlight
on and off until the end of her life. Against the advice of her friends
in Dawson, the owner of the Fairview Hotel did agree to wed "Count"
Charles Eugene Carbonneau. She knew he was a slippery fellow: in her
oral memoir, she made the awkward comment, "I had to get rid of the
pest somehow, so we [got] married." The ceremony took place back
in Dawson on October 1, 1900, with a reception at the Fairview Hotel
for 250 guests. For a couple of years, she enjoyed being "Countess

Carbonneau." The Carbonneaus took lavish trips to Europe, financed by Belinda's Klondike millions. One season, they rented an apartment on the Champs Élysées in Paris. The following year, they took a house in Monte Carlo.

Belinda soon realized that Charles had married her for her money and that he was running through it at an alarming clip. She tried to protect her various properties from her husband by bringing her father, John Mulrooney, up to Dawson and signing them over to him. Then, she extricated as many of her business affairs from Charles's clutches as she could, and in 1904 she moved to Fairbanks, Alaska, to try to rebuild her fortune. Both a mining partnership and a bank were quickly embroiled in lawsuits. When she filed for divorce from Charles in 1906, he retaliated by kidnapping one of her sisters and confining her to his hotel room. He talked himself out of a criminal conviction, and the divorce went through. "Belinda Gives up Her Title" read the headline in the *Yukon World*.

Belinda left the North in 1908 and moved to Yakima, Washington, where she planted an orchard and built an immense house that was quickly tagged Carbonneau Castle. She became a well-known local personality and enjoyed entertaining visiting dignitaries such as President Taft. But underneath the newly acquired sophistication was the same vengeful Belinda with a hair-trigger temper. When a former brother-in-law sued her for alleged embezzlement, Belinda lured him to a Seattle hotel room and hired two men to horsewhip him until his back bled. She was fined $150.

Belinda Mulrooney's life spiraled downhill. In the 1920s, she was forced to sell her castle and orchard, working first as a housekeeper and then as a seamstress. When she was eighty-five she moved into a nursing home, where she enjoyed a tot of whiskey and two cigarettes each day. She died there in 1967, aged ninety-five.

The British journalist Flora Shaw never again had the chance to show the stamina and verve she demonstrated in the Klondike. Once back in London in the fall of 1898, she resumed her post as colonial editor for the *Times*. The British government paid to print and circulate a pamphlet that reproduced her articles on the Boer War—articles that asserted Britain's sovereignty in South Africa and argued for the extension of the British Empire. But in 1900, Flora resigned from the newspaper for health reasons. Two years later, she married Sir Frederick John Dealtry Lugard, a high-ranking colonial administrator in the mold of Flora's other hero, Cecil Rhodes.

Flora's husband subsequently became Baron Lugard, governor of Hong Kong (1907–1912) and governor general of Nigeria (1912–1919). The Lugards were of one mind about the importance of Empire and the significance of their contribution to it. In 1904, Flora wrote to her husband, "To have helped to rouse the British public to a sense of Imperial responsibility and an appeal of Imperial greatness, to have had a good share in saving Australia from Bankruptcy, to have prevented the Dutch from taking South Africa, to have kept the French within bounds in West Africa, to have directed a flow of capital and immigration to Canada, to have got the Pacific cable joining Canada and Australia made, are all matters that I am proud and glad to have had my part in."

As Lady Lugard, Flora traveled extensively, raised money for the University of Hong Kong, and worked on behalf of Belgian refugees in World War I. A vehement opponent of women's suffrage, she became a Dame of the British Empire in 1916, and died in England in 1929.

Flora Shaw's biographers, Dorothy O. Helly and Helen Callaway, who wrote the entry for Dame Flora Louise Lugard in the *Oxford Dictionary of National Biography,* have argued that Flora's significance has been underrated. She was, they suggest, "a very important figure in the history of British imperialism, but a figure who because she was a *woman,* [has] been ignored by male historians of empire, and because she was an *imperialist,* [has] not yet been deemed worthy of recovering by feminist historians." Even within their own lifetimes, both Lugards saw the tides of history turn against them and the imperial project for which they had worked so hard. In January 1920, Leonard Woolf published *Empire and Commerce in Africa: A Study in Economic Imperialism.* One of the villains of his story was Sir Frederick Lugard. "Psychologically," wrote Woolf, "there is no difference between Captain Lugard and the people in past centuries who burnt and tortured men and women from the highest of religious motives."

Superintendent Samuel Benfield Steele, who had commanded the red-coated Mounties in Dawson, benefited enormously from his months in the North. Despite the ignominy of his recall, his misfortunes were blamed entirely on his political bosses, and his own career quickly picked up. Within months of leaving Dawson, he had also left the North-West Mounted Police. The Canadian financier Donald Smith, recently ennobled as Lord Strathcona, offered him the command of a British army unit to be recruited in Canada and to fight in the Boer War. In charge of Lord Strathcona's Horse on the veldt, Steele enhanced his reputation as an authoritarian commander. Years later, one of his subordinates recalled how Steele ordered a dozen men suffering from hemorrhoids to gallop flat out for five miles on the grounds that this would burst them and make them bleed.

Sam stayed less than a year with Lord Strathcona's regiment. He was then offered a divisional command in the new South African Constabulary. The Steele family spent five years in South Africa while Sam drew on his Dawson experience for this policing job. He won the confidence of the Boer farmers by ensuring that his police officers provided practical services to them, acting as game wardens, veterinarians, census takers, and license issuers.

Sam returned to Canada in 1907, took a role in the Canadian militia, and began to write his memoirs. But old soldiers never die, and when World War I broke out in August 1914, he was eager for a military command. Although he was sixty-three and widely considered too old for a front-line position, he managed to wangle an administrative post as commanding officer of a Canadian training camp in southeastern England and the titular position of command of all Canadian troops in England. With a chestful of medals, he was knighted in January 1918. A year later, just after his seventieth birthday, he died in England during the flu epidemic. A group of his friends had a death mask made, with the intention of commissioning a statue. But the statue never materialized; by the 1920s, a spit 'n' polish soldier like Steele had become a dinosaur. In the *Dictionary of Canadian Biography,* Professor Rod Macleod suggests that Steele "was like one of those organisms so perfectly adapted to their environment that a change in external conditions results in extinction. The Great War had so changed Canada and the world that in 1919 Steele's exploits no longer seemed significant."

Sam Steele was buried in St. John's Anglican Cathedral cemetery in Winnipeg. Vain till the last, he had managed to lop three years off his age. Although he was probably born in 1848, the splendid gravestone gives his dates as 1852 to 1919. His most important legacy is, without doubt, the heroic reputation he established for the Canadian Mounties in the West.

Father Judge, the selfless Jesuit priest, also lives on in public memory, although only within the Yukon. There he is still recalled as the Saint of Dawson. He is one of the few Gold Rush veterans whose Dawson grave is marked by a stone memorial close to the river rather than a simple wooden cross on the hillside. Two years after his death, his faithful congregation took up a collection for a monument to the priest and commissioned a gravestone to be floated down the Yukon. It arrived, according to the *Yukon Catholic* newspaper, in November 1903, and was erected beside the altar of his beloved church. Carved on the white marble in Latin were the words "Here lies the body of Father Wm. H. Judge, S. J., a man full of charity, who, with the co-operation of all, here first erected a house for the sick and a temple for God; and who, being mourned by all, died piously in the Lord, the 16th of January, 1899."

Father Judge's hospital and church burned down a few years later, and a new St. Mary's Roman Catholic Church was built several blocks to the south of the original buildings. Although the Jesuit's memory is celebrated in the church, where pictures of his hospital hang, his grave-stone sits neglected today in a grassy pocket of land beyond Dawson's ferry terminal.

Postscript
The Spell of the Yukon

I SPENT APRIL, MAY, AND JUNE of 2008 in Dawson City. Today, it feels like a shabby film set—a pale version of the raucous, rough-and-tumble boomtown of the 1890s. Yet over a century later, it still exerts a mysterious charm.

The Yukon River surges relentlessly past the waterfront, powerful in its chilly immensity, on its 1,400-mile journey to the Bering Sea. Under the midnight sun, the surrounding hills seem saturated with light—pulsing in the thin, dry air. Despite modern communications, the town's remoteness remains overwhelming. There are no fast food chains—no Kentucky Fried Chicken, Starbucks, or Tim Hortons to reassure outsiders that even within a few hours drive of the Arctic Circle, they are not too far from urban props. The roads remain unpaved. In the Bonanza Market I saw stubble-chinned prospectors, in from the creeks, purchasing enough groceries to feed themselves for several weeks.

There are more subtle echoes of the past, too, in the culture of the place. Dawson City remains the end of the road, and many of its residents were happy to tell me that they had "escaped" to the North from jobs, marriages, and lives that didn't work out. I learned not to ask "What do you do?" As Father Judge discovered, you still ask "What is your story?" The town's year-round population continues to be numerically unbalanced: according to a local filmmaker, permanent residents consist of 1,500 people and 3,000 dogs. Men outnumber women, but as a burlesque dancer told me, "The odds are good, but the goods are odd." While I was in the North, talk of smoking bans and seat belt laws elicited subversive guffaws. The heirs of Swiftwater Bill still partied prodigiously, especially in the dark winter months. (The only saloon open year round is the Pit, which has two rooms. One, the Armpit, is open during the day, the other, the Snakepit, opens at night.)

Like many a small town, Dawson is the kind of large-hearted community that organizes benefits for residents in trouble, just as it once organized benefits for Father Judge. On the notice board at Bombay Peggy's, the bar where (like Jack London in the Monte Carlo) I heard the best stories, there were regular announcements of fundraisers for people down on their luck. Dawson shares with other small, resource-based towns studded across northern Canada a hostility to the south and a sense of its own uniqueness. But Dawson is truly unique because of the legacy of the Gold Rush. Some of the original buildings continue to give mute testimony to past glory. The most poignant are wooden structures, like St. Andrew's Church, which have tilted at crazy angles as the permafrost under them has melted and subsided at different rates. Doors bulge, lopsided roofs slide, walls collapse inward, and there isn't a single straight lintel.

The physical legacy of the Gold Rush had all but dissolved by the 1960s. Then, spurred by the success of Berton's *Klondike* and renewed interest in northern resources and sovereignty, the Canadian government decided to revive Dawson, with its colorful past, for the future. Historians researched the town's heritage and its unique buildings. Many of the latter were restored and began to attract summer coach-loads of tourists, brought in by Holland America Lines. The Palace Grand Theatre reopened for summer touring productions. Today, for four months a year, the cancan dancers in Diamond Tooth Gertie's saloon are as energetic and exuberant as their predecessors—those famous sisters Jacqueline and Rosalinde, a.k.a. Vaseline and Glycerine. Meanwhile, the territorial administration building, which lost its raison d'être when the territorial capital was moved to Whitehorse in 1953, reopened as a museum in 1962.

At the same time, the rights of the local First Nation were finally recognized. The Klondike valley had once belonged to the Hän people, who had been brutally ejected from their ancestral lands and robbed of its mineral treasures. Confined to the small reserve known as Moosehide Village, three miles downstream from Dawson, Hän elders spent most of the twentieth century watching southerners plunder their hunting grounds, ship their children off to residential schools, and destroy their way of life. By the end of the century, such actions had come to be regarded not as the consequences of spreading "civilization" but as unethical and cruel violations of human rights. Land claims have been settled with most of the Yukon's First Nations, and compensation paid for the traumas of recent history. Since the early 1990s, the Hän people from the Klondike region have called themselves the Tr'ondëk Hwëch'in, and today they constitute about one-third of Dawson's residents. One of the few modern buildings in town is their Dänojà Zho Cultural Centre, based on traditional Hän construction, where tourists can learn a very different story from that presented in Diamond Tooth Gertie's saloon.

Today, 50,000 visitors a year flock to Dawson City during its brief tourist season. They visit the Palace Grand Theatre, the commissioner's residence, the Dänojà Zho Cultural Centre, and the Discovery Claim, where Carmack found his first nugget. In the gift shops, they purchase the works of Jack London, Robert Service, and Pierre Berton. The three writers' ghosts live on in the little town, each with a cabin that is on every tourist's itinerary. The Jack London cabin is a reconstruction of the one on the Stewart River on which he is supposed to have carved "Jack London, Miner Author" during the bitter winter of 1897. The Dawson version contains half the logs from which the original Stewart River cabin was built; the other half were shipped to Oakland, California, where another Jack London cabin sits on the waterfront. The

Robert Service cabin is the actual building where the poet lived between 1908 and 1912. Both are just along Eighth Avenue from Berton House, where Pierre Berton was raised between 1920 and 1930.

Thanks to Berton family generosity, Berton House is now a writers' retreat, where I spent my Dawson sojourn and asked a question: Behind the fictions and the mythology, what was the Gold Rush really like for its participants? London, Service, and Berton caught the communal frenzy that drove people to risk their lives for yellow metal. They relished the mock heroics and madness of the crowds. But history is the sum total of individual lives. I was interested in the experience of a few characters in this large historical drama. I wanted to jigsaw together real stories to illuminate, over a century later, life in Dawson City as the town grew from 300 to 300,000 in less than two years.

One of the first things that caught my eye in Dawson, painted on the side of a building opposite Klondike Kate's restaurant, was the first verse of Service's "Spell of the Yukon":

> *I wanted the gold, and I sought it;*
> *I scrabbled and mucked like a slave.*
> *Was it famine or scurvy, I fought it;*
> *I hurled my youth into a grave.*
> *I wanted the gold, and I got it—*
> *Came out with a fortune last fall,—*
> *Yet somehow life's not what I thought it,*
> *And somehow the gold isn't all.*

So few stampeders in the 1890s found gold, and yet like a modern wilderness adventure the Klondike provided for many—including my six subjects—a personal epiphany.

FOR THE MOST PART, I have kept the price of goods and services and the yield of the gold mines in 1890s values throughout this book. How much are these sums worth today? This question is almost impossible to answer in any meaningful way by a single estimate, because the value of labor and various commodities has changed in different ways. Moreover, monetary units have fluctuated in relation to one another: £1 was worth $5 in the 1890s but hovers around $1.40 today.

Gold is the easiest commodity for which to make comparisons over time. When a Klondike miner presented an ounce of gold dust to a bank in 1898, depending on its purity he would receive between $16 and $18. The official price was $18.96. Today, the value of an ounce of gold dust is well over $1,100. So a rough calculation to update the value of Klondike gold is to multiply 1898 values by sixty. Thus Bill Haskell's $25,000 purse would be worth around $1.5 million today. And the total payout from the Klondike gold fields between 1896 and 1909, which was estimated at $120 million at the time, now would be worth over $7 billion.

As far as other items are concerned, a rule of thumb is to base calculations on the gradual increase in the consumer price index over the intervening years. The CPI allows us to compare the cost—then and now—of things most of us buy, such as food, housing, transportation, and so on. Changes in the CPI suggest that since $100 in 1896 was worth a little over $2,600 in today's money, one should multiply 1896 amounts by twenty-six. Using that multiplier, the $1,500 Bill Haskell and Joe Meeker spent to outfit themselves for the Klondike is the equivalent of about $39,000 in today's terms. I have taken the conversion factor of twenty-six from the helpful and reliable website www.measuringworth.com. The site computes how much an American dollar or a British pound from a specified year is worth in current terms.

The CPI is not always a good guide to the relative value of other items, such as laborers' wages, for which meaningful comparisons are more complex. What can be said, however, is that the shortage of labor in the North meant Klondike wages in 1898 ran as high as five times the average daily wage in the United States. So even stampeders who did not find their own pot of gold could, if they spent a winter on a claim and left Dawson without blowing their take, return home feeling rich. No wonder gold dust was tossed around in Dawson saloons with such abandon. Nuggets must have felt like Monopoly money to people earning more in a day than they could earn Outside in a week.

Another figure that Klondike stampeders loved to quote is the number of degrees below zero registered on a thermometer. In 1898, thermometers used the Fahrenheit scale, on which the freezing point is 32 degrees. In general, I have preferred to use the phrase "degrees below freezing" to clarify temperatures, but I am also aware that the quoted figures are often rough guesses. Prospectors in the North developed their own sturdy system to measure degrees of cold. Homemade trail thermometers consisted of small pill bottles fitted into holes in a block of wood. According to an old-timer known as Sourdough Ray, the first bottle contained mercury, which froze at 40 degrees below water's freezing point; the next held kerosene, which froze at 50 below; the third had Jamaica ginger, which froze at 55 below; next Perry Davis' Pain Killer (containing opiates and alcohol), which solidified at 72 degrees below; and the last, St. Jacob's Oil (another patented painkiller containing ether, alcohol, and turpentine), was one he never saw frozen at all.

Images reproduced throughout the text have not been altered or manipulated in any way beyond standard cropping and resizing.

ACKNOWLEDGMENTS

DAWSON: My most heartfelt thanks go to Elsa Franklin and the Writers Trust of Canada for selecting me to become writer-in-residence at Berton House Writers' Retreat, Dawson City, in 2008. The Trust's James Davies organized everything for me, including transport for my dog, Jake, which was beyond the call of duty. My three months in Dawson were invaluable as I got to know the landscape and the town, and explored the rich resources of the Parks Canada offices, the Tr'ondëk Hwëch'in Heritage Centre, and the Dawson City Museum. Particular thanks to Laura Mann in the Museum, Miriam Haveman in the Dawson Library, Dawne Mitchell at Jack London's cabin, and Leslie Piercy from Parks Canada. I was fortunate in being able to draw on the expertise of two local historians: John Gould and Dick North. Tara Christie explained modern mining practices to me. David Fraser, Karen MacKay, Valerie Salez and Jesse Mitchell, Dan and Betty Davidson, Rachel Wiegers, Anne Rust D'Eye, Eldo Enns, Karen Dubois, and Dan and Laurie Sokolowski were generous with time and friendship. The highlight of my Dawson sojourn was the trip down the Yukon River, for which I can never thank Gordon MacRae and Maureen Abbott enough. Particular thanks to Lulu Keating, the brilliant filmmaker who made so much happen.

WHITEHORSE: Carl and Liz Rumscheidt offered both hospitality and friendship. Thank you. The Nancy McPherson/Sally McLean network embraced me: thanks to Pat Halladay, Audrey McLaughlin, Laurel Parry, and Mary Cafferty. At the Yukon Archives, Leslie Buchan and Donna Darbyshire showed me material I could never have found on my own. Susan Twist helped with photo research. Dave Neufeld, Parks Canada's Yukon historian, shared his extraordinary knowledge of the Gold Rush era. And Rick and Maureen Nielsen showed me the most exciting aspects of Yukon mountains and fashion. I will never forget my airborne luge down the Chilkoot Pass.

BERKELEY: David Kessler at the Bancroft Library guided me through the process of accessing the Helen Lyon Hawkins Papers, which include the Belinda Mulrooney memoir. Damaris Moore welcomed me to the Library Development Office at Berkeley. Susie Schlesinger and Michael Ondaatje made my visit to Jack London's ranch memorable.

OXFORD: Dr. Ken Orosz at the University of Maine at Farmington generously led me to Flora Shaw's letters in the Brackenbury Papers, and John Pinfold at Rhodes House helped me locate them.

EDMONTON: The staff at the Bruce Peel Special Collections Library at the University of Alberta went out of their way to make Sam Steele's newly acquired Yukon correspondence available to me; many thanks to Special Collections Librarian Jeannine Green, and Robert Desmarais, Mary Flynn, and Jeff Papineau. I greatly appreciated sitting next to Dr. Rod Macleod, who was happy to share his knowledge of the legendary Sam and to help with Steele's handwriting. He was also kind enough to review the Steele chapters. Dr. Merrill Distad, Associate Director of Libraries at the Cameron Library, was particularly helpful, and Shona Cook made living in a student residence bearable.

OTTAWA: As usual, I found the staff at Library and Archives Canada exceptionally helpful, especially the former chief archivist, Dr. Ian Wilson. I appreciated being able to draw on the encyclopedic knowledge of Jim Burant, Chief of the Archives and Special Collections.

Many other people were generous with time and resources while I was knitting together six disparate stories. In Toronto, Phil Lind allowed me to work in his private collection of Gold Rush materials, which is comprehensive, unrivaled, and tremendously exciting. In London, Peter Stone gave me materials about the White Pass Railway. In Ottawa, Chris Randall was generous with technical assistance.

Special thanks to readers who suggested further dimensions for the book, directed me to new research, corrected my more egregious errors (those that remain are entirely mine), and offered encouragement. They include Ernest and Marta Hillen, Maurice Podrey, Patricia Potts, Dr. Sandy Campbell, Dr. Duncan McDowell, and Dr. Bill Waiser. I would also like to thank the usual suspects: Wendy Bryans, Maureen Boyd, Judith Moses, and especially my airborne friend, Cathy Beehan. My three sons, Alexander, Nicholas, and Oliver, infected me with their spirit of adventure and, as usual, my husband, George Anderson, was generous with time, attention, and excellent advice. He was also a great companion on our Yukon road trip.

At HarperCollins Canada, Phyllis Bruce is the best editor anybody could hope to have, and she is backed up by a remarkable team: Noelle Zitzer, Camilla Blakeley, Ruth Pincoe, Greg Tabor, Dawn Huck, Margaret Nozuka, and Melissa Nowakowski. I was given a warm welcome to Counterpoint Press, Berkeley, California, by editor Roxanna Aliaga. My agent, John Pearce, at Westwood Creative Artists was helpful at every stage of the process.

Finally, I am grateful to the Office of Cultural Affairs in the City of Ottawa and to the Canada Council, for financial assistance. Their continued support of writers is not only a reflection of the importance of Canadian stories in a global culture: it is also of inestimable value to recipients.

SOURCES

Events, characters, and dialogue are taken directly from primary sources.

Chapters 1–5

Most of the information in the early chapters comes from William Haskell's *Two Years in the Klondike and Alaskan Gold-Fields, 1896–1898: A Thrilling Narrative of Life in the Gold Mines and Camps* (1898; repr., Fairbanks: University of Alaska Press, 1998). Additional details about placer mining, the journey north, and Yukon vegetation come from the memoirs of other prospectors, listed in the bibliography. Two useful official sources were George M. Dawson, *Report on an Exploration in the Yukon District, N.W.T., and Adjacent Northern Portion of British Columbia, 1887* (Ottawa: Geological Survey of Canada, 1898) and William Ogilvie, "Lecture on the Yukon Gold Fields (Canada)," Victoria *Daily Colonist,* November 6, 1897. "Life in the Klondike Gold Fields," by J. Lincoln Steffens, appeared in *McClure's Magazine,* September 1897. I also relied for many details on *The Klondike Stampede* (1900; repr., Vancouver: UBC Press, 1994) by the excellent reporter Tappan Adney.

Two later sources that capture the frenzy of the search for gold are Kathryn Winslow's *Big Pan-Out: The Klondike Story* (London: Travel Book Club, 1953) and *Klondike: The Last Great Gold Rush, 1896–1899,* the 1972 revised edition of Pierre Berton's bestseller *Klondike: The Life and Death of the Last Great Gold Rush* (Toronto: McClelland and Stewart, 1958). Hal J. Guest, a Parks Canada historian, produced three fascinating and sober research reports on Dawson City: "Dawson City, San Francisco of the North or Boomtown in a Bog: A Literature Review," Manuscript Report Series no. 241 (Parks Canada, 1978); "A History of the City of Dawson, Yukon Territory 1896–1920," Microfiche Report Series no. 7 (Parks Canada, 1981); and "A Socioeconomic History of the Klondike Goldfields 1896–1966," Microfiche Report Series no. 181 (Parks Canada, 1985). Information about Yukon's Hän people came from two books I borrowed from the Tr'ondëk Hwëch'in Heritage Centre in Dawson: Helene Dobrowolsky's *Hammerstones: A History of the Tr'ondëk Hwëch'in* (Dawson City: Tr'ondëk Hwëch'in, 2003) and *Han, People of the River,* by Craig Mishler and William E. Simeone (Fairbanks: University of Alaska Press, 2004).

For insights into the impact of the Gold Rush on First Nations, particularly the Hän and Tlingit peoples, I turned to Julie Cruikshank, "Images of Society in Klondike Gold Rush Narratives: Skookum Jim and the Discovery of Gold," *Ethnohistory* 39, no. 1 (Winter 1992): 20–41. The various versions of the first discovery of Klondike gold reflect the malleability of history. Cruikshank argues that "neither oral nor written versions can be treated simply as historical evidence to be sifted for 'facts'; furthermore, combining the two kinds of account does not really give us a synthesis, the 'real story.'" Events and power relationships are too complex, she argues, to accept only one kind of record. "Instead, both kinds of account have to be understood as windows on the way the past is constructed and discussed in different contexts, from the perspectives of actors enmeshed in culturally distinct networks of social relationships."

Chapter 6

Father William Judge appears in the memoirs of several prospectors, but the most important source for his story is the book his brother, Charles, wrote: *An American Missionary: A Record of the Work of Rev. William H. Judge,* 4th ed. (Ossining, NY: Catholic Foreign Missionary Society, 1907). This includes several first-person accounts of the priest collected after the Jesuit's death. Information about nineteenth-century missionary activity comes from *Pax Britannica: The Climax of an Empire,* by James Morris (London: Faber and Faber, 1968).

The bathing habits of Dawson's residents are described in Edward E. P. Morgan's *God's Loaded Dice, Alaska 1897–1930* (Caldwell, ID: Caxton Printers, 1948).

Chapter 7

In 1927–1928, Belinda Mulrooney dictated her memoirs to journalist Helen Lyon Hawkins of Spokane, Washington. Ms Hawkins never found a publisher for the subsequent book, which she provisionally titled "Miss Mulrooney, Queen of the Klondike." Ms Hawkins's notes and manuscript are now lodged in the Bancroft Library, at the University of California, Berkeley. I discovered these papers thanks to the excellent biography of Belinda by Melanie J. Mayer and Robert N. DeArmond, *Staking Her Claim: The Life of Belinda Mulrooney, Klondike and Alaska Entrepreneur* (Athens: Ohio University Press, 2000). Belinda was in her late fifties when she described her adventures, but her voice comes through loud and clear—blunt, humorous, ruthless. Ms Hawkins could barely keep up with her subject's exuberant narrative: two archival boxes are full of random, hastily scribbled notes (BANC MSS 77/81).

In the Dawson City Museum there is a rich collection of newspaper clippings about Mulrooney. Many of them are interviews with an elderly Mulrooney, on yellowing newsprint and detailing Belinda's carefully edited version of her life. Belinda's plans to build at Grand Forks and the opposition she faced are described in Frederick Palmer's *In the*

Klondike (New York: Scribner's, 1899), 141–47, and in Norman Bolotin's *Klondike Lost: A Decade of Photographs by Kinsey & Kinsey* (Anchorage: Alaska Northwest Publishing, 1980).

Melinda Mayer's *Klondike Women: True Tales of the 1897–98 Gold Rush* (Athens: Ohio University Press, 1989) amplified my understanding of the life of women stampeders and the different levels of "respectability."

Chapter 8

Tappan Adney was the source for much of the circumstantial detail about the scenes in California when the first Klondikers arrived. The role of the Hearst papers is touched on in Ken Whyte's *The Uncrowned King: The Sensational Rise of William Randolph Hearst* (Toronto: Random House, 2008). There was also valuable information in Guest's "Dawson City, San Francisco of the North or Boomtown in a Bog."

For biographical information about Jack London, I relied on Russ Kingman's *A Pictorial Life of Jack London* (New York: Crown Publishers, 1979); the Introduction to *The Letters of Jack London*, vol. 1, *1896–1905*, ed. Earle Labor, Robert C. Leitz III, and I. Milo Shepard (Stanford, CA: Stanford University Press, 1988); and Alex Kershaw's *Jack London, A Life* (London: St. Martin's Press, 1977). However, the last-mentioned places the Klondike in Alaska. Charmian London, Jack's widow, wrote several memoirs of her marriage, including *The Book of Jack London* (New York: The Century Company, 1921), and *Jack London and His Times, An Unconventional Biography* (Seattle: University of Washington Press, 1939). Two excellent sources on London's Yukon experiences are Franklin Walker's *Jack London and the Klondike: The Genesis of an American Writer* (San Marino, CA: Huntington Library, 1966, 1994) and Dick North's *Sailor on Snowshoes: Tracking Jack London's Northern Trail* (Madeira Park, BC: Harbour Publishing, 2006). The Klondike diary of Fred Thompson was produced as a pamphlet entitled *To the Yukon with Jack London* by the Los Angeles Zamorano Club in 1980, edited by David Mike Hamilton.

All the Jack London stories and books from which I quote are still in print.

Chapter 9

Details of Belinda Mulrooney's spat with Alex McDonald, including verbatim conversations, come from Belinda's unpublished memoir. Information about Jack London's activities comes from his widow's books and Kingman's *Pictorial Life*. Edward E. P. Morgan described Dawson saloons in *God's Loaded Dice*.

Chapter 10

Miners' nicknames come from an unpublished memoir by John Grieve Lind, a stampeder from Ontario who became a Klondike millionaire. Descriptions of the Grand Forks Hotel menu come from Morgan's *God's Loaded Dice,* and details of the hotel bedding from Jeremiah Lynch's *Three Years in the Klondike* (1904), republished in 1967 with an excellent historical introduction by Dale L. Morgan (Chicago: Lakeside Press, R. R. Donnelley and Sons, 1967). The plight of scurvy sufferers is vividly depicted in Kathryn Winslow's *Big Pan-Out*.

Recollections of Jack London from his Split-Up Island companions are taken from secondary sources, particularly those by Franklin Walker and Charmian London already cited, and from Emil Jensen's unpublished account, "Jack London at Stewart River," in the London Collection at the Henry E. Huntington Library, San Marino, California.

Chapter 11

The story of Belinda, Big Alex, and the boots is told in Belinda's memoir and retold in Mayer and DeArmond, *Staking Her Claim*, and Stephen Franklin, "She Was the Richest Woman in the Klondike," *Weekend Magazine* 12, no. 27 (1962): 22–23, 28–29.

Tappan Adney, in *The Klondike Stampede*, described ice-out in the spring of 1898, and information about health issues is included in M. K. Lux, "Disease and the Growth of Dawson City: The Seamy Underside of a Legend," in *The Northern Review* (Summer/Winter 1989): 96–117.

The turf war between the Oblates and the Jesuits was explored by George Edward Gartrell in "The Work of the Churches in the Yukon during the Era of the Klondike Gold Rush" (MA thesis, University of Western Ontario, 1970).

Chapter 12

Freda Maloof appears in Jack London's stories "The Wife of a King" (included in *The Son of the Wolf*, collected stories published in 1900) and "The Scorn of Women" (*Overland Monthly*, May 1901). His story "The One Thousand Dozen" (included in *The Faith of Men*, collected stories published in 1904) has as its theme the shortage of eggs. Charmian London reprinted Jack's journal of his trip down the Yukon in Chapter 16 of *The Book of Jack London*. Jack's account of the trip, "From Dawson to the Sea," appeared in the *Buffalo Express* newspaper on June 4, 1899.

The nuggets in the cuspidors anecdote can be found in an unpublished memoir by Ethel Anderson Becker, held in the Dawson City Museum archives.

Chapter 13

The early days of Dawson newspapers, and particularly Eugene Allen's *Klondike Nugget*, are vividly described in Russell A. Bankson's *The Klondike Nugget* (Caldwell, ID: Caxton Printers, 1935). From this point onward, the *Klondike Nugget* and the *Yukon Midnight*

Sun (available on microfilm at Library and Archives Canada) are invaluable sources. I also relied on Edward F. Bush, "The *Dawson Daily News:* Journalism on Canada's Last Frontier," Manuscript Report Series no. 48 (Parks Canada, 1971).

Jeremiah Lynch, the San Francisco financier who arrived this summer, mentioned Dawson's iniquitous interest rates in his memoir, *Three Years in the Klondike*. The best sources for banking activities in Dawson City are Victor Ross, *A History of the Canadian Bank of Commerce*, vol. 2 (Toronto: Oxford University Press, 1922); Percy C. Stevenson, *The Yukon Adventure* (New York: Yorktown Press, 1932); and Craig R. McIvor, *Canadian Monetary, Banking and Fiscal Development* (Toronto: Macmillan of Canada, 1958). Two unpublished Parks Canada reports contained a wealth of information: Richard Stuart, "The Bank of British North America, Dawson, Yukon, 1898–1968," Manuscript Report Series no. 324 (Parks Canada, 1979); and Edward F. Bush, "Banking in the Klondike 1898–1968," Manuscript Report Series no. 118 (Parks Canada, 1973). Duncan MacDowall's *Quick to the Frontier* (Toronto: McClelland and Stewart, 1993) explores the strengths of Canada's chartered banks (in this case, the Royal Bank) in the late nineteenth century.

Chapter 14

The increase in the number of steamers on the Yukon River in 1898 is noted in "The Postal History of Yukon Territory," by Rob G. Woodall, an unpublished manuscript in the private Lind Collection. Mary E. Hitchcock described the northern trip that she undertook with Edith Van Buren in *Two Women in the Klondike* (New York: Putnam, 1899). Neville A. D. Armstrong described the typhoid epidemic in "Klondike Memories," *The Beaver* (June 1951): 44–47.

The main source for the story of Flora Shaw's trip to the Yukon, in Chapters 14, 15, and 16, is her unpublished correspondence with her sister Lulu and her editor, Moberly Bell, which is included in the Brackenbury Papers in Oxford University's Bodleian Library. They are housed, appropriately enough, in Rhodes House, headquarters of the Rhodes Trust, which was established by Flora's hero, Cecil Rhodes. There is also a biography by E. Moberly Bell: *Flora Shaw* (London: Constable, 1947). Other sources include an unpublished manuscript by Joshua Gagnon, "Flora Shaw (Lady Lugard), Paving the Way for Women: From Struggling Writer to Powerful Journalist and Political Activist"; Stephen Usherwood and Elizabeth Usherwood, "A Lady in the Gold Fields," *The Beaver* (October–November 1997): 27–32; and the *Dictionary of National Biography*, vol. 34 (Oxford, New York, and Toronto: Oxford University Press, 2004), 725–27.

For background on Flora Shaw and her times, I used *The History of The Times*, vol. 3, by S. Morison and others (London: The Times, 1947); Joanna Trollope's *Britannia's Daughters* (London: Hutchinson, 1983); James Morris's *Pax Britannica*; and Lawrence James's *The Rise and Fall of the British Empire* (London: Little, Brown, 1994).

Martha Louise Black described her encounter with Flora at Bennett Lake in her memoir *My Ninety Years*, edited and updated by Flo Whyhard (Anchorage: Alaska Northwest Publishing, 1976).

Chapter 15

Flora Shaw's "Letters from Canada" are available on the *Times* microfilms: I read them in Library and Archives Canada.

Information about Dawson's social life comes from Jeremiah Lynch, *Three Years in the Klondike,* and Mary E. Hitchcock, *Two Women in the Klondike,* and information about Grand Forks from Norman Bolotin, *Klondike Lost.* The anecdote about Father Judge's chess games comes from *Sourdough Gold: The Log of a Yukon Adventure* by Mary Lee Davis (Boston: Wilde, 1933). Lewis Green explains Canadian mining regulations in *The Gold Hustlers: Dredging the Klondike 1898–1966* (Anchorage: Alaska Northwest Publishing, 1977).

Chapter 16

Harold Innis described the number of claims in the Yukon in *Settlement and the Mining Frontier,* vol. 9 of *Canadian Frontiers of Settlement* (Toronto: Macmillan Company of Canada, 1936). Details about the White Pass and Yukon Railway are taken from Wendy Vaizey's *A Brief History of Close Brothers* (London: Privately published, 1995). Benjamin Craig's unpublished diary is held by the Yukon Archives in Whitehorse.

The papers of Samuel Benfield Steele have recently been acquired by the Bruce Peel Special Collections Library at the University of Alberta, in Edmonton. The collection includes an extensive amount of material, including official reports, correspondence, diaries, journals, photographs, military memorabilia, and scrapbooks. I focused exclusively on Steele's eighteen months in the North. When I consulted his letters from the Yukon to his wife, I was one of the first people to read them since Marie herself slipped them out of their envelopes. All the Steele quotations in Chapters 16, 17, 18, and 19 come from this collection.

For background on Steele and the North-West Mounted Police, I consulted Steele's own memoir, *Forty Years in Canada: Reminiscences of the Great North-West, with Some Account of His Service in South Africa* (1915; repr. Toronto: Prospero, 2000) and Robert Stewart's *Sam Steele, Lion of the Frontier,* 2nd ed. rev. (Regina: Centax Books/Publishing Solutions, PrintWest Group, 1999). I also relied on R. C. Macleod's *The NWMP and Law Enforcement 1873–1905* (Toronto: University of Toronto Press, 1976) and Macleod's essay on Steele in the *Dictionary of Canadian Biography* online. I found useful information on the policing of the Alaska–Yukon border in Richard J. Friesen, "The Chilkoot Pass and the Great Gold Rush of 1898," Manuscript Report Series no. 236 (Parks Canada, 1978).

Chapter 17

Mary Lee Davis included the moose steak anecdote and Father Judge's conversation with Dr. Jim in *Sourdough Gold*. The quotation from Solomon Schuldenfrei comes from an unpublished manuscript in the Yukon Archives (Solomon and Rebecca Schuldenfrei fonds, 84/47, MSS 166). General information about Dawson in this chapter comes from Guest, "A History of the City of Dawson, Yukon Territory, 1896–1920." The story about Nigger Jim comes from Victor Ross's *A History of the Canadian Bank of Commerce*. The culinary imagination of the Fairview chefs is described in an unpublished history of the Yukon Order of Pioneers, shown to me by its author, John Gould, a Dawson historian.

The details of Father Judge's death come from Father Charles Judge, *An American Missionary*, and contemporary accounts in the *Klondike Nugget*.

Chapter 18

In addition to the Mulrooney memoir, the Steele Papers, and Russell Bankson's *The Klondike Nugget*, sources for this chapter include *Red Light Revelations: A Peek at Dawson's Risqué Ladies, Yukon Territory, 1898–1900* (Spokane, WA: Chickadee Publishing, 2001), by Jay Moynahan; and Jeremiah Lynch's *Three Years in the Klondike*. The plight of David Doig, manager of the Bank of British North America, is described in Stuart's "The Bank of British North America, Dawson, Yukon, 1898–1968." The story of Faith Fenton is told in Jill Downie's *A Passionate Pen: The Life and Times of Faith Fenton* (Toronto: HarperCollins, 1996).

Chapter 19

In addition to all the Steele and Mulrooney sources listed above, I drew much information about the end of the Gold Rush from the *Klondike Nugget*. The anecdote about the impecunious banker comes from Stevenson, *The Yukon Adventure*. For information about various political figures, including Clifford Sifton and Sir Charles Tupper, I relied on the *Dictionary of Canadian Biography*.

Chapter 20

Franklin Walker's *Jack London and the Klondike* traces the uses to which Jack London put his Yukon experiences. Other useful sources include "'The Kipling of the Klondike': Naturalism in London's Early Fiction" by Earl J. Wilcox, in *Jack London Newsletter* 6, no. 1 (January–April 1973): 1–12; and Jonathan Auerbach, *Male Call: Becoming Jack London* (Durham, NC: Duke University Press, 1996). Quotations from E. L. Doctorow come from *Jack London, Hemingway and the Constitution: Selected Essays 1977–1992* (New York: Random House, 1993).

I drew material on Robert Service from Service's own memoir, *Ploughman of the Moon: An Adventure into Memory* (New York: Dodd Mead, 1945); and Enid Mallory's *Robert Service: Under the Spell of the Yukon*, 2nd ed. (Victoria, BC: Heritage House, 2008). Two useful biographical sources were Carl F. Klinck, *Robert Service, A Biography* (Toronto: McGraw-Hill Ryerson, 1976) and Pierre Berton's *Prisoners of the North* (New York: Carroll and Graf; Toronto: Doubleday Canada, 2004).

The best source on Pierre Berton, other than his own works, is Brian McKillop's *Pierre Berton, A Biography* (Toronto: McClelland and Stewart, 2008).

Afterlives

The comment about Lord Lugard by Leonard Woolf comes from Victoria Glendinning's *Leonard Woolf, A Life* (London: Simon and Schuster UK, 2006). Information about Sam Steele in South Africa can be found in Sandra Gwyn's *Tapestry of War: A Private View of Canadians in the Great War* (Toronto: HarperCollins Canada, 1992).

SELECTED BIBLIOGRAPHY

Adney, Tappan. *The Klondike Stampede.* 1900. Reprint, Vancouver: UBC Press, 1994.

Backhouse, Frances. *Women of the Klondike.* Vancouver: Whitecap Books, 1995.

Bankson, Russell A. *The Klondike Nugget.* Caldwell, ID: Caxton Printers, 1935.

Bell, E. M. *Flora Shaw.* London: Constable, 1947.

Berton, Pierre. *Klondike: The Life and Death of the Last Great Gold Rush.* Toronto: McClelland & Stewart, 1958.

————. *Klondike: The Last Great Gold Rush, 1896–1899.* Rev. ed. Toronto: McClelland & Stewart, 1972.

Black, Martha Louise. *Klondike Days.* Whitehorse, YK: Acme Press, n.d.

————. *My Ninety Years,* Edited by Flo Whyhard. Anchorage: Alaska Northwest Publishing, 1976. First published as *My Seventy Years* in 1938 by Thomas Nelson.

Bolotin, Norman. *Klondike Lost: A Decade of Photographs by Kinsey & Kinsey.* Anchorage: Alaska Northwest Publishing, 1980.

Bush, Edward F. "Banking in the Klondike 1898–1968." Manuscript Report Series no. 118. Parks Canada, 1973.

————. "The *Dawson Daily News:* Journalism on Canada's Last Frontier." Manuscript Report Series no. 48. Parks Canada, 1971.

Coates, Ken S., and William R. Morrison. *Land of the Midnight Sun: A History of the Yukon.* Montreal and Kingston: McGill-Queen's University Press, 2005.

Cruikshank, Julie. *Reading Voices / Dan Dha Ts'edenintth'se: Oral and Written Interpretations of the Yukon's Past.* Vancouver: Douglas and McIntyre, 1991.

Dawson, George M. *Report on an Exploration in the Yukon District, N.W.T., and Adjacent Northern Portion of British Columbia, 1887.* Ottawa: Geological Survey of Canada, 1898.

Dobrowolsky, Helene. *Hammerstones: A History of the Tr'ondëck Hwëch'in.* Dawson City: Tr'ondëck Hwëch'in, 2003.

Downie, Jill. *A Passionate Pen: The Life and Times of Faith Fenton.* Toronto: HarperCollins, 1996.

Duncan, Jennifer. *Frontier Spirit: The Brave Women of the Klondike.* Toronto: Doubleday Canada, 2000.

Fetherling, Douglas. *The Gold Crusades: A Social History of Gold Rushes, 1849–1929.* Toronto: Macmillan of Canada, 1988.

Friesen, Richard J. "The Chilkoot Pass and the Great Gold Rush of 1898." Manuscript Report Series no. 236. Parks Canada, 1978.

Gould, John A. *Frozen Gold: A Treatise on Early Klondike Mining Technology, Methods and History.* Missoula, MT: Pictorial Histories Publishing, 2001.

Green, Lewis. *The Gold Hustlers: Dredging the Klondike 1898–1966.* Anchorage: Alaska Northwest Publishing, 1977.

Guest, Hal J. "Dawson City, San Francisco of the North or Boomtown in a Bog: A Literature Review." Manuscript Report Series no. 241. Parks Canada, 1978.

———. "A History of the City of Dawson, Yukon Territory 1896–1920." Microfiche Report Series no. 7. Parks Canada, 1981.

———. "A Socioeconomic History of the Klondike Goldfields 1896–1966." Microfiche Report Series no. 181. Parks Canada, 1985.

Hamilton, Walter R. *The Yukon Story: A Sourdough's Record of Goldrush Days and Yukon Progress from the Earliest Times to the Present Day.* Vancouver: Mitchell Press, 1964.

Haskell, William. *Two Years in the Klondike and Alaskan Gold-Fields, 1896–1898: A Thrilling Narrative of Life in the Gold Mines and Camps.* 1898. Reprint, Fairbanks: University of Alaska Press, 1998.

Hitchcock, Mary E. *Two Women in the Klondike.* New York: Putnam, 1899.

Innis, Harold A. *Settlement and the Mining Frontier.* Vol. 9 of *Canadian Frontiers of Settlement.* Toronto: Macmillan Company of Canada, 1936.

Judge, Rev. Charles J. *An American Missionary: A Record of the Work of Rev. William H. Judge.* 4th ed. Ossining, NY: Catholic Foreign Missionary Society, 1907.

Kitchener L. D. *Flag over the North.* Seattle: Superior, 1954.

Leonard, John W. *The Gold Fields of the Klondike: Fortune Seekers' Guide to the Yukon Region of Alaska and British America: The Story as Told by Ladue, Berry, Phiscator and Other Gold Finders.* London: Unwin, 1897.

Lynch, Jeremiah. *Three Years in the Klondike.* Edited and with historical introduction by Dale L. Morgan. Chicago: Lakeside Press, R. R. Donnelley & Sons, 1967. First published 1904 by Arnold.

Macleod, R. C. *The NWMP and Law Enforcement 1873–1905.* Toronto: University of Toronto Press, 1976.

Martin, Stoddart. *California Writers: Jack London, John Steinbeck, the Tough Guys.* London: Macmillan, 1983.

Mayer, Melanie J. *Klondike Women: True Tales of the 1897–98 Gold Rush.* Athens: Ohio University Press, 1989.

Mayer, Melanie J., and Robert N. DeArmond. *Staking Her Claim: The Life of Belinda Mulrooney, Klondike and Alaska Entrepreneur.* Athens: Ohio University Press, 2000.

Miner, Bruce. *Alaska: Its History and Resources, Gold Fields, Routes and Scenery.* 2nd ed. rev. New York: Putnam, 1899.

Mishler, Craig, and William E. Simeone. *Hān, People of the River.* Fairbanks: University of Alaska Press, 2004.

Moessner, Victoria Joan, and Joanne E. Gates, eds. *The Alaska–Klondike Diary of Elizabeth Robins, 1900.* Fairbanks: University of Alaska Press, 1999.

Moore, Carolyn. *Our Land, Too: Women of Canada and the Northwest, 1860–1914.* Whitehorse: Department of Education, Government of the Yukon, 1992.

Morgan, Edward E. P. *God's Loaded Dice, Alaska 1897–1930.* Caldwell, ID: Caxton Printers, 1948.

Morgan, Lael. *Good Time Girls of the Alaska–Yukon Gold Rush.* Vancouver: Whitecap Books, 1998.

Morris, James. *Pax Britannica: The Climax of an Empire.* London: Faber and Faber, 1968.

Morrison, William R. *True North, The Yukon and Northwest Territories.* Illustrated History of Canada series. Toronto: Oxford University Press, 1998.

Neufeld, David, and Frank Norris. *Chilkoot Trail: Heritage Route to the Klondike.* Whitehorse, YK: Lost Moose, 1996.

Ogilvie, William. *Early Days on the Yukon and the Story of Its Gold Finds.* Ottawa: Thorburn and Abbott, 1913.

———. "Lecture on the Yukon Gold Fields (Canada)." Delivered Victoria, BC, November 5, 1897. Victoria *Daily Colonist,* November 6, 1897.

Palmer, Frederick. *In the Klondike.* New York: Scribner's, 1899.

———. *With My Own Eyes,* New York: A. L. Burt, 1932.

Porsild, Charlene. *Gamblers and Dreamers: Women, Men, and Community in the Klondike.* Vancouver and Toronto: UBC Press, 1998.

Price, Julius M. *From Euston to Klondike: The Narrative of a Journey through British Columbia and the North-West Territory in the Summer of 1898.* London: Sampson Low, 1898.

Shaw, Flora. "Klondike." *Journal of the Royal Colonial Institute* (January 31, 1899): 186–235.

Sinclair, James M. *Mission: Klondike.* Vancouver: Mitchell Press, 1978.

Steele, Samuel B. *Forty Years in Canada: Reminiscences of the Great Northwest, with Some Account of His Service in South Africa.* 1915. Reprint, Toronto: Prospero, 2000.

Steffens, J. Lincoln. "Life in the Klondike Gold Fields." *McClure's Magazine,* September 1897.

Stevenson, Percy C. *The Yukon Adventure.* New York: Yorktown Press, 1932.

Stewart, Robert. *Sam Steele, Lion of the Frontier.* 2nd ed. rev. Regina: Centax Books/ Publishing Solutions, PrintWest Group, 1999.

Stuart, Richard. "The Bank of British North America, Dawson, Yukon, 1898–1968." Manuscript Report Series no. 324. Parks Canada, 1979.

Thornton, Thomas F. *Klondike Gold Rush National Historic Park, Ethnographic Overview and Assessment.* Final report, August 2004. National Park Service, Alaska Regional Office.

Tyrrell, Edith. *I Was There: A Book of Reminiscences.* Toronto: Ryerson Press, 1938.

Walden, Arthur T. *A Dog Puncher on the Yukon.* Boston: Houghton Mifflin, 1928.

Wiedemann, Thomas. *Cheechako into Sourdough.* Portland, OR: Binfords, 1942.

Winslow, Kathryn. *Big Pan-Out: The Klondike Story.* London: Travel Book Club, 1953.

Illustration Credits

All maps by Dawn Huck.

Front cover: McCord Museum MP 1979.111.212
Back cover: Yukon Archives, Dawson City Museum and Historical Society, collection 6390

p. ii, McCord Museum MP 1979.111.212

p. vi, McCord Museum MP 1979.111.18

p. 18, Library and Archives Canada C-028647

p. 24, Library and Archives Canada PA-149815

p. 31, Library and Archives Canada C-068898

p. 33, Library and Archives Canada C-059904

p. 35, McCord Museum MP 0000.103.44

p. 39, Library and Archives Canada C-016459

p. 47, McCord Museum MP 1979.111.121

p. 51, Library and Archives Canada PA-016277

p. 59, McCord Museum MP 0000.111.27

p. 71, Library and Archives Canada PA-013397

p. 75, University of Washington Libraries, Special Collections, Hegg 794

p. 78, University of Washington Libraries, Special Collections, Hegg 709

p. 85, Library and Archives Canada C-007513

p. 97, Library and Archives Canada C-014478

p. 102, Yakima Valley Museum 2002-800-003

p. 113, Bancroft Library, University of California, Berkeley brk 00010293-24a

p. 116, University of Washington Libraries, Special Collections, UW 26986

p. 123, Library and Archives Canada C-022015

p. 127, Bancroft Library, University of California, Berkeley Jack London 1876-1916, Group 1

p. 131, University of Washington Libraries, Special Collections, A. Curtis 46104

p. 133, University of Washington Libraries, Special Collections, LaRoche 2033

p. 146, Library and Archives Canada PA-013402

p. 150, McCord Museum MP 000.103.32

p. 154, Library and Archives Canada C-014259

p. 174, Library and Archives Canada PA-13284

p. 190, University of Washington Libraries, Special Collections, UW26618

p. 199, Library and Archives Canada PA-016544

p. 205, Library and Archives Canada C-000666

p. 207, Library and Archives Canada C-14477

p. 210, University of Washington Libraries, Special Collections, UW26724

p. 223, author's collection

p. 227, Library and Archives Canada PA-013424

p. 234, Library and Archives Canada PA-013428

p. 235, Library and Archives Canada C-018637

p. 236, Library and Archives Canada C-005393

p. 239, Yakima Valley Museum 2003-800-022

p. 244, Vancouver Public Library, Special Collections, VPL 32866A

p. 248, Library and Archives Canada e010772007

p. 263, Vancouver Public Library, Special Collections, VPL 32648

p. 268, Yukon Archives, Bill Roozeboom collection 6289

p. 273, Vancouver Public Library, Special Collections, VPL 32975

p. 281, Yukon Archives, Robert McLennan fonds, 6487

p. 290, Bruce Peel Special Collections Library, University of Alberta

p. 293, Library and Archives Canada C-022074

p. 302, Vancouver Public Library, Special Collections, VPL 9803

p. 307, Bruce Peel Special Collections Library, University of Alberta

p. 320, Bruce Peel Special Collections Library, University of Alberta

p. 322, Bruce Peel Special Collections Library, University of Alberta

p. 328, Vancouver Public Library, Special Collections, VPL 32655

p. 331, Bruce Peel Special Collections Library, University of Alberta

p. 334, Library and Archives Canada PA-01625

p. 344, Vancouver Public Library, Special Collections, VPL 32789

p. 345, Library and Archives Canada C-014258

p. 347, Bruce Peel Special Collections Library, University of Alberta

p. 361, Library and Archives Canada PA-178389

p. 366, Library and Archives Canada PA-102415

pp. 368–69, Vancouver Public Library, Special Collections, VPL 32668

Index

A page reference in *italics* indicates the presence of an illustration. An italic *m* following a page reference indicates a location on a map.